Waterfalls of Stars

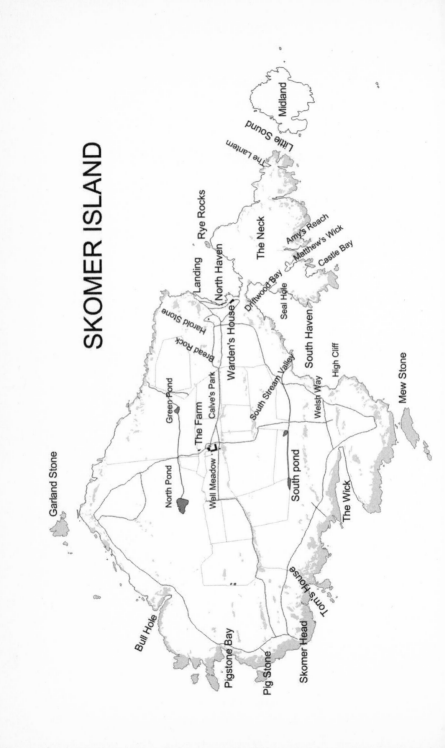

SKOMER ISLAND

Garland Stone

Bull Hole

North Pond

Green Pond

The Farm

Calve's Park

Well Meadow

Warden's House

Bread Rock

Harold Stone

Landing

North Haven

Rye Rocks

Driftwood Bay

Seal Hole

The Neck

Amy's Reach

Matthew's Wick

Castle Bay

The Lantern

Little Sound

Midland

South Stream Valley

South Haven

South pond

Welsh Way

High Cliff

The Wick

Mew Stone

Tom's House

Pigstone Bay

Pig Stone

Skomer Head

Rosanne Alexander

Waterfalls of Stars

My Ten Years on the Island of Skomer

Seren is the book imprint of
Poetry Wales Press Ltd,
57 Nolton Street, Bridgend, Wales, CF31 3AE

www.serenbooks.com
facebook.com/SerenBooks
Twitter: @SerenBooks

ISBN: 978-1-78172-380-7

A CIP record for this title is available from the British Library.

The publisher acknowledges the financial assistance of the Welsh Books Council.

Cover photograph: © Mike Alexander

Printed by Akcent Media Ltd

For Mike
Without you none of this could have happened.

Skomer is managed by the Wildlife Trust of South and West Wales. In recognition of their invaluable work in protecting our most precious landscapes and wildlife, the author is donating 10% of the royalties from this book to the Trust.

ONE

Even now, the slightest thing can take me back: the way the sunlight catches in the turn of a wave or a distant bird call, half-heard, snagged in the breeze. Then, in that moment between eye-blinks, I am there, on a cliff top at the edge of the Atlantic.

But, however hard my imagination tries to pull me back, I know that I will never see Skomer again. For ten years the island was my home, though I wonder now if home is too gentle a word to describe somewhere so resolutely wild. Only the perspective of time has let me remember the rawness I glimpsed in those early days, before my eyes were closed to anything but perfection. I realised within a few days of arriving how much Skomer would come to mean to me and that when I left it would have to be for ever. Islands are not like other places: they are shaped by their isolation. I had become so much part of that solitude that I could never go back as a visitor from the outside.

It seems strange to think that I had never even heard the name of Skomer until I met Mike. I was straight out of school, newly enrolled at college and just taking those first steps into adulthood. Mike was a very grown-up seven years older. I caught my first glimpse of him soon after arriving at the college, which was a rambling, ramshackle old house with scattered outbuildings in the grounds. I was sitting on the low wall of an open porch when the door of a building opposite burst open to emit a cloud of thick, white smoke, and Mike materialized theatrically through the swirling mist. Had I known him as well then as I do now, I might almost have suspected him of engineering such a dramatic entrance, but at the time I saw something faintly demonic in this fiery person as he turned, still haloed in smoke, to give me a menacing glare. It was not the sort of introduction guaranteed to win the heart of a timid eighteen-year-old.

From that point things deteriorated. Every time our paths crossed I had the distinct impression that the customary glare had grown a shade more intimidating, and I wondered vaguely why he had taken such an instant dislike to me. It was several weeks later that we first spoke to each other. We found ourselves at an impromptu party that, in the spirit of shamelessly blatant match-making, seemed to have been thrown for the sole purpose of stranding us in a room together. I was surprised at how well we got on, and within a few weeks I found it hard to imagine a time when Mike had not been part of my life. I had the slightly unsettling feeling that we already shared a past, as though we were drawing from a huge pool of unspoken understanding.

More than anything, Mike talked to me about Skomer, the island he had discovered as a thirteen-year-old boy. It had ensnared him with the same spellbinding power that it would eventually hold over me. He had been taken there on a day trip by a particularly sympathetic schoolteacher who had asked the class if anyone wanted to join the outing one Saturday. Mike was not the sort of boy who would have chosen to spend his weekends in the company of a teacher, but he was intrigued by the prospect of a boat journey and decided to go along. In the end, it was not the boat but the island that captivated him completely.

He spent the next few summers there, working as a volunteer and dreaming of the time when he would be old enough to throw off the responsibilities of school and take up permanent residence as warden of the nature reserve. Skomer is an island that can do that: despite its history of occupation stretching back thousands of years, it can make you believe that it has been waiting only for you. It has never been, could never be, loved quite as much by anyone else. I knew that from the way Mike described those perfect summers of the past, and I realised that he had managed to instil in me a vague, unsettling nostalgia for something I had never even known.

By the time we reached the third year in college, our frivolous, carefree relationship had begun to take on a sharper edge. The end was in sight. It seemed inevitable that, after college, life would take us in different directions. Perhaps if I had been older it could have worked, but we were the right people at the wrong time. I had a lot more growing up to do before I was ready to settle down, and I truly believed that we had met ten years too soon.

Then it happened: one of those moments around which your whole life pivots, when the decision you take will send you into a completely different future. Mike was so excited that the words came out in a disjointed stream.

'It's in the paper,' he shouted breathlessly, as soon as he was through the door. 'An advertisement for a job. They're looking for a new warden of Skomer. It's got to be two people. They need a couple to take it on.'

I felt a faint, claustrophobic panic closing round me, and I knew that nothing would ever be the same again. I was about to shatter Mike's long-held dream, and I doubted that we would survive it. A rift would open between us and, even if we didn't notice it at first, every stress would tear it wider.

'What do you think?'

Mike was still fizzing with excitement, waiting for my answer. What I actually thought was that nothing would persuade me to go there. I was young and irresponsible. I needed friends and nice clothes, music and films. I was certainly not about to decamp to an existence of mud and isolation and wellington boots. What I said, desperately backing away from the prospect without being too unkind, was,

'Well, if we did apply for it, what do you think the chances of getting it would be?'

'Oh, absolutely no chance.' Mike was insistent. 'I've been away from this sort of thing for too long. They'll want someone who's more in touch.'

I breathed again, light-headed with the realisation that I had been set free, completely unaware that was the moment when our lives went spinning off into another orbit.

'All right,' I said firmly. 'Let's go for it.'

It was easy to be decisive when there was nothing much at stake. I saw it as an act of pure altruism, but one that I could make without any sacrifice since it was obvious that I would never be called on to support my words with actions. Anyway, I reasoned to myself, how could I be cruel enough to say no to someone who is gazing with awe at a lifetime's ambition?

'Of course,' Mike was suddenly hesitant. 'You realise we'd have to get married.'

That was simply confirmation of all my worst fears about the situation. It strengthened my resolve that the whole thing could never actually happen. I was only twenty, and marriage was out of the question. I had an arbitrary rule carried over from childhood that I would have to reach the extremely advanced age of twenty-seven before I would even allow myself to consider the subject.

We spent the evening composing our letter of application. Among many other things, Mike had been assistant warden on Skomer's neighbouring island of Skokholm, warden of the Calf of Man Bird Observatory, and also of the Canadian Long Point Bird Observatory. As we assembled this information on paper his experience began to look frighteningly relevant.

'How does this sound?' Mike said, reading out part of a sentence in a formal voice. '. . . and if appointed we will get married before taking up the post.'

I winced without letting it show on my face.

'Couldn't you put something a bit more vague, like suggesting that we'll get engaged?'

'No!' Mike insisted. 'The advertisement says they want a married couple. The competition is going to be incredibly strong, and we don't want to spoil our chances. If we don't look right on paper we won't even get as far as the interview.'

It seems odd now, but back in 1976 that sort of thing really mattered.

'Oh, all right,' I conceded miserably.

We had to do it his way. It was his fantasy, not mine. And it didn't really matter. Since it was just an exercise in appeasement, it was hardly worth getting in a state over.

Once the letter of application was sent, and Mike had taken that first positive step towards his dream, he couldn't think about anything else. He described it endlessly: the bays and isolated beaches, the cliffs encrusted with birds, flowers that covered the island soaking it in perfume. The odd thing was to discover that I felt exactly the same. Despite the apparent sacrifices of leaving the mainland behind, I realised that Skomer was the first thing that I had ever wanted with any real passion. It was terrifying because we were spurring each other on, encouraging ourselves to believe that it was really going to happen. We kept making plans, talking about this distant mirage as though it were something tangible and attainable, and I was appalled at the way we were tempting fate, building ourselves up for such bitter disappointment.

I was right to be cautious. As the weeks went by, and we heard nothing, we had to concede defeat. Finally, Mike put into words what we both already knew.

'It's not going to happen,' he said. 'It's nearly March now, and the new warden will have to be in place by the beginning of the month. They must have already held the interviews and appointed someone. They haven't bothered to let us know, that's all.'

'Are you sure?' I asked.

'I'm afraid so.'

The world had never seemed a greyer, bleaker place. I felt as though I had lost something absolutely irreplaceable. I had swapped the sea-cliffs, the fields of bluebells, the swish of waves against the side of a boat, for drab streets full of drizzle and exhaust fumes, full of people curled in on themselves to shut out the dreary winter weather.

And then the letter came, giving the date for the interview a few days away. Elation bloomed with renewed vigour after being cut back so hard. We dissected our lack of information obsessively. Perhaps our chances were now as good as one in five, one in ten? It was still too much to hope for.

The night before the interview was predictably sleepless. Outside, a drunk was swearing noisily and incoherently in the street. His aggression was unnerving, and he didn't stop until the pain of smashing a window with his fist had brought him to his senses. There was something about that futile incident that made isolation seem so appealing.

I must have slept eventually because I woke with a feeling of nauseating apprehension that was worse than the cumulative total of every new beginning in my life. There would be no time for a gentle slide into disappointment: the new season had already arrived, and Skomer was still empty and waiting. The decision would be made immediately, and that certainty could end all our hopes.

Following the morning interview, we waited in a car park in the deserted town of Haverfordwest, where the shops were strictly adhering to half-day closing. There was nothing to distract us, to blur those endless seconds, minutes and hours until the afternoon was over and we would face the awful finality of knowing. Never had time slithered by with such wilful sluggishness. When, at last, we returned to the offices of the West Wales Naturalists' Trust to discover that we were the chosen ones, I realised that the ecstasy I had rehearsed so many times was tempered with terror. I listened numbly as the words sifted through my mind, vague and fluttering like a snowstorm. In an instant, my expectations had changed, because fantasy never includes harsh, cold practicalities. Imagining can always be done on your own terms. The reality was that we were being given just ten days to leave college and dismantle our former existence, ten days to pack and prepare for our departure. And, yes, that one overriding condition still applied: somewhere among all that, we were expected to fit in a wedding.

As we drove home I was so happy that my thoughts were spinning out of control, making me feel dizzy, but I was also shocked at having done something so momentous. I felt like the spoilt child who pleads that she will never ask for anything again if she can just have this one thing, but the moment the wish is granted she asks for something else. I had my wish, but the thing I really wanted was more time. With even one day's breathing space before I had to start throwing my life into confusion I could have gone on pretending that everything was all right.

'Why does it have to be done in such a rush?' I asked Mike, as the car sped through the darkening countryside. 'I mean, ten days to get ready, after we've waited so long.'

'They need us out there as quickly as possible.' Mike seemed unfazed by the drama. 'After all, Skomer's a seabird reserve. It's the beginning of March and the bird breeding season's already starting. Someone needs to be on the island.'

I was clutching a piece of paper headed 'Terms and Conditions of Employment'. We had been so carried away with discussing the practicalities of what had to be achieved over the next few days it had been overlooked. I began to scan quickly down the page.

'Oh no!' I gasped. 'This is terrible! The pay for the year is only £1200.'

The truth was that we had wanted the job so desperately we hadn't thought about pay, though I had never imagined it could be quite that bad. For a second I was seriously questioning the whole thing.

'It'll be okay,' Mike said briskly, without even pausing to do the most cursory mental arithmetic.

'But it's impossible,' I said. 'We can't manage on that. We'll be worse off than if we were on a student grant.'

'How can you talk about being worse off when you're going somewhere like Skomer?' Mike shouted. He sounded formal and distant. 'Do you really expect to judge the quality of your life by how much money you've got?'

'I didn't mean it like that . . .'

My voice trailed away miserably. Mike was cross with me for spoiling that supremely happy moment, so I decided to stop quibbling about the details and simply have faith in what we were doing.

Besides, if I had one big worry it wasn't the money but my parents. I hadn't told them about applying for the job; there had seemed no point in alarming them about something that was never going to happen. Now, with the astounding haste that had been imposed on us, we would have to get married the following week. There would be no time for breaking the news gently. I would have to tell them everything - Skomer, leaving college, getting married - in one great indigestible chunk. It wasn't going to be easy.

The next day we embarked on our frantic sequence of preparations, but where do you begin in planning for the unknown? Almost everything from the day before had instantly lost its relevance: dresses, smart shoes, coats that wouldn't withstand a force eight gale; records never to be played again, except as dated echoes from another era; anything that needed to be plugged in to an electricity supply. All these things were packed away for storage, although, at the time, I would have been devastated to realise that it would be more than ten years before I was to see them again.

The biggest problem was knowing what we needed to replace everything that was being cast aside. Food was the immediate priority. We decided to think in terms of buying enough to last for the first three months, which seemed a near impossibility to someone like me, who was used to stocking up only for the next few hours. We would have no electricity, and therefore no deep-freeze, which meant that we would have to rely heavily on tinned and dried food, the sort of things I would never normally have thought of buying. My ideas were exhausted almost before I had begun. We visited a local mill and bought two sacks of flour for making bread. Potatoes, hard white cabbage and unwashed carrots came in similar quantities. But then what? Still not even the ingredients for a single meal. Dried peas, lentils and porridge oats might see us through emergencies. We found delightful oddities, such as tinned butter, and some inedible disasters, like dried cabbage. In desperation, we blew our budget on a whole gammon, guaranteed to keep for six months (though we must have done something wrong because we found ourselves slicing off furry patches of green mould within a couple of weeks).

Mostly, it felt like a wonderful and exciting adventure, though occasionally I was jolted by the enormity of what we were doing. It was the oddest things that opened up the chinks for those little stabs of doubt, such as when Mike and I were packing late one evening. The routine was familiar by then: layer of polythene, heavy cardboard box, second layer of polythene, few yards of packing tape, cross hatch of sturdy string. All this was meant to ensure that everything survived the sea crossing in an open boat and the inevitable manhandling up and down the beaches on either side.

I was kneeling on the floor beside a pile of neatly folded clothes, looking for a suitable place to stow them. Suddenly, Mike grabbed one of my shirts, scrunched it into a ball, and wedged it down the side of a box.

'Don't do that,' I squealed, snatching back the shirt and trying to shake it smooth. 'I won't have an iron there. I'll never get these creases out.'

'I need it for padding,' Mike said, ramming my shirt back into the box. 'We're going to an island. You won't be able to worry about what you look like.'

And for a moment I was startled and apprehensive all over again to think how different things would be. I would, after all, still be the same person, and it was hard to imagine that I would find the courage to leave every last scrap of vanity behind, along with everything else.

It seemed almost extraneous with so much to think about, but we had to find time for the wedding. With the minimum notice allowed by law, we had arranged to be married by licence in Carmarthen, where we were living as students. It was the only way we could fit the wedding into the time available. We didn't remember to buy the ring until about four o'clock on the day before the ceremony, but, with only three jewellers in town, it shouldn't have taken too long. I chose with care, settling on a plain, narrow band of pale gold with a bevelled edge. It was slim and delicate, beautiful in its simplicity, but when the assistant eased it out of its velvet setting I was overwhelmed with disappointment. It was far too big for me.

'Oh, don't worry,' the assistant reassured me, obviously faintly amused by my naiveté. 'We can have it altered to fit. It'll be ready within the week.'

By the time we reached the last of the three jewellers I was reduced to holding up my ring finger and asking if they had anything to fit. As with the other two shops, all the rings in stock were much too big, but as soon as they heard of our predicament they agreed to do the necessary alterations on the spot. It was a small shop, with little choice, and I ended up with a thick, bulbous hoop of garish yellow gold, very much of its time, but so uncomfortable that I never actually wore it.

It was in that shop that I had another one of those reminders that we were already moving into a kinder, more benign way of life. When we returned half an hour later to collect the ring, it was accompanied by a gift-wrapped wedding present that was probably worth more than the ring itself. Everywhere, people became caught up in the romance of our story and went out of their way to help us.

With so much to do, there was no question of devoting a whole day to getting married. Our wedding day was also market day, which would be a good opportunity to stock up on some of the things we needed, including tools and young plants for the vegetable garden we planned to make on the island. Carmarthen is a small, grey, traditional town - not dour grey, but more like a soft, enfolding mist — a place where it would be almost impossible not to feel welcome. The market was the highlight of this gentle, changeless place, a treasure trove of farm butter, sea-scented cockles, fatty bacon, flannel shirts and outsize long johns. We spent the morning wandering among the throngs of respectably-hatted elderly ladies and farmers whose faces were bright with the polish of outdoors, so enjoying a last nostalgic glimpse into this time capsule that we almost forgot to be in a hurry. It was not until the afternoon that we found time to turn our attention to the wedding.

I didn't enjoy getting married, but then I had never expected to. In the tide of euphoria that had swept us along, sometimes almost submerging us, I hadn't lost sight of reality. Despite everything, I could see quite clearly that I was far too young to be making such commitment. I spent the day with a feeling of guilt, like a cold, glass marble wedged in the back of my throat, because I felt I had let my parents down so badly. I knew that what was happening could not have been further from the wedding they had always imagined for their eldest daughter. And yet they dealt with the situation, stoically doing their best to organise some sort of reception in the few days that were available, without uttering a single word of complaint.

The worst thing was that I could imagine how it must have looked to them. They would have been sure that I was acting on a whim and about to make a complete mess of my life. I wished that I could have found a way to tell them that I knew exactly what I was doing and that it was the right thing, but those words would have sounded arrogant and unconsidered. Of course, I couldn't have told them that everything was going to turn out well, no one ever knows that, but I would have liked them to realise that I understood the risks and that there was no other choice.

I had seen a different path, and I had taken a few steps down it to get a better look, but, suddenly, there was no turning back. It wasn't stubbornness or recklessness. It was because I thought I had glimpsed something infinitely brighter and more exciting ahead of me. I had been given the sort of opportunity that comes only once in any lifetime. If I had hesitated, and gone back to the well-worn path, that lack of courage would have haunted me forever. I didn't say any of that because, at the time, I had no words to express those feelings, and simply insisting that I was right would only seem to confirm the fact that I was being wilful and rebellious. I also knew that my mother had no way to express her disappointment without driving a wedge between us, so we all said nothing and just got on with it, but I have never looked back to that day with even a moment's regret.

Because of the restrictions of time and geography, the only guests were immediate family and friends from college. I think my parents must eventually have forgiven me for forcing them into this haphazard arrangement. Many years later, during the infinitely intricate preparations for my sister's white wedding, my father realised what a lucky escape he'd had with mine. Gleaming weakly through the fog of time, this day had become the shining example of how things should be done.

Given that it was a wedding, the day was oddly coloured by a slightly funereal sense of finality and farewells. All the unspoken words of friendships that had seemed to stretch idly ahead without any limit of time had to be compressed into a few remaining days. Our imminent departure evoked feelings of sentimental intimacy, and the fact that we were losing this companionship made it suddenly so much more valuable. We were leaving and closing the door behind us because, once we were gone, there would be no phone calls, no casual visits.

Our makeshift honeymoon was a night in a homely little hotel room, made glamorous by the addition of a bottle of champagne in a clinking bucket of ice. It was a surprise present from my parents, who had insisted we must escape from the boxes of packing and bare floorboards that we had expected to face at the end of the day. In the morning, I tried to snatch a few minutes from the prevailing chaos to linger over the toast and marmalade, but, to my dismay, before I could butter a second slice Mike was already heading for the door. He was in a hurry because we were due to meet the coastguard at St Ann's Head for instruction in emergency procedures.

We drove to the furthest tip of south west Wales, where the land reaches out into the Atlantic Ocean. Eventually, we arrived at the village of Dale, which lay hugging the shores of its harbour in the most impossibly picturesque way. The village had turned its face away from the elements, giving enough shelter to allow that wonderfully contradictory landscape of trees slipping down the hillside until they almost met the sea. It was quiet at the end of winter, with only brightly coloured buoys speckling the calm water where the boats should have been.

As we climbed up and away from the village, out onto the windswept headland, distant views began to open around us. The day was grey but bright, making the sea glistening and silvery.

'We'll be able to see Skomer soon,' Mike said.

Then, suddenly, there it was, a tiny splinter of land amid all that sparkling water. I felt a twist of excitement deep inside, so powerful that it startled me.

'Oh, it's beautiful,' I said, hardly able to believe that I was looking at my new home.

And yet, when we reached the coastguard station, with the diamond-chequered panes of the nearby lighthouse gazing out across the ocean, I found that I was beginning to believe in the reality of it all. There was such an atmosphere of the sea; I could taste it, touch it, hear it. The sound of gulls and rough-edged waves echoed round the cliffs; the air was damp with salt. It had a sort of captivating bleakness that I was already starting to love.

Our first lesson was in single-handed cliff rescue (which, translated into reality, presumably meant me hauling Mike, unconscious and dangling precariously on the end of a rope, up a sheer rock face). We stood on the cliff top in a steady bluster of wind, which I would soon learn to categorize as the mildest of breezes. My oilskins, the cheapest we could find in Milford Docks, were doing a good job of keeping out the weather. The bemused men at the chandlers on the fish dock had rummaged round in the attic to find me an undersized set of waterproofs (and I liked to imagine that they had been waiting there for a young boy on his first job out on the trawlers). They were dark blue, rather than the usual vibrant yellow, but the unaccustomed oddness of such clothing still made me feel glaringly overdressed. In time, they would come to feel like a second skin, their stiff newness growing soft and pliable and comfortable, almost moulded to my own shape after years of wear.

As I watched the heavy metal stakes being pounded into the shallow soil with a sledgehammer, my mind slipped involuntarily into a closed position, as it does with anything that I think I can't understand. I only hoped that no one's life would ever depend on me being able to tie the right sort of knot. It was a relief when that part of the exercise was over and we moved on to learning the technique for firing distress flares. I felt immediately that this would be a much more useful piece of knowledge to acquire. If I were alone and in trouble I wouldn't bother with ropes and stakes, I would simply summon help. I didn't know then how much of our time would be spent in conditions that would make outside help impossible.

Mike fired the first flare. It swished into the air with the elegance of a bonfire-night rocket, blazing against the sky with a dazzling, fluorescent red. It was obviously so easy it seemed a bit odd that we needed to practise, but I was happy to take my turn. I freed up the trigger mechanism as instructed and began to squeeze cautiously, my eyes half closed, waiting for the sudden impact.

'Hold it away from your face,' said a voice from behind me.

I took the advice to heart. Slowly, without any conscious movement on my part, the flare began to tilt away from me. By the time the explosion came, the flare was pointing horizontally and the fizzing ball of light went scudding across the open fields, sending a couple of startled horses cantering in the opposite direction. My hand was still tingling from the impact, as though the fiery cascade from a sparkler was spitting through my fingertips. The assembled coastguards nodded politely, as if to imply that the exercise had been an unmitigated success, but I knew that Mike was making a mental note to tease me about it as soon as we were alone.

We went inside to be introduced to our brand new radio, which would be our only link with the real world beyond the island. It was a little hand-held thing, with a microphone, on a curly wire, clipped to the side of its blue canvas carrying case. Then, in the days before mobile phones, when most small marine VHF radios were the size of a couple of shoe boxes, it appeared to be almost a miracle of miniaturisation. We were dispatched to different rooms to practise communicating by pressing and releasing the talk button, and putting the 'overs' and 'outs' in the right places: batting the conversation backwards and forwards like a tennis ball, because it was impossible to talk and receive at the same time. (Although it was standard radio language, in all the years that followed, I never could bring myself to say 'roger', which I thought would sound hopelessly pretentious in the mouth of an amateur like me.)

'Can you hear me, over?' came the voice of the coastguard calling me on the radio from the next room.

The trouble was, I could hear him, but it was nothing to do with the radio, which remained stubbornly silent, refusing even to make an authentic-sounding crackle.

'Can you hear me, over?'

The increasingly frustrated shouts were coming straight through the wall without any help from this wonderful new technology, and I was tempted just to shout back with my reply. As someone fiddled solicitously with the knobs on my lifeless radio, I seemed to be the only one to have noticed the painfully comic nature of the situation. I stared down at my hands, twiddling my strange, shiny wedding ring, concentrating my thoughts on it to distract myself from the aching need to laugh.

We left with sacks of ropes, hefty metal stakes, sledge-hammer, flares and rescue stretcher, as well as our radio; another car full of stuff to be added to our growing mound of essential provisions. There were only two more days left before we were due to pile those polythene-covered parcels into a boat and leave the mainland behind. It seemed like a good time to start panicking. I made endless lists, adding things as I remembered them, crossing off everything that was already packed and waiting for our departure. I still needed a cookbook, something old-fashioned and all-encompassing that would tell me how to turn those sacks of flour into loaves of bread.

'We've got to get an axe,' Mike insisted. 'We'll need it for chopping firewood. And don't forget matches and some extra torch batteries.'

'Needles and cotton,' I said out loud as I added them to the bottom of the list, and then as an afterthought scribbled down 'writing paper'.

'There must be so many things that are almost essential,' I said, 'and if you forget just one of them it could make life really miserable. I mean, imagine having to go for months without any soap or salt or coffee.'

I have no idea how we managed to do everything in those ten days, but somehow we did, so it was rather demoralizing to discover that it had been a waste of time. The day before our planned departure on the 14th of March, Mike phoned the boatman to make the final arrangements. One glimpse of his face told me that it was not good news.

'We won't be going anywhere tomorrow,' Mike said miserably. 'The weather's far too rough.'

From where we were, miles inland, wind and waves and tides seemed remote and inexplicable. I did not understand then that the breezes that feel so insignificant in town, as they scatter leaves and debris down paved streets, could turn the sea into a boiling white froth and make any journey in a small boat impossible.

Though it was hard to believe, after all our efforts had been channelled so single-mindedly towards that day, we were stranded. We were left, surrounded by our piles of luggage, with nowhere to go. The trappings of our old life had been dispersed and disposed of; the new life was sealed up in boxes, not yet ready to be opened. We were in a no-man's land, caught between the past and the future. Perhaps it was good for us to realise that we were leaving behind an existence of timetables and certainties, and moving into one where the weather might disrupt our plans for days, or even weeks, at a time.

We ended up in Lockley Lodge, a wooden house on the slopes above Martin's Haven, the nearest sheltered bay on the mainland to Skomer. It was owned by our employers, the West Wales Naturalists' Trust, who were happy for us to stay there while we waited to cross to the island. From outside, the cream-coloured building looked quite picturesque. Inside, the overwhelming impression was of mouse droppings: every surface was blackened by a film of gritty particles.

Our hoard of essentials filled the three small rooms. We had to pile every-thing several feet high, leaving narrow alleyways between the polythene packages to allow us to move from room to room. The ubiquitous blackness of polythene and mouse droppings felt extraordinarily bleak. We comforted ourselves that this depressing interlude would last for no more than a day or two.

When I was in the bedroom hunting out our sleeping bags, I noticed that one of the wooden exterior walls was flapping in the wind, like washing on a line. I could see fluttering strips of daylight in the corner where the two walls met. It was going to be a cold night.

In the morning, we discovered that the mice had launched an assault on our boxes of food, tearing away at the plastic and cardboard to reach the contents. It meant a total reconstruction of the edifices we had built, so that the boxes containing food could be kept in the bedroom with us. Before settling down for the night, we made sure that our shoes, and any other suitably heavy, unbreakable objects, were within easy reach of the bed. Then, when it sounded as though the mice were becoming too successful in their tunnelling activities, we could hurl something in the direction of the noise, which brought a brief respite from the onslaught. As an uncharacteristically thick, white frost settled in outside, the combination of mice and draughty, flapping walls didn't make for a dream honeymoon.

In fact, it was a difficult period altogether. We had spent every last penny preparing for our departure, and there was nothing left, even to buy food. Our first pay cheque was a month away, we had no credit cards and our bank would not contemplate a loan. We were in the ridiculous position of being surrounded by three months' supply of provisions and yet with nothing to eat, because we refused to break into the parcels that we had packed so carefully to be opened on Skomer. For most of that period we survived on slices of toast cooked in front of the little glowing square of an ancient, cream-enamelled electric fire. One of the culinary highlights was when we boiled up a mangel-wurzel (meant for animal food), that we had found discarded at the edge of a field, and discovered that it had a surprisingly pleasant and delicate flavour.

So we waited as the days stretched out into weeks, while the wind stayed at gale force and the sea was in uproar. Our domestic circumstances were so gloomy, and the waiting so tedious, that I couldn't understand why, each time the crossing was delayed, I felt a faint ripple of relief, an internal sigh of gratitude for at least one more day of normality. For another twenty-four hours I would remain in contact with cars and electricity and telephones; the shops would still be there for those insignificant forgotten things that I remembered in the middle of the night with cold panic. I suppose that what we had, despite its shortcomings, was at least a known quantity. The next step would be into the unknown.

Every day we walked from our wooden refuge up onto the headland looking out towards Skomer. The wind was cold and the weather permanently grey. The steep cliffs of the island looked almost black. Pale light silvered the veil of mist thrown up around it by the waves, so that it was half-hidden behind its own protective barrier. For the first time, I felt afraid of it. Amid so much excitement and trepidation I had thought almost entirely about the things we needed to do. Only now that we had reached the calm of waiting was I considering what it would really mean to leave the mainland behind.

The cliffs below hissed and thundered with the sound of surf. Between us and Skomer lay the tiny island of Midland. It split the stretch of open water in two so that the waves forced their way through on either side of it, frothing and churning like rapids on a river. I had never seen the power of tides like that before.

'It looks so close, but so unreachable,' I said.

'The island could never be so special if it was easy to get to,' Mike replied. 'It's the isolation that makes it what it is.'

I had thought that if I really hated it, if the loneliness and deprivations became unbearable, I could leave in three months. That was the length of notice required before we could abandon the job. But I knew then, as we stood there looking across the sea, that, whatever happened, I would have to stay for a year. It wouldn't be fair to give up after a few months: not fair to the island, or to me, or, least of all, to Mike. I had come to realise, just from the raw wildness of what we were looking at, that it would take time. I would have to work at coming to terms with such a harsh existence. Then, if I survived those twelve months, it would be an adventure that I could look back on for the rest of my life with a certain amount of pride that I had actually had the courage to do it.

TWO

It was over two weeks later than planned when we began carrying our supplies down the stony beach at Martin's Haven. The wind had dropped at last; the air was motionless, speckled with pinprick drops of moisture that smudged everything into muted shades of grey, and the flattening effect of the mist made the water look silky calm. But at the very edge, where the sea scoured up against the pebbles, there was still the irritable turbulence that lingers in the aftermath of a storm. The shallow cliffs around the bay were fringed with white, marking that point of endless conflict between land and sea.

With the tide quite high, it did not take long to carry the first of the black packages to the edge of the waves. I was suddenly extremely glad that Mike had insisted on each box being secured with string. Without that handhold, the slippery plastic would have been almost unmanageable. A small group of people had come to see us safely across to the island, and with their help the mound of luggage piling up on the pebbles grew quickly. The difficult bit was transferring everything to the dinghy as it wallowed in the flounce of surf that churned against the shore. As I waded into the water I was aware of the odd sensations of the sea, something that would eventually become too common-place even to notice. The weight of the water was momentarily startling as it crushed my boots against my legs and clung like wet concrete, resisting every step. Worse still was the way the pebbles of the steep shingle bank clattered and rolled from beneath my feet with the suck of each retreating wave, trying to unbalance me.

After such a promising start, I realised that my first impressions had been naively optimistic. The dinghy, piled high and looking precariously top-heavy, crept across the undulating waves towards the waiting boat. For all that effort, one dinghy-load seemed to have made no impact on the looming mass of black polythene.

The tide was dropping with remarkable speed. Everything that had been deposited precisely at the water's edge was soon left sprawling aimlessly in the middle of the beach. It would all have to be moved again . . . and again. We spent the morning leap-frogging everything down the beach in pursuit of the swiftly sinking sea.

At that time I thought only in terms of the tide being in or out; I did not realise how much variation there could be in the height of a tide and therefore, by contrast, in its lowest ebb. This was a very big tide indeed. The water drained away, like a bath emptying, until the waves, sapped of their strength, were sliding languidly against the gently shelving pebbles at the bottom of the beach. And then the tide kept on going out. The water oozed back from the sea bed to reveal an uninviting strip of slippery, green pebbles and an obstacle course of boulders draped in stringy, brown weed. That was when things started to become really uncomfortable.

I was soft then, not used to any kind of hard, physical work. A Calor gas cylinder took so much effort to lift that the muscles in my face twitched with the strain. It wouldn't take many months to build my strength, but that was no consolation at the time. I made my way towards the dinghy with a sack of potatoes, eel-skinned in black polythene, clasped in a desperate bear hug, while my feet skidded out of control across the blanket of weed, jamming painfully against every rock that got in their way.

It was such a relief when I realised that our apparently inexhaustible supply of packages had dwindled almost to nothing. By the time we left the mainland behind it was well into the afternoon. The boat rocked smoothly over the curves of grey water, which were all that remained of the storm-waves that had dominated the past few weeks. The island showed only as layers of shadow through the blur of mist. It was the dullest and most unflattering of lights. I knew that I should have been seeing it on a bright, blue day, with enough breeze to highlight the cliffs with white surf. But it hardly mattered; it looked wonderful to me. That single, decisive step of loading our belongings onto the boat had transformed my fear back into excitement. I was already beginning to feel that slightly possessive bond which meant that Skomer could never be less than perfect in my eyes.

Apart from the boat engine, it was very quiet: no wind, few birds, just one or two gulls flickering bright against the dullness, trailing long, wailing calls in their wake. I stood leaning against the rail at the front of the boat trying to take it all in; the smell and the taste of the sea air, its soft dampness against my face. Everything seemed so intense, because it was the start of something new. This was mine now, not something I would visit and then leave behind.

Suddenly, Mike was beside me.

'Can you see it?' he asked. I looked up, crinkling my eyes, trying to make them see through the haze. 'There, above the bay. It's our house.'

And then I caught sight of it. It was amazing. Never before had I seen a house quite so close to a cliff edge. Long, low and wooden, there was a whisper of grand garden shed about it, but, simply by virtue of its position, it was one of the most spectacular houses I had ever seen.

The boat turned into North Haven, and we were ready to start unloading onto the beach below the house. Mike and I went first, with Mike rowing us ashore in the dinghy. It came to rest with a hollow thump against the half-submerged rocks, with their fleshy ribbons of weed rising and falling in the flow of the water. As I stood up to get out, the dinghy wobbled precariously, and I was distracted by a chorus of shouts from the boat. The confused sounds echoed against the cliffs so that I couldn't understand what they were trying to say. Mike's reactions were faster; from among the echoes he somehow unravelled the message that our arrival at our new home needed more ceremony. He leapt up and scooped me into the air. I gave a gasp of alarm and clung to him as the dinghy struggled to regain its equilibrium. Then I realised that he was stepping out into the shallow, soupy mixture of seaweed and water that surrounded us. As he bounded across the slick of weed that fringed the beach, I closed my eyes in expectation of a bruising crash as we sprawled onto the stones. A second later I was back on my feet standing, slightly disoriented, on the pebbles. A great cheer from the boat resonated through the empty bay, and I felt a smile lighting up my face, like the sun emerging from the clouds. After so much planning and preparation, waiting and worrying, I had finally set foot on the island.

As if to spoil that moment, those packages began to reappear. The dinghy shuttled back and forth, painstakingly recreating the same daunting mound that we had spent most of the day carrying from Martin's Haven. By the time everything was unloaded, the afternoon was over; the boat and our helpers had to return to the mainland. I felt hopeless standing there, dwarfed by that seemingly immovable mountain.

'Don't worry,' someone said kindly as they were leaving. 'It stays light until gone eight now. That should give you plenty of time.'

I had a strange longing to stand and watch as the boat, our last link with civilisation, dissolved into the fog, but there was too much to do.

'I'll go and get the tractor,' Mike said confidently. 'Once we've got that we'll be able to move all this in no time.'

'Thank goodness for that,' I said. 'I couldn't face carrying this lot any further.'

I'd had nothing to eat or drink all day, and that brief lull had given me enough time to realise how tired and desperately thirsty I felt.

'Start moving this stuff up the beach before the tide comes in,' Mike called back as he began to walk up the path.

Fortunately, I did not realise the significance of that remark.

After lingering briefly at its lowest ebb, the tide had changed direction and was advancing very rapidly. I soon realised that if I carried each package to the top of the beach most of them would be inundated before I had time to move them. I could move each one only a few yards, until the whole heap was shifted, and then start again. As the incoming tide gathered speed so did I. Before long, I was forced to run with each load as I snatched it from the edge of the water. If there had been time, I would have sat down and wept with tiredness and frustration. I had picked them up and put them down so many times that I came to know each package intimately, and my heart sank at the deceptively small ones that clung to the ground as I tried to lift them.

Where was Mike? I stared up at the cliff top, but all I could see was a tangle of ivy leaves and the sky beyond. I could not spare even a few minutes to go and look for him because I was trapped on a revolving treadmill of packages. If I stopped, the tide would overtake me.

It was several hours later when Mike re-emerged from hiding. Just when everything was safely heaped on the slipway above the tide line, I heard the distant roar of the tractor. Eventually, it came into view, bouncing and clattering down the long track to the beach and looking devastatingly close to the cliff edge. All the silent rage that I had been fermenting dissipated into relief at the prospect of being rescued. At last the tractor was going to take over.

'Sorry it took such a long time,' Mike called above the engine noise as he reached the concrete slipway. 'The tractor battery was flat. I couldn't get it started.'

'I suppose we should have expected as much, really,' I said. 'You can hardly expect to come to a deserted island and find everything waiting for you in working order.'

'No,' Mike agreed briskly. 'Anyway, we've lost so much time already, we'd better get the tractor loaded up.'

'Is that it?'

I had only just noticed the hopelessly small carrying box on the back of the tractor.

'I'm afraid so,' Mike said as we began trying to cram some of the packages onto the tractor. 'You start carrying stuff up to the house. Otherwise it'll take all night.'

I watched miserably as the tractor growled out a puff of exhaust smoke and began to pull itself doggedly up the steep track. Just as I thought I had finished, the hard part was about to begin.

There is an art to carrying heavy loads up the side of a cliff. The principle is similar to winding spaghetti onto a fork, in that you should always start with less than you think you can manage. This is actually much more difficult than it sounds, bearing in mind that every armful left behind will mean another climb up the cliff. At first, I piled on as much as I could possibly hold, and then started walking. The problem was that the weight increased with each step of the climb, and by about half way up became unmanageable.

I set off, following the tractor up a track that felt almost vertical. As the tractor continued round on a broad loop towards the house, I veered off up a set of wooden steps and onto a narrow footpath that took a more direct route. The light, crumbly soil all around me was honeycombed with rabbit holes. Every couple of feet the ground opened up to reveal the black, empty mouth of a burrow. It made the simple act of walking extremely complicated, and if I inadvertently stepped off the path, even solid-looking ground was likely to give way beneath my feet where an underground tunnel came too close to the surface. This would have been unnerving in any circumstances, but with a heavy box, encased in slippery plastic, clasped tight to my chest preventing me from even seeing my feet, I could feel the anxiety tensing through my already aching muscles.

As I neared the house, the cliff edge cut in so close that it almost touched the path. I couldn't risk one step out of place. By the time I was able to let the box slide down on to the doorstep, my legs were trembling from fear and exhaustion. I could hear the tractor approaching, coming down from the hill above. As soon as it stopped Mike was calling to me.

'Have you seen the house yet?'

All day I had been simmering with curiosity to see the house, but the strain of the last few hours had dulled my enthusiasm. Then, when I saw Mike jumping down from the tractor and rushing towards me, it was inevitable that I would catch his excitement.

The L-shaped building, with huge windows, was clad in overlapping layers of cedar shingles. It was north-facing but, because of its position, at the edge of a narrow sliver of land where the island was almost cut in two by huge bays on either side, there were views of the sea both to the north and the south. The only door into the house was sheltered in the inside angle of the L. I crossed the shallow steps - broad, curved segments of a circle, cobbled with sea-smoothed beach pebbles - and entered my home for the first time.

The interior did not in any way resemble the primitive log cabin that I had imagined. It was obvious that, while I had been stuck on the beach, Mike had already found time to look round.

'Wait till you see the kitchen,' he called, racing ahead of me up the hallway.

It was a large room with windows on two sides, and I was vaguely shocked by its normality, which extended to a stainless steel sink with proper taps. But, really, it was impossible to walk into that room and see anything but the view. We were so high and so close to the edge that the windows looked straight down on to the sea. It was like being a bird soaring over the cliff tops. The rocky slopes of North Haven curved protectively around the bay in front of the house and then gave way to open sea. There was nothing else that day, no far off glimpse of land. The distance had been swallowed up, so that the greyness of the water melted imperceptibly into the greyness of the sky. The fading light had smoothed the sea, which spread below us like softly crumpled cloth.

The temptation to stand and stare was crushed by the thought of those packages waiting on the slipway. As we made a quick tour of the other rooms I realised that the house was bigger than I expected: four good-sized bedrooms, as well as a living room and a study. It was very bare, just the minimum of tables, chairs and beds, with plain wooden floors. But it had a nice feel to it, and in that setting I could not imagine needing anything other than simplicity. Given that it had been standing empty for the past five months, the house looked remarkably fresh and clean: no dust, no mould and, above all, no mouse droppings.

Mike was shuffling through a large bunch of keys.

'This door's still locked,' he said, 'and I can't find the key.'

After a lot of trial and error, one of the keys turned and the door swung open. I was amazed to see a perfectly ordinary bathroom. Up until that point I'd had some vague notion of carrying buckets from a well. I was disappointed that this stark, white bathroom suite did not fit with my romantic notions of isolation, although I would quickly come to see it as the one concession to normality I was glad not to have left behind.

'Come on,' Mike said. 'We'll have to get on before the light goes completely.'

On my first climb up the cliff path I had thought that I could not possibly do it again, but the brief rest had allowed my legs to stop shaking, and I was able to convince myself that I could manage one more load. It was the same each time. As I felt my way cautiously forward, concentrating on each laborious step, I knew that I was squeezing out every last drop of energy, but when I had shed the heavy load and was wandering back down to the beach I felt ready to try once more. By the time I had completed a few more trips the light was gone, and I was proud of the fact that my confidence had grown so much I could continue to pick a precarious route between the cliff edge and the ubiquitous burrows even in the dark.

Darkness, I discovered, is not an absolute thing. It can go on getting darker. And Skomer has its very own quality of darkness. On a cloudy, slightly hazy night, without the intrusion of even the most distant of artificial lights, the blackness thickens to the point of feeling almost tangible. There was no point in thinking of trying to manipulate a torch along with the slippery packages, so I had to rely on my other senses. It was difficult to concentrate on what I was carrying when my efforts were diverted towards finding a safe place to put my feet. Inevitably, something fell and landed with a thump next to me. I looked all round, but it was too dark to find anything. In the end, I decided that whatever was lost would have to stay there until morning. I tried to shuffle the black plastic more securely in my arms and then set off again. I had not gone far when something else thudded to the ground at my feet and, after a brief search, that too had to be abandoned until the morning. I was beginning to feel cross with myself and blamed the tiredness for making me so clumsy.

The next ascent of the cliff was even worse. I became convinced that there were things moving all around me. It was almost as if the ground itself had come to life. I kept hearing scurrying noises, the sound of something rustling through the dead bracken. But whenever I stopped to listen, the noise came from a different direction, as though it was coming from everywhere at once. And there were more of those thudding noises, some close and some further away. I felt uncomfortable with my own anxiety, and couldn't help remembering the way so many people had tried to warn me about the unsettling effects of isolation.

I knew that I was being irrational, but I gathered up my next load with more reluctance than ever. By the time I reached the narrow path along the cliff top, I had an overwhelming sense of being surrounded by something indefinable. Even the air was somehow shimmering with almost imperceptible sound. Then I heard a noise that was definitely real. It was a gurgling, strangled cry, a few tentative, high-pitched notes, coming from the ground very close to me. The clarity of the noise was startling, but at least I knew that I was not imagining it. Almost at once, there was another cry, further away but bolder and more distinct. Then came a sudden swooshing, close to my ear. My head jerked back with a reflex action, though I had no idea what I was ducking from. There was a shadowy flash near my face, but whatever it was veered off before making contact. All I felt was the whisper of air rushing against my skin.

The calls quickly spread from the ground to the air, growing stronger and more insistent. Streams of gurgling, bubbling, inharmonious notes were pouring over each other. I could hear the changing tone as they screeched towards me and then skimmed past. The whole island was erupting with noise and movement, and all I could do was keep going, creeping through the darkness as quickly as I dared.

When I reached the house I was ready to give up. I stood inside the shelter of its L-shaped walls and watched the lights of the tractor undulating down the rutted track towards me. As soon as the engine noise died away I walked round to the side of the house to meet Mike. He was ecstatic.

'Have you seen the shearwaters?' he called.

He grabbed a torch from the back of the tractor and shone it upwards, threading it back and forth across the sky. Birds flickered in and out of the pale beam, catching in the light for a moment before vanishing again into the anonymity of darkness. There must have been hundreds of them, filling the air above us like the swarm of gulls that follows a fishing boat.

'Where did they come from?' I asked in amazement.

'Right under your feet,' Mike said. 'They've been inside these burrows that you've been walking over. Or they've been out at sea, waiting until it gets really dark before they could risk coming back to the island.'

'It's incredible. To think the island was so quiet when we arrived, and yet these birds have been here all along.'

'Do you want to have a closer look?'

As we walked back towards the house the torch beam raked across the bank picking out dozens of birds speckling the dark vegetation.

'It's strange the way they sit there,' I said. 'They don't seem to be the slightest bit disturbed by the light shining on them.'

'No, it doesn't bother them. Do you want to see?'

He went bounding off up the bank and returned a few seconds later with a shearwater in his hand. The bird was calm, hardly bothering to struggle free.

'How did you do that?' I asked. 'I can't believe that a bird would sit there and let you pick it up.'

I leant forward to take a closer look. It was about the size of pigeon, but much more slender, with a sleek black head paling to white under the chin, and dark eyes that glinted in the torch light. The back and wings were black, the breast pure, unblemished white: too perfectly smooth to give the appearance of individual feathers. The bird seemed gentle and solemn in its serenity. I wanted to stroke the top of its head with my finger, but I felt it would be too much of an imposition for something so detached and dignified.

The number of birds in the air and on the ground was increasing by the minute. Mike told me there were over a hundred thousand pairs of shearwaters nesting on the island, and our house was in the middle of one of the densest colonies. Even surrounded by such an obvious manifestation of their presence, it was a number I found hard to contemplate, but as I made my way back down to the beach I began to get some idea of what it really meant. The birds were so thick on the ground that it was hard to walk.

The more I walked among them, the more obvious it became that the birds had no fear of being trodden on. They scattered themselves carelessly underfoot, and the responsibility for evasion was all mine. My sensibilities were less robust. I was unnerved by the prospect of being hit by a flying shearwater. They whistled past with dizzying speed, so fast that I could barely see them, and was left only with the faint murmur of wing-beats in my ears. They materialized from the blackness a few feet in front of my face, the white of their breasts just palely visible, and then were gone again, swallowed up by the dark. Every single time one came uncomfortably close I flinched in expectation of the impact. It was becoming a serious impediment to the slow progress I was already making, and I knew I had to force myself to ignore them. I convinced myself that they were much more accustomed to finding their way in the dark than I was. Their powers of navigation were no doubt faultless down to the smallest fraction of an inch. This apparent clumsiness was no more than my own inept interpretation of their remarkable flying skills.

It worked. I walked on boldly with my head held high, and when the inevitable happened I didn't see it coming at all. The glimmer of white at the corner of my eye was almost simultaneous with the crash. I just felt the thump on the side of my head. There was a crunch as my neck jarred sideways and a giddy ringing that I could feel and hear as a single sensation. The bird fell to the ground and shuffled off into the undergrowth. I touched the side of my head, which was still too numb and buzzing for me to tell if I had really been hurt, but there was no blood, so I assumed that I must be all right and continued shakily on my way.

It was nearly midnight when we agreed that we couldn't do any more that night. Once we had made sure that everything left down at the slipway was above the tide line, there was no reason why it shouldn't be safe until the morning, since it had been packed to withstand the weather. It was a strange concept, leaving our possessions heaped at the top of the beach, but on a deserted island we had no need to worry about security. As I walked back up the cliff for the last time that day, the tiredness became suddenly overwhelming. I waited for a few minutes, listening to the noise of thousands of birds calling at once. The sheer intensity of sound is almost impossible to describe. The calls were a tuneless, high-pitched warbling, rising and falling in a series of short bursts. Together, they meshed into a fog of noise that smothered everything. As birds flew close, their individual calls broke through clear and sharp, a flash of sound like the beam of a lighthouse briefly penetrating the haze. I had imagined a place of such peace and silence; this all-pervasive noise seemed unbelievable and slightly daunting. I seriously wondered if I would ever sleep again.

Inside the house, I began tearing my way through the layers of plastic in search of something to eat. The boxes had been labelled but, as I discovered, it was not a precise art. A box marked food might contain only salt and enormous packets of dried vegetables: nothing of any immediate interest. Eventually, I disinterred a pack of sausages and put them on to cook. Although I had not eaten all day, any feelings of hunger had been discarded long since. My only sensations were of exhaustion and a raging thirst. I rummaged a bit more in the boxes, but the longed-for coffee remained sadly elusive. Surely, in my whole life, I had never been quite so tired. I could happily have gone straight to bed without eating, but our first night on Skomer deserved better than that, so we ate the sausages and opened our one precious bottle of wine. We had arrived, and that alone needed to be celebrated.

For sleeping, we chose a room at the shortest, most exposed, tip of the L, with two walls made almost entirely of windows facing south and east, and no curtains. The latter seemed a fairly insignificant consideration under the circumstances. It was a large room with bare floorboards and a strange-looking fireplace at one end, made of beach boulders set in concrete. There was nothing else, apart from the bed and a bedside cabinet, where I laid out a few of my things to mask the emptiness.

The thin, foam mattress felt supremely comfortable. As soon as I lay still, the aching in my muscles stopped. Far below us there was a rhythmic, rasping whisper of waves against shingle. But we were high up, drifting among the clouds of birds. I shouldn't have worried about the shearwaters keeping me awake. Already, in my mind, their discordant calls had taken on the soft tones of a lullaby. As I closed my eyes and listened, I thought what a unique and wonderful feeling it was just to be able to hear them. There was something about that reassuring cacophony that made me feel welcome, as though I had come home.

THREE

By the following morning the mist had lifted. The light filled our bedroom, and I had a sense of perfect warmth and comfort, more intense than I could ever remember. It seemed like a good omen, as though everything was going to be all right here. The feeling was so blissful that I did not want to move and risk breaking the spell. The only niggling unease came from remembering that there were still so many of those awful packages down on the slipway waiting to be carried up.

When I forced myself to get up, I realised why I had not wanted to move. Everything hurt. Muscles from my neck to my calves seemed to have short-ened and stiffened in the night. They felt like ancient elastic bands that had hardened and perished with age to the point where they had lost their stretch. Just standing up was like wrenching them into impossible contortions. But those insignificant aches couldn't burst the bubble of excitement I felt inside. I ran straight into the kitchen, where the lino was cold against my bare feet. The view had expanded enormously since the twilight of the previous evening. Half–submerged rocks strung out across the mouth of North Haven made beautiful shapes in the water, and the cliffs were subtly washed with the gradu-ated colours of lichen, flowing from black, at sea level, up to vibrant golden yellow. The horizon had slid away opening up miles of sea, beyond which it was possible to decipher the shapes of the Preseli Mountains rising from the mainland. The sun had climbed high enough to be spilling splashes of red and gold, which caught briefly against the turning waves. It filled me with an almost tearful sense of wonder, and I told myself then that, no matter how long we stayed, this view was something that I must never learn take for granted.

There was so much to be done immediately that it was three days before I was able to see any more of the island, but it didn't matter: what little I had seen was almost too much to take in. After a night's sleep and in daylight, transporting the rest of our things up to the house was not nearly as difficult as I had feared. We had to unpack everything quickly since it had been thoroughly doused in seawater. It felt like a lifetime ago that we had packed those boxes, and it was like unwrapping Christmas presents as it emerged unscathed, without so much as a cracked egg. I had found Mike's idea of packing irritatingly excessive, with its layers of padding and waterproofing, but then I had no idea what an arduous journey lay ahead. Now, as our things reappeared in their new setting, I felt desperately grateful for his foresight. It would have been a dispiriting start to find ourselves sorting through boxes of wet and broken remains.

On our first excursion we walked up through the centre of the island. Although our house was perched on the cliff edge, the land behind continued to slope upwards. This gave us some shelter from the prevailing south-westerly winds, but also meant that every walk began with an uphill climb. I became hardened to it in time, but at first I felt the strain on my already tortured leg muscles. As we left the spectacular coastline behind, I couldn't help noticing that the interior of the island looked bleak. Then, I could just about see the island's faults, but soon I would become too besotted not to love it in all its seasons. Although it was early April, there was nothing about the vegetation that seemed to suggest winter might be over. Everything was battered, faded and flattened. Wind-scorched grass had been eaten to almost nothing by hungry rabbits. Dead bracken had been beaten down and leached of colour by a succession of winter storms until it gave the appearance of having set into a hard, dry crust, covering much of the island.

One of the things that struck me most forcibly about that first impression of the island was the number of corpses. The short turf was littered with the remains of shearwaters: a pair of wings with the rest of the body picked down to white bone; a skull with that distinctive black, curved beak. Mike told me about an article written in the early 1900s. To protect Skomer's anonymity it had been named only as Golgotha - the place of skulls. I could see why.

I found it faintly shocking to see this place, that I had so fondly imagined as a safe refuge, strewn with dead birds, to see the shearwaters, that I had watched over the past few nights crowding onto the island with such stunning effect, lying torn apart. I protested to Mike with childlike fury.

'But why? Why are so many of them being killed?'

'In a place like this that's so full of life, there has to be death.'

It was a brilliant answer that put everything into perspective, and it was something that I had to remind myself of frequently during our years there. If we were to live so close to nature, we would inevitably be surrounded by death. I had never seen anywhere so crammed full of living things. This scattering of dead birds was insignificant compared to the tens of thousands of shearwaters that would cover the island again at nightfall. It was a balance that I would learn to accept.

Despite these very obvious signs of predation, Skomer was one of the few places that offered the Manx shearwaters enough safety to risk coming on land. They were perfectly adapted for life at sea; their vulnerability on land was made obvious by the way we were able to walk among them and pick them up. Skomer was a haven away from people, but, more importantly, the island had no ground predators. There was nothing, from a rat to a fox, that could stalk the adult birds or raid the burrows for eggs and chicks. It gave the island a precious and fragile status.

Somehow, in all its history of occupation, Skomer had escaped the sort of invasion that has devastated so many other small islands. No stray rats had stowed away in the farming or building supplies carried to the island. No boat negotiating the treacherous tide races had discharged its live cargo as it foundered against the island's cliffs. The island had been lucky over the centuries, and we would have to remain permanently vigilant to make sure that luck would hold.

The only threat of attack came from the air: a raven or a great black-backed gull could easily take an adult shearwater. That was why they waited for night-fall to emerge, when these predators were no longer flying. Even a moonlit night could provide enough illumination to guide an airborne hunter to its prey.

As we walked, Mike pointed out the landmarks.

'That's called the Bread Rock,' he said, as we passed a large outcrop on our right.

I was fascinated to learn that every field, and even the more prominent rocks, had a name. The slope levelled out past the Bread Rock, and we came into an area of large fields. The centre of the island is relatively flat, and the view suddenly opened up ahead of us. A long, straight track stretched between the fields leading up to the old farmhouse with its group of outbuildings. Apart from our own house, these were the only buildings on the island. As we approached them, the extent of the decay became more and more apparent. There was no roof on the house, just the silhouette of the gables, dark against the sky.

The house and farm buildings formed three sides of a square, while the whole complex was enclosed and sheltered by high stone walls. The first glimpse as we passed through the gateway into the farmyard was a startling contrast to the windswept drabness of the rest of the island. Hidden by those walls was a secret garden. The lawn was dense, velvety green, clipped short and neat. And everywhere were cascading clumps of daffodils, particularly in front of the house where they formed unbroken banks that shimmered like a curve of sunlit water pouring over a weir. The house itself was imposing, dour almost. Its square, uncompromising shape was veneered with slate tiles, overlapping like the scales of a butterfly's wing. In the early spring light it was violet-grey, like bruised storm clouds, and the daffodils shone like shafts of sunlight at its feet.

I had the strangest feeling of trespassing. It was like being in someone else's garden. Despite the dilapidation of the house, the farmyard looked too well cared for to be completely deserted, but it was only the rabbits that kept the lawn so neatly cropped and the flowers, planted decades before, had thrived untended.

'It was beautiful once,' Mike said. 'A real Victorian home.'

(We later found some intricately carved legs from the billiard table abandoned in a shed: a tiny of shard from the dark and richly furnished interior of its heyday.)

'Do you remember it?' I asked.

'No. It was almost a ruin when I first came, although we used to sit in the back kitchen which still had a roof.'

I stared, trying to imagine the days of its glorious past. The contrast was quite melancholy. The windows gaped blankly and, though the interior walls remained, still marking out the pattern of the rooms, they were choked with fallen debris making it impossible to walk inside. The few remaining joists from the upper floors had all but broken free and dangled dangerously overhead. It looked bleakly romantic, but I longed to find some sense of it having been a happy place.

The only part of the complex of buildings that still had a roof was faced with a row of half a dozen deep blue doors.

'What are these?' I asked.

'They're called the chalets. They were the old cow sheds. It's where visitors and voluntary assistants can stay in the summer.'

I opened one of the doors. The roughly partitioned room had a bare concrete floor and contained only an old iron bedstead.

'You'd have to be quite dedicated to stay here,' I said.

Mike had already turned his attention towards the corner of the farmyard.

'Look at this. It's the island's only tree, a black poplar.'

The branches arched elegantly above the rabbit lawn, with a promise of summer shade, but its crown was severely sheared away, in line with the top of the surrounding walls. The winds cutting across the island had prevented the tree from stretching up into the sky beyond that protective shelter, and so it had remained all its life cowering in its own little haven of calm.

We walked out behind the house, where the land sloped away giving us an open outlook all the way to the north coast. The reddish browns of damp bracken made a stunning contrast to the intense blue-grey of the sea beyond, as we stared out at a view that went on forever.

'I've got a surprise for you,' Mike called as he disappeared through a bramble-clogged gap in one of the walls.

A minute or two later he reappeared, crashing through the mesh of under-growth, cupping a tiny animal in the palms of his hands. He held it out towards me and the creature sat calmly washing its face and whiskers, quite uncon-cerned. Its fur was polished Titian, like a conker caught in the evening sun, and it had liquid eyes, glossy as a bead of black ink.

'What is it?' I asked.

'It's a Skomer vole,' Mike said. 'It's unique to the island; you won't find one of these anywhere else in the world.'

He placed it carefully into my outstretched hands and I felt the minute pressure of its cold little feet wandering over my skin.

I was used to wildlife as something to be glimpsed in the distance; the idea of birds and animals that could be gathered up from the ground without showing the slightest distress felt more like something out of a children's story.

'Why doesn't it mind me holding it?' I asked, as the vole began to explore its way up its way up my arm towards my shoulder.

'Well, they just happen to be tame. As an isolated island group, these voles have had very few predators. Some people say that's why they don't have the same response to danger that you would find in mainland animals.'

'You mean his mother never told him to watch out for people?'

'Something like that.'

That was as far as we went that day. My first exploration of the island had been brief but memorable. There was so much settling in still to be done that we returned the vole to its place among the worn, wintry vegetation and made our way reluctantly back home.

FOUR

The rest of the island was gradually revealed over the coming days, weeks, and even years. It was not a large island, only a couple of miles long and a mile wide, but it would never be possible to know it completely, and there was always something still to be discovered, right up to the very end. In those early days the revelations were spectacular: shaded inlets that turned the sea deep, glossy green, towering offshore rocks fringed with seals, a soaring arch of natural stone made dazzling gold by its crust of lichen.

Discovering the island brought a range of emotions, but I was surprised to realise that the strongest of these was relief that I had finally arrived, as though this was what I had been waiting for, what my whole life had been leading towards. I did not experience any of the feelings of strangeness and desolation that I had expected. It was so easy, like slipping back into the routine of some hazy, forgotten past. I just knew that I had reached the place where I was meant to be.

Sometimes when I woke in the morning I was scared to move, afraid that if I left that half-dreaming state the island would be gone, and only the old reality would remain. It seemed ridiculous that it could be true. It was as though I had stretched out my hand and with one gentle, almost tentative, push had sent my life in a different direction. Less than a month before I had been single, a student, vaguely concerned about the uncertainties of the future. Now I had left that existence behind, just walked away from it, taking almost nothing with me. It was hard to believe that everything had changed so suddenly and so completely, and that I had found what I had always wanted without ever realising it.

It was sometime during the first week on Skomer that I developed the anxiety that would haunt me for the rest of my time there. It terrified me to realise that one day I would have to leave. No matter how far in the future, eventually it would happen. All thoughts of being brave and trying to bear it for a year were gone. I talked to Mike about it a few days after we arrived.

'I think if we could,' I said, 'I'd like to stay for ten years.'

Ten years. It was an arbitrary number plucked from nowhere, but I knew exactly what I was trying to say. I was young enough to believe that a decade was reassuringly infinite. Because the truth was, I had already made up my mind that I wanted to stay forever.

Despite the misgivings that had troubled me while we were on the mainland, once we arrived there was nothing that I missed. We had been transplanted so dramatically from one place to another that it was almost impossible to make any comparisons with the past. Our life on the island was complete in itself; I never saw it as lacking in anything. All the things we had left behind would have been inappropriate in that new setting. My greatest fear, loneliness, did not materialise. I can't explain why, except to say that my love for the island seemed to compensate for everything else. Over the years, one of the questions I was most often asked was how I coped with the loneliness of isolation. I couldn't answer because, although I was sure I had once understood it, the longer I spent on the island the more difficult I found it even to imagine how loneliness might feel.

In a more practical sense, the thing I should have missed was electricity, but, again, that was something from the past that had no place in the present. It was something that didn't exist, not something that was missing. Living without electricity is not like suffering a power cut on the mainland, when everything you rely on suddenly lets you down. And yet, while my conscious thoughts didn't dwell on electricity, my hand made an odd little reflex action to reach for a light switch every time I walked into a darkened room. That happened, almost without fail, for several months, but I liked the warm, mellow glow from the gas lights, and, gradually, we learnt to leave boxes of matches at strategic points around the house where we could feel for them in the dark.

Within a few days of arriving, I had no choice but to give in to the insatiable demands of bread-making. It was an inescapable necessity that would have to be repeated every two or three days. I had come equipped with various recipes from friends, together with my brand new copy of Mrs Beeton, but all the helpful advice had served only to cloud the subject in a daunting mystique. I was beginning to see it as an art that only the chosen few could ever hope to master. It was a formidable responsibility because, even if I produced loaves that crashed brick-like from their tins, we would have no alternative for the foreseeable future but to eat them.

The house could still be very cold in those early spring days, especially since we had no heating and the twisted metal window frames let in every passing gust of wind. Bread-making gave me the ideal excuse to drag the huge, old paraffin heater into the kitchen and burn up some of the precious fuel. We might be able to put up with the cold, but the soft, pallid dough definitely needed to be treated with more respect and, as my recipes insisted, protected from draughts. It was a battle of wills with the paraffin heater, trying to encourage it to produce a noticeable amount of heat without sending out streams of sooty smoke and black smuts.

There was something unfailingly satisfying about the way the dough transformed itself. It started off sticky and unformed, clinging irritatingly to the bowl and to my fingers. Then, after a few minutes kneading, the tussle between me and the dough was won. The ingredients coalesced and began to squash and flow beneath my pummelling knuckles. I could tell when it was ready, just by the feel. It became smooth and dry to the touch, and the plump cushion bounced back into shape when it was squeezed. Sometimes, if I was busy or if my arms were aching, I was tempted to stop when the dough was almost there, when it felt smooth but not quite springy enough. It was a mistake, though, because the bread never rose so well or had such a good texture. No part of the process could be hurried; I was slowly learning the patience essential to anyone who intends to spend a long period of time on a small island.

Then came the enjoyable part, shaping and proving the loaves, watching them rise, smelling them baking and, finally, tapping the golden brown crusts in search of the hollow sound that comes from a properly cooked loaf. I always felt a sense of pride as I turned my finished loaves out onto the cooling rack, and I can still remember a batch of fresh, warm rolls eaten with just-melting butter and tinned sardines as one of the most delicious things I have ever tasted. That, though, probably says more about our general level of deprivation than the intrinsic quality of the sardines. When we had been buying our supplies we had been so intent on trying to find things that would endure months of storage and still produce an acceptable meal that we had entirely forgotten about the frivolous nature of food. It is about pleasure as much as survival and, once the enjoyment was removed from eating, I was amazed to discover what an enduring obsession food could become.

We had allowed ourselves no treats: no tins of fruit, no biscuits, or chocolate, or crisps. This was mainly due to an acute shortage of finances, which had forced us to concentrate on the necessities, but it was also because we had found it almost impossible to overturn thought processes that had been channelled towards buying fresh food on a daily basis. Faced with such a radical change it had been difficult to form any coherent plan. One of our most outstanding disasters was the catering pack of dried cabbage, which, after cooking, turned into an exact replica of school-dinner cabbage, complete with the black bits that we used to call flies. In fact, even with the dried cabbage, no amount of careful inspection ever managed to convince me that they weren't flies. Another memorable failure was the dried, textured soya protein, that I assumed was supposed to bear some vague resemblance to meat, but which emerged from the cooking process looking and tasting like screwed up bundles of marinated pink tissue paper.

After a short time, I developed raging food cravings, which was a new experience for me. These all-consuming longings were fuelled by the knowledge that they were insatiable. Sometimes the urge became so great that I found myself running halfway across the island to get home and indulge myself by looking at a favourite picture of a chocolate cake.

The result was that we embarked on a hopelessly unhealthy diet. I discovered that just about anything tasted nice if it was inside a pie, and so that became the preferred way of cooking everything, from cheese to baked beans to corned beef. Our sacks of flour, which had seemed ridiculously over-cautious, began to diminish with unsettling speed. The only saving grace was that our active, outdoor way of life meant that I was able to survive on a diet of pies without converting those extra calories into fat.

Before we left the mainland there were already distinct signs of spring; on the island we appeared to have stepped back at least a month. Everything remained determinedly dormant. For weeks I peered hopefully into the tangled cages of dead bracken for signs of anything coming to life. Then when spring arrived it seemed to come with the speed and power of a tidal wave breaking over the island, and suddenly it was brilliant with colour. I had never seen anywhere so overwhelmed by wild flowers.

Delicate, white sea campion fringed the island like a scattering of snow. The scent was deliciously fresh, faintly spicy, exactly how a flower should smell, and, with so many in bloom together, the perfume drifted in invisible clouds. The isthmus that ran beside the house joined the main part of the island to a smaller area, known as The Neck. It was wonderful to stand on that thread of land surrounded by sea, with almost limitless views to north and south. The sea campion covered it from edge to edge, and the floral scent was mixed with sharp, salty sea breezes and the faint ammonia of seabirds in a way that will always remain for me the definitive smell of a sea cliff.

The sense of discovery that I felt in those early weeks never quite went away. Spring, in particular, always brought that exciting feeling of newness. There was something liberating about being on Skomer, as though we had slipped the chains of adulthood and could explore with childlike freedom. I often thought what a perfect place it would have been to have grown up, and felt sad that I had come so late to the island.

The seashore provided endless scope for exploration, particularly at low tide. I loved the rock pools with their wine gum splodges of sea anemones in sunlit red and green. Mike was infuriatingly sure-footed over the slithery sheets of weed that were exposed at low tide, and he invariably left me standing as I wavered cautiously in his wake. I looked on in envy as he darted along the tide line, stopping and watching occasionally, like a hunting animal, then snatching a fish out of the water with his hands, and giving me a quick glimpse before allowing it to slide back beneath the waves. My favourite was the tompot blenny, which was a vibrant goldfish-orange, with fat, pouting lips and feathery eyebrows, like little fronds of coral.

I suppose that most people can remember one special summer that, for some reason, stays with them forever; mine was that first summer on Skomer. It was exceptional even in its own right, so hot and still and sunny that the certainty of one unclouded day following another was never in question, a summer destined to find its place in record books. It began in May, quite inauspiciously, with a fluffy, cotton wool sea fog that wrapped itself around the island and clung on tenaciously for a week. It was desperately frustrating to see probably the only good weather of the year disappearing into the fog. We could tell that it was sunny by looking up through the mist at the brilliant whiteness above. And we could feel the unpleasant heat seeping humidly through. I knew from the radio that the rest of Britain was basking in a heat wave, and was sure that a typical summer wouldn't allow for more than a week of this weather before the rain set in again.

I shouldn't have worried; the mist lifted spectacularly and the sun came pouring down. On the first sunny day I was out on the Neck, counting gulls. The sun was so blisteringly hot that the moment it arrived I covered myself up with a long-sleeved shirt. Even so, at the end of the day I found a neat, white imprint of my bra where the sun had singed my skin through the material of my shirt. It was an indication of what was to come. The sun on Skomer was formidably powerful, probably because it reflected from the rocks and the water all around. Mike turned deep, dark brown, with pale creases at the corners of his eyes from squinting into the dazzling light, while his hair was bleached white-blond in striking contrast. My skin never went any darker than faintly cooked toast, but at least it didn't burn.

By the time the sun arrived, the landscape had undergone the most dramatic change. Great sweeping tracts of the island had turned blue. It had begun gradually as a faint lilac mist drifting over the distant slopes, so insubstantial that it could have been a trick of the light. Then, like an incoming tide flooding over the last dead remnants of winter, the pools of dusky indigo had spilled across the island. Everywhere that had once been smothered by the dried up stems of bracken was inundated by bluebells. In places they stretched for acre upon acre, ending only when the slope of the land gave the illusion of meeting the sea. I could stare out across a view made of nothing but blocks of colour, from the dense, purplish bluebells, to the hard aquamarine sea and then the translucent turquoise of the sky, each trying to out-compete the others as the purest form of blue.

On the cliff tops faint shadows of pink were intensifying, like the first hesitant trickle of dawn soaking into the sky. The thrift flowers grew from rounded hummocks of fine green leaves, covering the plant completely until there appeared to be nothing but a mound of pink. They clustered so closely together that each individual tussock became part of the foamy cloud of colour. There was a guilty pleasure in walking over them, feeling the resilient plants springing beneath my feet, but I preferred just to sit cushioned among the flowers. All around was a patchwork of pink, some paler, some darker, the changing colours as subtle as the dappling of sunlight. I could sink into a mattress of flowers and watch them pour gently away over the cliff top so that they appeared to go on forever, and there would be nothing else but the sound of waves and of seabirds skimming erratically past.

The one thing that left the thrift marginally short of perfection was its lack of smell. Such a vibrantly beautiful flower seemed to deserve a flamboyant scent. But perhaps when the bluebells were in full flower, anything else might have been superfluous. In the heat of the day, with the sun drawing the last dregs of moisture out of the soil, the smell of bluebells came percolating up through the air like a humid mist.

By evening, the accumulated intensity of unrelieved sunshine began to feel stifling. The greatest luxury was to launch our boat and float out to sea, where the air was always cool. Then, as we approached the island again, the bubble of warm air trapped above the land came drifting down to meet us, thick and treacly with the perfume of so many flowers.

It was at about that time that the first day-visitors began to arrive. They were later than usual because the old converted lifeboat that transported them from the mainland had been laid up undergoing repairs. It was odd seeing a thin stream of people trickling off the boat onto my island. I desperately didn't want to resent them, but I found it difficult not to feel possessive about Skomer. It was a relief to discover that I actually enjoyed being able to show people what was so special about the island, and their enthusiasm only confirmed my feelings. Besides, by late afternoon everyone was gone, and the best time was still to come, when the island came back to life after the sleepy heat of the day.

The problem was that having people on the island took away that sense of a carefree existence. We became aware of time again as our days were regimented by the arrival of the boat. Everything suddenly felt fragile: the burrows laced through the dry crumbling earth, the cliffs smothered with birds. Though most of our visitors showed absolute respect for the island, the potential for accidental damage still worried me. As it turned out, the only real trouble came from the occasional attempt to steal birds' eggs and the determined photographers who tried to get too close to the nesting seabirds. The safety of the visitors was perhaps even more of a concern. Since we were in sole charge of the island, I felt a constant niggling anxiety that someone would be hurt in a fall, or simply collapse in the overwhelming heat.

Apart from day visitors, there were two or three postgraduate students who spent several months each year studying the birds, and a small number of voluntary assistants who generally stayed for a week or two to help with the work of the island. Mike had told me not to be concerned about the prospect of people coming to the island because Skomer usually brought out the best in everyone. And he was right. Over the years we were privileged to meet some of the kindest and most generous people I have ever known. With many of them it was clear, almost on first acquaintance, that they were destined to become lifelong friends. Whatever needed doing, someone was on hand to help. It made things almost too easy, lulled us into a false sense of security and let us forget, for a time, about the reality of living on an island.

It was inexperience that allowed us to take the water supply for granted. Early in June, Mike and I were passing the tank, which was filled by a spring on the slope above the house. He went over and listened.

'That sounds odd,' he said.

I joined him, pressing my ear against the tank. It sounded hollow with just the faintest reverberation, like the echo of a dripping tap.

'It seems to be empty,' Mike said, looking concerned.

We began to unscrew the numerous bolts that held the inspection hatch in place. When we managed to look inside, there was nothing but a great, ringing emptiness. The pool of water at the bottom was being replenished only drip by drip.

'Well, that's it then,' Mike said. 'No more baths or showers until we get some rain.'

This news was received with dismay by the students, who had their own self-contained quarters next to our house, but I thought that it would be no more than a minor irritation for a week or two. Fortunately, none of us realised then that the ban would have to remain in place until October.

Once boat contact with the mainland was established, one of our first priorities was to get some chickens. The boatman, Terry Davies, who also ran a smallholding, was happy to advise us and arranged to buy some suitable birds. We made repairs to one of the old sheds at the farm, put up perches, and filled the nest boxes with straw. We even found an old, white china egg in the cellar of our house, which we tucked prominently into the straw to give the newcomers some encouragement.

The chickens, when they arrived, were absolutely beautiful. Their feathers were greenish black, shining with a rainbow iridescence, and round their necks were collars of fiery gold. We couldn't wait to release them from the packing cases into their new quarters. On their first night Mike and I wandered up to the farm to find them settling down to sleep, sitting clucking and gurgling in a comfortable huddle. As solicitous new owners we picked them off the ground and sat them on their perches. There were no foxes or other predators to worry about, but we felt responsible for training them in proper, chicken-like behaviour.

We had bought them as point-of-lay pullets, which I took rather too literally. My innocence concerning all things connected with poultry led me to believe that point-of-lay meant that the eggs would arrive the following day. I was up at the farm early the next morning, searching excitedly through the straw. All I found, of course, was the china egg. As I watched the chickens scratch appreciatively at the grain that I had scattered over the ground, I decided that they were feeling disorientated after the boat journey, and would soon be ready to lay.

'You'll have settled down by tomorrow, won't you?' I said.

The chickens, though preoccupied, seemed to cluck faintly in assent.

I made the same expectant search the next morning, and the next, though my patience was not rewarded for another six weeks. The chickens, however, eggs or no eggs, were a good buy. They were completely free range, with a whole island to roam over, and yet they never left the farm complex where they burbled and scrabbled contentedly around the grassy yards. They brought the place to life, obliterating that air of desertion. Whenever we approached the farm, they ran clucking to meet us, jostling together as a single entity, greeting us like an enthusiastic dog rediscovering its owner after a long day's absence.

It was about three months after we first arrived that the opportunity arose for me to visit the mainland. It would be a fleeting visit, just long enough to buy a few essentials, but I was incredibly excited. When we had been struggling with our dreary food supplies I had dreamt of all the things I would like to buy and, somehow, the idea of shopping had become invested with a magic that it couldn't possibly possess. I spent the crossing transfixed by the rafts of seabirds drifting across our path. As the boat approached them the clusters of birds divided, skimming aside in a splash of watery trails, or diving below the surface and dissolving into a faint silvery plume. I was ecstatically happy to think my life had changed so much that this was now the prelude to something as mundane as buying food.

A few hours later I was back on the island with my head throbbing, determined to see as little as I could of the mainland in future. It had been awful. I had found the speed of the car terrifying, even at twenty-five miles an hour, and being in a street surrounded by so many people was unnerving. The air oozing up from the hot pavements, hazy with traffic fumes, had made me feel that I was going to suffocate. Soon, I was aware of a sensation like a hammer pounding inside my head behind my right eyebrow. By the time I returned to the relative cool of the sea-washed island, I knew that I would only visit the mainland again as a matter of absolute necessity. All visions of the exciting face of civilisation across the water were gone, and that aversion only grew over the years.

Until I went to Skomer, I had never seen so many rabbits in my life. The island was awash with them. I noticed it most in the evenings, particularly if we were walking up towards the farm as the light was failing. Beyond the Bread Rock, where the land levelled out, the broad, open fields gave an uninterrupted view of the rabbits enjoying a late graze before darkness set in. It seemed to start with a single animal, the one that was closest, or most alert, the first one to run from our approach. And then, like wave upon wave of falling dominoes, a ripple spread across the field. Dozens of shadow-brown creatures, almost absorbed by the twilight, began to run. They had been invisible in their stillness but, as soon as they started to move, they materialized, as if from nowhere, into a gently shifting sea of rabbits.

Rabbits had originally been taken to Skomer to be farmed, about seven hundred years previously. They once provided a good source of income, but had been little troubled by people in recent years and, in the absence of foxes or any other ground predators, the rabbits thrived. In such a hot, dry summer there seemed to be simply too many rabbits and not enough food. Some of the slopes around the cliff edges were slowly reverting to scorched, brown earth. They looked terrifyingly vulnerable with their intricate lacework of burrows stripped bare. In places, the sandy soil trickled away, like time through an hourglass. It would have been impossible to walk over the hollow crust of earth without collapsing the burrows and crashing onto the chicks hatching out underground.

The vegetable garden that we had begun with such high hopes back in April was slowly shrivelling. We had established it in the old walled garden at the farm, the only place sheltered from the salt winds. Previous residents of the island had fenced off a good-sized area, burying the wire right down to bedrock to exclude the burrowing rabbits. Without this, any attempt at gardening would have been out of the question. Even so, it was a very dispiriting process during that inhospitable summer, with every drop of water having to be carried several hundred yards from the well behind the farm.

I had never been able to find any enthusiasm for gardening under any circumstances, and there was nothing about the challenges of gardening on Skomer that was going to change my mind. After the hot and dusty walk through the centre of the island to the garden, I had no motivation left for weeding. I would far rather have walked on out to the cliffs to find the fresh breezes and watch the seabirds. Mike, on the other hand, I was convinced had a genetic predisposition for it. His father was a prize-winning vegetable grower, and I was sure that Mike must have an innate knowledge of how things should be done. Added to that, he was not one to be beaten by circumstances once he had set his mind on something, so, against the odds, our garden had every chance of surviving.

Despite my positive thinking, the early signs were not good. Young plants, nurtured in our sunny rooms at home, were instantly demolished once their tender young shoots were settled into the earth.

'It's those Skomer voles,' Mike shouted, as we arrived, yet again, to find a depleted garden. 'Look at this!' he snarled, pointing to a few ragged remnants of green protruding from the soil. 'That's my broad bean plants totally destroyed. It's pointless. All this hard work, and nothing to show for it. I don't know why I bother.'

He was so cross that I felt somehow responsible for the situation.

'Well,' I said lamely, 'we can keep out rabbits, but there's not much we can do about the voles.'

'Huh!' he said, in a we'll-see-about-that sort of voice.

Mike went stamping off to gather further evidence. I tried staring with my eyes screwed up, to blur the chewed rows into slightly more complete stripes of green. Then I wondered if this might be a good time to abandon the whole enterprise. The problem was that the only alternative to home-grown vegetables was something nasty out of a packet.

'Come over here!' Mike called in a tone of voice that made me think he suspected my treacherous thoughts. 'It isn't a vole doing this,' he said, pointing to a row of half-eaten lettuces. 'There are rabbits getting in here.'

'There can't be,' I insisted. 'We check the fence every time we come. We'd see if there was anything wrong with it.'

'Well, they must be getting in somewhere, and if I get my hands on them, they'll be sorry.'

We looked again, examining every inch of the fence for any sign of a burrow where the rabbits might have tunnelled from the dull brown desert outside into our artificial oasis.

'I think we can be pretty certain that there are no rabbits getting in here,' I said at last.

Mike looked suspicious, but even he couldn't deny the evidence of his own eyes.

We went back to weeding, and my mind wandered off in search of something more interesting. I was soon diverted by the discovery of a slow-worm, which allowed me to abandon the gardening in order to rescue it from any possible encounter with a spade. I picked it up from the dry earth and it felt beautifully smooth and warm as it coiled snake-like through my fingers. Its skin was golden, almost metallic in the sunlight, patterned with black markings. I held it up to study the fascinating perfection of its tiny face, and was particularly impressed by the miniature forked tongue that flickered occasionally into view. Everything about it said snake, although it was, in fact, a legless lizard. Skomer has no snakes, which I found particularly comforting as we waded through the whisper-dry undergrowth or delved our hands carelessly into burrows to look for birds. I took the slow worm to the edge of the garden and watched it writhe safely out of sight with a fluid twist of its body.

'There! Behind you! Grab it!'

Startled by a sudden shout from Mike, I looked round and saw something flitting between the lettuces. Before I had even managed to make a convincing dive in the right direction, the thing was gone, lost among the leaves.

'Oh, too slow,' Mike groaned dismissively. 'There it is again! I'll have it this time!'

He darted between the rows of peas with impressive speed, and the rabbit was about to find itself cornered against the high stone wall. It was only a baby, a few inches long, and I couldn't help feeling sorry for it, despite the destruction it was capable of causing. Mike dived, but the rabbit made a dazzling right-angle turn, leaving him floundering in the earth. I took up the chase, while the rabbit disappeared neatly into the tent of runner beans.

'Where's it gone?' Mike asked, regaining his composure.

'Somewhere in here,' I said, indicating the wigwam of bamboo canes.

'You mean you've lost it?'

'Not exactly,' I lied.

'Well it's not getting away this time. You take that end and I'll watch the other.'

After a few minutes of tense stand-off, the rabbit made a high-speed exit between my ankles, leaving me snatching feebly into thin air. Mike stormed after it with barely concealed exasperation. I followed in his wake, hoping to redeem myself. The rabbit careered towards the corner of the garden, and it looked as though we were about to win. We were closing in on it, and there was no room left for escape. To my horror, it didn't stop running but hurled itself straight into the wooden fence post. The force of the impact catapulted it backwards and it lay dead, stretched out on the dry, crumbled earth.

'Oh dear,' I said, already wishing that we had left the poor thing alone. 'Why ever did it do that?'

'I think it was trying to get out,' Mike said. 'Look, there's a tiny gap where the fence post meets the wall. That must be where it got in. I never imagined that it would be possible for a rabbit to get in there when we were checking the fence, but this one's so tiny it must have been able to squeeze through.'

He picked the rabbit off the ground, all thoughts of retribution gone. It lay on its back in the palm of Mike's hand, its body limp, drooping white paws framing the lifeless face. Mike gently stroked its forehead with the tip of his finger. We both felt terrible. The rabbit looked so perfect; there was no blood, no obvious injury. As we watched, I thought I noticed a slight twitching of its nose, and few moments later it opened its eyes. Then it sat up with all four feet planted on Mike's hand, as though it had forgotten its earlier persecution.

Mike carried it back to the middle of the garden, picked his best remaining lettuce seedling, and fed it to the rabbit leaf by leaf.

'There can't be much wrong with it if it's got an appetite like that,' Mike said with satisfaction.

'I thought you were ready to kill it a couple of minutes ago,' I replied.

When the lettuce was finished, Mike set the rabbit carefully down on the grass outside the fence and it hopped off into the undergrowth.

'It'll be back tonight,' I said. 'And it'll bring its friends.'

'Oh well,' Mike said, his earlier rage seemingly forgotten. 'That's part of gardening. You have to take the setbacks or you'll never get anywhere.'

The sea that surrounded Skomer that summer was as gorgeous as a desert island fantasy. The weather was so persistently calm that the water was permanently a glisteningly translucent turquoise. There were no waves, just a pale, fizzing trail of bubbles at the very edge of the water where it touched against the shingle. I had always thought of British seas as dense and opaque, with an undertone of grey even on the bluest of days, and the surface forever broken by fractious little waves. These pellucid waters reminded me of something I had only seen in pictures of far-off places. It was breathtaking looking down from the cliff top into the bays below; the sand and the rocks and the seaweed, seen the through the clear water, shimmered in a stunning kaleidoscope of patterns and colours, with everything stained faintly blue-green. In the stillness, we could see fish swimming and spider crabs, with their enormously long legs and spiky bodies, wandering idly across the seabed.

In the absence of any bath water, regular dips in the sea seemed almost as much of an obligation as a recreation, despite the fact that I felt much more sticky and unclean after a plunge in salt water. I could never quite believe how unpleasant the cold water actually felt. All day, as the sun scorched the back of my neck, and the soles of my feet felt as though they were melting into the ground, I stared longingly at the cool water, waiting for the quiet of the evening when I could plunge below the surface and wash away the clinging

heat. It was difficult to bring myself to accept that the reality of that longed-
for sensation was almost unbearable.

The sea around Skomer was more achingly cold than anything I had experienced before. As a little blip in the ocean, surrounded by restless currents,
there was none of the warming effect of the land that I would have enjoyed
on my childhood dips at the seaside. It was impossible to enter the water there
without feeling the breath snag in back of my throat and thinking 'never again',
but its appearance was so limpidly enticing that I fell victim to its temptations
over and over again. Then, as the first sensation of shock subsided, I was won
over. I became lost in the fascination of that different world, following my
ghostly pale hands as they parted a trail though the shuddering fronds of
seaweed. Wearing a mask and snorkel I could swim down to where the fish
flitted among the weed. And if I moved slowly, without causing too much
disturbance, I could become an object of interest to the occasional curious
puffin as they swum towards me for a closer look. The birds looked astoundingly beautiful under water. When they dived below the surface, air trapped
against their dark feathers formed a silvery skin. Just for a moment, we would
be held together as I watched them watching me through the flickering under-
sea light.

Back in those early years, the summer boat service had a gloriously random
feel to it. With the boatman and his son doubling up as farmers, we might not
see the boat for days when more pressing matters, like the harvest, intervened.
It must have been frustrating for anyone trying to visit the island, but I
cherished that element of uncertainty, the reminder that, however good the
weather, we were still isolated.

It was essential that we met every visitor as they arrived, to help them
understand the island's wildlife and, above all, to explain the extreme fragility
of some of the more vulnerable areas. A single person wandering at random
among the burrows or venturing too close to the cliff nesting colonies could
cause damage. Since we had no way of knowing whether the boat would run,
we spent many hours sitting on the cliffs above North Haven, watching for it
to come into view around the distant headland of Wooltack Point. When she
did appear, the *Sharron* was an impressive sight: an old lifeboat, painted royal
blue and white, glinting in the hard sunlight. She was a sturdy wooden boat
with remarkably graceful lines, built long before the First World War and
originally designed to be powered mainly by oars. Even now that she had been
fitted with a relatively modern engine she maintained a dignified serenity as

she cut across the sea leaving a slowly unfolding trail of ripples in her wake.

Our niche for boat watching, set back into the slopes above North Haven, seemed to draw in every scrap of heat, sucking it up like blotting paper. I half expected to see the air around me shimmer with the sheer intensity of it. It was hot enough to bring the secretive lizards out of their hiding places to stretch out and bathe in the downpour of sun. Often, it was only the noise of desiccated grasses swaying and rustling as the lizards darted out that drew our attention to them. If we took care not to disturb them, they would remain sitting companionably alongside us, blending almost invisibly into the sun-baked rocks, as we all kept vigil for the boat.

Butterflies wandered aimlessly, as if dizzied by the heat, meandering with the same random motion as blossom scattering from a cherry tree. They came to rest on our arms and legs, brushing our skin with their powdery wings. All around us crickets and grasshoppers - some brilliant green, some splashed with orange - were springing with such beguiling speed that they seemed to materialize and vanish again like part of a conjuring trick. The air was misted by their gently abrasive rasping sound, which mingled sleepily with the faint graze of water against the shingle. The combination of sights and sounds made me feel that I had been transported not just a short stretch across the sea but far, far away from a British summer. It had an exotic strangeness that was beyond my experience.

Nothing could cut more sharply through this soporific atmosphere than the arrival of the choughs. First came the clear, exultant notes, rebounding against the rocks with a sound of brash self-confidence. We always had to look up; it was an irresistible sound that couldn't be ignored. And there they would be, a cluster of sleek, black birds pirouetting and somersaulting through the sky, eclipsing everything. Of all the birds I ever saw, they were the ones that really made flying look fun. Some made it look easy, but none showed the fluid grace of such effortless acrobatic skills. Choughs were unmistakable, even in silhouette, with their up-flicked wing feathers splayed like outstretched fingers, but their most striking features were the bright red legs and curved beak. For a few seconds they filled the bay with their presence and then, as their calls slipped echoing into the distance, they left behind an empty space that nothing else could fill.

Spectacular though that summer weather was, it probably went on for too long. By August, the island looked depleted in the relentless heat. Velvet green paths had become strips of dust, and the vegetation was singed paper-dry. We became increasingly disturbed by the risk of fire. One glowing cigarette end thrown aside by a visitor might be all it took. With tens of thousands of shearwaters in their underground burrows, I could hardly bear to think of the damage a fire might cause. I became highly attuned to the smell of smoke, and seemed to sense it half a dozen times a day. Sometimes it was so real that I ran in search of it with the heat and panic choking in my throat, but it was always a false alarm. I think that in the absolute calm, the hot, dry, scorched smell was carrying across from the mainland.

As the drought sapped the colour from the land, one splash of brilliance remained to the west of the farm where chrome-yellow ragwort billowed across the fields, like something that had drawn the intensity from the sun and was reflecting it back. The iridescence of insect wings simmered among the flowers and, in the stillness, the buzzing air sounded heavy with heat. The profusion of ragwort provided ideal conditions for the vivid black and yellow caterpillars of the cinnabar moth, which clustered and crawled among the leaves. I was completely captivated by the moths themselves which, earlier in the year, had flecked the sky like drops of vermilion rain.

That month I celebrated my twenty-first birthday, and my parents came to visit. We crossed in our open boat to Martin's Haven while the early morning was still colourless. They and my sister Pippa stood in a huddle on the pebbles, as though barely expecting anyone to arrive at this deserted place. Their things were neatly packed, much of it in my father's old naval kitbags, and I was touched to see so much that was him in this meticulous preparation. The boat grazed the stones almost silently in the stillness and I jumped down, smiling, awkward. We hadn't seen or spoken to each other since the wedding: nothing but bright, superficial letters passing between us. I still wasn't sure how they felt about it.

As I came close, their appearance shocked me. They looked slightly alien; their skin was so pale it was almost translucent.

'It's because we've been travelling all night and we're tired,' my mother said defensively when I mentioned it later.

But it was more than that: we lived in different worlds now. I hadn't noticed how weathered and sun-bleached we had become, how everyone we knew matched that pattern.

When the boat turned into the mouth of North Haven everything had changed. My gentle cliffs had grown taller and more forbidding again. The island, I noticed, was exhausted and singed by drought. Mike cut the engine and we drifted towards the landing beach. As the noise died I suddenly heard the gulls swirling overhead, shamefully raucous. I was seeing it through their eyes and nothing looked quite right. No one spoke, as though we were all stunned by this first glimpse of a new place, and I could feel them hating it.

'You're very lucky,' my mother finally said.

They felt like the kindest words she had ever spoken, and I knew then that I had been forgiven for the anguish I must have caused them over the previous months.

My birthday presents seemed to consist mainly of bedsheets, and Mike hadn't been able to get me anything but an old-fashioned flowery card from Marloes Post Office. I smiled bravely, but it felt like a gentle slap on the wrist, as though my mother was telling me that if I chose to be an adult I must put away childish things. I was probably being unfair, though. They didn't know me any more: who I would be or how to relate to me in this new place. They couldn't imagine me being as I was, wanting the same things, but I did. I would have liked perfume, or jewellery or something nice to wear, just like any other twenty-one-year-old.

Under the circumstances, my birthday dinner was the best possible. We had Champagne, something I had rarely tasted before, almost too fizzy-dry to drink, but lovely for its exoticness. My parents had somehow managed to find a whole chicken encased in an enormous tin. There were scruffy vegetable from the garden, tinned prawns to start and finally my mother's homemade Christmas pudding, with cream from yet another tin.

As soon as August was over, everything went quiet. The *Sharron* continued to run, but there were only a few of end-of-season visitors. It all felt peaceful again. As the evening brought a faint cooling of the air, Mike and I sat on the isthmus, gazing down into South Haven at two female seals drifting languidly in the bay. They floated almost upright, with their noses above the water. The sea highlighted their pale silver dappling, and smoothed the blubbery plump-ness of their beach-bound bodies to streamlined elegance. Through the water I could see the rippled sand of the seabed, with the flicker of light and shade washed across it in mesmeric patterns by the faint movement of the sea. Imprinted onto the sand were the two wandering shadows of the seals. The mingled colours of golden sand and weak blue sea created a translucent, liquid green. The water was so clear, so lacking in substance, that it seemed impos-sible for the seals to remain suspended in that nothingness. They rose above the seabed like helium balloons tethered to their own shadows.

The heat of the day was gone from the sun, and I felt it soft and warm against my face. Everything was quiet except for the muted calls of gulls lapping against the cliffs, and there was not a flutter of breeze. I closed my eyes for a second to lock that moment into my memory forever, because I knew that I would never find a time or a place more perfect than this one.

FIVE

I have often heard talk of the calm before the storm, but I couldn't believe how violently that summer came to an end. We had become accustomed to a sea without waves. The intense stillness, that had seemed so odd at first, had grown to be my understanding of how a Skomer summer would always be. I had forgotten about storms; they belonged to the far off realms of winter.

It was the end of the first week in September, the morning after we had watched the seals, and we were waiting for the boat. For once, there was no doubt that it would come because things were winding down for the end of summer and the last three visitors from the chalets at the farm were due to leave that day. We were in North Haven expecting the *Sharron* to appear from behind the headland, flaring occasional darts of brightness from the morning sun. The absolute flatness of the sea was broken only by the tides racing through the sounds. Where the waters from north and south met, the colour of the sea changed; sapphire touched against aquamarine in distinct pools. I watched the drifting tides idly, as I had watched them so many times that summer.

By mid-morning we were beginning to invent reasons for ourselves as to why the boat should be late. We were vaguely puzzled, but no more than that. Over the past few months we had forced ourselves into a slower pace of life. It had been frustrating at first, but gradually Skomer had imposed its own rhythm, and we no longer fought against it. If we had to wait for the boat, we waited as long as necessary. Besides, there was no hardship in gazing out across the gently shimmering expanse of blue, watching for any sign of movement.

'What's that?' Mike said at last.

I turned to follow the direction of his gaze. Several miles to the north there was a hard, white line cutting across the oily smoothness of the sea. Behind it the water looked dark and ruffled, flecked with a restless shudder of white.

'What on earth can be causing that?' I asked.

'I think it must be a storm,' Mike said. 'And it's coming this way fast.'

It was true. The white line was ploughing across the water towards us, churning everything in its wake. I might expect to see a squall of rain approaching, with the shadowy strands reaching down from the clouds to touch the sea, but I would never have imagined that it was possible to watch the arrival of something as invisible as a gale.

'We'd better get back to the house,' Mike said.

And we both began to run, without having any clear idea why.

A few minutes later the wind hit. It thumped against the walls of the house with a single, juddering blow and then roared around us. The blue-glass water of North Haven turned instantly to a shivering white froth. Tiny, unformed waves bit into the surface, and a hazy smear of salt spray was dragged horizontally above them. Shortly afterwards the rain arrived: exploding across the windows in hard, heavy drops, which soon became a solid stream of water washing against the glass.

It was obvious immediately that there would be no chance of the boat running that day, so we were free to enjoy the novelty of a storm, which, in its early hours, was exciting. At first, despite the strength of the wind, the sea remained oddly flat. The force of the air seemed to be crushing the waves down, leaving only streaks of white drawn across the surface in the direction of the wind. Then, gradually, the fragmented wavelets began to gain momentum, gathering themselves together into longer, smoother ridges of water.

The wind was shaking the house so aggressively that the water in the sink splashed with its own miniature waves as I did the washing up, and when I tried to drain the sink, the air forcing its way into the pipes sent the water gurgling up from the plughole, like a fountain. It was my first real storm on Skomer; I had to get out and experience it for myself, to see the waves disintegrating against the cliffs and feel the rain spilling over the parched island.

I put on my heavy, blue oilskins and cautiously opened the door. Inside the angle of the L-shaped house, facing away from the wind, everything was calm. I could feel the roar of the rain-soaked air ripping overhead, and see the bracken on the hill above twisting and writhing in its grip, but where I stood there was a pocket of unnatural stillness. For the first time in months it was cool again. I edged my way along the wall of the house and stepped out into the open. A barrage of needle-sharp raindrops stabbed into my face; the air pressed like a smothering hand over my nose and mouth. I turned my head away, struggling to breathe, and felt the angry drumming of the rain against the hood of my oilskins. Momentarily overwhelmed, I pulled back into the shelter of the house.

At least now that I knew what I was facing I could be better prepared. Taking a deep breath I forced my way out into the storm. I kept my head bowed forward, one hand protecting my eyes from the prickling rain. My oilskins were dragging against my body, snatching and whipping like a loose sail. I leant hard into the wind and felt it supporting my weight as though I was touching a solid object. After a few faltering steps my balance disintegrated, and I was pushed backwards into the summer dust that was turning to melted-chocolate mud. From that undignified position I recognised defeat.

Leaning on the kitchen window sill, peering out through the cold, dewy glass, I had to make do with second best. The storm was compulsive, both fascinating and unsettling. It was impossible to carry on with anything else and ignore it. We watched the sea gradually building as the waves clustered together, growing in size and strength. The larger they grew, the more tantalisingly slowly they seemed to move. Their surfaces were taut and shiny, like flowing strands of molten glass. That brilliant, lit-from-within clarity of the day before was gone. The water was pale greenish-grey and cloudy once more, like an ordinary sea, but where the waves stretched into steep curves they turned clear and glossy so that it was possible to see right into the heart of them. Deep inside was the last of the radiant blueness left over from summer. The wave tops were being snatched away, streaming out like plumes of white smoke carried horizontally by the wind. Everything was becoming smudged by the glistening salt that misted the air and frosted the windows.

By late afternoon, the waves had grown to a size that I had neither seen nor imagined possible. It took only a few of those huge, curling waves to fill the whole of North Haven, a space that could have been scattered with hundreds of normal breakers. I was mesmerised with disbelief by the enormous troughs between the waves, which scooped so deep into the water that they looked as though they would reach down to the seabed. From the cliff top I had no perspective, so I tried to compare the sea in my mind to something familiar like the *Sharron*. It was only then that I saw the true size of the waves; they were too immense to allow me to create an imaginary picture of a boat in the bay. I could only see the *Sharron* slipping down into one of those watery gullies and being swallowed up entirely.

'Do you think the *Sharron*'s still in Martin's Haven?' I asked Mike.

'I guess she must be. The storm came up so quickly there would have been no chance to run for shelter.'

'How long could she survive in a sea like this?'

'I don't know. I'm afraid I wouldn't give much for her chances.'

It took all the pleasure out of watching the storm. It should have been so exhilarating, but I could only think of the *Sharron* trapped among the ferment of boiling foam, just off shore, but beyond help. Each time a wave exploded at the base of the cliff I could see the water pouring across the *Sharron*'s deck.

Each time a particularly vicious gust of wind punched the house, so that the timbers creaked like aching joints, I could feel the *Sharron* snatching and bucking against her mooring ropes

By high tide the air was so saturated with rain and sea, it seemed as though the waves were breaking over the house. I could feel the pounding of the surf against the cliffs running through me with a deep, rumbling shudder, like the faint resonance of an earthquake. Water flailed against the windows in rhythmic pulses; perhaps spray mingled with rain, perhaps the very tips of the waves reaching up as far as the house. It was impossible to tell. The warped, metal window frames were being given an ideal chance to show their inadequacies, and the rain began to pour through.

I somehow believed that the storm would fade with coming of darkness. It seemed only natural that such incredible power would quickly burn itself out. The light disappeared with surprising speed, soaking away into the thick cloud and the hazy, waterlogged air. The arrival of night felt disconcertingly abrupt after so many long, clear summer evenings when the afterglow lingered, mirrored in the sea. The darkness made everything so much worse: the sudden catch of the wind as it shook the house, the far-off thump of collapsing waves, the spray against the windows glinting cold and white in the gaslight. We were cast adrift, with the dangers no longer recognisable. It was easy to imagine the shattering of waves as the sound of the cliff falling away, or the creaking house actually moving on its foundations. We had to keep looking out to persuade ourselves that everything was still all right, peering through the darkness to catch sight of the faint, luminous glow of surf below.

Then the shearwaters arrived, tumbling and crashing into the chaos. The first thud against the house made us both start, but then they followed one after another. Confused by the mist of rain and spray, carried by the persuasive stream of wind, the birds slammed helplessly into the walls and roof. We were used to the occasional bird hitting the house, but never like that before, and never with such force. I remembered those benign summer nights when the muted bump of a single bird colliding with the wooden shingles had seemed shocking. We always rushed out to find the injured bird only to discover it vaguely dazed and ready to fly away. But this was different.

I started to cross to the window to see if I could glimpse any dead or injured birds lying on the ground outside. At that moment something white flashed at the window in front of me, followed by a crash that made the room reflected in the glass swim like an image on water.

'That was close,' I said. 'I can't believe the glass bent like that without break-ing.'

That was the first of many shearwaters to come raining into the windows. I was expecting the glass to splinter, bringing the storm ripping into the room, and was sickened by the realisation that each blow was a living body.

'I think the lights might be attracting them,' Mike said at last. 'It'd probably be better if we turned them out and went to bed.'

I listened in the darkness to all the known and unknown noises that made it impossible to relax. My muscles tensed with each shearwater strike, each shifting sigh of the house, and yet somehow, eventually, I slept. When I woke the light was watery grey, and I could hear that the storm was beginning to slip away. I pushed back the bed covers and walked through into the kitchen. I sensed at once the dullness; the brilliance of that wonderful summer had been washed away. The rain and spray had cleared from the sky and I could see out across St Brides Bay to where the slow, powerful sweep of the waves was already being tamed. Northerly winds, as we were to discover, were fierce and sudden, but their anger was soon forgotten. They didn't have the reach of southerlies and westerlies to build the mountainous swell waves that might take days to subside.

Mike appeared.

'We should go and have a look round outside,' he said.

The first thing I expected to find was dead and dying shearwaters. We walked the perimeter of the house; there was not a single bird. I stretched my hand out to touch the wooden walls, wondering if they could be springy enough to let the birds bounce off without hurting themselves.

We went down to the beach. The track was gouged into deep gullies where the summer-dry earth had been sluiced away. The beach was unrecognisable; the smooth, shingle clearing that linked the slipway with the sea was gone. The smaller stones had been scoured out, leaving huge boulders emerging like rocky outcrops from a sea of gravely sand. Part of the concrete slipway had broken away; its ragged end had been undermined, and was left jutting precariously unsupported.

'Well,' Mike said. 'That's going to make launching the boat difficult.'

'I think impossible might be a better word.'

As we made our way back up to the house I wondered how the tractor was going to negotiate a track with ruts that looked more than axle deep. We were discovering that there was something demoralising about the aftermath of a storm. All that was left was the bedraggled devastation, with none of the drama of being caught in the middle of it.

We spent the day trying to do the first makeshift repairs to the beach so that at least we had some sort of pathway to take the boat to the sea. By the afternoon, the waves had dropped away so much that we found ourselves glancing up frequently, half expecting the *Sharron* to come into view around Rye Rocks. Perhaps it was an unrealistic expectation, but even a day later it was hard to believe how bad the storm had been.

That evening we had a report from the coastguard that a red distress flare had been seen off the north-west coast of the island. We went out and did what we could to search from the cliff tops. The waves sounded powerful as they fell and echoed against the rocks below. Darkness magnified the sounds. I felt frightened for what we might find, anxious for anyone who might be in trouble along that turbulent stretch of coast.

Eventually, at two in the morning, it was conceded that the whole thing had been a false alarm. Whoever it was that had reported the red flare, though well-meaning, was obviously mistaken. We went to bed tired, and bemused that such a search could have been sparked by an over-active imagination.

The following morning, Mike called the coastguard for our regular daily radio check, and they passed on a message asking if we could arrange to bring the stranded visitors to the mainland. It sounded like bad news; certainly the *Sharron* was out of action. Our only remaining hope was that she was damaged rather than lost.

Still on the island were a small group of undergraduates from Cardiff University, three visitors at the chalets, and Norman McCanch, an off-duty lighthouse keeper whose idea of a holiday was to surround himself with sea and birds. The students were intending to stay for a second week, which left only three people needing immediate evacuation.

Our own boating arrangements were precarious, consisting of a small, flat-bottomed dory that belly-flopped over the smallest of waves with spine-jarring force and an outboard motor that was on the mainland, where it had spent most of the summer patiently awaiting repair. All we had were two low horse-power Seagull engines, which had only ever been intended as backup for the main engine.

Mike was not prepared to carry passengers using the under-powered Seagulls, so he crossed alone to try to borrow a more suitable engine. When he returned a couple of hours later I was waiting on the beach in North Haven, with the water lapping round my feet. I caught the boat as it came on shore, holding it clear of the rocks.

'How was it?' I asked.

'The crossing was fine. Just a bit of swell on the water. But it was terrible coming into Martin's Haven. I could see at once that the *Sharron* was gone. And then, as I was passing the place where her mooring used to be, I realised she was still there. I looked down and I could make out the colours of her hull shimmering up through the water.'

'That's awful,' I said miserably. 'Do you think there's any chance they'll be able to save her?'

'I doubt it. She must be starting to break up by now.'

She had clung on until eleven o'clock at night, and her mooring had held, despite the force of the sea, but in the deep hollows between the waves she had dropped almost to the seabed, smashing her hull repeatedly against an old mooring block that should have been safely submerged. Then the thick wooden post that held her anchor rope had snapped, leaving the tether trapped in one of the side cleats and swinging her broadside into the waves. Perhaps it only hastened the inevitable but the *Sharron* was swamped by the sea and sank. I knew that she was only wood and metal, but the sum of her parts was more than that. She had history and character, and she would be sadly missed.

'Poor Terry,' I said. 'Did he watch her go?'

'He couldn't keep away, even though there was nothing he could do.'

I felt a lump in my throat as though I was going to cry. I never understood how boats could inspire so much affection.

'Look.' Mike tried to distract me. 'I've only borrowed this engine, and I've got to return it by the end of the day. Our engine isn't ready and I can't really risk coming back to the island without it. With the *Sharron* gone we're going to be on our own for the rest of the winter. If there's any chance of getting our engine ready quickly I might have to stay on the mainland overnight and bring it back tomorrow.'

And there it was: the awful mistake, the one you learn from and never make again, if you are lucky enough to be given a second chance.

'All right,' I said reluctantly, but in complete complicity with the sin that was being committed.

Our boat was loaded with its passengers, and Norman McCanch acting as willing crew. I watched it slip smoothly across North Haven and out into the long, rolling swell beyond the shelter. The boat looked small against the open sea, but the waves had no strength left in them; they were just the last exhausted remnants of the storm. I stood on the beach until it was out of sight, and then began to walk slowly back up the steep track. The island felt disturbingly empty. Mike was gone, and I had no idea when he would be back, whether it would be that day or the next. And that was the mistake we had made. The boat would make its return journey with no one to watch or wait for it, no one to notice if it failed to arrive.

But I did watch and wait. From late afternoon I stared out of the kitchen window willing my eyes to pick out the one substantial fleck of white that would not fade and vanish like all the other ephemeral flutterings of turbulence that spangled the water. The moment I caught sight of the boat I would be ready to run, to be there on the beach to catch it before the waves could smash it against the newly exposed rocks.

No amount of staring could force anything to materialize from the greyness. For the first time since we came to Skomer, I ate my evening meal alone. As I washed up, my position at the sink gave me the perfect vantage point to continue watching the bay. It was nine o'clock, almost dark. Eventually, and reluctantly, I put a match to the gas light. The flame jumped with a sputtering gasp around the mantle, and then died back to a soothing hiss. A soft warm glow spread across the room. I knew that by lighting the gas I had conceded that Mike would not come home that night. When I turned back to the window the outside was gone. All I could see was a cold, black copy of the room reflected in the glass. No more staring, no more waiting: it was too late. I was sure that Mike would not have set off from the mainland once the light had started to fade. I would go into the sitting room, maybe light a fire. The cool dampness of the air felt so odd after the endless summer.

As I began to move away from the window I saw a pinprick of red, sharp enough to burn its way right through the mirror image of the room. Was it really coming from the outside, or was it an optical illusion, a reflection of something closer at hand? I ran back to the window and threw it open. The spot of luminous red remained, but there was nothing but blackness surrounding it, nothing to give me any bearings, any idea of space or distance. Then, as my eyes began to focus, it was gone, faded without trace. I stared at the dark, indecipherable blankness, and I waited, but nothing else happened.

Eventually, I closed the window and tried to think what I should do. I had definitely seen something, and yet it had been over so quickly that I was beginning to have doubts. I went through it again in my mind. There had been a red light: red, the colour of danger. The only logical explanation was that I had seen a distress flare. But all I could think of was the previous night. Then I had wondered how it had been possible to create a false alarm that sent so many people out searching; now it seemed like the easiest thing imaginable.

I was tempted to dismiss that momentary flicker of red as no more than a trick of the light, to forget about it, to go and find some firewood. I wasn't going to spark off an emergency without good reason. Then I imagined how it might feel to be alone in the dark sea, desperately hoping that someone might have seen that call for help. I had no choice. I switched on the marine VHF radio and unclipped the microphone.

'Milford Haven Coastguard, this is Skomer One, over.'

'Skomer One, Milford Haven Coastguard, over.'

'Milford Haven Coastguard, I've seen a red light low down on the water, somewhere off North Haven, over.'

There was only a short pause before the voice came back to me.

'We're launching the Angle lifeboat.'

I was shocked. I couldn't believe that my few muddled words could have such devastating effect. I went over it again in my mind, trying to convince myself that I really had seen a flare. The thing that worried me was that the light I had seen was close to the water, whereas I would have expected to see a parachute flare, like the ones we had used in practice at St Ann's Head, which would have held the light suspended high in the sky. The only possibility was that it was hand-held flare. I knew such things existed because I had seen Mike set off some out of date ones to dispose of them. Then it hit me in one jarring realisation. Mike was carrying those flares; he was the one signalling for help.

Once I had made the link it seemed ridiculous that I hadn't thought of it before. I was so firmly convinced that Mike wouldn't be at sea in the dark that the only connection I had made was with the false alarm of the night before. But in that terrible moment of understanding I knew. I was absolutely certain that Mike was somewhere out there in the dark. Once the coastguards had checked Martin's Haven and told me that the island boat was not there, I couldn't cling on to any shadowy pretence of hope.

All I could do was wait. I needed to be outside, to experience the darkness, the cool, misty air against my skin, the shivering gusts of wind. It was the only way that I felt I could really understand what was going on. I took the VHF radio and went out onto the cliffs above North Haven. I was able to hear fizzing, broken voices, but I knew that what was available to me on the radio was only a tiny fragment of the whole. I heard that a second boat, the St David's lifeboat, was being launched, but the weather was too bad to call out the helicopter. That was in the days before the local RAF search and rescue helicopters were equipped with radar, and without it the clouded blackness that night was impenetrable. As I stared into the dark it was so featureless that it shimmered against my eyes, with the vague movement of water droplets clogging the air. But apart from that there was nothing, not even a sense of scale or perspective. It was like staring into a void.

Eventually, I was able to make out the lights of the lifeboat. The long, pale beam of the searchlight was caught and held suspended by the mist. Occasionally, as it made its slow, purposeful sweep across the water, the brilliance flickered straight into my face. I had to blink and look away because my eyes, made sensitive by sitting so long in the dark, were dazzled by the harshness of the light. The fact that I could actually feel the light touching me, singling me out as I sat on the cliff top, made the whole thing feel so close that all those miles and miles of empty sea looked comfortingly small. It was an illusion, of course, but it I wanted to believe it.

The radio buzzed with a new surge of drama. One of the cliff rescue parties on the mainland had found the wreckage of a boat. It sounded like the beginning of the worst possible news. The radio signal kept breaking up, leaving only split and crackling scraps of sentences, with my imagination working too hard trying to fill in the details. The words I kept hearing were, 'please use land line'. I knew at once that they were trying to hide something from me, though, more logically, they were just avoiding the frustrations of a poor radio signal. They had probably forgotten about me waiting in the dark, quietly listening to everything that was going on.

I had not noticed the rain growing heavier. The mist had solidified into a dense, penetrating drizzle. It was saturating my hair, dusting my skin. Suddenly I had an awful thought: the radio must be kept dry. I undid my coat and slipped the radio inside, leaving an opening at the collar for the sound to escape. The cold air slid down round my neck making me shiver. I remembered that it was when we had first visited the coastguards at St Ann's Head that we had been warned to keep the radio dry. That had been the morning after our wedding, and now we had been married exactly six months to the day.

I didn't know what time it was when Professor Bellamy came to find me, except that it was late, and I was cold; the wind was beginning to accumulate that distant, overhead roar, and the waves were once more washing noisily

against the cliffs. Professor Bellamy was accompanying the Cardiff undergraduates; he was a man whose contribution to island life we had already come to
value, whose ideas and enthusiasm were part of the constant process of learning that Skomer gave us. His intention was to persuade me that I should go
back to the house. He was right. There was nothing I could do to help by sitting
out on the cliff, but I needed to feel the wind and the rain and the darkness,
the same wind and rain and dark that Mike was experiencing. Without the
occasional glint of a searchlight making bright reflections across the sea I would
have nothing to cling on to. I would be cut off. These were ridiculous ideas,
not ones that could be translated into meaningful words, but I was determined
not to move. Prof's arrival, though, was enough of an interruption to make
me realise that I couldn't afford to risk the radio in the rain any longer. Without
it my isolation would be unbearable. I had to leave the cliff top.

Back in the kitchen, the mellow gaslights felt painfully harsh. Separated
from the darkness that had held me enclosed in my own thoughts I was startled
back to some sort of normality. I was beginning to realise from the scraps of
information coming through the radio that the boat wreckage had been a false
alarm; it was debris that had been in the water for a while, nothing to do with
the present search.

Time moved as though it had snagged against an obstacle: two o'clock,
three o'clock. Prof and I chatted as though everything was normal, as though
it wasn't the middle of the night and we weren't both diverting three-quarters
of our attention towards the silent radio. Then, suddenly, there came a flurry
of activity. A boat had been located close to the cliffs on the far side of St
Brides Bay. I was no longer piecing together scraps of half-heard information.
The call came from the coastguards directly to me, keeping me in touch as
soon as there was some positive news.

'Can you see them both? Are they all right?' I asked.

I could feel the panic rising inside me now that an end was in sight. I had
been willing them to find the boat, and now for the first time I considered
the possibility that it might be empty.

'They appear to be fine,' came the reply from the coastguard. 'They're both
shouting their heads off to make sure we've seen them.'

I could actually hear the smile in his voice. And they deserved a few smiles
of triumph, all of them involved in the rescue, after what they had been
through that night.

The boat had washed so far inshore that it was one of the cliff rescue parties, not a lifeboat, that finally spotted it. I could hear over the radio the last stages of the rescue as the boat was dragged to safety. It made compulsive, if fractured, listening. I heard descriptions of white parachute flares being fired to illuminate the scene, and I wished that I was still out on the cliffs, able to catch a glimpse of the distant light. It seemed to take a very long time as I stood in the bright kitchen staring at the empty window, able only to imagine the moon-pale surf breaking and dragging against the darkness of the rocks, highlighting them, drawing them out from their invisibility. I could feel the splash of water, the boat rearing fitfully in the waves, the hollow, echoing boom of hard surfaces as the hull bounced against the rocks. It would be so easy for it to go wrong: the missed footing, slipping against the glassy weed away from safety.

And then it was over. I heard that Mike and Norman were both ashore. Following almost immediately in the wake of that relief was an undercurrent of bleakness. I was alone; Prof had gone and the radio was silent. It was early morning, and I knew I should sleep, but those hours of unbearable imagining had left their shadows behind.

I went to bed because it seemed like the only possible thing to do at that time, but I lay there with a sense of wakefulness that was as cold and stark as I feared it would be. I knew almost nothing about what had happened; there were only empty spaces where the questions kept echoing round and round.

SIX

By morning, the wind, which had been gathering strength throughout the night, had reached a full gale. The sea was a dense slate-blue, bright and brittle, flickering random tongues of white. All the insubstantial translucence of summer had vanished. It looked hard and formidable, no longer to be treated casually as we had when we drifted aimlessly across its surface to find some pocket of evening coolness, or trailing hooks to catch a few mackerel.

There would be no crossing that day, or for several days to come. They were days in which Mike and I couldn't exchange the briefest of words, at a time when I felt that even the sound of his voice could have answered a lot of the questions that were waiting, unresolved. It was a reminder of what we had done in choosing such isolation.

Mike finally brought the damaged boat limping home. We would have a lot of work to do on it.

'Are you all right?' he asked as I met him on the beach.

'Yes. Are you?'

'Of course,' he replied.

I noticed that he had a spark of exhilaration, while I still felt drained. It made me wonder if adventures are more distressing for those who experience them at second hand, who have too much time and little enough information to piece together the most elaborate fears.

'So, what happened? How did it go wrong?' I asked as soon as we were back in the kitchen.

'Well, once I realised that there was no chance of getting our main engine, I decided to come straight back that evening while the sea was calm. I had our two Seagull engines, and there was plenty of daylight left, so there didn't appear to be any problem.'

'That sounds ominously optimistic.'

'Yes, it does with hindsight. We were about half way across Jack Sound when the engine packed up, and the tide was running very strongly. I had a quick look to see if I could fix it, and found that the points had burnt out, but that was okay because we had a spare engine. The trouble was, the minute we lost power the current was throwing us all over the place. Norman was trying to hold the boat steady with the oars while I changed the engine, but the waves were coming from all directions at once. A huge wave swamped us, and once those Seagull engines are soaked there's no chance of starting them. So there we were with two engines and neither of them working.'

'It seems almost impossible for things to go so badly wrong when you're so close to home.'

'Well, that's what we thought. We weren't worried at first, because we thought we'd row the last bit home.'

'I feel so awful. If I'd walked across to the far side of North Haven I'd probably have seen you.'

'You weren't to know. It was my fault for being so vague. In future, you'll always know exactly when I'm expected back.'

'So why didn't you make it?'

'If we'd been in a traditional style boat, I think we could have rowed back easily, and that would have been the end of the story. But that flat-bottomed dory skittered over the waves, and we couldn't make any headway. In the end, we decided to row together, sitting side by side and taking an oar each, but with the extra power of both of us rowing, instead of propelling the boat forward the bows dipped under the water. The boat flooded; it was full to the top, like a floating bath tub.'

'You must have been freezing.'

'We were. You wouldn't believe how quickly the cold gets to you. We started to bale out the water, but our fingers got so numb we lost the baler over the side. That was when we realised that we needed help, and we let off the first distress flare. We were trying to be careful, waiting to see if there was an answering flare to let us know we'd been seen. But it wasn't until the last flare had been fired that we knew that we'd been spotted, so we had no flares left to show our position. By then it was dark, the wind was picking up and we were drifting fast in the current.'

'It must have been terrifying.'

'The worst thing was that we could see the lifeboat with its searchlight sweeping across the sea. It came so close, and we were shouting and waving, trying to attract attention, but gradually it started to move further away. That was devastating, because we knew it wouldn't repeat the same search pattern for hours, if at all. We really started to lose heart at that point.'

'I was watching the lifeboat too. It seemed to light up the whole sea.'

'Eventually we found that we'd drifted right across the bay. We'd lost the shelter of the island and were catching the full force of the wind, which was pushing us onto a cluster of offshore rocks. We were afraid the boat might break up, and we were about to scramble out onto the rocks in the hope that we might be picked up from there. Then we saw the lights of the cliff rescue team, and tried to row towards them. They were amazing, you know. Some of them waded up to their waists in the water to drag us ashore, because we were so exhausted by then we couldn't even row the last few yards.'

'So what on earth did you do then? It must have been at least three o'clock in the morning.'

'Yes, we were cold and wet and exhausted, and all I wanted to do was to go home. But we were very lucky. Do you remember Joe, the Chief Coastguard we met at St Ann's Head? Well, he took us back to his house for the night, and his wife got out of bed to cook bacon and eggs for us.'

'At that time in the morning? What an incredible thing to do.'

'I know. It's overwhelming the way all those people helped.'

I was touched as the details of the story gradually unfolded. Perhaps one of the great unrecognised heroes was George Sturley, a Marloes boatman from one of the old fishing families. He had been dragged from his house, still in his carpet slippers, to give the benefit of his local knowledge of tides and currents. He pinpointed the exact spot where they were found, even though it was miles from where they went missing.

'Anyway,' Mike went on. 'It gave me a chance to do some thinking. In case anything awful ever happens again, I bought you this.'

He handed me a manila envelope containing a life insurance policy.

A few days later, a boat was hired to make the long journey from within the shelter of Milford Haven to collect Professor Bellamy and the students. We were suddenly alone. The loss of the *Sharron* had made it feel so abrupt and unplanned that I was apprehensive. It reminded me of those first misgivings I had experienced at the thought of leaving the mainland. After such long and gentle welcome, the island had shown us its serious side, and it left me feeling faintly subdued. We had arrived with the spring opening out in front of us, bringing birds and flowers and improving weather. Now, I looked ahead to shortening days, with the last of the birds abandoning the island, and the prospect of being confined by a sea that I no longer trusted.

Mike put his arm round me as we stood at the water's edge in North Haven watching the last boat of the year disappear. At our feet the sea was restless, snatching at the pebbles with a clatter that reverberated against the empty cliffs. The sea is always restless; it made me realise how unnatural the stillness of the summer had been.

We began to walk up the steep track towards the house. A rabbit dashed from nowhere right across our path. We both started at the sudden movement and then smiled at our own stupidity. Amid such absolute solitude any noise or movement felt out of place, but we would get used to it.

We quickly learned that there were just two seasons on Skomer. In time, we came to speak only of summer and winter, and we both knew exactly what we meant. Summer was when the passenger boat ran and visitors came, when the island was bright with flowers and the cliffs were alive with thousands of strident seabirds. Winter began early in September, when most of the seabirds had left and the vegetation was already fading: the boat stopped running, the island was quiet except for the roar of wind and waves, and we never saw another person.

We didn't immediately recognise that first winter. Despite the storm, I thought that the last dregs of summer were still to come, the mellow slide into autumn. The signs were promising. The rain that followed in the wake of that intensely dry weather brought a startling revival to the landscape. Around the cliff tops, the driest slopes were transformed, almost magically. In the heat, the vegetation had shrivelled and finally vanished, leaving the burrows looking naked and fragile in the sand-pale soil. Within a few days of the rain, a fine green haze bloomed across the burnt slopes, like a newly seeded lawn.

But my hopes of an Indian summer were unrealistic. On our little windswept fleck in the Atlantic Ocean winter came early and spring came late. The storm had carried not just rainwater, but drenching salt spray washing over the island. The forests of green bracken, scorched by the salt, quickly blackened and died. The brilliant purple and red fuchsia flowers at the gateway to the farmyard had been torn loose and smashed to the ground, where they lay for a while, like an intricately-woven oriental rug, before their colours withered away. The succession of storms that was typical of that time of year had soon crushed the vegetation into a uniform brown crust, so that the island began to look very much as it had when we arrived in April, before the winter had begun to give way to any signs of spring.

Time had a different quality that year: decelerated by the complete newness of everything. The hot, still summer had seemed to last forever, and now winter was stretching slowly ahead of us. The evenings had been so light, with so much to be done outside, that I hadn't properly appreciated the effects of cold and dark without electricity. The house had a feeling of summer about it: an idealised place where the reality of winter had never been considered.

There were no carpets, just polished floorboards. The enormous windows, that let in the light and the views, left a hundred entry points for wheedling draughts, and the thin cotton curtains did nothing to hold them back. During the daytime we had no heating, and simply piled on more jumpers as the weather grew colder. When the cold had penetrated every layer and reached right down to the skin, the only solution was to go outside. It was always warm walking - eventually - no matter how bad the day.

The island was rarely peaceful. All summer the thousands of competing bird calls set up a clamour that shut out the smaller sounds. Then the winter brought the constant shifting of wind and waves, the rhythmic churning of beach shingle dragging against the shore, and through that blur of noise cut the high-pitched wail of seals. It was a lonely sound, despite the fact that, as summer ended, the seals gathered in large, though not very sociable, groups on the beaches and offshore rocks. There was something about the calls that was sad and faintly human, which I suppose was what made them so powerful. Most of the hundreds of seals that we saw were using the island as somewhere to haul out of the sea and rest, but a few came to give birth to their pups.

It must have been the solitude that drew them, because none of the beaches offered ideal conditions for a pup. Apart from the caves, there was nowhere that would not be inundated during a particularly high tide or severe storm. The newborn pups were intensely thin, with a cry so like the sound of a human baby that it could penetrate your heart. When they first arrived, damp and disorientated, with the white fur slicked smooth against their bodies, their eyes looked huge and hollow. But as the sea breezes dried the fur, it became thick and fluffy, disguising the bony angularity of the body, rounding out the face and softening the eyes, so that they melted into pools of liquid darkness.

For much of the time the pups were content to sleep, nestled into the safest corners they could find, right at the top of the beach. But if they were awake and hungry, they might cry incessantly until they were fed. The noise became so unsettling that I couldn't help scanning the waves, anxiously hoping to pick out the sleek head of a returning mother.

I was fascinated by everything about the seals, from their minor squabbles to the way they luxuriated so conspicuously in sleep. If one of them was asleep on an offshore rock in the face of an incoming tide, it would fight to the very end to avoid losing that hard-won fragment of comfort. As the patch of rock was inundated, the seal curled itself out of the reach of the water, gradually lifting its tail and head into the air until the whole body was twisted into a painful arc. When the rock finally disappeared from view, the seal gave the impression of balancing in this ridiculous position on the surface of the water with no visible means of support. It was a rare privilege to have such unrestricted access to a group of mammals, to be able to watch as the details of their existence unfolded. With seals, life is not hidden away in the hours of darkness, or tucked out of sight in underground hollows. It is all there to be seen: the fights, the births, the deaths.

If there was any time that I found adapting to island life difficult, it was during that first winter as the day length began to shrink away. I had always had an aggressive loathing for November, which left me feeling oppressed by the sudden onset of dark evenings. On Skomer, the natural influences were so much more intense. The changing of the seasons, the storms and droughts, the ebb and flow in the tide of flowers and seabirds, were the most important factors in our lives, and so the disappearing daylight began to assume an increasing dominance.

Throughout the summer, the gaslights had provided an impeccable service. It would have seemed a waste to go inside while there was still daylight, and so it was often not until ten or eleven at night that we finished outside and I cooked our meal. Then, as we ate, the gas simmered with a soft background light. The only criticism I could make was that the lamps gave off too much heat in a house that had been soaked in sun all day, and we were often forced to close the windows, as moths were attracted in from the outside to flutter destructively around the fragile gas mantles.

At four o'clock on a winter afternoon the gaslights felt quite different. When I first lit them they appeared bright and warm and mellow, but it was impossible to do anything that needed detailed concentration. If I tried to sew or paint, my hands threw a dense shadow over whatever I wanted to see, and any colour chosen under gaslight was sadly transformed by the cold light of day. It was a disappointing end to my plans for spending the long winter evenings painting. Fortunately, the light was clear enough for reading, although books became a precious commodity that had to be rationed. Often, I stopped at the last chapter and put the book aside for the luxury of knowing that it would be waiting for me the following night. Mike was incapable of such restraint. If he had a new book he devoured it in one gulp, even though it meant sitting up into the early hours of the morning, and knowing that the next evening he would be searching irritably through the bookshelves for anything he could bear to re-read.

Most evenings I had to set aside time for mending. At first, this seemed a slightly archaic practice, the sort of thing I would have sniggered at in the instructions for young housewives at the front of my copy of Mrs Beeton, but somehow it imposed itself on me. It began when I realised that we couldn't afford to throw away a good pair of socks just because of one small hole. Then I found myself forced to darn the elbows of my jumpers. As the thinning patches spread from the elbows up under the arms and then down the sides of the body, so, too, did my assiduous darning. Some of my favourite jumpers were almost equally divided between darn and original wool, but the soft, felty patches I had woven so painstakingly into place only added to their appeal, like the wear on an old teddy bear. When Mike's shirts all began to disintegrate at once I had to take evasive action. By carefully unpicking the stitching of a frayed collar I could turn it over and sew it back into place with its respectable face on show.

One unexpected discovery was the pleasure of listening to the radio. I mean really sitting and listening, rather than using it as a background noise. We used to settle ourselves down for the classic serial on Sunday evening with the same spellbound anticipation that used to accompany Listen with Mother when I was a child. Stories like The Moonstone and Vanity Fair made a far more vivid impression than any television programme ever had, because it came to life in my head.

The cold remained an enduring distraction during those winter evenings. Our foresight in carrying driftwood up the cliff throughout the summer, cutting, drying and storing it, had not provided us with the blissfully warm nights we had expected. The grey-tiled fireplace in the living room, the sort that might have graced any small, suburban house of a certain age, would probably have been quite efficient filled with a glowing bed of anthracite. But it only accommodated a couple of chunks of driftwood, which crackled and spluttered and roared, sending a thin plume of flames screeching up the chimney. With the fireguard in place, I don't think that any heat escaped into the room at all. Without the fireguard, the regular explosions sent a glistening red rain spitting across the room. We braved it for as long as we dared, until a dangerously close encounter inevitably weakened our resolve and the fireguard was pushed back into place.

With a larger fireplace we might have had time to let the logs settle down to a comfortable glow, but our scraps of wood were eaten up too quickly. The storms raging outside and the fire roaring inside colluded to create an indoor gale that came ripping in tiny ribbons up between the floorboards. On the worst nights I huddled at the fireside with my hair fluttering in the breeze. I took to wearing my father's old wartime flying jacket, with blankets wrapped round my legs.

I had forgotten how bitterly cold an unheated house could be. However ineffective the fire seemed, opening the door onto the glacial wilderness of the corridor beyond always came as a shock. I found myself sitting up later and later into the night rather than face the misery of the bathroom. In bed, I had to curl up tight, shivering against the slab of cold sheets until they had absorbed enough warmth to create their own little microclimate.

The cold was something we learned to live with. Running out of batteries for the radio, was the thing that I would have considered a severe hardship. Radio 4 was my constant companion, my ongoing education, my contact with the outside. Without it, I would have felt lost. The rest of the world was gradually changing, becoming detached from my memories, which remained frozen in time. I had no new visual images of people and places in the news. More and more, I had to construct my own impression of reality from what I heard on the radio.

Without any machinery to take away the drudgery, routine chores, like washing clothes, took up a disproportionate amount of time. A good radio programme could eliminate most of the boredom, but nothing could prevent the soggy, crinkled skin that resulted from having my hands immersed in soapy water for so long. The pile of washing-in-waiting seemed to grow throughout the winter; the more I took away, the bigger it got. It meant that I was committed to washing almost every day when the wind dropped below force six. Our hard, outdoor way of life provided an endless supply of very dirty clothes. I could spend half an hour on a single pair of trousers, scrubbing with a stiff brush against oily marks and ingrained knees until the palm of my hand blistered.

I came up with a brilliant invention to make my life easier. It was a sort of makeshift washing machine consisting of a large, plastic tub and a ship's flagpole. We found the flagpole washed up among the assorted beach-combings in South Haven. It was a smooth pole, about three feet long, topped by a rounded disc of wood with a couple of holes in it. I picked it up for its interesting look and feel, and carried it home, where it was left propped in a corner. I studied it a few times, turning the wood between my fingers, convinced it was trying to tell me something. Then I felt the dawning of inspiration. I filled a deep tub with soapy water, added the clothes, and plunged them up and down with the flagpole. I could see the dirt oozing out into the water as I pounded with growing enthusiasm. It was such an improvement on the old method that I convinced myself it was every bit as good as a washing machine, despite the lifting of heavy buckets of water and the fact that I still had to finish off with the scrubbing brush and then rinse everything several times over. I was disappointed to discover, years later, that someone else had actually invented the washing dolly long before I had.

Mike had found an old mangle in the cellar, which he cleaned and set up outside for me. There was something delightful about feeding in the heavy, wet clothes, which then emerged stiff and weightless, welded into paper-thin shapes, like shadows peeled from the ground. I had to position everything very carefully as it went into the mangle, to avoid sealing in too many indelible creases. My iron, which ran on gas, had a habit of roaring, spitting flames and generally terrorising me, so I had more or less given up ironing, and relied on careful handling at the washing stage to reduce crumpling to a minimum.

In the end, it wasn't the creases but the buttons that forced me to abandon the mangle. I grew so tired of scrabbling round trying to find replacements for buttons crushed between the rollers that I returned to the miserable method of wringing by hand, twisting the clothes into unwieldy skeins until the water ran down my arms, to be turned into ice-cold trails by the fresh wind.

I always had an immense feeling of pride as I stood back to watch a line full of washing snapping and writhing in the sea breeze. I knew that it was silly, but I couldn't help it. Washing pulled out of a machine is a tiny, unnoticed routine. My washing felt like yet another small skirmish fought and won. I had also discovered that running water is probably one of life's greatest luxuries, despite the fact that ours had barely lasted the summer. Lack of electricity was fairly insignificant, but the need to carry and heat every drop of water would have definitely counted as deprivation.

That winter I had my first experience of complete isolation: ten days without human contact. Mike had to go to the mainland for a series of meetings to plan for the coming year, and the preparation that it would take to leave the island empty, secured against the storms, seemed hopelessly daunting. Besides, I wanted to stay. It was my home, and I had no intention of abandoning it just because Mike was going away.

I have no idea why isolation should be regarded as inherently frightening, but it is. To me, Skomer was the safest place imaginable. I loved the island and felt, in some vague, irrational way, that the feeling was reciprocated. The barrier of sea was a safeguard, not a threat. And yet, over the previous months, I had been told so many cautionary tales about the dangers of isolation, stories that sometimes made the skin on the back of my neck tingle. There was the woman, left alone in the old farmhouse, who went mad after a week, the solitary workman found hanged in the barn because he took the sound of shearwaters for demons, and, the one that, for some reason, affected me most, the figure on the cliff top seen waving to the departing boat when the island was left empty. I didn't believe any of them but, annoyingly, they left their imprints, little whispering thoughts that wouldn't quite go away.

Once Mike had gone, every experience was intensified. The cliffs seemed higher and more dangerous, because I was acutely aware that one slip would leave me without help. The singing of a winter robin sounded more beautiful, as though it was deliberately interrupting my solitude. On my first afternoon alone, I walked to Skomer Head, the most westerly tip of the island, and stared out to sea. The water was sleekly calm, the air colourless, the horizon lost at some indeterminate point. Nothing between me and America, I thought, with a faint sense of awe. It was no wonder that the island felt small and vulnerable in the face of storms swelling up across those thousands of miles of open sea. That day, the weather was unnaturally still. It was rare to be able to stand on that exposed headland without the wind snatching my breath and flicking tendrils of hair into my eyes. I sat down on a convenient perch of rock and let my imagination wander out towards the horizon.

The light at sea is always the last to go. It retains a faint, luminous glow long after the sun has set. When I stood up and turned back inland I was shocked to see that it was almost dark. I felt a silly little stab of panic. I had the length of the island to cover to get home. What if I were to slip in the dark, catch my foot in a burrow, break my ankle? Who would come looking for me?

As I stood thinking about the walk back, the silence was split open by a long, sharp scream. I couldn't think clearly, except to tell myself that it was a woman's voice. For a moment, my rigid muscles wouldn't even let me turn to see what was happening. Then the scream came again, pushing me into action. Hardly daring to look, I moved my head very slowly and glimpsed a young rabbit being dragged from the ground by a buzzard, its desperate screams echoing into the twilight. I wanted to cry with relief but, instead, I started to run. It was too late for reason. That explosive mixture of panic and isolation had been shaken up and was starting to bubble over. I just wanted to get home, running recklessly through the dark.

Even reaching the house didn't bring an immediate reprieve. There was no easy flick of a light switch. The rooms and corridors had to be faced in darkness: feeling for the box of matches; turning on the lamp by touch; waiting for the hiss of gas through the pipes; the match broken in haste; fizzing, flickering shadows at the second try as the match spits into life; the dull flame leaping up around the mantle before dying back to brightness and safety.

The following afternoon, a heavy shower raked across North Haven. In its wake the sun burst brilliantly from behind the clouds, glistening against the deep, smudged grey of the retreating shower. A rainbow began to form, growing and brightening in the sparkling air. It strengthened into an unbroken arc over North Haven. Outside the bow the sky was as heavy as blued steel; inside it was bright, smoky white. As I watched, the rainbow continued to grow, the curve stretching down below the level of the cliffs until it joined in a perfect circle above the bay. It looked impossible, unreal. Within the glowing halo of colours, the light swelled to a dazzling silver. I was almost mesmerised, as though I was having some sort of vision. I wanted to run, to call for Mike. I needed someone else to see it too. And then it was gone, dissolved away into the dull sky. I realised then that nothing is completely wonderful if it can't be shared.

For day after day I didn't speak at all. I began to make a point of talking to the chickens to break the silence.

'Hello there. How are you?' I called, as they came waddling at top speed down the track, ecstatically pleased to see me. 'Hello Eustacia! Hello Mehitabel! Where's Zuleika?'

(I strongly believed that, since chickens had so little going for them in the way of intelligence, they at least deserved the dignity of the grandest possible names.) They lost interest in me once the grain was scattered, with all their attention diverted towards scratching and clucking at the ground, but I stayed until the meal was finished, just to have some company.

That was the only time I spoke, apart from my twice-daily radio check with the coastguard, when my voice sometimes fractured embarrassingly through lack of use. As auxiliary coastguards we were among the few people licensed to use marine VHF radios on land, but our use of these priority channels precluded any idle chatter. The frequencies had to be kept open for emergen-

cies, and our communications focused on a few essential words. I only discovered years later that when I was alone on the island Mike used to telephone
the coastguards to ensure that I had made contact, but sometimes my radio
had failed and sometimes my calls weren't logged. In these instances, he used
to plead with the helicopter pilots at nearby RAF Brawdy to check for a light
in the kitchen window shining from the cliff top if they happened to be passing
by on exercises.

As the week drew to an end I was beginning to feel quite pleased with
myself. Mike was almost due back, and I had survived unscathed. It was when
I heard the shipping forecast that I realised things would not be going to plan.
The shipping forecast was compulsive listening, at least two or three times a
day, only this time it was the bringer of bad news. The predicted northerly
winds made it certain that Mike would not be coming home. I felt inordinately
disappointed, and ashamed of myself for being so weak.

The delay stretched out one day after another. My week alone had already
become ten days when the weather forecast deteriorated dramatically. I settled
down for yet another evening with nothing but the malevolent, spitting log
fire for company. In our 'summery' house the curtains in the living room were
blatantly non-functional: a decorative fringe, incapable of being drawn across
the window. Since one wall was mostly glass, it meant that I spent the evening
staring at a reflection of the room: not a cheerful mirror image, but glittering,
hard shapes set against a sombre backdrop of darkness. I recognised the sense
of vulnerability that this created as being left over from childhood. The
inescapable thought remained: while I couldn't see out, anything outside might
see in.

I managed to lose myself in a book, only to be startled back to reality by a
hard, insistent knocking at the front door. It was mind-numbingly, heart-
stoppingly impossible. No one could be on the island. It was late at night and
stormy outside; I was certain that I was totally cut off. To my surprise, feeling
my way through the fog of panic, I acted with absolute calm. From the kitchen
window the moon was bright enough to confirm what I already knew: the
waves were pushing hard onshore in a froth of foam, and there was no boat in
the bay. The knocking at the door came again, rapid and impatient. It was
definitely no trick of the wind.

I couldn't even switch a light on in the hallway, but I walked to the front
door and pulled it open decisively. There was no peering cautiously through a
half open slit, no tentative calling into the dark. It was essential to show from

the start that I was in control of the situation. For a moment I was blinking into an indecipherable blackness and then Mike threw his arms around me.

'Sorry,' he said. 'I didn't want to startle you, so I thought it was better to knock at the door rather than come barging in.'

'But the door is never locked,' I replied, trying not to be cross, 'and if you'd just called out so I could have heard your voice you wouldn't have scared me half so much.'

Mike had made the long trip round St Anne's Head, begging a lift in an old lifeboat that wouldn't flinch at such rough seas. They had come into South Haven, facing away from the weather, and, though he described the difficult landing with casual bravado, I noticed him limping up the hallway.

Despite the shock, I was glad that Mike had made it back before the weather deteriorated, and that I didn't face an indefinite period of waiting and watching alone. It was wonderful to have company again, someone to share the miracle of a rainbow, to make the storms feel more like an adventure than a threat, to sit with in rapt silence through the Sunday serial. I also appreciated some of those half-forgotten things that arrived with Mike from the mainland: fresh food, letters and a newspaper that was barely out of date.

When I looked back on those ten days alone, I began to convince myself that I had almost enjoyed them. To have been granted that amount of solitude was an exceptional opportunity. It was something that would have been almost impossible to achieve in any other way of life. In all that time, I had seen no one, not even a face on a television screen. I had had no conversation, even by phone. It had made me feel absorbed into my surroundings, more aware of them, more part of them. I realised that, through any amount of anxiety or discomfort, I had not for one moment wished myself anywhere else. I felt as though I had taken the final test of my ability to live in isolation, and passed. Somehow, that brief period alone had resolved the last of my problems. My lingering doubts about the bleakness of winter were gone. I knew that I was exactly where I wanted to be.

SEVEN

On Skomer, winter came to an abrupt end at a precise moment in the middle of March. That defining moment was the return of the puffins. Regardless of what the weather did, once the puffins were back there could be no denying that winter was behind us. Since we had arrived in the April of our first year, the puffins were settled in before us. The following year, we could hardly wait for that sign of new beginnings. Other seabirds were making regular visits back to the cliffs, but we were both convinced that there was something symbolic about the return of the puffins.

Some of the most mundane chores, like doing the washing, put me in an unparalleled puffin-watching position. My view from the kitchen sink took in the whole of North Haven and then stretched on almost forever across St Brides Bay. I was determined that if there was a puffin to be seen, I would be the one to discover it. Mike, with his terrifyingly acute vision and superior knowledge of wildlife, was always pointing out distant smudges that he had clearly seen and identified, but this victory was going to be mine. I kept a pair of binoculars next to the sink, and they were usually covered in dissolving clouds of soapsuds from where I had grabbed them with wet hands, or with a dusting of flour if I happened to be making bread. My poor distant vision, which melted everything into soft focus, created an unfortunate number of false alarms. I used the binoculars to study any vaguely unusual occurrence, from passing fishing boats to dramatic movements of the tide races, but the first puffin remained disappointingly elusive.

We had walked along the south coast as far as High Cliff, then inland to the farm, and back home following the long, straight track through the centre of the island. I was carrying a couple of fresh eggs, salvaged from the chicken shed. It was about three o'clock in the afternoon: grey but bright. I thought how much I appreciated those few extra minutes of light we were gaining daily. In the worst of winter we would already have been moving into cold twilight. Those things really mattered to us when our lives were shaped by the pattern of the days.

As we began to descend the steep slope behind the house Mike stopped abruptly.

'What's that?' he said distractedly. Then, after a pause, 'It's a puffin. The first puffin. They're back!'

I doubt that he would have seen it at all had the sea not been so calm. With the slightest breeze, the bird would have been lost among the flickering shadows that traced the wavelets. Mike handed me the binoculars, and then I saw it, a tiny fleck amid the vast sheen of greyish water. The sun broke through from beneath the heavy sky, so that the sea glinted like polished metal and the clouds, in contrast, turned to a soft, muted black. The light caught and glowed against the pure white of the puffin's breast feathers. The beak showed brilliant red, new and unnaturally perfect. Its reflection drifted out across the water in undulating bands of ripples. For a moment the puffin shone, like a bright memory of the summer that was gone. Then the light faded to the bleakness of a wintry afternoon and the bird all but vanished again.

We hugged each other for the sheer joy of seeing the puffin. Our lives had become very small. Everything we knew was confined within a little circle of sea. But far from being dull, it all mattered so much more. I couldn't remember anything on the mainland that would have created a pure sense of elation in a way that the puffins returning to Skomer could.

We walked down until we had reached the cliff top outside the house. Soon, thirty or forty birds had gathered in North Haven. Somehow, they were not quite what I expected. I remembered the previous summer, when the cliffs had been full of birds, tumbling, strutting, arguing. The knot of puffins far out in the bay seemed subdued and nervous, as though the winter had erased any familiarity with the island, and they came back now only reluctantly out of some irresistible sense of duty.

All afternoon, I glanced out regularly from the kitchen window. They gathered in growing numbers until there were two or three distinct groups of puffins clustered across the smooth water, dividing and reforming in spangled islands. Each time I looked, I expected to find them gone, but instead, at the end of the afternoon, they took to the air.

Puffins in flight do not display the effortless grace of most birds. Even becoming airborne is an exercise in pure determination. They began by building up speed, half running, half flying across the surface of the water. As they ran, their orange, webbed feet left trails of splashes, ephemeral pathways of footprints streaming out across the sleek calm. When they finally broke free into the air, the weak sunlight was trapped for a moment in the glittering cascades of droplets they left behind them.

Soon there was a thin stream of birds gliding above the cliff tops. As they circled one or two broke away, dipping low, almost hovering above the land, before being swept back into the tide of birds. I was sure that they were looking for their own burrows, seeking out that one precious shadow on the ground from among a thousand others. Out of so many seemingly anonymous burrows, most birds would return to the same one year after year, and they were so long-lived that some of these same individuals could have been acting out this ritual since before I was born.

Gradually, the number of birds making up the spinning circle dwindled with the fading light. By the time they left, not a single bird had ventured onto land. For the whole winter they had been at sea. After so long in their own element, where they were swift and agile, they were wary of returning to the land, which would make them instantly clumsy and vulnerable. Their entire lives would have been spent far out at sea if the need to breed did not force them on land.

The puffins arrived again the next afternoon. North Haven shimmered with the constant agitation of their movements as they shivered their wings, dipped their heads below the surface of the water, checked nervously all round. As evening came, they took to the air. Mike and I went out on to the cliff top to watch. It was still and bright and mild. We could hear the scrabbling splash of feet scurrying across the water, and the swish of wings fighting against gravity to stay aloft. The puffin's wings are barely big enough to carry it, and the rhythmic hum of the rapid wing beats is very distinctive; it is the sound of summer on Skomer. I always thought that puffins were among the few birds that made flying look like hard work. When I watched a gull soaring effort-lessly in the updrafts above the cliffs, controlling its flight with a barely perceptible flick of a wing, I often felt an intense longing to experience such freedom. But I never felt any envy as I watched the puffins struggling to reach the cliff tops.

We waited as the puffins began to fill the air around us. Most of the birds from the water had gathered into a huge circle that was wheeling dizzily above our heads. There was an undulating swooshing noise as the birds careered past, sometimes closer, sometimes further away. From our vantage point on the cliff top, I felt as though we were up among them.

'Look,' Mike called. 'That one's going to land.'

A short distance away, a puffin was clasping at the air just above the ground. Its wing beats had dropped dangerously low, as though it was about to stall and come crashing the final few feet to the ground. But at the last moment it plunged forward, gaining speed as it dropped below the cliff line, and then skimmed up to join the other birds. After a couple more circuits it was back.

'There,' Mike said. 'I'm sure that's the same bird. It's in precisely the same place as last time.'

I was willing it to land, out of some irrational desire to see the puffins actually back on the island again. The bird hesitated, faltered in mid-air, and then swooped away. On its fourth attempt it fell out of the sky, tumbling to the ground in what looked like an unplanned manoeuvre. For a second it froze, crouching low, wings still outstretched as if in flight, remaining suspended in some nervous uncertainty between land and air. Then, slowly, it folded its wings and stood upright, in final confirmation of having arrived on land. It scattered wary glances in all directions while shifting nervously from foot to foot, giving the impression that, after so long at sea, it could not bear the touch of warm, dry grass beneath its webs.

It was the only one that had dared to leave the sky. For a single bird to be pioneering alone like that was too intimidating. Almost immediately, it was gone again, throwing itself from the island in a flurry of wings. But that brave gesture broke the spell. One after another, dozens of birds came fluttering and crashing down. They stayed only long enough to make fleeting glances into their burrows, but it was the first stage in moving away from their solitary winter lives back to the colony.

The next afternoon I waited for the puffins, happy in the certainty that winter was over. But they did not come. There was not a single puffin, not one stray confused bird wandering into North Haven at the end of its long journey back. It was the same the next afternoon, and the next; the bay was still and empty. Then, the day after that, they were back again, more than ever. It was a blustery day, and the breeze made things easier for the puffins, lifting them into the sky so that they could appear to soar with some of the carefree fluidity of other birds. Instead of the usual uncontrolled crash landings, they could hang in the flow of air above the cliff top, lowering themselves gently and precisely to the ground.

They were quickly rediscovering their old burrows, finding their lifelong mate among all the other apparently indistinguishable birds. I thought that their greetings were touchingly euphoric as they faced each other and bowed, flicking their heads rapidly from side to side so that their beaks clashed. I knew that it was silly to read such emotion into it, but they did seem pleased to see each other. There was a real air of excitement as they bustled about, peering into burrows. They did everything in brisk little bursts of activity, and their slightly jerky movements, coupled with the shiny perfection of their appearance, made me think of rows of identical clockwork toys.

The puffin burrows needed tidying up after the winter. Some of them must have suffered earth falls, resulting in blocked tunnels and cramped nesting chambers, but part of it seemed to be about the puffin's instinct to dig. Each bird was stamping its own individuality onto the convoluted tunnels of earth. The compulsive digging produced some spectacular effects. Scrabbling with their large feet, like a dog burying a bone, the puffins sent fountains of soil spraying out of the burrow entrance. An inquisitive mate, poking its head into the burrow at the wrong moment, might find itself caught full in the face by one of these geysers of earth.

The puffins looked immaculate. They preened so assiduously that the individual feathers were moulded together into a smoothly polished surface. With their brightly coloured bill plates and feathers freshly acquired for the coming breeding season, they gleamed with a reborn newness, until they emerged from the burrow refurbishments with their white breasts caked in earth, their feathers damp and stringy.

I hated to see so much earth being excavated. The underground lacework of burrows was so fragile that, in places, it was impossible to walk across. I could imagine just one beakful of soil too many causing the whole intricate system to disintegrate. Along the isthmus, small wedges of crumbling cliff top slumped away every winter. This sometimes happened in periods of storms, when rainwater gushed into the burrows and wheedled its way through the ground until it could find an escape route to the sea. Even a minor cliff fall vibrated through the air with an explosive drum roll, as the debris crashed onto the beach below, to be churned into a muddy stain on the water and then finally consumed by the sea. The chances were that among that mess of fallen rock and earth would be the pocket of air that had once been a burrow.

I watched as one returning puffin made the discovery that its nest site, loyally defended for many years, had been among the debris long since obliterated by the tide. The entrance to the burrow was still there, but the part where the nest chamber should have been opened out into a patch of empty sky. The puffin entered the familiar tunnel, exited almost immediately through the raw hole in the side of the cliff and, supported by the wind, hovered at the exact spot that had once been the nest chamber. It repeated the process time after time, as though the memory of what should have been was stronger than the reality it now found.

Perhaps one of the reasons that it was the puffins, above all birds, that marked the turning point in the seasons was because we lived in the middle of a puffin colony, and so were more acutely aware of their comings and goings. With the lengthening days keeping us busier in the evenings we had reinstated tea to fill the gap between lunch and an increasingly late dinner. As I was slipping bread under the grill for an early evening snack, I heard a rapid pattering above my head. I turned to Mike and grinned.

'That's when I know the puffins have really settled in, when they start clattering about on the roof again.'

There was another short staccato of puffin feet as one of them ran down the wooden shingles and back up to the vantage point of the apex.

'I know,' Mike agreed. 'It's a lovely noise isn't it?'

It was not unusual to have a dozen or more puffins promenading along the rooftop, and the fights sounded ferocious as they resounded against the hard surfaces overhead.

The settling in and courtship of the puffins was combined with only the most perfunctory of nest building. There were no intricately woven structures; a few scraps of vegetation scattered over the burrow floor were all that was necessary. But the puffins managed to achieve even these casual improvements with a certain amount of eye-catching style. The nest material often consisted of beakfuls of flowers, which were paraded ostentatiously before being taken below ground. There could be few sights in nature more endearingly pictur- esque than the puffins standing at their burrow entrances, gazing out to sea, with bouquets of thrift and sea campion clutched in their beaks.

The *Sharron* proved to be irretrievable. When she had sunk she landed on the mooring block and her hull had split open. With no chance of salvage, she was burnt where she lay, at low tide on Martin's Haven beach. Her brass fittings melted and flowed in shining pools among the pebbles. As it cooled, the metal and stone fused together, their shapes harmonising into miniature sculptures. Mike brought one of these surprisingly elegant objects back to the island, and we kept it as a memento of the boat we had been so fond of.

The *Sharron*'s replacement, another lifeboat, called the *Arklow*, needed a lot of work to convert her to a passenger-carrying vessel. It was a slow process, and she was not ready until early summer, so we enjoyed another extended period of solitude that year. The *Arklow* was painted vivid red, and her decks were open, except for the stark little wheelhouse perched incon- gruously at the stern, looking like a telephone box that had lost its way. The reflections of her bright new paintwork sparkled in fragments across the waves, like a drift of autumn leaves, but I could never see her as anything but functional rather than beautiful, and we never grew to love her as we had the *Sharron*.

I think I had always known that no summer could compete with the first one. It was the most spectacular introduction that I could have had to the island. With a second year reaching out ahead of me there should have been something wonderful about being able to anticipate the changes in the season, in the same way as we had waited for the puffins, but having it mapped out in my mind seemed to be to wish it away. In looking ahead I was hurrying past what was already there. Every day I looked for the first bluebell, finally discovering one, as in future years I always would, on the warm, sheltered slopes of South Valley. Soon after that, a wash of dilute indigo saturated the whole island. Gulls' nests scattered among the crackle-dry bracken were suddenly afloat in the hazy blueness. The pale birds had reflected the drabness of winter bracken, but now their pristine white plumage almost sparkled against the contrast of clear, bright colour.

Once the puffins had laid their eggs a quieter period followed. Each pair of birds had a single, white, roundish egg hidden away below ground, and their relatively carefree existence was curtailed by the need to remain constantly incubating the egg. During the daytime the colonies were largely deserted, since the birds temporarily released from the burrows were likely to be out at sea feeding. But in May, the hatching of the eggs brought the cliff tops vibrantly back to life. From first light until the last shadows soaked away into the landscape, puffins were scudding in to land with streams of slim, silvery fish fluttering from their beaks.

Along with this fresh surge of activity among the breeding birds there was a gradual influx of younger puffins, not yet matured into the full responsibilities of adulthood. The fringes of the island became more crowded with puffins than at any time during the year. Two, three and four year old birds, still too young to breed, return in successive summers, mostly to the cliffs that they fledged from, to look and learn. Though they had grown into perfect replica puffins, they were just distinguishable from the older birds by their beaks, which were slimmer and less ridged. With nothing more pressing to occupy them, these birds kept themselves permanently busy as full-time spectators, and if there was one thing that intrigued them it was a really good fight. Though they became less common as the season progressed, conflicts between the adult birds sometimes degenerated into dramatic, but rarely damaging, brawls. These involved wrestling with their beaks locked together, while tangled wings thrashed against the ground. They became so absorbed in the battle that the two interlocked birds sometimes plummeted over the cliff edge, still intent on the skirmish. It was often not until the rocks below were sweeping dangerously close that they broke apart and flew to safety with only their pride severely battered. Like gangs of excited children in a school playground the young puffins ran *en masse* to get the best view of each emerging contest. Any adult interactions were essential watching for the immature birds. When a pair greeted each other with a kiss of beaks, it had to be done in front of a large and appreciative audience. With shameless curiosity the youngsters craned their necks forward until their own beaks were almost part of the flirtatious clash between the paired birds.

This was the time of year when, for me, the island reached its peak, when the flowers and birds came together in a fleeting, unsurpassable brilliance. But as soon as the bluebells were at their best I began to imagine that, already, I could see them fading. There was a slight purplish dustiness about them, a barely perceptible tarnishing of that purity. The red campion began to grow up through them, and the pink mixed with the blue, like watercolour streaked over wet paper. The new shade of pale amethyst was still beautiful, but it was no longer the special colour of those first summer days. I wanted to rush out and grab armfuls of the flowers. I wanted to hang on to them and stop them slipping away so fast. I hated the way it was moving so quickly.

The previous year had been as endless as a childhood summer, pulled and stretched by the novelty that surrounded me. I could have picked out every single day and remembered its unique quality. Each flicker of change was a precious experience. Everything was a first; nothing was lost in the haze of routine. Now the days were losing their distinction, piling up, with one overlaying another so that the memories were blurred.

Before long, I began to notice that the cliffs were growing quieter: despite every effort of my willpower, the summer was drifting away.

'The razorbills and guillemots are leaving already, aren't they?' I said miserably to Mike as we sat on the grass overlooking High Cliff.

The rocky ledges were streaked white from constant use, but the gaps in the lines of birds were beginning to show. He reached out and took my hand.

'You shouldn't feel sad to see them go. It's what it's all about, the end of another successful breeding season. I tell you what. We'll come out tonight and watch the chicks fledge. It's better if you can see a purpose to them leaving.'

We left the house that evening as the twilight was turning the air cloud-grey. It was still light enough to see, but the perspectives were flattened out, colours washed away. The cliffs were echoing with insistent, high-pitched cheeping sounds, cutting through the simmering frenzy of growling adults. We settled ourselves down to watch. The water was dappled with adult birds, white breasts glimmering faintly, dark backs barely more than shadows. A razorbill chick was visible, high on a rocky ledge, close to where we were. Usually they were difficult to see, tucked out of sight behind a protective parent bird. Now, in full view, it looked almost unreal: a tiny version of the adult, a few inches high. Its behaviour was desperately agitated, running about the ledge and cheeping wildly. Several times it went to the edge of the precipice, as if it might fall, but at the last moment it rushed for safety at the back of the ledge.

Such agitation was not surprising. The chick appeared to know exactly what was expected of it. Throughout its two or three weeks of life it had been nurtured and protected. And now this. It was being forced to leave the solid security of the cliff for a leap into the unknown. The chick retreated again from the rim of the ledge and stood with its back turned to the beckoning whisper of the sea. At last, the chick scampered to the brink of its only known world, and then launched itself out into nothingness. To me, it was an act of the most pure and innocent faith. There would be no way back, and alone it would face death, but it trusted unequivocally that its parent would find and defend it.

As the chick fell it opened out its wings, but it did not soar. The tiny, unfinished wings could only slow its fall. A jutting piece of rock caught the chick, and it turned a somersault in the air before tumbling on its way. Though it seemed to fall endlessly, in an instant it hit the base of the cliff and scrambled into the water. It was unhurt; the lightness of its body and the resistance of its wings against the air had been enough to soften the landing. Almost at once, the adult bird was at its side, and in that moment it had accepted the responsibility of leading the chick out into an environment that might overwhelm it. The rocky niche had provided some sort of defensible sanctuary, but now the fledgling had to be protected from a whole sea full of dangers. The nervousness in the adult was obvious. Its head flicked constantly round, even dipping below the surface of the water, searching every corner of its existence.

The clamour of the gulls was diminishing; a few birds wheeled idly overhead, spilling out long, querulous wails, unaware of the scrap of food making its escape in the dull water below them. During the daytime their calls were everywhere, but the approaching darkness had subdued them. It was a window of relative safety for the fledging chicks, while there was just enough light left in the sky, but after the gulls had stopped hunting. And there was the urgency. The chicks had to be as far away from the island as possible before the dawn, a few hours away, could rouse the gulls. Using its untried leg muscles and perfect seagoing feet, the fledgling swam with fierce determination, heading towards the mouth of the bay.

I watched the fleeing adult and chick until they became indistinguishable from the greyness. Around us guillemots and razorbills were still calling, and an occasional chick tumbled quietly into the water. I found it almost painfully moving and inexplicably melancholy. There was an ache in my throat that might have turned to tears if I had tried to talk. It wasn't just sadness that the birds were leaving. I couldn't tell what it was: perhaps the bravery and determination of the chick, the loyalty of the adult, the fact that so many of the fledglings would not survive the vast challenge of the ocean. We waited until the darkness fell silent.

The following morning the cliffs were noticeably emptier. The same process was repeated over the next few nights until there was hardly a guillemot or a razorbill to be seen. I stared across at the cliffs. The contrast with the noise and activity of the last few weeks was so profound that I felt I could hear the bare rocks ringing with silence. All summer, the deep, throaty growls had rippled from one bird to the next as they joined in the uproar, and the hum of wing beats had laced through the air. Now the whitened cliffs made shining reflections in the milky turquoise sea. It looked desolate, and yet Mike was right. This was what it was about: another successful season, another wave of young birds safely fledged. It was true that they would not all live long enough to return as adults, but at least there was hope.

When the birds were crowded together on the cliffs they were terrifyingly vulnerable. Mike and I both had a profound dread of some catastrophe striking them while they were on the island, supposedly under our protection. I used to watch the distant shapes of oil tankers sliding into the mouth of Milford Haven and I knew that each one carried the tiny seed of a potential disaster.

Although the disappearance of the cliff-nesting birds felt like some sort of turning point towards the end of the season, we were only just on the brink of high summer, with the temperate spring weather giving way to some of the hottest days of the year. That summer, like most others, had its own minia-

ture heatwave woven into the normal highs and lows of wind, rain and intermittent brightness. Though sea breezes were an almost constant presence, an
island without shade or shelter could still feel overwhelmed by the inescapable
force of the sun. Shards of blistering heat echoed back from the sea and rocks
all around. Sunlight pressed like a weight on the top of my head, trickling
down through my hair until it burnt its way through to the skin. With so much
time spent working outside, the endless sunshine could become not liberating
but oppressive, making me slow and clumsy. It felt as though the energy was
melting out of my body until it oozed in puddles round my feet.

A few days into the heatwave I found it impossible to think of cold as
anything but pleasurable. I would happily have walked barefoot through a
snowdrift. Trying to remember the torments of winter - cold bed-sheets,
persistent, wheedling draughts - defeated my imagination; the only true
discomfort was being hot. I was surprised, then, to find that half way through
another of these aggressively sun-drenched days I was forced to admit defeat
and go back to the house for something warmer to wear. The sun was still
shining but the heat had drained from the air.

As soon as I got home I pulled on a jumper, feeling the wool strange but
comforting against my bare arms, and walked through into the kitchen. The
atmosphere outside was changing. The colour of the air had thickened to
pinkish-grey, which made it appear drab and dusty. I turned and looked to the
south. Clouds were pouring over the horizon, wallowing in the sky like black
ink dripped into clear water. Within a few minutes the rain arrived, long,
silvered strands clustered together as densely as the shimmering curtain of a
waterfall. The clouds had ripped open, releasing a deluge that was all the more
dramatic coming as it did out of a pure blue summer day. Water flowed over
the dry ground without soaking in, spilling a mirror-bright film across the
short turf and gathering dust from the paths into muddy rivulets.

I began to notice that the gulls were behaving strangely. They were flocking
above the isthmus, hovering in the air and screeching in that irritable, aggressive way of theirs. I looked out through a blur of rain, trying to interpret the
unfocused images. From amid the melee of wings, birds were swooping down
towards the ground, as though they were hunting. But hunting what? I never
trusted the gulls and this curious behaviour was making me uneasy. I decided
to go out and look.

As I walked towards the isthmus I saw a gull wrestling something dull-grey
and shapeless in its beak. Other birds whined around it, angry and jealous,

ready to take advantage of any weakness to steal the prize. I was appalled to realise that this coveted object was a chick, and I began to run in some vain hope of saving it. The gaggle of birds melted away still mewing their irritation, but I was too late: the chick was gone.

Mike arrived on the tractor.

'What's going on?' he called.

'I don't know. Something's disturbing the gulls, and they got hold of a chick somehow.'

He jumped down and stood beside me.

'Look!' Mike said a few moments later. 'There are more chicks out of the burrows. That's what the gulls are after.'

Along the isthmus a scattering of bewildered puffin chicks lay sprawled on the damp ground. The surge of water had come flooding from the slopes above, gushing through the burrows and washing the chicks out into the open. Overhead, the gulls were churning themselves into a frenzy of excitement at this unexpected rash of food.

'Quick,' Mike shouted. 'We've got to get the chicks back before the gulls find them.'

I grabbed the nearest ball of bedraggled fluff. With the cloud of down shrunken smooth against its body it looked very small and, deprived of this natural insulation, the dampness made it feel feverishly hot. A gull swooped low, skimming close to my head, whining out its longing for the chick, and I waved my arm furiously to ward it off. Already, the water had subsided, leaving only strands of debris from the burrow mouth drizzled across the ground like the trace of a flooded river. I knelt down in the mud and reached deep into the darkness to place the chick inside.

We ran along the cliff top to retrieve the last of the saturated waifs and make sure they were safely back underground. With no more chicks to entice them, the gulls sailed smoothly away on the invisible airborne tides, mewling with half-hearted rage. Everything was quiet and normal again. I watched the dense slab of rain as it moved off across the sea. In its wake the depleted sun cast a cool brilliance over the rain-varnished landscape. My wet hair had an uncomfortable, clinging stickiness and my arms were muddy up to the shoulders. I shivered with a feeling of deep cold, and found myself remembering fondly the pure, unrestrained sunshine we had just lost.

That summer, perhaps as an antidote to the quiet left by the departing birds, Wellington arrived. The subject arose one morning over breakfast.

'They're rounding up the goats on Skokholm today,' Mike said, extremely casually.

Skokholm was our nearest neighbour, a small island about three miles away. As well as its beautiful red sandstone cliffs and populations of seabirds, it had a herd of goats. Taken to the island to supply fresh milk, the goats had long since been abandoned and now wandered freely. Most years they were rounded up, and a few of the young animals were removed to prevent the herd from expanding too much and causing damage.

'The boat is going to call in here on the way to Skokholm,' Mike went on, 'so I thought I'd go over and give them a hand catching the goats.'

'That should be interesting.' I grinned at the amusing image of agile goats and frayed tempers. 'So what do they do with the poor things once they've caught them?'

'Don't worry. They make sure they find homes for them.'

'Oh, that's good.'

'Actually, I was wondering if we might have one.'

My mood of vague amusement changed immediately. I was adamant.

'Absolutely not!' I said firmly. 'What on earth would we want a goat for?'

'Well . . . I don't know. It would be handy for milk.'

'I'm used to the taste of long life milk now, and I certainly don't need goat's milk.'

The *Arklow* pulled away from North Haven with Mike on board smiling and waving, obviously relishing the prospect of an adventure. I smiled and waved back, relieved that we had sorted out the goat issue before it had gone any further.

It was late when the boat returned. I was in my customary place at the kitchen window, painstakingly scrubbing the tiny potatoes that I had unearthed from the garden. It was a tedious chore made almost pleasant by the view of North Haven stretching out below me on a beautiful, still evening. I heard the soft hum of an engine and looked up to see the *Arklow* skimming across the bay, close in to Rye Rocks. She glided gently up against the cliff at the bottom of the landing steps, and the ripples she had created sent her own reflection washing in broken patterns across the bay.

I watched as Mike leapt nimbly across onto the rocks, followed by a young and very nervous goat. It must need to stretch its legs before they finish the journey to the mainland, I thought calmly. Then I had the strangest impression that the boat was pulling away from the cliff. I grabbed the binoculars with muddy hands. It *was* pulling away, and Mike was waving cheerfully up at me as he stood there with one small goat. Through the little tunnel of vision I watched as he lifted the animal and swung it across his shoulders. I was irrationally angry. Stopping only to drag my boots on, I began to run frantically, ignoring the closeness of the path to the cliff edge, and the burrows beneath my feet waiting to trip me up. I had the idea that I could nip the whole thing in the bud, if only I could get to the landing while the boat was within shouting distance.

Boats move incredibly slowly, but I was slower still, slipping and panting over the sandy ground. The boat was shrinking rapidly into the distance as it made its way back to the mainland. It was futile now, but I was too incensed to stop running. I reached the top of the cliff, hot and cross, at precisely the same time that Mike arrived from below, with the goat draped like a stole around his shoulders.

'What is that?' I demanded furiously, glaring at the terrified animal.

Mike's broad grin didn't falter, even for a moment.

'It's a present for you,' he said.

I am ashamed to admit that I was disarmed by the sheer audacity, and by the sight of those anxious amber eyes gazing at me from Mike's shoulder.

'You *knew* I didn't want a goat,' I shouted, trying to sound crosser than I really was.

We walked slowly back along the narrow the path and tethered the goat close to the house. She was not a particularly beautiful animal, with her ragged, tobacco-coloured coat and extraordinarily spindly legs. Her mouth was curved permanently into a faintly knowing grin.

'How did we end up with this one?' I asked.

'Well, no one else wanted her. The others were much prettier.'

She moved as far away from us as the tether would allow and screamed with terror, or anger, or both. I edged cautiously towards her, holding out a tentative hand of friendship, but she stayed forever out of my reach, bucking and rearing against the rope. I suppose I should have left her in peace, but I hated to see her so alone on that first night away from the herd. I gathered up a huge bouquet of all the plants I thought might appeal to a goat and sat down close to her, holding the offering with an outstretched arm. At once she stopped screaming and eyed me with interest. I should have known that greed is the all-conquering sin in a goat. She extended her neck, and even her lips, so that she could eat while keeping as much distance from me as possible.

Showing immense delicacy, she selected the tastiest blooms with her surprisingly agile lips and then chewed them with a contented sideways motion.

After that there was no looking back. I wouldn't say that we became friends exactly, but I think she began to accept me as one of the herd.

'What's she called?' I asked Mike, as the goat watched us sitting on the doorstep the next morning putting on our boots.

Mike thought for a moment.

'Wellington,' he replied.

'How do you know?'

'Because she's such an old boot.'

'Oh, that's cruel,' I laughed.

But the name stuck, and Wellington she was ever after. It proved to be a name she thoroughly deserved.

After the idyllic unreality of the previous year, we learnt that normal summer weather was capable of throwing little flounces of bad temper. These sudden and unpredictable squalls of irritability could pass as quickly as they came, leaving everything serene and unruffled again. I was in the kitchen one night, finishing off the washing-up sometime after midnight, when the still air began to break up into choppy little waves of northerly wind lapping up against the house. The atmosphere thickened with mist the colour of black ink. Almost at once, the soft blanket of shearwater calls was spiked with hard sounds of birds colliding against the house. It was something so familiar that I barely noticed it at first, but then the shearwaters, disorientated by the dense, hazy darkness and surfing helplessly on the tide of wind, began to pummel more violently into the walls. I felt my muscles tensing in sympathy.

There was a half-seen flicker of light and a noise so overwhelming that I thought it must be coming from inside my own head. From somewhere a rain, silver-bright and hard, was pouring over my face. Without time for thought my hands pressed over my eyes, protecting my skin. I was paralysed, unable to move as the sharpness of the noise jarred against my senses. When the rain stopped I tentatively uncoiled from inside myself. All around me the floor shone like a lake of cracked ice. Wind was spilling into the kitchen through the raw void in front of me, and a single white feather lay on the draining board. For a second the numbness of my thoughts left me able only to wonder how so much glass could have come from one broken window. Then as I became more rational I stared at my hands and cautiously touched my face, barely able to believe that there was no blood.

I turned very slowly, not daring to move my feet, which remained imprisoned by the splinters of glass. A shearwater had smashed through the window with such force that it had come to rest by the far wall. Despite the feelings of disorientation that were buzzing round my head, my greatest concern was to see if the shearwater was all right. At that moment Mike, who had been enjoying an uncharacteristically early night, appeared at the doorway, still half-submerged in the confusion of sleep. The sight of me, the bird and the sea of glass gave all the explanation that was necessary. He crunched across the room and picked up the shearwater. The feathers were smooth and unruffled, the skin completely ungrazed. With typical shearwater resilience it had launched itself like a missile through the pane of glass and emerged unscathed. Mike took it outside and left it on the doorstep to fly away when it was ready.

Back in the kitchen we assessed the damage. One broken window: a nuisance not a tragedy, although I was already mentally wrestling with the complications of carrying a large, brittle-thin film of glass on a blustery boat journey. It was then that Mike noticed the pies. I had baked extra and left them cooling on the worktop where their golden crusts had been pierced by glassy arrowheads. The disaster was instantly thrown into a new perspective. A mere broken window could be overlooked, but the destruction of the pies was unforgivable. Mike disappeared without a word. He came back carrying the shearwater, which he had retrieved from the doorstep, and held it up to give it a good look at the glittering pie crusts.

'There!' Mike said in the sort of tones usually reserved for a particularly recalcitrant two-year-old. 'Look what you've done.'

The shearwater stared at the scene of its crime, but appeared determinedly unrepentant.

Although we never saw another summer as hot and still as our first on Skomer, neither was there one that came to such a dramatic end. The second summer faded gently and predictably away. Early in September, Terry decided to take the *Arklow* away to sheltered moorings, and we began our second winter. As a parting gift he brought us a large bag of coal, having heard our miserable accounts of the driftwood fires.

September weather could be the best of the year, sparklingly clear, with a hard-edged sea touching on an unimaginably distant horizon. As soon as we were alone, we both realised how much we had been looking forward to that time. I had no more fear of winter; I just loved the sense of absolute peace that came when the island was ours again.

One of the places that highlighted the mood of those tranquil, end of summer days was North Valley. It had a feel and an atmosphere that set it apart from the rest of the island. The swampy, shallow dish of land opened out into the shining reflections of Green Pond, and beyond that, where the trickle of clear, peaty-gold water overflowed from the pond, the valley suddenly took shape. Its steep sides provided enough shelter for a thicket of blackthorn to grow in a narrow wedge along the bottom of the hollow. The gnarled, finger-thin twigs were interlaced like the clasp of a thousand bony knuckles, forming a single dome of branches, with its leafy canopy carved by the wind to the shapes of water-smoothed stone. Beneath this drift of vegetation the stream disappeared, and could only be heard trickling between the boulders as it made its way down to the sea.

There was a feeling of nostalgia in the soft, bubbling whisper of water against stone and the carefree sound of small birds, as though the valley was full of half-forgotten memories from summers long past. It was something we rarely heard amid Skomer's insistent uproar of weather and seabirds. In this sheltered haven the last of the season's migrating sedge warblers and whitethroats tumbled through the undergrowth. The pure energy of their song hung suspended in the stillness. Frequently they vanished into the thicket of blackthorn, but the drumming of wings traced out their paths as clearly as a brightly coloured thread woven through the branches.

It was the time of year to clamber down the overgrown valley out towards the edge of the island where hoops of brambles barred our way like coils of barbed wire. Berries the colour of a bottle of crimson ink held up to the sun dripped among the thorns. Overripe fruits had fallen and splashed over the leaves below. They were sweet and juicy enough to be worth the risk of tearing our clothes and skin. One followed another until our fingers were dyed with the indelible inky stain. If there were enough, we collected some to take home. The art of bottling fruit was another one of those odd, old-fashioned skills that I had learnt out of necessity. The shiny jars sitting on the larder shelf gave me a particular sense of pleasure because I knew that I had preserved not just the fruit, but the fading brilliance of summer, to be poured out again on a drab winter day.

One of the best discoveries of late summer was that brief period when the night-time sea sparkled with phosphorescence. Any sharp disturbance sent a firework display of sparks cascading through the water. It was spectacular enough for us to walk down to North Haven beach in the dark just to sweep our hands through the sequinned water or kick our feet against the black waves and watch them explode into a confetti of bright flares. On the rare occasions that we took the boat out at night, the propeller cut a glittering trail through the water. It all added to the feeling that Skomer had almost endless layers to be unravelled, more than anywhere I had ever known.

As Wellington settled in, she took on something of the role of a pet dog, only with none of the abject deference. There was no longer any need to keep her tethered, since she could be guaranteed to stay within earshot of a rattled food bowl. When not busy, she slept in the shelter that Mike had built for her close to the house, though she bitterly resented the fact that we had our own superior accommodation, which she would have preferred to share. She learnt how to open the front door by hurling herself at it with great force, and we were occasionally startled by a resonating thud followed by the clatter of hooves on floorboards. As we dragged her outside she bleated with heart-rending fury, digging her hooves in to make herself immovable as she curled back her lips and bared her teeth, nibbling destructively at the walls until the last moment before ejection. It made me wonder if all goats were genetically predisposed to cause maximum irritation.

She had taken to joining us on our walks, quite uninvited. In fact, even if we wanted to go without her, it was impossible to sneak past without being seen. The trouble was that, while a dog might be amenable and grateful to be taken for a walk, Wellington was simply in charge. All walks had to be taken in single file, with Mike in front, Wellington in the middle and me invariably bringing up the rear. If we strayed from these rules and tried to walk side by side she threw the most dazzling tantrums, rearing up on her hind legs like a wild stallion and butting us. We discovered that the only way to curb these attacks was to lay her on her side and hold her firmly down, which seemed to convince her for a while that she was not the dominant goat in the herd. During these periods of relative calm, her open confrontation shrank to the occasional surreptitious flick of the head so as to jab her horn into a vulnerable thigh as she passed.

The previous hot, dry summer, followed by torrential rain, had produced a gloriously abundant crop of mushrooms. First to appear were the parasol mushrooms, fat globes on stalks, which opened out into enormous, shaggy-topped umbrellas. When I sliced them up ready to cook they looked supremely appetizing, the flesh so richly brown that my fantasies turned them into thick slabs of fried steak. In the pan they shrivelled and seeped and turned grey.

Eventually, they shrank to a disappointing scraping of sludge at the bottom of the pan and tasted of nothing in particular.

The quietly unpretentious field mushrooms were delicious. The creamy white domes bulged unobtrusively through the short turf, particularly in the open, grassy fields behind the farm. There were so many of them that we were forced to take a bin-bag to carry them home. We could easily find enough to fill the frying pan several times over, and make a whole meal of mushrooms.

Although our second summer could not have been more different to the first, there was no question in our minds that the mushroom crop would not arrive in exactly the same way. We were disappointed. After our first foray we arrived home trailing a large bag with one or two mushrooms rattling round in the bottom. After that, we realised that the only receptacle we were likely to need was an empty pocket, and the resulting mushrooms never constituted more than a garnish on the side of the plate.

Wellington insisted on coming mushroom picking, and on these occasions she contrived to be more annoying than ever. At first, we thought that her infuriating behaviour must be no more than unfortunate coincidence. After all, we would hardly have expected a goat to have such an unerring ability to anticipate and frustrate our plans.

It began with the sighting of the first mushroom, a single pale disc amid the smooth green of so much rabbit-cropped turf. Mike, whose keen eyes were guaranteed to beat me to any new discovery, called out triumphantly.

'Look, there's one!'

I began to move towards it, but Wellington, looking up from her idle browsing of a piece of ivy, raced ahead of me. When she reached the mushroom, her dextrous lips stretched out and coiled round the tender flesh, plucking it delicately into her mouth.

'Oh no!' I complained. 'Why did she take that, out of all the things she could have eaten in this field? I'm sure she's never been interested in mushrooms before. There aren't enough mushrooms that we can afford for Wellington to eat them.'

It just seemed like bad luck that Wellington had noticed the mushroom at the same time as us and, for some odd reason, had decided to eat it. But the next mushroom excited as much interest as the last. Mike pointed at the mushroom. Wellington charged towards it. I followed in rapid pursuit of scrawny goat, arriving in time to see the mushroom vanish, as if it had been sucked into the nozzle of a vacuum cleaner.

'Oh Wellington!' I said crossly. 'What did you have to do that for?' She gave me one of those peculiar, enigmatic grins. 'Surely she can't have done it on purpose?' I said to Mike.

'Only one way to find out,' he replied.

The next mushroom Mike indicated to me silently. Then, for Wellington's benefit, he called out, 'Look, over there,' while pointing ostentatiously in the wrong direction. I hurried down the false trail with Wellington barging her way ahead of me, while Mike strolled casually over to pick the mushroom.

'I never realised you were such an intelligent goat,' I said to Wellington as she gave me a petulant little butt in protest at the fruitless search. 'Though, fortunately, not too intelligent.'

By repeating this performance, we managed to pick a meagre pocketful of mushrooms, and I am glad to say that there are some instances in which goats never learn.

The mushrooms were more than a minor luxury as far as we were concerned. Our vegetable garden, having been defeated by a summer of dry, salty winds, rabbits and voles, had nothing left to offer. Mushrooms were one of our few remaining sources of fresh food.

Towards the end of September, winter settled in with a vengeance. The weather began to pummel in from the south-west, rain-soaked and restless. We listened to the shipping forecast several times a day and were always rewarded with a gale warning for our sea area. The thick smudge of rain enfolded us like a blanket. I used to lean my elbows against the kitchen windowsill to watch the dizzying patterns of raindrops as they swirled horizontally across the isthmus. It was compulsive. Everything had been washed away and our isolation was complete.

From inside the house the weather looked unbearable. If we could force ourselves outside, it was not just bearable but exhilarating. I could feel the storm driving right through my skin, infusing me with energy. Sometimes, as we fought to stay upright, we found ourselves laughing out loud at the lunacy of pitting ourselves against such weather. It took more preparation than usual to face the outside. I had to plait my hair tightly because the slightest stray strand would snap against my face like a whip and sting my eyes. We made masks out of strips of stockinet, cutting out holes for the eyes and mouth, to protect ourselves from the raindrops that stabbed into our skin like needles, and the necks of our waterproofs were stuffed with clean rags to soak up the rain that was inevitably driven inside.

When we walked close to the cliff edge we could feel the deep, juddering vibration as the waves surged against rock, but it was almost impossible to see anything. If we had the strength to lean out into the wind there was only a cloud of dazzling, salt-bright haze where the breaking waves should have been. The force of the wind swept my breath away and made the skin on my face tremble. The effect soon became so suffocating that I had to pull back from the cliff edge and gulp down mouthfuls of air.

The sack of coal had given us a couple of weeks of blissful warmth before the battle with the snarling, spitting driftwood resumed. As the evenings closed in on us, and we were reduced to hunting round for something to read, I discovered a copy of Thomas Hardy's *Under the Greenwood Tree* among our books. After a rather disillusioning encounter with *Tess of the d'Urbervilles* at the age of thirteen, I had avoided Hardy, but this time I was captivated. Over the next few years I read all his books, some of them several times, until finally I opened the last unread book, *The Hand of Ethelberta*. I realised then how awful it would be to know that, for the rest of my life, there would be no new Thomas Hardy to look forward to, so I put the book away and have never read it.

During that winter, as Thomas Hardy led on to Jane Austen and the Bronte sisters, I found myself slipping into a sort of unreality. We had been cut off for so long that it was becoming difficult to remember what day, even what month, it was. More and more, I felt cast adrift in a time that belonged to no particular decade. I knew that somewhere there were cars and shops and televisions and streetlights, but I felt much closer to the lives that existed in the books I read. I could believe in them far more easily than the increasingly remote world over the water. Sometimes, I stared across the sea and tried to convince myself that there really were people over there, rushing to catch trains, stuck in traffic jams, late for meetings. It seemed faintly incredible, and I wondered if I would ever be able to go back to all that. The idea was becoming frightening; I realised that I preferred the solid, dependable truth of books.

We tried to stick to the rule of holding three months' supply of food. This was a fairly arbitrary amount since we had never worked out what three months' worth of food actually looked like, but it was one of those ideas that we had clung to fondly since our earliest days on Skomer. Now, for the first time, these vague theories were being put to the test. By the beginning of November, with no fresh supplies since the end of September, food was becoming a problem, and the weather was showing no sign of relenting.

I think that we could have held out for the full three months if it had simply been a matter of survival. We had almost endless supplies of staples, like rice, porridge and lentils, but our pampered appetites craved more than that. Recklessly, we had eaten the best things first, in the hope of better weather to come. We never quite believed that the gales would go on for weeks without a pause.

There was enough flour left to make bread, but it had begun to taste bitter, and I was secretly afraid that it might have grown some invisible, poisonous mould. I think the damp had got to it. The house felt dry to me but, in truth, the sea-damp of salty air was everywhere: in our clothes, our food, everything. Then, worse still, I found white maggoty things in the flour. I sifted them out and said nothing to Mike. After all, we had little choice but to eat it, and there was no reason for both of us to have to swallow those nasty, wriggling images along with each mouthful of bread.

In desperation, the garden had been dug over several times to unearth every last tiny, hidden potato. The final straw as far as I was concerned was when the onions ran out. I hadn't noticed until they were gone that they were the magic ingredient that could make almost anything taste nice. The growing darkness of the shortening days seemed to focus our minds on food, and random cravings became intrusive. There were whole days when I couldn't stop thinking about crisps or ice cream, and I had worn the ink off the pages of my cake recipes by thumbing through them too often.

One lunch time, with a batch of the bitter dough still rising under a tea towel, there was only one thick crust of bread left. I decided to leave it for Mike, and went through the cupboard in search of something for myself.

'What's that you're eating?' Mike asked, as he trimmed the mould from our small remaining piece of cheese.

'Instant mashed potato,' I replied.

'Instant mashed potato and what?'

'Just instant mashed potato.'

The weather settled into an irritating pattern of clearing and calming each night, and then deteriorating again by morning. Day after day we woke to the sound of the foghorn bellowing out from Skokholm lighthouse. It was a dreary sound, if only because it promised another day of gloomy half-light. The fine, pinprick rain jabbed against the windows in a series of irregular gusts and, even though we knew that the storms were far less daunting than they looked from the inside, there were days when we barely made it outside. The winter was a time partly for writing up the summer's work, and when every trace of a view had been absorbed by the thick, misty rain, it was easy to find an excuse to stay indoors. We always regretted it, though; we had become used to an outdoor way of life, and a whole day confined left us feeling restless and unsettled.

The only positive thing about the weather pattern was that when the wind dropped at night we could sit by the spluttering driftwood fire without the usual draughts scudding through the room. But even when the wind receded the waves remained. They continued to beat against the island in huge, slow surges built up by the weeks of storms. The gales ripped away the other sounds, and it was only when the wind fell light that we could hear the power in the sea. The shingle, caught by the waves, flowed like a slush of crushed ice, rasping as it spilled up and down the beach.

As the tide dropped, seals began to haul out of the water onto North Haven beach, immediately below our living room window. We heard the drag of their bodies across the pebbles as more and more of them left the churning waves for the stillness of the land. Their howls skimmed over the perpetual clamour of sea sounds. As the seals settled down to sleep, we could hear hostilities breaking out as one inadvertently invaded the fragment of solitude belonging to another. Everything came drifting up clearly through the hard night air: the throaty snarls, the tumbling, ricocheting pebbles dislodged by the skirmishes.

From the fireside we listened to the unfolding dramas until we couldn't resist going out to look. The daytime clouds had peeled back from the sky, uncovering a brilliant, almost-round moon, with a light strong enough to cast shadows and make the sea shine. We tried to creep silently, but the more carefully we moved, the more noise we made. Just the snapping of plant stems beneath our feet sounded harsh and intrusive. If the seals had suspected that we were there, they would have immediately abandoned the land. We even checked the direction of the last traces of breeze to make sure that our scent would not be carried towards the beach. Then, when we had reached the cliff edge, the darkness let us stand and watch in a way that would have been impossible during the daytime.

There is something beautiful about seals by moonlight, an ethereal elegance that uncompromising daylight snatches away from them. Seals are sleek and agile, but only in the water. The moment they slump out of the waves on to the pebbles, their bodies become recalcitrant things overwhelmed by gravity. They move across the beach with a lolloping shuffle, bouncing against the stones with a force that sets the blubber shuddering beneath their skin. In the bluish moonlight they acquired the beauty of marble sculptures, solid but streamlined. Their wails, echoing through the silvery air, gave the illusion of being almost tuneful as they bickered restlessly, searching for the most comfortable spot on the shingle.

Once the seals had given us the impetus to leave the fire and go outside, we often felt such a craving for air and exercise that we continued to walk for some distance round the island. I loved walking on the cliffs at night. It was best not to use a torch; its dazzling brightness dulled our eyes to everything else and kept us confined within the narrow beam of light. As we grew accustomed to the dark, the landscape opened out around us. The thick band of surf that rimmed South Haven glowed white, and even the distant sea had a faint luminosity, so that it was possible to see for miles. Overhead, the clouds, still heavy with rain, had broken apart and were tumbling in great dark chunks across the sky. It was liberating to touch the breeze and taste the air, without feeling it as some crushing power that we needed to shelter from. And yet I almost knew that by morning the sky would have closed in again and storm-force winds would make the prospect of standing and gazing at the view unthinkable.

We desperately needed to get to the mainland for supplies, and Mike was forever staring out of the window, searching for the slightest hint that the weather might be improving enough for us to make the crossing. My rational self ached for fresh food, but, deep down, I didn't want to go. The longer I stayed away from the mainland, the more I dreaded any contact with it. If the forecast suggested a lull in the weather, I was tempted to disappear early in the morning to make sure that it would be too late to make the crossing by the time I was found. The days were so short that only an early start would ensure that we were back before dark. But it didn't happen: as one week followed another, the shipping forecast remained the same, gale force, storm force, severe storm force. The only thing that we managed to avoid was hurricane force. There was no need for me to hide away.

When the weather moderated it was well into November and, much as I wanted to, I didn't dare jeopardise this one chance. We had had no fresh supplies since September. Mike, never at his best first thing in the morning, threw the kitchen window wide open and leaned out into the cool, damp air. There was no wind and the heavy atmosphere veiled everything with its smooth greyness.

'Right,' Mike said decisively. 'We're going.'

I had been ready with excuses, but I knew that they were pointless. However hard I tried, even I couldn't find a trace of white water out beyond the haven, and this might be the best opportunity we would get for weeks.

'I'll take the tractor and meet you down at the landing,' Mike said, obviously enlivened by the excitement.

The starting of the tractor sounded like a triumphant roar, reflecting Mike's enthusiasm. I wandered miserably down to the beach, like a reluctant child on the way to school. I really didn't want to leave the island, and, apart from anything else, we would have a row. Mike would be bossy and I would be petulant. He would stay dry and I would be soaked to the skin. That was the way it invariably was.

I began to assemble things from the boatshed on the jetty: life-jackets, flares, oars, anchor. I could hear the tractor rumbling down the hill towards me, bringing the inevitable still closer.

'Right then, let's get moving,' Mike called as he jumped down from the tractor.

His brisk efficiency was already beginning to annoy me.

After Mike's boating disaster the previous year, the disgraced flat-bottomed dory was eventually replaced by a smaller boat, made of fibreglass but of a trusty, old-fashioned, clinker-built design. At only thirteen feet, it may have been little more than two bathtubs long, but it rode the sea properly, cutting through the waves instead of bouncing over them, which meant that we (and our supplies) could remain relatively dry during the crossing. It was also light enough for us to manhandle down the beach with slightly less grazed skin and scuffed tempers than before. Even so, it was never easy launching the boat in the winter unless the tide was exceptionally high. The storms scoured away our smooth pebble runway leaving the path to the sea strewn with rocks.

When the boat was finally afloat at the edge of the water, I held it while Mike loaded it and secured the engine. Our previous outboard had proved so unreliable that we had reverted to the old Seagull engines. They were tiny, antiquated-looking things that bore no relationship to a modern engine, but were so simple that Mike could maintain them entirely on the island, without ever having to send them to the mainland for repair. It was true that they didn't provide the ideal solution. The strength of some of the tide races round the island easily outstripped them, and sometimes, in a mutinous moment, they spluttered to a halt leaving us adrift in the dangerous waters of the sounds. But, given the prohibitive costs of buying and maintaining a powerful new engine, it seemed like the only option.

I waited until the waves were with me, gave the boat one hefty shove off shore, and jumped in as it started to move. As soon as we were in deep enough water, the engine sprang obediently into life with a yank of the starter cord, and quickly pulled us out of danger, away from the rocks and turbulence of the beach. As we moved further into the bay, the boat was rocked by long, shallow curves of water loping across North Haven. It was just a kind of gentle, seasick motion, nothing to get alarmed about. The journey looked set to be dull and nondescript.

The engine pushed us slowly and steadily across the water, rattling away with the unfailing rhythm of a trusty old sewing machine. I glanced up at Mike as he held on to the tiller. He was staring at the sea ahead of us with a smile of anticipation. I turned back towards the house on the cliff top, thinking how much I would have liked to be still inside, looking out.

As we passed Rye Rocks, leaving the shelter of North Haven behind, an enormous freak wave came looming out of nowhere. It was a huge slab of slate-grey water that seemed to obliterate the sky. Mike swung the boat quickly, so that the wave wouldn't catch us side on. I was sitting at the front of the boat facing back towards the stern. My view consisted entirely of that mass of water, piled high above us and approaching fast. Mike, grimly determined and steering straight ahead, had the advantage of not being able to see the wave bearing down on us. I was transfixed, certain that the mound of water was about to collapse on top of the boat. Though I wanted to look away I couldn't.

But instead of hitting us, the wave slid gently beneath the boat lifting us higher and higher. I began to feel a little safer as I realised that the water wasn't going to break over us, but that confidence disintegrated as the wave crest approached with a surge of speed. The boat was being catapulted forward like a surfboard. We built up a sickening momentum, quite beyond the aspirations of our tiny engine. Then, as suddenly as it had caught us up, the wave abandoned us. It passed beneath the boat and we were left slipping away down its retreating slope. We had lost speed so rapidly, and the wave was sweeping so quickly ahead of us, that it felt as though we were actually sliding backwards.

The feeling of relief at having survived unscathed never had time to materialize. As the wave moved away it opened up the view. My theory of the single freak wave was in tatters. There was another one coming along, maybe bigger than the last. Mike was still staring fixedly ahead, intent on steering.

'There's another one right behind us,' I shouted.

Mike glanced back and then carried on without the slightest change in expression. As we began to feel the lift of the next wave he called,

'Get the flares out and hang on to them.'

I scrabbled in the front compartment of the boat, finding it almost impossible to turn my eyes from the sea. It was like facing a wild animal waiting to pounce and trying to summon up the courage to look away. I snatched the waterproof canister and wedged it between my knees so that I could use both hands to prise the lid open. Once I had found the distress flares I clung on to them until my knuckles turned white.

We were surfing again, skimming helplessly along the peak, and then left floundering, seemingly without power, as the great wave lumbered past. As we sank into the trough between the waves the sea closed in around us, and there was nothing but the steep slopes of water on either side. I pulled the waist strap of my life-jacket tighter as the next wave approached. With each one I couldn't believe that we would ride over it rather than being swallowed into it. As we were lifted onto the top of the wave, the view expanded until I could see a wilderness of untamed water stretching out behind us. The ridges and furrows went on forever, an inexhaustible succession of waves waiting their turn to batter our little boat.

I had never been in a sea like that one. They were not wind-driven waves, just the legacy of weeks of storms that had gathered up the water into an enormous, rolling swell. As a result, there was very little white water, just these smooth mountains of sea. That was how we had been deceived when we looked out of the kitchen window to the sea beyond North Haven. Our mental wave index had come to rely too heavily on the presence of white water. Storms meant surf; uniform grey implied calm. The dull, hazy atmosphere had blotted out the contours, making the water look flat and safe. Now we were suffering the consequences of being too trusting of the beguiling sea. I couldn't remember ever having been so frightened before. All I wanted was to go back into the shelter of North Haven, but I knew that it was too late for that. We were only surviving the waves because they were hitting us end on. If one of them caught us from the side there was every chance that the boat would flip over or be swamped. That made turning back impossible; we had no choice but to go on.

As we came closer to the mainland, the effect of tides and currents was changing the nature of the waves. They were growing larger all the time. Waves out in the open sea are gentle compared to waves butting up against rocks. We could hear the sea now, exploding against the cliffs of the mainland. The air was echoing and vibrating, as if with one perpetual thunderclap. The dense foam was boiling up round the base of the cliffs and then swilling out to obliterate the offshore rocks. Everything above was veiled with a steely sheen of vaporized sea. I was convinced that if the engine cut out at that point we would be lost. Amid such chaotic power it was hard to imagine how the boat could survive for more than a few minutes before being splintered on the rocks.

Then I caught my first glimpse of Martin's Haven, the only landing point for miles. It should have been our refuge, but it was seething with white water. I knew at once that we couldn't land there. The waves were forcing us to keep heading towards the shore, but we had nowhere to go. Suddenly I felt the boat being wrenched sideways and I looked back towards Mike to see what was wrong. I realised that he was trying to turn the boat. We were caught in the pause between two waves. The water was stretched taut like a skin, smooth and shiny, slow as molten glass. It was a terrifying momentary illusion of calm as the oncoming wave swelled up above us. I stared at Mike, unable to speak. There was a look of the most fixed determination on his face. I couldn't believe that he would take us side-on into the wave; we would never make it. We slid endlessly across the curve of oily-calm water, while the wave above was almost frozen, collapsing onto us noiselessly and with infinite slowness, as though it had all the time in the world. Then, from total hopelessness, I began to think that we might have the faintest chance. The boat was beginning to straighten out as the wave crest hit us and with one violent lurch we were over. Time began to move again, and the turbulent sounds came back to fill the silence.

As we had approached the mainland and the waves had grown in size, so too had the troughs between them. Mike had realised that there might be time to turn the boat in the lull of one of these troughs. It was our last chance before we were driven too close inshore, and he took it.

I hadn't realised how easy our outward journey had been. All that time we had been going with the waves, been carried along by them. Now the waves were against us and we faced each one head-on, like a clash of wills. The speed of the water pouring towards us negated the power of our engine. We came almost to a standstill as we pushed against the wave, inching our way up the steep slope. When we reached the pinnacle, the prow of the boat rose up into the air and kept on going until the balance of weight finally tipped. We fell forward with a juddering crack and found ourselves tobogganing down the opposite face of the wave.

It was so quick that, immediately, the next wave was upon us and we were climbing again. I could hear the engine churning with all its might, trying to force us forward, while we remained suspended, locked into the force of the wave. I wanted to cry, but it was too serious for that. I had to remain calm.

'I love you,' Mike called from the back of the boat.

That confirmed my worst fears; he didn't think our chances were very good either.

All my efforts were concentrated into willing the engine to keep going. I listened hard to the sound it made, feeling the breath catch in my throat with every slight variation in tone. In my experience, outboard motors didn't simply run like a car engine. They were temperamental. A bit of grit, a splash of seawater, could be enough to make them choke and die. Even though we had a spare engine, it would have been impossible to swap them once we were floundering powerless amid those waves.

I found the oddest comfort in promising myself the luxury of crying. If my feet touched land again, I would allow myself to wallow in the stream of tears that I could feel building inside me like a physical pressure. In the meantime, we kept on running into the waves, knowing that each time we toppled with spine-jarring force over the crest we had taken one more step closer to home. It was only when we turned into North Haven and the sea became suddenly, miraculously calm, that I felt the muscles in my chest slacken and I was able to breathe freely again.

The boat nudged gently against the beach and I jumped down to hold it steady. For a moment I thought that my legs would not take my weight; they felt floppy, as though the bones had melted. I clung on to the side of the boat for support, letting it rock quietly to and fro. I didn't cry at all. Already I was beginning to forget quite how awful it had been. I laughed a little, that slightly hysterical how-could-you-do-that-to-me kind of laugh, but mostly we just got on with the practicalities of dragging the boat up the beach and securing it against the next storm.

That feeling of relief at still being alive didn't last long. When we had been in the boat, I had convinced myself that I would never want anything else if only I could feel the calm of solid ground again. But soon after the unsuccessful trip a sense of frustration set in. We actually felt disappointed that we had come so close, and yet been forced to return home empty handed: back to our porridge and powdered potato.

Our food cupboard was a tiny room lined on all sides with shelves. It even had its own gas light on the ceiling. Usually, the shelves were stacked high with provisions, and I had no need of the light because I knew where to put my hand on anything. Now the cupboard was distressingly empty. Occasionally, during that really lean period, Mike would light the gas mantle, take a chair, and settle himself inside the cupboard. I wasn't sure if he was dreaming of better times or searching for inspiration. I suppose that it was odd behaviour but, at the time, since I could empathise completely with his pining for real food, it didn't seem particularly strange.

'I haven't got a clue what to cook for dinner tonight,' I said one evening as I joined Mike sitting gloomily in the cupboard.

'What's that on the top shelf?' he asked.

There was a cluster of tins with rust-spotted labels, almost out of reach.

'Oh, that's really horrible things that I put up there out of the way.'

'We might not be feeling so choosy now.'

I'd looked through them so many times before that I knew it was a waste of time, but I reached one of the tins down just to placate him.

'Ugh! Butter beans!' I said, wrinkling my nose in an I-told-you-so way. I tried another just to prove my point. 'Yuk! Tinned pears!'

Even the thought of that peculiar combination of squashiness and grittiness set my teeth on edge. Mike looked suitably defeated. Then, unexpectedly, his face lit up.

'I know!' He leapt to his feet and clutched me by the shoulders. 'You could make a pear sponge.'

'For dinner? You can't have pudding for dinner.'

But even as I dismissed the idea, the thought of warm, golden sponge was becoming unbearably tempting.

'Oh go on!' Mike squeezed my shoulders tighter. 'It'd be delicious.'

Just as I could almost smell it baking, as I was preparing to allow myself to be persuaded, reality struck in the most disastrous way.

'I can't,' I wailed. 'I haven't got any eggs.' I reached for the egg box, my hands trembling with anticipation. 'We have! We've got two eggs!'

'Thank goodness for the chickens.'

They had certainly earned their keep. Since we had run out of chicken food, it justified all the times in recent weeks when I'd had to go hunting through our supplies, selecting the less palatable things, and asking Mike, 'Shall we give this to the chickens, or eat it ourselves?'. And I instantly forgave them for the mornings I had spent waiting outside the shed for an obliging hen to lay, so that we could have an egg each for breakfast.

We began to trawl through the cupboard, embellishing the brilliant plan. I found a jar of cinnamon and sniffed the delectable contents.

'I'll make a cinnamon sponge. It'll be perfect with the pears.'

But it was Mike who really struck gold.

'Look at this! I've found a packet of chocolate custard.'

'Oh!' I drooled. 'Pear and cinnamon sponge with chocolate sauce.'

I started straight away. It was the first time in ages that I had felt any enthu-siasm for cooking. I arranged the pears artistically along the bottom of the tin and scraped every last speck of sponge mixture on top, determined that this was going to be a masterpiece. Almost as soon as I put the baking tin into the oven the smell of warm spice began to emerge. I started to tidy the kitchen, basking in the scent as I gathered up the dirty mixing bowl and the pear tin. The longing for that meltingly fresh sponge, just crisp on the outside, and drowning in chocolate sauce, was beginning to make my stomach ache with hunger. Pudding instead of dinner; it had a childish wickedness that made it even better. As I was about to throw the empty tin into the bin I noticed one last slice of pear clinging to the bottom. I couldn't afford to waste it, but it wouldn't be too late to push it down into the soft sponge mixture. When I opened the oven door to retrieve the sponge, a deliciously aromatic cloud wafted over me. I closed my eyes for a moment to savour the sensation. It had the same bright, uplifting feeling as the first warm sun of spring touching my face.

As I caught hold of the baking tin my hand touched against the hot oven shelf. Quite involuntarily, the burn caused my arm to jerk away from the source of danger. My elbow crashed hard into the table leg behind me: the baking tin leapt from my grasp and reeled through the air. As the tin hit the lino upside down, an explosion of fresh-baked fragrance filled the room. A primitive, animal-like wail of despair came from somewhere deep inside me, followed by a tidal wave of tears. The tin finally skidded to a halt at the end of a sticky golden stream. The mixture was at that awkward stage: hot and runny, before it had started making any attempt to set. Every last trace of it had oozed out of the tin.

At the sound of my wailing Mike came rushing into the room, to see the thing in which we had invested such ridiculous anticipation spread messily across the floor.

'I couldn't help it,' I howled. 'I burnt my hand.'

To my surprise, Mike didn't shout. He obviously recognised that the situation was too desperately serious for that. In fact, he didn't say a word as he scraped up the gooey puddle that still smelt tantalizingly desirable.

'I can't make another one,' I blurted out in little convulsive sobs, when I had recovered enough to speak. 'There are no more eggs.'

Mike remained stoically calm, as though such tragedies happened every day.

The longer we waited to cross to mainland the more I panicked about forgetting something vital, until I had recurrent nightmares about returning home empty handed. After so much solitude I found the mainland completely disorientating, and all I could think about was getting back to the island before dark or before the weather turned. Our failed excursion had only confirmed my prejudices against boating, but the more I grew to hate these shopping trips, the more ecstatic I was when they were over. When we finally made the crossing, it was one of my favourite moments to be back in the kitchen just as the last light of the day was disappearing, opening my sea-spattered boxes of food, filling the larder shelves. I felt it deep inside: a quietly euphoric sense of liberation. Whatever the weather did, we wouldn't have to think about launching the boat again for weeks. And for days to come, the simple tastes of fresh bread or potatoes would seem extraordinary.

Perhaps the greatest satisfaction came from being able to condemn the last of the bitter flour and downgrade it to chicken feed. I made it into loaves, without even bothering to sift out the maggots. In fact, I am sure that if the chickens could have passed an opinion on the subject, they would have insisted that it was the maggots that really gave the bread its flavour.

EIGHT

Though they were by no means the most severe, the storms of that winter were more relentless than any we were to experience during our years on Skomer. Eventually the season turned, and the return of the puffins, slipping tentatively back from their exile at sea, confirmed that the winter was over. Birds were spectacularly reliable in providing the stability that shaped our year. As they settled in, their fleeting visits became more frequent, until the fringes of the island were permanently clouded with seabirds.

During the breeding season, perhaps the single most impressive sight on Skomer was the Wick, an inlet on the south coast of the island. One of its faces was a tall, sheer cliff of black basalt carved with horizontal ledges that could have been made purely for the convenience of nesting seabirds. Facing the cliff, on the other side of a narrow strip of seawater, were enormous slabs of smooth rock that veered at a giddying angle down to meet the sea, giving the whole thing an appealingly lop-sided appearance. The cliff sent a deep shade across the ribbon of enclosed water so that it had its own incomparable colour, green and sleek as polished jade.

Among the cushiony, thrift-covered banks there was a hidden tunnel that dipped down into the earth and then opened out onto the stone slabs, which provided a perfect amphitheatre for viewing the teeming cliff across the narrow stretch of water. Passing through the tunnel was to leave behind an ordinary summer day and then emerge in a different place. As we stepped out onto the slopes of rock from the cool, cloistered silence of the tunnel, the sound and the smell of massed seabirds enveloped us, shimmering all around like the harsh glare of sunlight on rocks. A sudden, stifling heat fizzed through the confined atmosphere. The smell was pungent, catching in the back of my throat with the sharpness of ammonia. At first I found it nauseating but, with time, as it became associated with the charge of excitement that came from being surrounded seabirds, I almost grew to like it.

With so many birds crowded onto the cliff, the instant impression was of chaos, of confused comings and goings and raucous, squabbling voices. The strident growling of guillemots and razorbills had an undertone that seemed faintly angry, while the mewing of kittiwakes echoed round and round, sounding plaintive and urgent. Only the streams of chuckling notes from the fulmars soared cheerfully free. Like the puffins, guillemots and razorbills are thickset birds with wings that appear undersized for the weight they have to carry. To overcome this disadvantage their wings beat hard and fast, drumming against the sky. White swirls of kittiwakes, like splinters of sea foam caught in the wind, circled distractedly before returning to the cliffs, while fulmars slid serenely along the rivers of air.

And yet, underpinning this confusion, everything was meticulously planned. Nest sites were precisely chosen and jealously guarded. Each bird fitted into the pattern of the cliff, like the only possible piece in a jigsaw. Guillemots arranged themselves along the cliff ledges, wing almost touching wing. When the time came, they laid their eggs onto the bare rock. While they were at the colony the individual birds became part of a group that functioned in harmony, and, in protecting themselves, they protected each other. If they were anxious or disturbed, the guillemots responded by bobbing their heads. The message spread like a whisper, until the anxiety was communicated down through the group of birds, and they all stood bowing to one another. These preliminary warnings prepared them to face the threat of predators and also made it less likely that they would be seized by panic, which could have sent eggs or chicks tumbling from the cliff as birds scrabbled to escape.

The shade and shelter of the steep Wick cliff made a window into sea. Leaning on the soft mounds of thrift, we could look down into the seemingly infinite depths that were shiny-green, like the light through a champagne bottle. Against it, the stark white feathers of the birds flared with the brilliance of stars in a darkening sky. The sea was lit up by whole constellations of puffins, guillemots and razorbills. When the birds dived beneath the surface, a film of air cocooned them in a thin layer of liquid silver. We watched them threading their sparkling trails through the water and then rise to the surface, to be abruptly transformed from glistening metallic creatures to ordinary flesh and blood.

In the late spring days, when the cliffs were overflowing with birds, and flowers were everywhere, saturating the air with their scent, the island almost touched perfection, but I sometimes thought that the shearwaters, more than any other bird, captured the true essence of Skomer. Nothing was more uniquely memorable than the dramatic influx of shearwaters on a moonless night. The birds seemed to wait for some critical degree of darkness, but once that point was reached they materialized, as if from nowhere, filling the sky. From out of the stillness and silence, the familiar crashing and caterwauling enveloped the house almost instantly.

We never lost sight of the fact that what we had was truly special. Something like a quarter of the world's population of shearwaters came to the island during the breeding season. The experience of being surrounded by storms of seabirds pouring through the darkness was disconcertingly moving, and something that I could barely have imagined before we came to Skomer. Since my first timid discovery of these birds, it was hard to believe how much the shearwaters had become part of life, cannoning off the windows and gurgling noisily in their tens of thousands.

At the end of winter, shearwaters returned to the island, rediscovering the burrows that they shared with a faithful mate. Then, just as we had grown accustomed to the surge of noise, relative peace returned. The female birds deserted the island for one brief period of freedom and sustained feeding before they returned to lay their single egg. For the shearwaters an exceptionally long breeding season stretched ahead, which would tie them to the island until August or September.

It was when the birds returned and settled in that they began to make their presence felt inside our house. When it was first built, nest boxes had been established in the cellar, with convenient entry points on the outside, to compensate the shearwaters for the burrows that had disappeared beneath the building. Over the years before our arrival the nest boxes had been removed, leaving the shearwaters with free access to the cellar. It was not unusual for one of us, rummaging round in the cellar, to uncover a bewildered bird patiently incubating an egg in a little niche beneath something we had stored there. Fortunately, shearwaters are surprisingly resilient when disturbed and never deserted their eggs as a result of these accidental intrusions.

We were so cautious about using the cellar during the summer, that the shearwaters probably had far greater scope for disrupting our peace. The male and female shearwaters shared the incubation and, since a break for feeding involved a long trip out to sea, the bird left behind could become very restless. This restlessness was often translated into calls which lasted throughout the hours of darkness. The shearwater's call is loud, unmelodic and tuned to a gratingly high pitch. With the closest cellar-dwelling birds no more than a foot or two below our bed, separated only by a layer of floorboards, their potential for causing irritation was enormous. When I first heard this shrill sound bubbling up through the floor it was hard to believe that the bird was not in the bedroom with us, and my amused fascination was mixed with a faint apprehension.

On sleepless nights, Mike could be unreasonably sensitive to this noise. By three or four o'clock in the morning he sometimes became quite vocal himself.

'If that bird doesn't shut up, I'll go down there and wring its neck,' he growled from under a pile of dishevelled bedclothes.

'You don't really mean that,' I muttered back sleepily.

The truth was that I really enjoyed having the shearwaters so close. I always tried to listen as I lay in bed, but usually as soon as I closed my eyes it was morning. If I could stay awake, I found the shearwaters' convoluted squeals comfortably reassuring, but for Mike it was not until the barely perceptible glow of dawn lulled the shearwaters into silence that he was left in peace.

In foggy or windy weather, we came to expect the added disturbance of shearwaters performing crash-landings against the house. Moonless nights brought the greatest numbers of birds. When we were out on nights like these, we needed to be permanently alert and ready to duck as the caterwauling birds sliced past our heads. We gradually developed some sort of sixth sense, since by the time we actually saw the birds looming palely out of the darkness it was too late to avoid the collision. It became too easy to build up an image of these birds as clumsy, noisy, faintly comical and lacking in grace. But that would have been unreasonable, because the reality was so different.

It was tempting to judge everything from our own perspective, since every time we were close to the shearwaters they had left their own environment to enter our alien place. On the island they appeared slightly ludicrous because they were always vulnerable, always fighting against the handicap of bodies built for survival away from land. They are so well adapted to life at sea that their legs are right at the back of their bodies, ideal for swimming, but on land they cannot stand or walk. Though they can fly with remarkable strength and skill, it is difficult for them to launch themselves once they are grounded. To minimise the risk of predation they wait for the safety of darkness, blundering blindly through an environment that emphasises their weaknesses. Shearwaters need to be seen in their own true element, the sea. There they are transformed, almost miraculously, into the most elegantly accomplished birds.

Throughout the hours of daylight the shearwaters effectively vanished. Though I had seen this metamorphosis hundreds of times, I still found it almost impossible to imagine the vast numbers of birds hidden down burrows, or waiting far out at sea. The first signs of them returning to the island came in the evening. We stood on the cliff top above North Haven as the pinkish light of the sun was beginning to soak into the clouds. Puffins were all around us, wings thrumming against the air, feet splashing the water in little bursts of energy. The shearwaters were so far away that we could only see them with binoculars but, once I knew what to look for, I could make out the dark pools of gathering birds, drifting like cloud-shadows across the distant sea.

'Let's take the boat out and have a look,' Mike said.

Our visits to the rafting shearwaters were rare and special occasions. I always regretted that pressures of time allowed us so few of these stunning encounters, and yet, because of their scarcity, they were all the more precious.

In summer everything seemed so easy. The boat ducked effortlessly into the gentle waves where the high tide lapped against the slipway. The engine started first time and we went spluttering as delicately as possible through the sheets of puffins clustering in North Haven. At our approach they either ran, scattering paths of sparkling footprints across the water in front of us as they became airborne, or they dived, vanishing with barely a splash.

When we had left the puffins behind we were able to pick up more speed. The guillemots and razorbills speckling the water became fewer as the island began to shrink into the distance. A couple of miles at sea are immeasurably longer than the same distance over land: across the permanently shifting surface of the water our headway was barely perceptible. The sounds of the island disappeared and the sun sank, slipping away into the chalk-smudged air before breaking free again in dazzling rays beneath the cloud. The low sun highlighted the ridges and furrows of clouds that stretched out across the sky in the same rippled patterns as a sandy beach abandoned by retreating waves. Seeing the clouds lit up from below reversed the natural perspective of sun shining down from above, making the scene look unreal.

With the waves fragmenting the distant view, the shearwaters were more elusive than they had appeared from the cliff top. Mike was standing up in the boat searching out the rafting birds.

'Almost there!' he called.

Suddenly the engine cut out and the most powerful silence flooded around us. There was nothing but the faintly echoing slap of the waves as they cradled the boat. The drone of the engine had become so pervasive that I had stopped noticing it, and it was only when the noise disappeared that I recognised the startling quality of silence. I looked back towards Mike to see why we had stopped.

'We're so close now, I don't want the engine noise to frighten the birds,' he said. 'We'll row the rest of the way.'

The oars moved with a soft, regular swish, and the boat slid forward in a series of smooth pulses. Each time the oars were lifted, streams of sea water rained down from the wooden paddles. The droplets trapped the last red glow of the sun so that they flowed like liquid light. When we had almost reached the raft of shearwaters, Mike stowed the oars and left the boat to drift, wallowing against the shallow waves, following its own course.

The birds were so still and silent that I hardly dared to breathe. The slightest noise would be so out of place amid the tranquillity that they would surely panic. Almost imperceptibly, we were carried on the insistent rocking motion of the waves closer to the birds. The contrast with the shearwaters that I saw at night on the island was so immense that they were barely recognisable. The only sound to be heard was an occasional soft cheeping noise. There was none of the discordant warbling that filled the darkness on Skomer.

A pathway of light rippled as it stretched out towards us across the sea from the glowing arc of sun on the horizon. The scorching flare of daytime, so painfully brilliant that it hid the sun from view, was extinguished. The sun was cooling now, like a fading ember, white-hot in the centre dimming to red at its rim, so that it appeared as a solid, three-dimensional shape.

At some signal, unrecognisable to us, the swarm of shearwaters rose in a single, unified movement. We were enveloped by them and became, briefly, part of the spangled cloud of birds. They flew with streamlined precision, gliding effortlessly, flipping from side to side, dipping first one wing then the other so low that it appeared to brush the surface of the water. As they swirled all around us the white underside and black back flickered alternately into view, so that the birds sparked from black to white and back again. The air whispered with the sound of wings, but there were no calls.

As the shearwaters circled us, I was transfixed, transported from my world into theirs. Then, all at once, they moved away. I watched the shadowy flock drift out across the water until, with gentle synchronicity, the mist of birds settled again: individuals in such perfect sympathy that they appeared to coalesce into a single entity.

The intensity of being enclosed by this carousel of birds had been hypnotic and I was disappointed to lose them. I turned back towards Mike.

'Can we follow them?' I asked.

He looked across towards the horizon where the last bright fragment of sun had been doused by the sea. The remains of the fiery brilliance were caught by the clouds, which soared red-streaked across the sky.

'I think we'll have to be heading back before we lose the light,' he said.

The greyness of the sea was washed with pink, but the distant hulk of the mainland was turning black. I wasn't worried, though; I knew that the sea would hold the light long enough to take us home.

We would be back on the island before the shearwaters, but when it was completely dark, they would follow. As they came crashing into the island with their tuneless squalling, I would still find it hard to remember them as those silent, graceful birds we had just seen.

After most of the cliff-nesting seabirds had fledged, the shearwater chicks remained inside the burrows, their period of cosseted protection far from over. Night after night, tiny acts of individual courage were replayed on the cliffs, as flightless guillemot and razorbill chicks plunged from the safety of the ledges. And each day the bleached white cliffs were left a little emptier and a little more silent, gradually fading to no more than a memory of what summer had been. By contrast, the nights were busier than ever with shear-waters tumbling exuberantly from the sky, ready to regurgitate their precious cargoes of fish for the tens of thousands of chicks waiting below ground.

The island had such a network of interwoven burrows just below its surface, it was inevitable that, occasionally, the ground beneath my feet disap-peared and I went crashing through into one of these holes. This was particularly so in summer as the earth became drier and more crumbly. It happened again as I was crossing the isthmus. I dug frantically at the soil with my hands, ridiculously squeamish about what I might find. Then my fingers touched the soft down and, easing my hands round, I was able to lift the chick out: poor, sleepy, bemused thing, caked with dirt. Brushing the crumbs of earth away, I checked the eyes and beak, head and neck, running my fingers along the legs and wings looking for breaks. Nothing: there never was. All the shearwaters I inadvertently squashed came out unscathed. For such delicate-looking birds they were improbably robust

I set about rebuilding the burrow, determined that when the parent returned with a slurry of warm, oily fish it would find everything as it should be. Such a ludicrous looking thing, I thought, as I gave the chick one last brush, ready to put it back: a great puffball of wispy grey down with a slender, black beak protruding from it, and eyes glinting through the haze of fluff. It was also enormous. Although the froth of down made it look bigger than it really was, there was no disguising its weight. It was solid fat, having grown on its rich diet to be larger than the parent birds. At its peak, an exceptionally large chick may be almost twice as heavy as an adult.

'Sorry,' I said. 'That must have been a bit of a shock. You can go back to sleep now.'

I leant down into the tunnel and left the chick to wait for nightfall.

The departure of the shearwater chicks was very different to the half-grown guillemots and razorbills we had watched so often fledging from the cliff ledges when the days were at their longest. The shearwaters stayed right through the summer, and it was not until September that the nights grew quiet. From inside the house, it felt as though the shearwaters were gone: no more calling, no more birds crashing into the windows. Outside, apart from the odd silence, everything looked almost normal; there were still thousands of birds scattered across the ground. The change had come about because most of the adults had been replaced by chicks that, having shed their down, looked almost indistinguishable from their parents. The look might have been identical, but the moment I picked one off the ground the difference was obvious. The young birds were soft, plump and docile, while the adults were lean and taut, their muscles powerful from the thousands of miles they had flown.

I thought that shearwaters had the most disillusioning of starts in life. They are exceptionally pampered chicks, fed by two attentive parents until, eventually, the chick is deserted. By the time the young birds venture above ground, their parents have left, soon to embark on the migration that will take them half way across the world. As they stretch out their wings after a brief lifetime in the confinement of a burrow the young birds are already facing the future alone.

There was a pyramid-shaped rock at the corner of the path on the hill above our house that was a favourite gathering place for the young shearwaters, and we used to wander up there late at night to watch. The slope of the rock was shallow enough for the shearwaters to shuffle their way to the top. At the pinnacle, a foot or two off the ground, they flapped their long wings against the night sky, feeling untried muscles for the first time. But it was a short-lived freedom. There was always another bird waiting to topple the victor from the peak, and the plump little birds remained earthbound, to find their way back to their burrows before dawn brought the gulls to the skies.

Over the days of their abandonment the young birds lost weight through starvation, and gained confidence by testing their wings against the resistance of the air. There came a point where the game of scrambling for the highest pinnacle was no longer play, because eventually those wings would have to prove themselves. For each bird there was a time when it had to open up its wings and fly. Although this was what the whole of their lives had been leading towards, to us, as we stood vigil at the pyramid rock, it appeared to happen with bewildering speed. One moment the chick was stretching its wings: the next it was caught in the up-draughts and soaring skywards. We glimpsed this exultant sweep of flight for only a split second before the bird was absorbed into the darkness. No matter how many times I watched, that sense of awe was always tinged with a faint sadness.

I feared for every single one of them setting out alone into the night. At a couple of months old, they seemed too fragile for what lay ahead. As those soft, un-calloused feet left the rock, I knew that it would be at least two years before they touched land again. The fledglings would fly alone, with no adult guidance, for thousands of miles to the seas off South America. And if they survived those two years at sea, most would make their way back, finding, among those all but infinite miles of empty ocean, the same tiny island that they fledged from.

That was why I felt an ache of sympathy every time I saw one of those birds unfold its wings and leave behind everything that was familiar. I bent down and picked a bird off the ground, felt its softness and warmth, its perfect, undamaged feathers, the absolute newness that betrayed its lack of experience.

'How will you manage out there?' I asked, replacing it for perhaps its last few seconds on solid ground.

How could it possibly know what it had to do next? How did a bird that had never seen anything but the darkness of a Welsh island find the shores of South America? How would it know when it was time to return? I had held in my hand a tiny miracle with some sort of wisdom far beyond my own.

Night after night the shearwaters fledged, and their numbers diminished until, by early October, we were forced to hunt for the last remaining birds. It was such a contrast to the summer nights when we had been tripping over them and ducking as they crashed into us. I regretted the times I had heard the birds calling outside but decided that I was too tired to go and look. As perhaps the last bird of the season vanished into the darkness, I wondered how I could have taken any of this for granted, even for a single moment.

With September moving towards October the scattering of seal pups being born in bays around the island began to increase. That year we grew particularly fond of two pups in North Haven. They were such individuals, with such starkly contrasting characters, that we couldn't help being drawn to them. The first to arrive was Barrel-Rat. We had never named a pup before, and tried to avoid becoming sentimental about these wild animals, but there was something about this one that caught our imaginations. He was the most contented pup I had ever known, sleeping his life away in an attitude of total bliss.

This placidity was probably more to do with the obsessively doting mother than the inherent nature of the pup. Seals have enormously varying responses to the demands of motherhood. Some disappear, leaving the newborn pup alone on the beach crying helplessly for hours at a time, and will only come ashore for the minimum period necessary to feed it. Most remain just offshore with their heads bobbing above the water, holding the beached pup almost constantly in their gaze. At the first cry of distress these mothers come splashing through the breaking waves, scattering showers of clattering pebbles in their urgent progress up the beach. After feeding the pup they might stay for an hour or so, sleeping close by, before returning to the water.

Barrel-Rat's mother had found her vocation, embracing motherhood as a full time occupation. She was almost always to be seen on the beach, watching over the sleeping pup, feeding it as soon as it woke. The pup grew with almost astounding speed: day by day he became visibly fatter, but no less eager for food. By the time he was two weeks old, Barrel-Rat had progressed from being merely plump to positively fat. First his neck disappeared, then the flesh rippled into thick rolls around his chin.

At that stage, his mother could have abandoned him. After only two or three weeks of maternal care pups are left to find their own way in life. Barrel-Rat had certainly grown strong enough to face independence, leaving his mother free to go back to sea and catch fish as the mood took her. But she stayed, continuing to feed the pup into a state of comfortable obesity. His life was so perfect that he had no need even to move; he simply luxuriated on his patch of stones under the cliff at the top of the beach, where the tide rarely reached.

It was about that time that Nipper was born. As soon as I left the house in the morning I knew that another pup had arrived during the night. The newborn-baby cries coming up from the beach were very distinctive, and when I looked down I saw the arc of brilliant white fur against the darkness of glistening wet stones. I could easily pick out the mother as the one sleek head among all the others in the sea that was turned constantly towards the pup. Nipper was as active and inquisitive as Barrel-Rat was permanently sleepy. He explored the beach restlessly, collecting an occasional slap from the flipper of another seal if he nosed against it too persistently.

When he was a couple of days old, Nipper realised that he was no longer content to wait quietly and watch his mother return to the sea after she had fed him. He followed her down the beach, calling noisily, shuffling himself forward as his flippers snatched against the skittering stones. At the water's edge the adult seal slid through the ruffle of white water, while Nipper hesitated. Tingling soft bubbles of surf brushed around him. He turned, as though he might go back, but his awkward movements sent him slithering sideways down the shelving bank of shingle. As he scrabbled to cling on, the waves lifted and held him, breaking his link with the land. He had slipped uncertainly into this new element and now he had no choice but to swim. His uncoordinated body writhed with such enthusiasm that he spun himself round in a circle. Whether they came at two days or six weeks old, I found those first soaring moments of weightless freedom profoundly moving.

At first Nipper could only meander aimlessly, unable to steer properly because the front and back halves of his body fought against each other. Each little flick of his muscles sent him twisting erratically through the water. But within a couple of days he had discovered his coordination and the slickness of his movements implied more experience than his brief life could have given him. He played with his mother, teasing her with his agility. Although adult seals are strong swimmers, able to hold themselves steady against the most overwhelming waves, she couldn't match the mobility of the pup's tiny body.

From the top of the cliff I could see the brightness of his coat shimmering like a mirage through the chalky turquoise water as he dived beneath the melting outline of his mother. The two animals twisted and looped around each other with the grace of an underwater dance. And then, when the playing was over and the pup hauled itself back onto the beach, it was like a spell breaking. The weight of his body pinned him down and every movement was once more an effort. Barrel-Rat had not experienced that freedom, always shunning the incoming tide, preferring sleep and the known world. I could see how easy it would be never to discover that there was something better beyond our own little patch of stones.

We were surrounded by so much life on Skomer that, inevitably, death was commonplace. It was the lesson I had learned from Mike the first time I had walked across the island and seen so many dead shearwaters. We had to accept the natural sequence of life and death; our concern was for the wider pattern of survival, not to grieve for every individual. I knew that, but still there were times when I shed tears over some small, white, furry body battered in the storms, or a perpetually crying pup abandoned by its mother. No amount of calculated objectivity could stop me from growing attached to the seal pups, and those two in North Haven were special. Special because they were there each day, from the moment we first looked out of the kitchen window until the sky turned dark and their pale fur looked faintly incandescent in the twilight. But it was more than that. There was something in each of them that shone out: Nipper with his playful daring, Barrel-Rat's permanent contentment and the endearing devotion of his mother.

In early October, we experienced some beautiful days, a fleeting Indian summer that was still and bright. It was a delightful contrast to the previous year when the sea had been so wild for so long. Then, our lack of supplies had seemed insignificant compared to watching the seal pups being swept from the beaches and knowing that we could do nothing. The arrival of seals and storms on the island was something that seemed to coincide. In my mind, the seals were always fighting the weather, forcing their way through the surges of foam to find some patch of calm on the beaches beyond.

This peaceful atmosphere was contagious. I felt it and so did the seals. It made me happy to see them wallowing in the tranquillity, drifting with their noses tilted up towards the sun, or lying in that indeterminate strip where the invisibly crystalline sea became beach, allowing the slow, limpid waves to rock them gently.

Although we lived surrounded by seals, I was disappointed never to have seen the birth of a pup. I knew that this was unlikely since pups are almost invariably born during the hours of darkness, but simply by being so elusive it took on an almost mystical quality. Every time I looked down onto the seal beaches there was a faint hope at the back of my mind that I might happen upon the one exception that proved the rule.

We had been for a late afternoon check round the island, enjoying a day that had an almost unnatural feel of summer about it. As we walked back down the track behind the house I heard that familiar baby call. I had become so accustomed to the sound that I hardly noticed it, and carried on talking. Mike cut across me.

'What's that noise?' he asked, grabbing my arm so that I stopped walking. We both stood still and listened.

'Oh, it's only a seal pup,' I said dismissively, and began walking again. Mike looked through the binoculars.

'There!' he said. 'At the top of North Haven. It's another pup.'

'That wasn't there when we went out a couple of hours ago,' I sighed. 'It's only just been born, and we've missed it.'

We rushed down the track until we reached the cliff edge. The pup certainly was newly arrived, wet and scrawny, with the pink cord still clearly visible. Despite its inexperience, it cried as though it had had endless practice, producing an impossible amount of noise from such a tiny body. A few feet away the mother slept peacefully, her conscience untroubled by the wailing. We watched for a long time hoping to see the pup's first feed, but nothing happened.

Back in the house, I lit the gas under the kettle. Standing by the stove I had a perfect view of the seal pup from the side window of the kitchen. Eventually, the cow seal shifted herself, lifted her head from the pebbles and gazed briefly at the howling pup. Then, wriggling her shuddering blubber noisily against the pebbles, she rolled onto her side. She encouraged the pup to feed, caressing its head roughly with her foreflipper, so that the claws drew grooves through the damp fur.

The only problem with our brief return to summer was that it removed the barrier between us and the mainland. The sea was so smoothly accessible I could hardly believe that the previous year we had been stormbound throughout October. I knew from that bitter experience that it was only sensible to stock up for the winter while we still had the chance, but it didn't make the prospect any more pleasant.

In the morning, I went out to have another look at the new pup, although, in such ideal weather conditions, I had no worries about it surviving the night. I watched for a while as it slept, one foreflipper curled comfortably over its nose, and then returned reluctantly to the house because I knew that Mike would be keen to get started for the mainland.

As I walked down to the boat there were perhaps half a dozen seals staring at me from the water. They followed my progress, swimming alongside to ensure that they maintained the best view. Around their glossy, black heads, the morning sun sparked off the water in haloes of fluttering stars. The air was still, and the waves stroked against the shore like the faint rustle of a taffeta skirt. It was a day to be here on the island, not rushing off to the mainland. It didn't matter that my whole life was here, even one day away from it felt wasted.

Down on the concrete slipway, a newly moulted seal pup, about six weeks old, was fast asleep and snoring gently. He was pure mole-black, with a coat as dense and fine as velvet. The colouring was unusually dark; the first coat to emerge from under the white baby fur is usually dappled grey. He was sleeping exactly where we needed to take the boat, and there was no way round him. As I was wondering whether I had the heart to disturb him, Mike arrived on the tractor.

'Come on!' he called, seeing me idling on the slipway, hands in pockets. 'Why aren't you getting the stuff down from the shed?'

At that moment the seal was instantly awake and snarling furiously, baring teeth that would have put a guard dog to shame.

'I think we have a slight problem,' I said.

Mike jumped off the tractor and came down to join me. At his approach the seal snorted viciously.

'Yes, you're very fierce, aren't you?' Mike said affectionately, in a voice that would placate an anxious baby.

He might have been irritated with me for holding up proceedings, but a seal would be forgiven anything. The seal snarled again, stretching out his neck and opening his mouth in a deep throaty hiss, which gave us a wonderful view of his impressive teeth. Despite the fact that he could have inflicted a serious bite, we were not concerned about approaching the pup because he was not agile enough on land to represent any threat. Adult seals (with the occasional exception of protective mothers) were almost never aggressive, preferring to head for the sea rather than face confrontation, but the moulter hadn't yet learnt that he was supposed to be afraid of people, and he was not going to be dislodged without putting up a good defence of his position.

'Come on,' Mike said, 'don't you think it's time for your morning swim?'

The seal gurgled a bubbling hiss from the back of his throat, head thrust forward, round black eyes bulging with the effort. Mike took a step forward and the seal lunged provocatively to meet him.

'I'm afraid you can't stay here,' Mike went on, 'however comfortable you find this concrete.'

Eventually the seal gave up, slithering down to the sea with a last triumphant snort to show that he had won. I walked back up to the boat shed to collect the life jackets and flares, and it didn't occur to me that clearing a seal out of the way was anything other than a normal prelude to a shopping trip.

The boat slipped easily into the calm water. As we loaded it and fixed the engine in place, the retinue of seals that had followed my progress along the cliff watched from a few feet away, heads bobbing above the flimsy waves. They felt safe enough to come close: at the slightest frisson of danger they could have vanished, weaving their way invisibly through the water.

We drifted out into the bay and the engine started smartly with the first pull of the cord. The sound of the engine made the seals dive in flurry of simultaneous splashes, and then they surfaced again to satisfy their curiosity. They swam with us across the bay, playing in the turbulence of the propeller and streaming sunlit ripples in their wake. When we reached the open sea it was as peaceful as the sheltered bay had been. Even in summer, such halcyon days were rare.

I felt elated as we returned with a boat full of supplies. It was over, and we wouldn't have to go again for ages. For the first time in as long as I could remember there was no sense of urgency about getting home. The weather was absolutely calm and settled. The boat crept along under the cliffs with no threat from the waves as we explored the coast in a way that was usually only possible on the stillest of summer evenings. We passed The Lantern, a cave that cut right through the thinnest tip of the Neck so that the light shone from the far side of the island. The cliffs looked so different and felt so quiet with the birds gone. Seals basking on the rocks were untroubled by the slow sputter of the barely-ticking engine; they just raised their heads to watch us pass.

Back at the house, we unwrapped the black polythene parcels. Our preparations for that first crossing to the island had set the standard for every subsequent shopping trip. Whatever the weather, our supplies were packed to withstand a storm, because boat journeys were so unpredictable. As everything emerged from the boxes we laid it out on the kitchen table with childlike pride, relishing the wonderful things we had bought, things that in another life would have seemed commonplace. Occasionally, I glanced out of the window to check the pups. Nipper was wet, obviously having just returned from a swim, Barrel-Rat was under the adoring gaze of his mother, and the new pup was sleeping peacefully, so I was reassured that she must have been fed quite recently. Everything was perfect.

I began to rearrange the larder so that with the influx of fresh provisions nothing would be left forgotten at the back of the shelves to go stale. The radio was chattering in the background; it accompanied everything I did in the kitchen. The news came on. I wasn't even aware that I was listening to it until something I heard brought me to a standstill. It felt like a great hollowness opening up inside me. There had been an oil spill. A tanker had run aground on the Hats and Barrels and then continued on up the coast with a gash in its hull spilling oil. Mike and I turned to stare at each other; there was a mixture of denial and awful certainty churning through my thoughts. How could we be part of the national news? The Hats and Barrels was a series of rocks about fifteen miles away. They were guarded by a lighthouse, so a ship could only come to grief by taking a short cut inside the light.

I felt weak, intensely exhausted. I leaned my elbows against the window sill for support, letting my gaze rest on the pups below me on the beach. The brand new pup was still asleep, dreaming perhaps as it rubbed its flippers restlessly against its face. What was there to dream about with only a few hours' experience of life? It looked so white, so new, so completely untarnished.

'I never thought of an oil spill happening on a day like this,' I said, still in a state of vague disbelief. 'It was storms and fog that made me worry. But, look! Look at this!' Suddenly I was shouting. I could feel the anger rising, as I turned my head to look out across the bay. 'I can see for miles. I can see forever. How can anything go wrong on a day like this?'

'I don't know,' Mike said. 'Maybe that's the problem. I suppose when conditions are this good people start to get complacent because they can't imagine anything going wrong.'

I rested my head against the window frame, defeated again, staring at the pups.

'We'll be all right, won't we?' I said without much conviction. 'I mean, fifteen miles is a long way isn't it? It won't necessarily come here.'

'Well, I hope not but, unfortunately, all we can do is wait. There's nothing else we can do.' He put his arm round me. 'Try not to get too upset. At least the birds are gone. If they were still here we really would be in trouble, whether the oil reached us or not.'

The next day we walked to the most westerly point of the island and looked out across the expanse of ocean. To my utter dismay I found that we could actually see the oil. That put an end to my efforts at convincing myself that it was somehow remote; it seemed certain to reach us. The only question was how long we would have to wait.

It was my first experience of an oil spill and it was nothing like I imagined. I had been scanning the horizon for thick, black, tarry pools. What I actually saw were pale, milky patches on the water. It looked deceptively benign, as insubstantial as the sheen of oil on a wet road.

'So it's just a thin film on the surface?' I asked hopefully.

'I don't think so.'

Mike sounded serious. He had been involved in oil spills before, and had worked on oil pollution research. He had far more idea what to expect than I did.

The following day we suffered the backlash of our beautiful, still autumn weather; we woke to find ourselves trapped in a swathe of fog. When I looked down from the kitchen window I could barely make out the sea, which was as colourless as the air. It was oppressive, claustrophobic. We had thought that we could only wait and watch, but now even that had been taken from us.

We walked along the cliff tops, tracing the perimeter of the island, though we knew it was pointless. If the oil had been lapping at the base of the cliff we would not have been able to see it. We made our way up to the north coast, and then began to head west. The more I stared, the more impenetrable the fog became. It prickled and swam before my eyes in a shoal of constantly drifting specks. It was completely disorientating, especially for someone like me with no natural sense of direction. We were about three quarters of the way up the coast when I was jolted by a nauseating realisation. I stopped dead.

'What's that?' I asked.

'What?'

'Can't you smell it?'

Mike turned his face into the breeze.

'You're right. It's oil.'

'Oh no! So it must be coming closer. We definitely couldn't smell it yesterday. It could be anywhere; just off shore for all we know.'

By morning the fog had not lifted, but the smell was much more pervasive. It was everywhere, as soon as we opened the door to look outside. I felt irrationally menaced by the knowledge that the oil was somewhere out there in the fog, and yet I had no idea how close it was. In my bleaker moments I thought that the island might be encircled by a sea of oil. And then I told myself that it was never too late for a miracle. A storm from the right direction might still save us.

Later in the day, a faint breeze from the north began to gather strength. It signified change, but, without knowing how far the oil had travelled in the past days, we couldn't tell if this would be for better or worse. If the oil was still to the south or west it might be swept away, but if it was already off the north coast it would be carried straight on shore. The northerly wind was cool and fresh. It began to lift the mist a little. The sea turned dark slate-grey, flecked with white. As the twilight guttered and faded, the fog cleared enough for us to be able to see out beyond North Haven. In the dying light we could make out the place where the sea met the cliff at the entrance to the bay. The water had an odd, granular texture, like something that had curdled. Streaks of it were streaming round the cliff into North Haven. The more I stared, the more everything became the same indeterminate grey, until the light disappeared.

'Well,' I said, as if to fool myself, 'you couldn't call that an oil slick, could you? That was just a few stray blobs of oil.'

But all night I kept wondering how many of those blobs of oil were finding their way into North Haven.

In the morning, I rushed to the kitchen window at first light. The wind had swelled to a full gale, and long, white rolling waves were being driven into the bay. I stared at them, a blink away from tears of relief. Although everything was shaded in half-light, I was sure that the water was clear. As they stretched up, before disintegrating in a cascade of effervescence, the waves had a glossy, translucent smoothness. I could almost believe that the danger had passed. The gale had been blowing all night without pushing any oil on shore.

I went to the side window to check the pups. At first I couldn't understand what I was seeing. It was just obvious that something terrible had happened. The beach had gone, and in its place was something like a thick, brown drift of snow: a soft, blanketing thing that had smoothed away all the stones and contours. It was so clearly oil, and yet my mind didn't want to accept that explanation. Oil would be thin and sticky and black, coating things, not obliterating them.

I called to Mike.

'What is it?' I asked.

The light was still dull, still camouflaging everything; I continued to hold out some ridiculous hope.

'It's oil,' he said.

We dashed outside to the cliff edge, and it was then that I was able to see the three pups. They were so thickly smothered with oil that they were almost indistinguishable from the boulders on the beach. The only thing that marked them out as living creatures was their painfully piercing wails. Mike lost any pretence of composure; he shouted his anger at the oil with a rage that echoed back from the cliffs. I couldn't bear the combination of his fury and the awful sadness inside me. The seals below dissolved into watery blur, and all I could feel was the wind turning the tears into cold streaks against my skin.

The adult seals were gone: the ones that had playfully accompanied us on that last carefree boat journey; the ones that we heard every evening, howling and skirmishing, as we sat by the fire. They were gone, all but three: three heads bobbing in the clear water out beyond the oil; mothers staring up towards their beleaguered pups. All three were brown, though only stained with oil, not completely engulfed in it like the pups. At times they thrashed wildly in the water, using their flippers to try to claw the pain away from their eyes. The oil must have been burning them. They could have left like the others, but they would not go, not while their pups were stranded.

They were helpless, and we were helpless, too. That was the most overwhelming feeling. At that state of the tide there was no way round to the beach except by boat. With the waves hitting directly on shore the beach was a torrent of seething brown foam. It would have been impossible to land and, besides, there was nothing that we could usefully have done.

We went dismally back to the house and Mike called the coastguard. No answer. The frequencies we used were buzzing with activity. The oil was obviously coming on shore all around. Everyone was so preoccupied that we couldn't make ourselves heard. Mike called again and again. Nothing. Normally our direct channel to the coastguard was quiet, and calls were answered immediately as though someone waited day and night for that single call. I felt suddenly appalled by our isolation. How could we be alone with that terrible mess?

'This is hopeless,' Mike said at last. 'We'll go out and see what's happening on the rest of the island. At least we'll be in a better position to let the coast-guard know what's going on if we ever do get through.'

Outside, the wind was cold and penetrating, but I was almost too numb to notice. We walked briskly, silently. I felt the tears so close to the surface that any attempt to speak might allow them to escape. I couldn't stop thinking about the pups, but perhaps worse still was the realisation that we had only seen the effects of the oil in one bay. I was dreading what we would discover on the rest of the island.

With the gale coming in from the north, it was that side of the island we were most worried about. We were striding fast to reach the coast, heads bowed against the storm, intent only on our mission. The sound of our footsteps was ripped away by the wind. Then, somehow, a buzzard was there in front of us, looking up, startled: it had become aware of us at precisely the same moment that we had noticed it. The bird rose from the ground a couple of feet ahead of us, opening its huge wings and hanging for a second on the flailing gusts before being swept skyward. It was so astoundingly beautiful, its colour and detail highlighted by the impossible closeness, that I was mesmerised. Then, almost at once, I was shocked at myself for finding any sort of pleasure in such a wretched day.

As we came out onto the headland at the Garland Stone, for our first good view of the coastline, I could feel the apprehension twisting inside me. Staring across the choppy waves I almost believed that it was clear.

'I can't see any oil, can you?' I asked.

Mike was scanning the surface with binoculars.

'No, it looks really clean.'

Then I remembered my mistake when I first saw North Haven that morning.

'It must be trapped under the cliffs,' I said. 'Right below us.'

'It's possible,' Mike agreed. 'We'll have to check the whole coast.'

The further we walked up the coast, the more optimistic we became, until we were convinced that there was no more oil. It was a wonderful discovery after my nightmares about the island drifting in a sea of oil.

'Well,' said Mike, as we stood on the wind-rasped precipice of Skomer Head. 'I suppose we'd better get home and see what we can do about the oil in North Haven.'

'Yes, I suppose we had.'

I think we were both reluctant to go back and face it again.

The sense of deliverance following a lucky escape is often remarkably short-lived. Almost at once I found relief giving way to a feeling of bitter resentment.

'It's unbelievable,' I raged, running slightly to keep up with Mike's purposeful stride as we made our way back. 'I mean, seeing as we've got so little oil, why did the whole bloody lot of it have to end up on my pups?'

'I know. It doesn't seem fair, does it? Poor little things, just starting out in life.'

As we came over the ridge above the house, the wind hit us full in the face. I stared down at the ground, as if to shield my eyes, but, in reality, I couldn't face seeing the oil. We had both gone quiet again, worrying about what to do next, and I was listening intently in case the cries of the pups would be carried up on the wind.

Suddenly, Mike's pace slowed.

'There's someone at the house,' he said.

I looked up with a start. It was unnerving. We never saw anyone after early September. The sight of two people standing on the doorstep in the middle of a gale was so exceptional as to be almost unreal. Mike was racing forward again.

'It's Eric . . . Eric Cowell' he shouted with delight.

Eric was an old friend of Mike's who now worked as an ecologist in the oil industry. They greeted each other with affection, and a certain amount of disbelief on Mike's part.

'It's wonderful to see you, but what on earth are you doing here?' Mike asked.

'We heard you trying to call the coastguard this morning,' Eric said. 'We couldn't get through to you on the radio, so we thought we'd come out and see what's wrong.'

Mike glanced across at North Haven, which was still thick with foam.

'How did you manage to land?'

'Oh, we didn't come by boat. We came by helicopter,' Eric said. 'By the way, let me introduce Harry.'

We shook hands politely. Harry, thickset, red-haired and smiling, turned out to be one of the greatest assets you could possibly have in an oil spill.

'So,' Eric said, 'let's have a look at the problem.'

We didn't have far to walk, just a few yards to the edge of the isthmus where we could look down on the beach. The tide was receding, and the oil looked even worse now that more of the floating residue had been deposited on the stones. The pups were subdued, no longer crying, simply exhausted by the struggle to stay alive. The three brown heads of the mothers still rode determinedly above the waves. Harry was staring down at the oil with professional interest.

'Chocolate mousse,' he said. 'It's the result of this wave action. It churns the oil into an emulsion with the water and you end up with this. We call it chocolate mousse.'

Now that he came to mention it, it did look exactly like chocolate mousse.

Within a few minutes, the impossible and the irredeemable had begun to seem like entirely surmountable problems. There was no doubt that rapid intervention with dispersants while the sea was still rough would have the whole lot vanishing like magic. So there was hope; the oil would be gone long before the birds began to return.

We went back to the house for coffee.

'So what's the situation on the rest of the island?' Eric asked.

'Clear, as far as we can tell,' Mike said, 'but we've only checked the most obvious areas.'

'Maybe we'd better have a look round while we're here, then, just to make sure.'

Eric made a call on his radio and, almost immediately, a tiny, blue helicopter descended onto the isthmus, lowering itself as cautiously as a puffin in a gale.

We were introduced to Jim, the pilot, as we squeezed into a space that was about the same size as the interior of a very small car. When we were strapped in, the helicopter did a little leap and hopped over the edge of the isthmus. For what seemed like several minutes, it felt as though we were in free fall, and I realised that I had left my stomach somewhere above us. As we were about to hit the water, the helicopter lurched forward, skimming above the waves.

'Sorry about that,' Jim said, with an unrepentant grin. 'Just picking up speed.'

I had somehow been honoured with the front seat, and when I looked down I saw that the floor was actually a bubble of glass. Between my feet the waves were scrambling dizzily into a blur of speed. They were so close that I imagined being able to stretch my foot down and touch them. Then, as we rose higher, the view opened up. The island was spread out below us, absolutely familiar and yet completely unknown. The emphasis had changed; wider patterns of ancient fields and hut circles that we never saw properly from the ground were clearly defined. But the most important thing was the sparkling blueness of the water. No oil anywhere. On the north side, the sea was flecked with bustling white waves and the cliffs were thickly fringed with surf. On the south, sheltered by the island, everything was glisteningly smooth and summery.

The most disturbing thing about flying with a see-through floor was when we moved from land to sea. One moment the ground was just below us, then, as we crossed the edge of the cliff, a hundred foot chasm opened beneath my feet, and, for a split second, it felt as though we were dropping out of the sky. I loved it. Mike was forever losing patience with me for balancing too close to cliff edges, but this flirtation with high places was better than anything to be found on solid ground.

With rest of the island clear, the pups continued to be our main concern. When the tide had fallen far enough, we were able to make our way on foot round to the oil. The beach in North Haven is divided in two by a rocky promontory; the furthest part is accessible only at low tide, by slithering over boulders draped with brown, fleshy weed. The western edge of the beach, which we used to launch the boat, had remained clean. It was only on the eastern side, beyond the promontory, that the oil had become trapped.

As the tide dropped, and the floating oil was deposited, it lay over everything like a billowing quilt. The reality of coming into contact with that substance is hard to describe. To name it after something as innocuous as mousse was far too forgiving. It was dense and gluey, rather like wading through a giant tub of brown petroleum jelly, but far more heavy and clinging. In some places it was no more than inches deep, but in the natural hollows of the beach it sank into pools of perhaps a couple of feet, certainly too deep for us to negotiate wearing waders.

We found the youngest pup quite quickly. She was dead. In fact, as I stared down at her, it was impossible to imagine that she had ever been alive. She was so heavily coated in oil that there was nothing to suggest there had once been warm flesh under there. She was smooth and dark, like something made of stone, exquisitely carved and polished into flawless perfection. Shaded from the light of publicity, she would go un-mourned by anyone outside our small, bedraggled retinue. I wished that the whole world could have seen her starkly sculpted body as it lay on that isolated beach: a sad memorial to all the lives ever wasted in these pointless little tragedies.

Nipper was alive, but in trouble. His inherently restless nature had not been curbed by the arrival of the oil. He had continued to drag himself across the beach as best he could, probably searching for his mother. As he moved, the pebbles had clung to him so that his body was encrusted in a mass of oil and stones. His search had finally come to a halt when he had slithered into a pool of oil that had gathered round the base of a rock. He was defeated, unable to move and unable even to rest. The oil around him was so deep that he would have suffocated if he had tried to lie down. He was struggling to hold his head up, despite the weight of oil and stones pressing down on him, tempting him to give in.

We were able to free him from the oil and he was taken to an animal hospital on the mainland. He had been such a strong and determined animal from the day he was born; I saw him as one of nature's fighters. He might have been badly oiled, but I was absolutely confident that he was going to come through it. If any seal was going to survive such an ordeal, it was Nipper. This false optimism made it all the more distressing when he died a few days later.

Barrel-Rat waited for us patiently. I am sure that he could have had no thought of rescue, but his whole life had involved lying in one place watching reality unfold around him, and when the oil came he continued to do the same. He was as saturated in oil as the others, but because he was so fat and strong it did not appear to be such an unbearable burden to him. And because he had not moved too much, there were fewer stones clinging to him.

We rolled Barrel-Rat into a blanket and used it as a stretcher to carry him round to the landing beach. Once he was settled, we scraped away as much of the oil and stones as we could. This miserable task was made immeasurably easier by Barrel-Rat's placid nature. Apart from the occasional reproachful growl, he was remarkably co-operative. A bad-tempered pup of his size and strength would have made the process almost impossible. Cosmetically, the end result was not good. He was still brown and sticky, but no longer encumbered by the oil, and it seemed counter-productive to drench him in chemicals to clean away the last of the oil. Besides, if everything went well it should only be a short-term problem. Barrel-Rat was on the verge of moulting. Our hope was that, over the next week or so, he would shed his baby fur and most of the oil with it.

We knew that by moving Barrel-Rat away from his beach we were almost certainly severing the last link with his mother, but we had no choice. Leaving him in the oil was not an option. Anyway, he was ready for independence; every other pup I had seen of his age had already been abandoned. The extraordinary bond between Barrel-Rat and his mother must have been reaching its end, and we suspected that the pollution had driven her away. Although they had tried to brave the oil, there was no longer any sign of the three mothers. It would have been different for Nipper, he still needed feeding, but Barrel-Rat was fat enough to survive for several weeks without food. We left him at the top of the slipway tucked securely under the cliff and settling down to sleep.

In the evening, with the island quiet again, I felt every trace of optimism drain away. The oil was everywhere; I could smell it, taste it. The sensations were so bad that I didn't want to eat. To me, Skomer had always felt untouched by the outside; even the air was so clean and pure that every rock was encrusted with green and gold and grey lichen. I realised that, no matter what happened over the coming days, no one would be able to turn the clock back. The island had been violated, and nothing could ever take that away. I was being irrational, but it was probably an understandable reaction to the sight of something so precious being desecrated. When I tried to swallow to clear the imaginary taste of oil, I could feel the ache of something cold and hard, like a cube of ice caught in my throat. It was one of those sensations that I could remember from the worst times of childhood, when I was trying desperately not to cry.

The next day brought more bad news: no dispersants were to be used. The rare and fragile ecosystem around the island should not be assaulted with toxic chemicals. It was the right decision, but at that moment I just wanted the oil to be gone, no matter what it took. In truth, even if the will to use dispersants had been there, the time had already passed. The wind had dropped away over night, and the chemicals needed the churning action of a rough sea in order to work. The water was once again impossibly, unseasonably calm, and the oil lay draped in a flaccid mass across its surface.

Every tide had the same pattern. As the sea came in the oil lifted, spreading over the water in a thick, impenetrable sheet, and when the water ebbed away the oil was deposited again. It was unbearably frustrating, seeing both the permanence and the impermanence of the situation. When the oil was settled, it looked as though it would be there forever; when it was afloat I could visualise the whole lot being scooped away.

Although I had come to terms with the fact that there would be no magic wand to wave away the oil, the decidedly primitive solution that finally emerged was very disillusioning. I had naively imagined that all the money of the oil industry would have developed sophisticated remedies for these disasters. The last thing I expected was for twenty-five men armed with plastic sacks and shovels to arrive and start digging up our oil slick. The amount of oil on the beach was estimated at about two hundred tons; I didn't want to begin to imagine how many spadefuls that represented.

However bitter we felt about the oil companies, those feelings of resentment could not possibly extend to the people who came from BP to help us.

There was no feeling of 'them' and 'us'; we knew that they were on our side, one hundred percent. At first we had been incensed, feeling that we were sufficiently inaccessible to be ignored. We were sure that all the resources would be concentrated on the mainland, cleaning up beaches that lacked the urgency of our situation, but were more likely to attract bad publicity. Everything changed with the arrival of the helicopter. While Eric continued to co-ordinate things from the mainland, Harry returned daily to the island. With him came Frank, manager of the BP refinery at Milford Haven, a blunt, no-nonsense Scotsman: exactly the sort of person to get things moving. Though these were very senior people, their approach was entirely practical. There was no question of them standing back and directing operations. They were in the thick of it, plastered in oil along with everyone else.

The plastic bag method of oil removal was painfully slow. Each bag, filled with a couple of shovelfuls of oil, had to be ferried off the beach by dinghy and loaded onto a waiting barge. The barge took five hours to make the single trip to Milford Haven to off-load its cargo. That meant it had to spend all night travelling in order to be back in North Haven ready for work the following morning.

It would have been easy to become dispirited by the lack of progress. After a couple of days it was hard to see any change in the amount of oil left on the beach. It wasn't so bad in the daytime, there was such a sense of purpose that it carried us along, but in the evening, when North Haven was quiet again, the feeling of desolation came back. We went outside and stood on the cliff in the fading light. The air was soft and very mild for the time of year. When I leaned right forward I could make out Barrel-Rat sleeping at the bottom of the cliff. The fact that he had survived seemed disproportionately important. He was the brightness amid all that gloom, the proof that life would go on.

As we stood, absorbing the calm, I heard a faint rustling noise at the edge of the water. I looked down and saw a female seal quietly emerging through the shallow waves. She was almost invisible, her dappled coat just part of the mosaic of muted greys that were the sea and stones. Her movements were alert and purposeful: stretching her neck as high as it would go, bobbing her head to find the best view up the beach. Then, as though she had found what she was looking for, she began to move rapidly, dragging herself forward with her flippers, while the rest of her body followed on behind in a lumbering, wave-like motion. She went up to Barrel-Rat, reaching her muzzle forward to touch him and then stroking roughly at the top of his head, before rolling over onto her side to let him feed. It was his mother. Through the upheaval of the oil she had not given up hope of finding him again. It was one of those moments that sent a shiver of emotion tingling across my skin.

We saw Barrel-Rat's mother only a few more times and then she disappeared. I imagined that she was distressed by the abruptness of their separation and had come back to make sure that he was all right before she could finally allow herself to abandon him. That was fanciful, of course, my own uncompromisingly human interpretation, but I thought that we deserved one fairy-tale ending amid so much bleak reality.

The good news was that the shovels and plastic sacks were not the ultimate solution to our problem. We were going to be rescued by little machines that floated across the water devouring the oil with their whirring rotor blades. Since almost all the oil was lifted clear of the beach at high tide, the shovelling would soon be necessary only to perfect the finishing touches.

I was glad that so much optimism had not caused the mundane process of shovelling to be abandoned as we waited for the arrival of these machines, because they were defeated by the thick, adhesive consistency of the oil. They churned and gurgled in the water, leaving the oil untouched.

The idea persisted, however, that it should be easier to recover the oil from the sea than to scrape it from the stones. Floating booms were used to trap the oil and prevent it from settling back onto the beach with each outgoing tide. Unfortunately, our boat was the only one small enough to potter close in among the rocks where the oil lingered in brown, scummy sheets at high tide. Mike and Harry used a boom attached to the boat to capture puddles of floating oil and tow them further out into the bay. The boat was suffering; its hull was being cracked by the constant collisions as it bounced from rock to rock, and water was beginning to come seeping in. Though I was determined that we should win the fight with the oil, I could hardly bear to see our boat slowly disintegrating. I loved it, and it had given me such a sense of security since the departure of the hated dory. I watched in dismay as, like everything else that came anywhere near the oil, our gorgeous blue boat turned brown.

In the quiet of the evening, with the boats and people gone, our familiar and beautiful view was now dominated by the miniature captive slicks of oil, anchored down so that they couldn't escape and do any further damage. The booms were fluorescent-pink inflatable tubes that looped in a circle around the oil, and the effect of these things in North Haven was like giant oil-filled paddling pools drifting across the sea.

The seals were gradually returning. With the most volatile elements of the oil now evaporated away, it no longer seemed to hurt their eyes as it had in the first few days. When everything was peaceful at the end of the day, they came slipping back into North Haven to explore these oddly transformed surroundings. The booms were of particular interest. They inspected them carefully, nosing round the edge of the brilliantly coloured plastic. Then they dived below for a better look, and I could see the shape of their muzzles pushing from underneath against the oil, which gave the appearance of having set into a thick, rubbery skin that stretched without breaking. This exploration culminated in a particularly adventurous seal heaving itself over the lip of the boom and launching itself into the pool of oil. Instead of sinking in the mire, the force of the belly flop sent the seal skidding across the slippery, brown surface, catapulting it off the far end and back into the water. This manoeuvre met with such approval that the other seals were soon queuing up to take turns.

Under different circumstances I would have loved to watch them play, but seeing that disgusting pollution treated as a game seemed grotesque. I turned away to the side window of the kitchen and looked down at the oil remaining on the beach. After so many days of work, there was an enormous amount still to be cleared. The initial sense of shock had passed, and I simply felt despondent about the situation. I watched idly as a gull flew across the sky. Its spiritless wailing calls, like a reflection of my mood, echoed against the empty cliffs. It turned above the isthmus and then swooped low towards the beach. In a frozen moment of despair I realised that the pulse of its wings had slowed as its feet reached downward in preparation for landing. Almost at once, the flesh-pink webs touched the oil.

The bird must have known immediately that something was wrong. Its wings were barely folded across its back before it tried to fly again, but in that fraction of a second the oil had taken hold. As the wings stretched high into the air, the bird remained anchored. Panic caused the controlled pattern of wing beats to disintegrate. In the disorganised flurry of movement, the tip of one wing touched the oil. It was caught inextricably in the trap. Within moments the other wing was snared. All the furious flapping couldn't lift the bird, but only drag it down. In a fleeting, violent struggle the gull was gone, vanished without trace. The oil closed over its head smooth and glossy and unruffled.

Perhaps it was my prevailing sense of depression, but I found that fleeting incident profoundly disturbing. It was not so much a death but a complete obliteration, a denial of life. One moment there had been a bird gliding peacefully above the bay and the next there was nothing, not even the ragged remains of flesh and feathers. Its life had been cancelled out, as though it had counted for nothing. The idea that a living entity could just cease to exist triggered one of those dismal meditations on the fragility of life, which haunted me occasionally for years afterwards.

I focused on the one shining ray that was glinting through the clouds. There was something very exciting on the horizon in the shape of the *Bay Skimmer*. She was on her way to us from Ireland, and she was to be our salvation. Soon the mess and disruption would be nothing more than a memory, and we would return to peace and quiet. The *Bay Skimmer* was a brand new oil pollution control ship, so much at the cutting edge of technology that she had never been used before. Everything hung on her arrival.

The next morning Frank and Harry emerged from the helicopter looking uncharacteristically grim.

'What's wrong?' Mike asked.

'Oh, we've had a bit of a row with Head Office,' Frank said. 'They're claiming this whole operation's costing too much, and they've cancelled the *Bay Skimmer.*' He must have seen the look of misery on our faces. 'Oh, don't you worry,' he went on, fiercely. 'We've promised you that this beach will be cleaned, and we're not going back on that. I've told them that if the *Bay Skimmer* isn't out here immediately, I'll be up in London showing them where they can stick the oil.'

It was Skomer. I knew it was. The island had worked its magic on them as it did with everyone. Skomer had captivated these level-headed oilmen and turned them away from hard, financial reality into champions of our little, windswept island.

The arrival of the *Bay Skimmer* was every bit as wonderful as I had hoped it would be. She came gliding into North Haven with her shining reflections seeping out across the calm water. Compared to all the other boats, daubed and dingy from working in the oil, she was a glittering jewel. The captain, bringing her on her first ever mercy mission, was justly proud of his boat. Mike and Harry, wearing their customary shade of deep sludge, pulled alongside in our boat to discuss a plan of campaign. As soon as they touched the gunwale, the captain raced forward, waving his arms in horror, intent on repelling oily boarders. Negotiations had to be shouted between boats, while the captain of the *Bay Skimmer* busied himself with a cloth, wiping furiously at the prints of oily fingers. Poor man, I thought. After so many days of watching the way the oil smeared itself insidiously over everything, I knew that he was in for a miserable time if he had any thought of keeping his boat clean.

The captain's efforts to distance his vessel from the oil provided a rare moment of light relief. Since the grimy boats were not allowed alongside his ship, he attempted to walk out along one of the inflatable booms in order to communicate with Mike and Harry who were drifting nearby in the dinghy. It was about as hopeless as trying to walk on water; the boom instantly folded under his weight plunging him into the oil.

The fact that the captain of a pollution control vessel appeared to have an obsessive aversion to oil shouldn't really have mattered so long as the boat itself worked. The idea behind the *Bay Skimmer* was almost ludicrously simple. Her bows opened up to reveal a giant conveyor belt. As the boat was steered through the oil, the moving belt lifted it off the surface of the water and down into the hold. It reminded me of comic book technology: so impossibly logical that no one would ever think of it in real life. Perhaps that was why it hadn't been developed until now.

I couldn't wait to see the last of the oil sliding effortlessly out of sight. One of the miniature slicks was released from the booms while the *Bay Skimmer* chugged slowly and purposefully towards it. The bow doors were open and the conveyor belt was turning. Oil and boat were on a collision course and it gave me enormous pleasure to watch as the oil finally met its match. The boat began to plough through the oil and . . . nothing happened. The conveyor belt continued to turn, while remaining brilliantly, sparklingly clean. I had no idea what the conveyor belt was made of, but it appeared to be the only substance on earth to which the oil did not cling tenaciously. Every boat, every person, everything on the island that had been in the vicinity of the oil, quickly acquired that sticky, dipped-in-chocolate look, everything but the *Bay Skimmer*'s conveyor belt. I half suspected the captain of slathering it in a protective coat of polish.

It was a depressing moment. I don't think that any of us had ever questioned that the *Bay Skimmer* would be the answer, if only she was allowed to make it to the island. She was brand new and ludicrously expensive; with credentials like that, she had to work. As the realisation of the dismal failure that we were witnessing began to permeate the general sense of optimism, there was an uncomfortable mixture of dismay and embarrassment.

'Don't worry,' said those who knew something about oil. 'It's just a teething problem because the belt is so new. Once it gets a bit of oil on it, the rest will start to stick.'

There was a concerted effort to get the belt acclimatized to the oil. Mike and Harry, drifting in the dinghy across the open bows of the *Bay Skimmer*, grabbed handfuls of the stuff and plastered it onto the belt, scrubbing it in with ferocious zeal. Nothing would make it cling. In fact, the belt seemed actually to repel the oil, so that it slithered away leaving not even the faintest stain. Various solvents were used to clean the belt in order to make it less resistant, but still it treated the oil with disdain, shrugging it off with ease.

At the end of a frustrating day, Jim, the pilot, arrived with the helicopter to pick up Frank and Harry. He had come on the first day of the oil spill to ferry the BP officials down from London, and had stayed, despite having not so much as a change of clothes with him. His zany good humour made him a real morale booster. That evening he must have been kept waiting too long, because, after a minute or two, the helicopter disappeared. We could hear the roar of rotor blades, even see the squall of the downdraught fanning out across the sea, but there was no sign of the aircraft.

'What on earth's he up to now?' Frank asked.

A few minutes later the helicopter reappeared from below the cliff and parked on the isthmus. Jim came sauntering cheerfully across to us.

'What was that about?' Frank asked.

'Oh, just seeing if I could use the rotor blades to blow the oil trapped under the cliff out to sea.'

Good try, we all agreed. And, I thought, no more impossible in principle than the *Bay Skimmer*.

That should have been a low point, seeing the hopes we had invested in the *Bay Skimmer* melting away, but Barrel-Rat came to our rescue. He began to moult. Usually, the white coat comes away in wisps that drift in the air like thistle down, or, in the case of inactive animals like Barrel-Rat, gather in a soft carpet around the sleeping pup. But, because Barrel-Rat's fur was glued down and matted together by oil, when it was finally shed it cracked open and peeled away like a hard outer shell. From within that drab brown creature, a perfect, new, velvet pup broke free, with the same pristine beauty as a butterfly emerging from a chrysalis. Barrel-Rat's transformation was the incentive we needed to keep going.

The concept of being able to lift the oil straight from the surface of the water was not abandoned. A company with the delicious name of Dyfed Sludge supplied a sewage pump with a long hose to suck up the oil. The sturdy, old-fashioned pump was set chuntering away on the decks of the *Bay Skimmer* ready to send the oil gushing down into her holding tanks, which would be able to separate the oil and water. Once again, the intractable nature of the oil almost turned a good idea into total failure. The oil was so solid that it wouldn't go into the pump. In desperation, Mike began hacking at the oil with an oar, chopping it into chunks, like huge segments of withered brie, and feeding it piece by piece to the pump. At last, they had found something that worked. It was slow and tedious, but incalculably quicker than the shovel, and marked a turning point at which the battle began to swing in our favour.

This upturn in our fortunes was shattered by a deterioration in Barrel-Rat's condition. He had been content on the slipway, sleeping, or watching the comings and goings with an occasional indignant hiss if he felt himself to be unreasonably disturbed. He never left his comfortable resting place since he was still too fat to be troubled by any thoughts of hunger. Then, quite unexpectedly, his interest in life vanished; he became droopy and listless. We checked him carefully. He appeared to be in excellent condition, and I was afraid that if we could find no obvious cause for his illness he might sink into an irreversible decline. Then, when we had almost given up hope, Mike found a poisonous abscess under Barrel-Rat's foreflipper. It looked bad, but at least discovering the problem opened the door to finding a cure.

We had no experience of dealing with sick seal pups. They were born into such unforgiving conditions that there was usually a harsh dividing line between those that lived and those that succumbed rapidly to death. Eric launched himself with enthusiasm into the process of finding a cure for Barrel-Rat. He phoned round various zoos trying to track down a suitable antibiotic and, perhaps more importantly, obtaining detailed instructions on where, amid so much blubber, to inject a seal.

There can have been few seals that would have submitted to such treatment without a ferocious battle, but Barrel-Rat allowed himself to be pulled and prodded as the abscess was cleaned, and only gave a mildly reproving snort as the needle was jabbed into him. The reversal in his condition was almost immediate. Barrel-Rat quickly became his old sleepy but contented self: our bright symbol of hope.

The shovelling and pumping of oil continued with its own monotonous rhythm. The only change was that an end to the whole gloomy situation was definitely in view. The beach was beginning to re-emerge, uniformly brown, but no longer completely masked by the thick drifts of oil. The last remnants of the diminishing mess had to be hooped into deeper pools by the booms so that it could be lifted more easily with a spade.

The *Bay Skimmer* eventually left, having sucked up not a drop of our oil under her own power, and I never heard of her again. I don't know if she found an oil slick that was more to her taste, or if she was allowed to remain forever glisteningly new, without having to suffer the indignity of being covered in oil.

On the final day of the clean-up, Frank insisted that we should take a trip to the mainland in the helicopter and choose a new boat to replace our own, which was leaking hopelessly from the damage sustained in its clash with the oil. From snippets of overheard conversation I was beginning to suspect that he and Mike were hatching a plot.

'We'll get another boat exactly the same, won't we?' I asked Mike. 'I mean, we've managed so well with that one. I don't want to find ourselves struggling again with something we can barely manage to get in and out of the water.'

'Yes, of course we'll get another one the same,' he said, with rather less conviction than I would have liked.

The helicopter ride to the mainland was a bit of an adventure, as well as being an escape from the oil, which seemed to have dominated our lives forever. Jim, still on his extended one-day visit, greeted us with the usual profound enthusiasm. The rotor blades started to turn with a gently rising judder and suddenly the ground beneath my feet disappeared. Through the glass floor I watched as we plunged over the cliff edge down towards the oily beach. The descent halted just above sea level and the waves streaked beneath us. I looked up to find that we were exactly on a level with the men standing on the deck of the barge. For a moment their startled looks were frozen as we stared straight into each other's eyes, and then they flashed past. Jim, predictably, excused this manoeuvre as a necessary way of gaining speed, but I suspected that its main function was to test the calibre of the passengers. He was in typical good form explaining how nervous passengers usually made enquiries about what would happen if the engine failed. His response was to demonstrate by switching off the engine and letting the helicopter flutter quietly downwards.

Frank joined us at the boatyard, even though it was only a matter of point-ing out another boat just like our beautiful, blue thirteen-footer. I saw what we wanted straight away, but Mike and Frank went sightseeing along the rows of boats. They stopped by a much larger boat and sank into deep discussion of its finer points in what, I assumed, was a purely detached way. I wandered over.

'This one would suit you better,' Frank said. 'That boat you've got at the moment isn't big enough for the sort of seas you have around Skomer.'

As a former tanker captain, it was hardly surprising that he would say something like that.

'Yes, I know,' I answered. 'But we couldn't manage to get anything bigger up and down the beach.'

I expected Mike to join in, but he remained silent, confirming my suspicions that this was what they had both planned all along.

'It's not that much bigger,' Frank said. 'Only another three feet. But it'll make a huge difference to how it handles in the water.'

It didn't matter. They could scheme all they liked; I still had the trump card.

'I don't think our engines are big enough for a boat that size,' I replied.

'Oh, don't you worry about that,' Frank said, dismissively. 'We'll get you a decent engine.'

And somehow we came out of the boatyard having ordered, not the little blue boat I had set my heart on, but a huge white monster. I suppose, objectively, it was a nice boat: sleek and elegant. The trouble was that, unlike Mike and Frank, I couldn't visualise it cutting cleanly through the waves. I could only see it crashing and bouncing over the boulders of North Haven at low tide on a winter morning.

That marked the end of the tortuous operation to clean North Haven. The effect was remarkable. It had been undertaken with such conscientious dedication that the oil was reduced to no more than grimy streaks scumming the water. We were back to a situation that had seemed almost unimaginable a couple of weeks before. And throughout that time the wind had barely breathed. The sea had touched against the shore so gently that the work was able go on undisturbed. Not a single day had been lost to the weather. The oil had lain thick and smooth, rising and falling with the tides, never fractured or scattered by the waves. It was exceptional for a time of year when we would expect to be besieged by storms. Perhaps the fates were working with us, but it didn't feel like good fortune that the only significant oil to have come ashore throughout the incident was at North Haven and Martin's Haven.

The most important thing, though, was that the oil had gone. A similar accident in the spring would have devastated the island's seabird colonies. During the three days before the oil had been swept on shore, it had stretched for miles around the island, covering the areas where the auks would have been feeding and where the rafting shearwaters gathered. Even in October, when the island seemed to have been almost deserted by the birds, thousands were caught in the oil at sea and died. Although some attempt had been made to count them, the true number would never be known. Mike had seen countless barely recognisable corpses disappearing with the shovelfuls of oil. Though the casualties were few, just two seal pups and a relatively small number of birds, the pain and distress were unquantifiable, something on which no price could ever be put.

Financially, the cleaning of that section of beach, the removal of those two hundred tons of oil, had cost £400,000: an enormous sum of money then. It was irrelevant, of course, but, with Skomer running entirely on a few thousand pounds a year, I couldn't help thinking how much good that money could have done under different circumstances. But the thing that really shone from it all was the determination to put things right. I was full of admiration for the way everyone had held on and seen it through in the face of such disastrously mounting costs.

The boats in North Haven dwindled away, and finally we were alone again. I had longed for the whole thing to be over, but it left an overwhelming sense of anti-climax. The oil had gone, but not the shadow of its violation. In our three years on the island, nothing before had tarnished the atmosphere of that bright and beautiful place. The shock we felt was undoubtedly a loss of innocence: a warning of the island's fragility and our own powerlessness.

The seals didn't come back to North Haven beach. Even when all tangible presence of the oil was gone, they seemed to sense the change in the same way that we did. The bay was bleak and forsaken. I felt it most at night, sitting by the babbling driftwood fire, and knowing that something was wrong. There was no longer the soulful wailing of seals to harmonize with the random cracking of the embers smouldering in the grate. No more hissing voices and scattering of stones as the seals fought over some imagined intrusion.

Then, one morning, we went down to the slipway and found that Barrel-Rat was gone. It was exactly as it should be; at last he had broken free to find his own way. But I missed his reassuring presence, his disgruntled snorts if we accidentally woke him, his overflowing, blubbery robustness. The important thing, though, was that he was healthy and had recovered from the oil. Independence had been far too long in coming. He had finally launched himself from the safe niche at the top of the beach and let the cold waves enfold him, had discovered what it was to be liberated from the restrictions of his own body.

It was a happy ending, the last chapter of a miserable story. We stared out across opaque grey waves that were beginning to turn wintry. There was no sign of Barrel-Rat's smooth head, slicked by the polish of seawater. He had vanished completely. With the freedom of a whole ocean waiting to be discovered, we would probably never see him again. And yet, as we gazed at the empty bay, I knew that if this was really a happy ending, it should have felt very much better than it actually did.

NINE

As the winter drew to a close, we began to appreciate the value of the painstaking clean-up operation in North Haven. In Martin's Haven, the only beach on the mainland to be badly oiled, everything had been so much simpler. Though it was an isolated bay, reached only by an unsurfaced track, it was sufficiently accessible for heavy machinery to be brought in. Mechanical diggers had set to work, trundling across the beach and scooping up the oil in great gulps. The whole thing was over and forgotten while the Skomer team was still knee deep in oil, shovelling it into plastic sacks.

It was only the passage of time that began to demonstrate the value of the slow and cautious approach that had been imposed on Skomer by its remoteness. The heavy machinery used in Martin's Haven had ground the oil down into the pebbles. The cosmetically impressive result showed its weakness with every tide. Each incoming flood lifted the oil trapped in the pebbles and floated a milky, opalescent bloom across the surface of the water. Months later, as the seabirds were returning at the end of winter, we could see this oil from Skomer. It stretched in a broad, silky band from the mouth of Martin's Haven and extended a mile or two out into St Brides Bay.

The return of the first seabirds was not an ostentatious arrival like the coming of the puffins. In the dull light of early morning guillemots and razorbills were visiting briefly, to see the ledges again and to re-establish their places for the breeding season. And, to our great relief, they were coming back to clean water. Around the island, winter-grey seas glittered with stray sparks of sunlight, and there was no trace of oil washing out from North Haven.

Eventually, when the birds were settled in, there came the return of another migrant. Wellington had spent the cold, hungry days of winter staying on Terry's smallholding. As April brought lengthening days and milder air she came back to us. It was a happy reunion, thrown only slightly awry by the news that Wellington was pregnant. Mike and I smiled with gratitude that she had been so well cared for, at the same time hoping that our dismay was not showing through. This was not one of those accidental events resulting from an illicit encounter with a billy. Wellington had had a carefully pre-arranged meeting with a magnificent white Saanen, reputed to sire only female kids. It was just another one of those little acts of thoughtfulness of which we were so frequently on the receiving end. Although we saw Terry as a boatman, there was no doubt that, at heart, he was a farmer, and I suspected that someone with such leanings could only see an animal as being at its best when it was reproducing.

We led Wellington from the boat across to the house and, already, she was forgetting to be on her best behaviour. She wrenched away from the hand on her collar to snatch ravenously at the passing vegetation.

'Come on Wellington.' I gave a gentle tug. 'Let's get you back home.'

She responded by swinging her head round, to catch that tender point at the back of my knee with the point of her horn.

'This is terrible,' I said to Mike. 'Wellington's such a pain. Can you imagine how we'd manage with two or three more like her?'

'No,' Mike agreed. 'It doesn't bear thinking about, does it?'

Once Wellington was settled in, we made straight for our book on goat husbandry with its grainy, black and white pictures of perfectly-proportioned goats, all smiling and looking extremely good-natured, none of them bearing the slightest resemblance to Wellington. The most pressing task was to calculate a date for the arrival of the kids.

'Dreadful,' I groaned. 'It says here that the goat will choose a day for the birth at any time within a period of about two weeks. Imagine Wellington making the decisions. It's bound to be as inconvenient as she can make it.'

All we knew was that when the time came we would be waiting for a mild, humid, wind-free day.

The oil spill had brought us not only a new boat but also a new radio. Frank and Harry had been concerned by the problems we had in making contact using our portable radio, and insisted that we needed something better. We received a top-of-the-range ship's radio: huge, solid, green-enamelled and, with all its knobs and dials, delightfully old-fashioned looking. It was mounted on the kitchen wall by the window overlooking the beach where the oil had been, and wired through to a tractor battery in the cellar.

The new radio made our daily contact with the coastguard much more reliable, but one morning that spring, a routine call turned into something more disturbing. The coastguard at St Ann's Head was concerned about the source of an extremely bright light that they had seen on the island the previous night. I felt his words like a cold ripple of panic. Mike and I exchanged puzzled glances. There had been no lights on the island; we had nothing capable of generating a bright light. This explanation left the coastguard unconvinced. They had definitely seen a light, and he described its exact location on the island. The more insistent he grew about the certainty of the light, the more uncomfortable I began to feel.

'What was that about?' I asked, as soon as the radio fell silent.

Mike Shrugged. 'I don't know.'

'He thinks there was something here, doesn't he?'

'It sounds like it.'

The truth was that we both had a good idea what it was about. We were caught up in the Broad Haven Triangle, an area of Pembrokeshire that was said to be the target of a wave of alien visitations. The newspapers were fanning the flames with stories of lights in the sky and silver-suited figures roaming the countryside. It had generated an outbreak of mild hysteria locally. I had seen it as vaguely amusing and not at all sinister, but it suddenly began to feel a lot more threatening.

I tried to be rational.

'There couldn't have been a light. We don't have anything more powerful than a torch. No one's going to see that twelve miles away. Besides, neither of us left the house last night.'

'No, and there's no possibility of anyone seeing the house lights from that direction.'

The fact that we were able to dismiss any logical explanation so easily only made the whole thing worse.

'So, from the direction he described it, where exactly would the light have been?'

'Just up here, the other side of Captain Kites.'

I felt a shiver inside; only one steep slope and a few hundred yards separating us from whatever it was.

'What do we do now?' I asked.

'I don't know. Let's go and have a look.'

As we climbed the path rising up towards Captain Kites, and then followed the gentle incline down the other side, I was irrationally apprehensive about what we might find. I have no idea what we hoped to discover by looking at the empty space where something had been: a circle scorched into the turf, perhaps. We searched for disturbance to the vegetation, anything that might give us a clue as to what had happened there the previous night. Unsurprisingly, but disappointingly, there was nothing. It left the incident unfinished, and, despite my efforts to dismiss it from my mind, there remained a chink in my sense of security.

Wellington bloomed throughout her pregnancy, growing plump and, possibly, even slightly less bad-tempered. As the time for her to give birth approached, I half expected to go out one morning and find Wellington presenting us with the kids as a fait accompli. The more predictable reality was that I went out to give her her breakfast only to find that she had vanished. I didn't panic immediately because I knew she wouldn't have gone far. There was one foolproof way of bringing her home at a gallop. I grabbed her food bowl and rattled it loudly.

'Wellington! Wellington!' I called in my most appeasing voice, as I listened for the sound of greedy bleating accompanied by thundering hooves. Nothing. I wandered out onto the isthmus, calling and rattling at full volume, although by then I knew that something was not quite right. I went back to the house.

'I can't find Wellington,' I said miserably.

'Oh, she can't be far away,' Mike said.

'Honestly, I've looked all round, and she never goes out of earshot of her food bowl.'

We put our boots on and went back outside to continue the search. The sky was a thick, grey blanket: no clouds, no sun, just smooth, soft grey, with the atmosphere dense and warm beneath. Mike tried calling. The air was so still that his voice came echoing back from the cliffs. I glanced up at the sky and suddenly saw what was happening.

'Look,' I said. 'This is it.'

'What?'

'Wellington's day. The day she's chosen to have her kids. Humid and calm.'

'Oh no,' said Mike, 'and she's gone off somewhere to have them.'

'She wouldn't do that. She never goes anywhere without us.'

'Well she has this time. We'd better find her in case she's in trouble.'

We ran up the hill behind the house, calling breathlessly. At every moment I expected to hear an irritable answering bleat, but she remained silent, making no attempt to help us. Despite this lack of cooperation, we found her surprisingly quickly. We arrived panting at the top of Captain Kites, and there she was, tucked away in a hollow under a large outcrop of rock. She looked up vaguely, as though we were unwelcome strangers, and then looked away. There was no desperate wail of recognition that usually accompanied these reunions. We moved tentatively towards her. The place beneath the rock where she was sitting had been scooped out to form a sheltered dish. The soft, sandy soil was speckled with the imprints of her hooves.

'It looks like she's been coming here for a while to prepare this place,' Mike said. 'She hasn't dug all this today.'

There was something touching about the thought of selfish, irascible Wellington coming here alone and lovingly carving out this den for her kids.

'Shall we take her home?' I asked.

'No, best leave her. She knows what she's doing. Let's trust her judgement and see what happens.'

We settled ourselves down at a discrete distance to wait. Wellington sat with her vast belly splaying out sideways beneath her. She was obviously straining, and giving the distinct impression that something was about to happen.

'She's supposed to be standing up,' I whispered to Mike.

'How do you know,' he whispered back.

'It says so in the book.'

'You can't expect Wellington to do things by the book.'

So we waited and nothing happened. I looked at my watch.

'It's over half an hour,' I hissed.

'That's not long,' Mike replied.

'It says in the book that if nothing happens after half an hour, she's in trouble.'

'How much trouble?'

'I don't know. We're supposed to stand her on a slope with her front legs lower than her hind legs.'

We walked over and began to heave at Wellington. She heaved back. I have never understood how animals have the power to make themselves so completely immoveable, but Wellington wedged her bulk firmly against the earth and clung on limpet-like. With a great deal of wrenching we got her to her feet, manoeuvred her front legs downhill, and felt her slip through our grasp decisively back onto the ground.

'This is no good,' Mike said after a couple more tries. 'She's determined to stay sitting down. Are you sure about this standing on a slope stuff?'

'Absolutely. I was only reading it yesterday.'

Mike looked doubtful.

'Maybe you'd better dash back and get the book so that we can check what else it says.'

I stared down the steep slope towards the house, reluctant to leave at such a critical time.

'I'll stay here to keep an eye on Wellington,' Mike added.

I had noticed that whenever anything needed fetching from distant parts of the island Mike was invariably preoccupied with something more important. I took one last look back at Wellington and then set off at a run.

Soon I was struggling back up the incline, trying to read as I went so that I would be ready with the vital information the moment I arrived.

'It definitely says to stand her on a slope,' I called, as soon as I was close enough.

'Err . . . you're too late,' Mike said, with a faint smile of satisfaction.

I stared down into the dusty hollow to see an indistinguishable shape encased in what looked like a punctured balloon.

'You mean I've missed it?' I wailed. 'I've only been gone a few minutes.'

Wellington was showing only the vaguest of interest in the apparition.

'What is it?' I asked, as it slid out of its gelatinous cocoon.

'It's a nanny,' Mike said triumphantly.

'Thank goodness for that.'

A billy would have been a real problem; we couldn't have kept it and would have been unlikely to find a home for it. Soon after, a second kid came lurching effortlessly into the dust. After an almost imperceptible flicker of curiosity, Wellington ignored it. Mike lifted it trembling to its feet.

'Another nanny,' he called, as he showed it to Wellington.

She sniffed, but was clearly not as interested as she would have been in a bowl of food.

The little goats looked impossibly fragile. The angle of every bone seemed to show through the damp, clinging fur. Mike tucked one under each arm and began to carry them back towards the house. Wellington followed closely behind bleating crossly.

By the time the kids were dry and settled on new straw, Wellington was developing a profound fascination with them. She stared at them, unblinking, for whole minutes at a time, occasionally lowering her head towards them so that she could inhale their scent. She could be forgiven her brief interlude of pride. The kids were absolutely adorable. They were both pure white and, at first glance, very much like particularly skinny newborn lambs. But their fur was silky rather than woolly, and the curve of their mouths gave them a smile that was far more mischievous than any lamb's. They were immediately and insatiably active, tottering precariously on shiny black hooves, springing fearlessly on legs that looked too insubstantial to hold their weight.

Wellington was transformed almost instantly into a model of patience. The kids loved to climb. It was essential for them to reach the pinnacle of any convenient prominence, and then jostle for position until one lost its balance. In those early days of exploration, their mother's back represented the challenge of a mountain. They would clamber up, digging sharp little hooves into the furry slopes, and then joust with non-existent horns until one of them was sent skidding down the flanks. It was the sort of behaviour calculated to provoke a furious backlash from Wellington. At every moment I expected one of them to receive a painful sideswipe from her horns, but it never happened. She sat contentedly throughout the chaotic proceedings.

The two kids were virtually indistinguishable. We named them Boojum and Snark. The only obvious differences between them were in character: Snark was adventurous and outgoing, while Boojum was much more diffident. I searched for minor variations, so that I would always know who was who, and found that Snark had a scattering of faint black speckles on her nose. Mike had a much more ostentatious way of telling them apart. He discovered that if he bent down Snark would jump onto his back, planting two little hooves so firmly on each shoulder that she stayed put as he stood up again, and was able to ride round triumphantly, high in the air. Boojum, on the other hand, was far too shy to take advantage of the proffered shoulders. It was a fairly complicated method of identification, but almost infallible.

They were animals without fear of heights, happy to gambol to the very edge of the cliff and then dance with glee along its slippery, sandy margins. At the most precarious point, one of them was sure to leap in the air, flicking out its hind legs with a little sideways twist, in perfect imitation of a newborn lamb. At that point I would have to hold my breath and look away, while Mike went charging over to grab one in each hand and carry them back to the shelter.

The awful thing was that these perilous jaunts were not confined to the hours of daylight. After going to check on them in the middle of the night, Mike found them skipping with carefree delight along the crumbling precipices of the isthmus. It was an unfortunate discovery because it meant the end of unbroken sleep. From then on he had to get up several times a night to bring the goats in from the cliff. It would have been better if he had remained in contented ignorance of these night-time activities, because his efforts to keep them safe were almost certainly futile. I was convinced that the kids would be exploring the moonlit fringes of the bay long before Mike's head touched the pillow.

Their delight in life was infectious. The only negative aspect to having goat kids was that it became impossible to relax outside the house. If we tried to sit out on the large, curved doorstep to catch the last of the evening sun, it had to be done with a small white goat each on our laps. It wasn't, in fact, too much of a hardship because they were beautifully clean and unexpectedly fragrant animals. If I buried my face in the silky fur there was only a sweet, warm, grassy smell, without any hint of the muskiness of goat.

Their most lively time was in the last hour of daylight. There was something about the fading light that infused them with mischief, so that they became wild and full of energy. They indulged in play fighting that involved rearing up at each other on hind legs accompanied by some flamboyantly spectacular head butting. This usually culminated in a high-speed chase around the perimeter of the house, a hopelessly circular contest in which each goat played the role of both pursued and pursuer. The most entertaining trick was one of Snark's solo endeavours. She invented the most breathtaking acrobatic leap that involved charging directly at the house and then, at the last second, launching herself into the air so that all four hooves made contact with the wooden wall. Catapulted by the slight spring in the boards, she turned a complete back somersault before landing again squarely on the ground. The manoeuvre was so accomplished that it invariably sparked a ripple of applause from her audience of two.

As the months passed, I realised that I was slowly regaining my equilibrium in the aftermath of the oil. Without noticing it, I had somehow grown accustomed to the new white boat; perhaps it was only because summer made everything so much easier, but I was actually beginning to like it. With the days at their longest, the guillemots and razorbills were leaving. Each evening a new wave of departures left the cliffs looking noticeably emptier the following morning. It was an uncomfortably forceful reminder that summer was meandering idly away. That sublime period when daylight lingered far into the night, and the cliffs were crowded with birds, was such a tantalisingly ephemeral thing that I wanted to cling on to every last moment.

Now there was a particular poignancy in watching the birds leave. So many times I had looked down at the gauzy blue water as it swirled against the edge of the cliff and, for a second, the oil had been there again, a sticky-smooth blanket smothering and flattening the waves. I saw over and over again the gull that I had watched struggling and sinking, dissolving away into that haunting nothingness. Before, I had only imagined how it might feel to see a dozen, a hundred, even a thousand, birds dragging themselves deeper into the oil with every panic-stricken movement, but now I almost knew. I finally understood something that logic alone could never quite make me believe: however much I wanted the birds to stay, it was better they should go.

Besides, it was only the beginning of the end. It would be weeks before all the birds were gone. Puffins were still surrounding the house, returning from the sea with metallic rainbows of fish shimmering in their beaks. There were kittiwakes too, and while the cliffs still echoed with their calls the island remained steeped in the sound of summer.

Even when most of the birds were gone, the lingering kittiwakes made the cliffs seem spectacularly alive. Unlike other cliff-nesting birds, which settled for the cold, hard surfaces of ledges and crevices in the rock, kittiwakes built the most elaborate nests. In spring, they flew to the island's ponds to gather mud and grass, which they somehow cemented to the vertical cliff face. Through the most laborious process of construction, strand by strand, they created impossible, gravity-defying structures that clung to the stone facades, looking like miniature haystacks.

In the earliest stages of nest building the sheer drop of the cliff offered an almost unattainable starting point. I always remembered the first time I watched a kittiwake as it attempted to augment the first rudimentary scraps of nest already glued into place. It flew with grass streaming from its beak, trying to return to the little tuft of tangled vegetation on the side of the cliff. Over and over again it circled, scrabbling at the air with its feet as it tried to grasp the nest site, wings stretched out behind battling to hold itself steady against the emptiness. But each time, it lost its balance and fell away, swooping through the sky as it doubled back for another approach. I had no idea how many attempts had failed before the kittiwake finally made contact with the cliff but, in that moment of success, I saw the precious streamers of grass fall from its beak to flutter slowly and silently down to the sea.

The finished nests were a triumph. In the face of wind and rain and scorching sun, they remained throughout the summer, clasping defiantly above the giddying waves. The chicks that broke free from the eggs blundered into a precarious existence. After all the engineering work to hold the nest in place, the space left for occupation was more of a dented platform than a deep, protective cup.

The kittiwakes filled the Wick with noise and excitement. Brief periods of stillness were swept aside by intense flurries of activity. One of the best places on the whole island was to be on the slabs looking across at the intricately carved rock face, and letting these great waves of exultation wash over us. Every few minutes, clouds of birds came pouring out from the cliffs, swirling round the inlet several times before settling again. These blizzards were accompanied by explosions of calls. The kittiwake's cry is an attempt at its own name, with a long, drawn-out emphasis on the last syllable. Every call was magnified and repeated as it reverberated against the hard surfaces of rock and water. A hundred birds could sound like a thousand, as their shouts blended into the dramatically atmospheric harmony echoing from the cliffs.

The summer had been an uneventful one, without any extremes of weather, until August. The wind began to gather strength, and, though barely more than a stiff breeze, it came as a definite intrusion to the pattern of summer days. It coincided with the Fastnet Race, a yachting event that would normally have passed unnoticed as far as I was concerned. A couple of days after the slow building of the wind, there was a violent and unpredicted change in the weather. Within hours, the breeze had become a full-grown storm, with gusts of seventy to eighty miles an hour screaming across the island. The hundreds of yachts that had entered the race had reached the part of the course that stretched between the Scilly Isles and the Fastnet Rock, off the south-western tip of Ireland; not exactly close to us, but close enough to be sharing the same weather systems.

The Fastnet Race was instantly news. In the appalling conditions yachts were turning over or breaking up. Literally dozens of people had been plunged into the waves and were fighting to survive for long enough to be rescued. It was one of the rare times that I felt we were being directly touched by the news that came in from outside. Usually, we ran side by side with the real world, in a sort of parallel existence. Although I listened avidly to the radio, my perception of the news had changed, and the things I heard felt increasingly remote. If I saw pictures in newspapers I found them almost too unnervingly authentic.

This time, I didn't need a newspaper or a television to see the horror of the news reports. I only had to go outside to feel the battering, salt-sticky wind and see the waves breaking the surface of the sea into huge, jagged wedges. I knew what it was to be in a boat staring at the slow-motion power of a storm, and it was among the few truly terrifying experiences of my life.

From one of the more sheltered hollows on Skomer Head we looked out across the endless succession of waves. Their size was unfathomable with nothing to give them a sense of scale. The distance was softened by the mirage of salt-haze hovering like steam above the sea. For a long time we watched this beguilingly hypnotic rhythm in silence, as though leaving would be another small abandonment of all those lost at sea. I felt numb with sadness and disbelief. Finally, we began to walk back along the south coast. When we reached the Wick we found the inlet washed with spray. The nebulous froth had turned into something thick and solid, engulfing the surface of the water until there was nothing but whiteness. We had seen seas like that in winter, but never before in summer.

As the waves lumbered slowly, determinedly in from the sweeping wilderness of water, they appeared to grow in size against the perspective of the cliff. They came crashing into the open mouth of the Wick, each one creating an arc of water that swept in a smooth, continuous roll along the perpendicular rise of rock. The waves were compressed as the inlet narrowed, forcing the twisting surge of water to swell higher and higher up the cliff. The kittiwakes had built their nests far enough above the sea to escape the worst summer weather, but this storm was not something that experience had taught them to prepare for.

Birds sat stoically protecting their young as the waves licked to the very base of their refuge. It was a rising tide and, every so often, one outsized wave reached up into the cluster of nests, where some of the last remaining chicks were not yet ready to fly. In the moment that the nests, and their flightless occupants, were snatched away, fountains of birds rose up to safety though spangled droplets. The kittiwakes showed unwavering courage, waiting with their chicks until they were within a heartbeat of death, but, in the end, there was nothing they could do.

Almost imperceptibly, the waves crept further up the cliff, ruthlessly shaving away the nests, and in their wake everything was washed clean: no crusted stains of white, no debris of nests, just the obliteration of a whole summer. The cries of the birds were all but lost in the tangled roar of wind and water, but occasionally the sharpness of their wails cut through. And in those faint echoes I imagined that I could hear the sound of anguish.

But those were tiny catastrophes, insignificant compared to what was happening further out to sea. As the winds died down and the waves subsided, it emerged that more than a hundred and thirty competitors from the Fastnet Race had been rescued and fifteen drowned. For us, to watch from the periphery was one of the saddest and most sobering of experiences. Yet it was not an exceptional storm, simply sudden and unexpected in its ferocity, and, above all, out of its season, coming at a time when people, and even birds, were trusting in the weather to be a little more benign. It was a reaffirmation of what Skomer had already taught me, that the ultimate power of the sea lay in its unpredictability.

We had grown used to seeing the vegetation shrivelled into premature winter by the arrival of storms, but it was a new experience to see the birds swept away and to hear the effervescent calls of the kittiwakes abruptly cut off. We should have been able to see the scattering of birds gradually dwindle and to listen for the last lonely cries drifting among rocks. The promise of the final days of summer still to come had been taken away.

It left me watching more anxiously than ever for the arrival of the first seal pups. Once the seal season was underway, there could be nothing quite as spine-tingling as a visit to Seal Cave. This was an inlet with a tiny, inauspicious entrance in South Haven that opened out beneath the Neck into a surprisingly large cavern. My first visit there remains imprinted in my mind as one of those truly unforgettable moments of discovery. I have far fewer of those than I should; Skomer felt so immediately like home that most of my memories are ones of belonging rather than discovering.

The descent to the cave from the grassy slopes above was neither steep nor difficult, but for me it was particularly unnerving. The slab of vertical rock that formed the last short section of the route was running with water, sending a glossy film oozing over the glutinous green weed that coated the stone. I was unfazed by heights, but had a very low tolerance for slime. I couldn't bear anything unpredictable that threatened to snatch the ground from underneath my feet and throw it crashing up into my face. I lowered myself cautiously over the edge of the bank and down onto the sheer rock, feeling with my toes for any barely perceptible crevice in the stone which might give me some sort of grip. This painstakingly slow procedure was not helped by Mike's impatience. As someone whose feet clung to stone surfaces as if by some peculiar form of magnetism, he was immune to anything green and slithery, and baffled by my need to remain flattened against the rock face as I inched downward.

By the time I reached the shingly floor of the inlet my legs felt weak, like they had been deprived of some of the more important bones. Daylight disappeared as we walked into the tunnel that formed the entrance to the cave, forcing me to focus on the sounds coming from deep inside. Everything was amplified by the great hollow space in the rock, so that we could hear the seals breathing quite clearly, even though they were still some way off. The most disturbing thing was the fact that the sounds were so human. A comical shudder of snoring competed with the sort of agonized wailing that might come from some dank dungeon. The whole symphony was punctuated by the occasional heart-rending baby-cry of a pup. Any attempt at a stealthy approach was hopeless; in the resonant stillness our feet crunched forcefully over the pebbles of the narrow passageway.

The entrance we were using was also one of the seals' routes to the sea.

'If a seal tries to come down here, you'll have to get out of the way quickly,' Mike said. 'It might knock you over in its panic to escape if it feels trapped.'

My hands were touching rock walls on either side of the tunnel as I groped my way forward. There wasn't exactly a great deal of space.

'Get out of the way where?' I asked.

'Climb up the side. You'll manage if you have to.'

I was scared, and I could feel the fear twisting tighter inside me with each step further into the darkness and closer to the cave. But it was a deliciously exhilarating feeling of terror, the self-inflicted sort that comes from watching a painfully tense film.

After a few more steps, blinking and staring hard, trying to make use of any remaining dregs of light, there was a flare of noisy snarls and hisses. It sounded exactly like the fights I had seen so often on the open beaches. This was followed by the distinctive rhythmic sequence of crashing stones that indicated a seal moving very rapidly. And it was getting louder.

'It's coming this way,' Mike shouted. 'Move!'

I pressed both hands onto the smooth, perpendicular stone beside me and leapt against it. Somehow, my toes found a tiny sliver of a ledge a couple of feet above the ground and I perched there, clinging to the wave-polished rock with my fingertips. As my eyes grew more accustomed to the darkness, I was able to distinguish a dingy blob lumbering through the gloom. It was a huge, male seal throwing itself forward in a series of ungainly pulses, hitting the ground with such force that I could see each impact shudder through its body. For a ridiculous moment I had the feeling that it was charging at us, defending the protected inner sanctum from intruders. In the same instant the thought vanished as the seal thundered past, inches beneath my feet. From such a precariously close distance it was impressive: about eight feet long, with a charcoal-black coat, and solidly muscular neck and shoulders that were grazed with ancient scars. I stared down, knowing that I was as close as I was ever likely to get to such a formidable animal. A few seconds later, we heard a splash as the seal reached the safety of the water. It was obvious that we were not the cause of its fury, but merely bystanders as it fled from a humiliating defeat in some minor scuffle.

'That was amazing,' I said, laughing with relief as I slipped back down to ground level.

We walked on. By the time the tunnel was starting to open out into the cave, the last of the light was gone. The viscous blackness, clinging all around me, made each step feel faintly dangerous. From out of this blank space, a ferocious hissing noise erupted at our feet. I leapt back, and Mike switched his torch on. The beam fell upon the furious face of a fluffy, white seal pup, gargling the most persuasive of threats from deep within its throat.

'Oh dear,' said Mike, with a gentle affection that showed no respect for the pup's rage. 'Have we disturbed you?'

Bravely, the seal held its ground in guarding the entrance to the cave, where an older and wiser animal would have crashed to safety long before we came so close.

We made our way cautiously round the pup, leaving it snarling indignantly, and proceeded into the cave. The combined intensity of noise and darkness smothered my senses, allowing room only for a pricklingly alert anxiety. To avoid unsettling the seals, Mike used the torch only briefly, scanning across the plump, round bodies to make a quick count of the, mainly female, animals clustered into the cave. Then he let the beam brush across the high, curved rock above us. Glimpsing the soaring, domed roof for the first time, I felt something of the spiritual awe that comes from standing at the heart of a great creation.

We left almost immediately so as not to intrude any further into a place that so obviously belonged to the seals. Although we needed to go to the cave regularly to check on the pups, our visits were fleeting and strictly rationed to prevent unnecessary disturbance. This meant that the experience of each visit was heightened by a sense of anticipation. Even so, to my disappointment, it was impossible to recapture the fizzing aura of terror that accompanied my first visit. The mystery of the unknown was gone forever. The descent came to seem simple and the darkness, full of hidden sounds, no longer held me in a state of fearful suspense.

Eventually, it became so unthreatening that I was happy to make my way down to the cave alone when meetings on the mainland took Mike away from the island for a week or so each winter. In fact, I slightly revelled in the rebellion of doing something illicit. The most unsettling aspect, as I slunk into the darkness, was not fear of the cave but the knowledge that Mike would be appalled by these solitary expeditions. I eased my conscience by leaving an explanatory note on the kitchen table, which would be found if I failed to return. Afterwards, I took a guilty pleasure in crunching up the note and throwing it away, so that Mike need never know where I had been.

Since we could rarely go into the cave, I liked to sit on the cliff top at high tide above the water-filled entrance, watching the seals drifting in and out. This was particularly good on still, clear September days, when the water was deep-blue, hard and glittering, like a gemstone. Somehow, the sea swallowed up the light and drew it down into the shaded tunnel so that the water turned pale, radiant turquoise in contrast to the twilight. This luminescence shone out from within the seawater, spreading rippled waves of brightness over the shadowed stone archway above. Seals, gliding close by, with their noses above the water, or turning slow, exultant somersaults, were sometimes almost lost amid the searing white pools of molten sunlight that flowed around them sending dazzling sparks glinting into our eyes.

After the end of the first week in September we were unlikely to see anyone else on the island, and, if the weather was not too severe, September and October could be idyllic months. Once we were into November, our sense of isolation began to harden. Short days and bad weather made the process of being alone more serious, and yet, with each passing year, we came to love the winter a little more. We had grown to thrive on the challenges that made the summer seem uncomfortably safe by comparison. It was in the bleakness, the wildness, the need to draw on undiscovered depths of self-reliance, that we found a true understanding of island life.

Isolation can be the most secure feeling imaginable. There was never any need to lock our door. If we were out walking, coats, cameras or binoculars could be abandoned anywhere and collected again hours later. But if something broke our established patterns, the mere fact of being so alone intensified any drama. If anything should go wrong, particularly at night or in bad weather, we had no hope of immediate help. Mike used to play on this fact by arranging unexpected events to catch me out. It was an area where my sense of humour ran dry; I really couldn't see the funny side of a practical joke.

While I was cooking the evening meal, Mike, normally so devoid of patience, could find the perseverance to conceal himself almost indefinitely in the larder for the pleasure of leaping out at me, with his eyes rolling grotesquely, as I opened the door to find the next ingredient. He did this just rarely enough that I never remembered it might happen, and the sense of shock was always infuriating.

When he bought a new torch, Mike discovered that it could be set with a time delay, after which it would begin to emit a red flashing light. This was too much for him to resist.

'I'm just going next door,' He called as I was preparing dinner.

'Okay,' I replied, and I heard the door slam ostentatiously as he left.

'Next door' was the now-deserted laboratory, which Mike annexed in the winter as a woodworking studio. Soon after he left I began to have the uncomfortable sensation that there was something behind me. I turned round to see waves of eerie red light washing down the hallway. I paused for a moment to think of a logical explanation and then I called out Mike's name. No answer. I was on my own. I peered anxiously through the glass door into the hall. The light continued to pulse, making everything throb weakly red. Steeling myself, I opened the door and crept cautiously out into the hall where, at once, I saw the torch standing brazenly at the far end of the passage.

I stormed out of the front door and through the darkness, until I was blinking into the gaslights of the laboratory.

'Look,' I raged. 'That sort of thing isn't funny. You frightened the life out of me.'

But with the two of us standing there, safely cocooned among the scented wood shavings, my anger was already beginning to feel slightly ridiculous.

With the most elegant poetic justice, Mike's practical joke came back to haunt him only a few days later. One of the first good storms of the winter was building and I had gone to bed some time after midnight, lulled to sleep by the sound of the house creaking in the wind. Mike had stayed up, still wide-awake; the short November days were beginning to unsettle our sleeping patterns. I was too deeply asleep to have any idea of how much time had passed when I heard Mike whispering loudly from the bedroom doorway.

'Are you awake?' he hissed.

'No,' I said. And then added for the sake of authenticity, 'Not very.'

'I'd like you to come and look at something.'

'What now? Do I have to?'

'I think you should.'

I heaved myself reluctantly out of bed, following Mike, in my bare feet, across the polished floorboards to the cold kitchen lino. He stood by the open window staring out. I stared too. At first there was nothing. Then my gritty eyes focused on a small, intense light, flashing on the far side of North Haven.

'Can you see it?' Mike asked.

'Yes.'

'Thank goodness for that. I thought I must be imagining it.'

My initial jolt of fear had been tempered by the suspicion that this was another trick, but as soon as Mike spoke I could tell that he was genuinely scared. As the sleep cleared from my head it became obvious that he couldn't possibly have staged anything so elaborate.

'What could it be?' I asked, my throat beginning to feel uncomfortably tight.

'I don't know. I can't come up with a logical explanation.'

With the light adrift in an infinite darkness, it was difficult to pin it down to any specific location. After a lot of staring through binoculars, we decided that the beam was coming from Rye Rocks, the reef that ran across the north-eastern entrance to North Haven. It wasn't stationary, but wavering back and forth, and flicking on and off.

'It looks like someone waving a torch,' I said.

'It couldn't be. Even if someone was in trouble out there, they'd never get onto Rye Rocks in this storm. They'd be smashed to pieces.'

The possibility of a shipwreck seemed remote. We almost never saw a boat at that time of year; all the small boats were taken out of the water before the worst of the winter weather.

'What are we going to do?' I asked.

'I'll call the coastguard. Maybe they'll know something.'

Mike called Milford Haven. It was three in the morning, and the answering voice sounded slightly startled by this intrusion into the silent hours. I found it surprisingly comforting to hear that there was someone else out there, beyond the dense blackness that surrounded us.

'We have a light in North Haven,' Mike said into the radio, sounding deceptively calm and detached. 'Do you have any reports of anything happening?'

The fact that the coastguard was as baffled as we were was predictable, but unexpectedly disappointing. It was our only tenuous hope of an easy solution and, with that gone, I felt frighteningly alone.

'Well,' Mike said. 'We'll have to go and find out what it is.'

I dressed quickly, shivering with cold anxiety as I pulled on layers of jumpers, while Mike gathered up torches, flares and the portable radio.

As soon as we were outside, I could see goat eyes glowing red in the torch-light. Wellington had been instantly alerted by the sound of the front door, and immediately sensed the electrifying atmosphere of tension. The kids were tumbling round our feet, like puppies eager for a walk. We shrugged them aside and broke into a run. The goats came too.

The whole thing had an almost unbearable sense of urgency, mainly because I knew that the light didn't exist. There was no explanation for a light on the cliffs in the middle of a winter storm and, therefore, it couldn't be there. Logic told me that if the light wasn't real it would vanish before we reached it, simply melt away if we came too close. And I didn't want to live through the longest, darkest nights of winter with the unknown right outside my house, wondering what it was and waiting for it to come back. We needed to find it before it could get away, because that was the only way we would have peace of mind.

Normally, we avoided using torches if we were walking at night, preferring to let our eyes grow accustomed to the darkness so that we had a complete, if very dim, picture. That night there was no time to wait. Our surroundings were narrowed to the disorientating strobe of torchlight, as the beams lurched crazily in time to our footsteps. The wind was so strong that it was hard to run against it. Every step was like wading through water. Boojum and Snark were revelling in the adventure, running with us, pressing themselves so close that our legs became tangled with theirs. The wildness of the storm was stirring Wellington into a frenzy. She was racing ahead and then spinning round to confront us, rearing up on her hind legs, horns tossing from side to side. Her horned head with blazing red eyes had an unnerving look of evil.

'Get out of the way, Wellington,' I said crossly, pushing her aside as she lunged forward to butt me.

The push was received as a welcome response to her challenge, encouraging her to rear and throw her head in elaborate display, while managing to land the occasional bruising jab with her horns. And she got away with it, because we were both too distracted to stop her.

A couple of times I jarred my ankles slipping into burrows, but I carried on running, barely noticing the interruptions. I was finding it hard to breathe, because the wind was smothering my face and my chest was tight with exertion, or maybe panic. I didn't have enough breath left to speak, but I didn't need to. I knew exactly what Mike was thinking, and he understood precisely what was on my mind. We were remembering the time earlier in the year when the coastguard had seen a light on the island. It had haunted us to the point where it had become easier to dismiss it as some sort of optical illusion. Now that we had both seen this one, we would never be able to make it go away.

We reached a place on the cliff top that was as close as we could get to the light, which, instead of fading, had grown larger and clearer and brighter at our approach. We sank breathlessly to our knees and stared down. The light was vividly, undeniably there, suspended in the blackness, glinting against the surf, and yet we were no nearer to understanding what it was. From that distance its movement was much more clearly defined as it swept back and forth in an arc. In my mind, now, I could almost see someone holding it, swinging it at arm's length above his head, but through the darkness I could pick out nothing but that mesmeric spark. I had thought only of reaching the light and seeing what it was, but now that we were there, the mystery remained tantalisingly, hopelessly unresolved.

'What now?' I asked, feeling weak with exertion and dismay.

Mike called the coastguard for permission to fire a parachute flare. In a moment we would be able to see everything. The flare went shooting upwards with a noise like the air being ripped apart, and then exploded into the most dazzlingly clear, white light. The parachute opened and the light was suspended briefly. The bay flashed into view with startling clarity. My eyes, so used to the dark, blinked involuntarily at the painful brilliance. As I was starting to make out the shapes of the rocks below us, the darkness cut across them, like a black curtain falling back into place, as the flare burnt itself out. All that was left was the single point of brightness flicking teasingly through the dark.

'Did you see anything?' Mike asked.

'No,' I admitted miserably.

Mike sent another flare cutting into the sky. Our eyes were prepared this time for the abrupt cascade of light. The flare didn't seem so blindingly brilliant, and we were able to make use of the brief window of illumination. I saw the rocks, surrounded by surf, with the light swaying above them. In fact, I seemed to be staring at it, blankly, for ages before our artificial daylight fizzled out.

'What was it?' I asked

'Some sort of buoy with an intermittent beam attached to a long metal pole. It's obviously broken free from somewhere in the gales. It must have been carried for miles before it got caught up here.'

Mike called the coastguard to update them on this unexceptional discovery. In a state of dull inertia, we sat on the cliff still staring at the mysterious light, which had become instantly so mundane, wondering how it could ever have inspired such fear. It was perhaps four in the morning, but the surge of anxiety had left us uncomfortably detached from any thought of sleep. What should have been relief felt more like disappointment. As the light continued to pulse, suspended above the waves, we wandered slowly back home, and the goats, exhausted by the excitement, trailed reluctantly in our wake.

TEN

That winter was the last time we had to endure the bad-tempered spitting of the open fire. We demolished the dreary, grey-tiled fireplace and replaced it with a mellow quarry tile hearth and a wood-burning stove. For such a small change, it was remarkably life-enhancing. The only drawback was that the warmth of the living room highlighted the bleak chill in the rest of the house. The bathroom, by comparison, felt like an Arctic tundra, and I could only face slithering between the cold bed sheets by curling myself up in a tight knot so that my toes didn't have to explore the uncharted territory at the bottom of the bed.

Although the spring could still be cold, the wood-burning stove had to be reluctantly abandoned as the days lengthened. The light evenings kept us busy outside, and by the time I had cooked and we had eaten, it was too late to think of lighting the stove. But I missed it and, though we rarely found time to sit in the living room, I used to sneak in regularly to give the stove an admiring glance. The object of all this affection was an oblong, cast-iron box on legs, in matt, velvety black, decorated with Norwegian landscapes that were so ugly as to be beautiful.

One day, during one of these reveries, I was convinced that I heard a noise coming from the stove. I peered inside and saw nothing but a layer of cold ash. At the same time, the noise stopped, so I closed the door of the stove and forgot about it. But the next time I passed the room, the sound was unmistakable: a sort of scrabbling, animally noise. I crawled round the room, listening in corners, until I was persuaded that the wood-burning stove was the only possible source of the sound. I looked inside, shining a torch into every corner, while the faint haze of ash drifted in the beam. There was only silence and a glaring emptiness.

That evening, the noise was still there and the stove was still empty. I called Mike and he searched and he listened from all angles, and finally he agreed with me that there was a distinct sound emerging from the stove.

'There's only one place left to look,' Mike said. 'I'll have to take the whole top off.'

As he did so, a ball of soot erupted from inside and shot across the room. It was only when it came to rest that I recognised the completely black puffin. Like a magician's box, the stove appeared empty, but there was a tiny hidden compartment above the water heater at the top, which was revealed as Mike dismantled the stove. The puffin made a panicky attempt to fly towards the window, sending flurries of soot across the room, which, in honour of the wood-burning stove, had been freshly decorated in shades of dirt-magnet cream and finished with painstakingly hand-sewn ivory-coloured curtains.

Seeing our hard work about to be blackened, Mike launched himself with almost dizzying speed and caught the bird on his first lunge, folding its wings carefully back into place to prevent it from hurting itself. Once we were outside we dusted the puffin down and found that it was unharmed. Mike liberated the bird above the cliff, and it sped away as though some terrifying predator was on its tail. For a few moments the charcoal-black bird stood out from all the others; then it splashed down onto the sea where it was almost instantly clean again.

'I hope it'll be a bit more careful next time it goes exploring strange holes,' Mike said.

'Poor thing,' I agreed. 'It must have thought that it had found the ultimate burrow when it saw our chimney pot.'

Given the remoteness of our situation, it was surprising how much we seemed to be accepted as part of the community. Marloes, our nearest village, about three miles inland from Martin's Haven, was one of those places that had a way of enveloping everyone within its environs and tucking them securely under its wing. It was odd, though, to realise that some of the kindness we were shown stemmed from a faint sense of pity. While I still woke every morning to look out of the window with a feeling of wonder that I really had found myself living in this most perfect of all places, many of those across the water on the mainland believed that we had drawn life's short straw. They saw our existence, without television or human company, shops or even electric light, as one of extreme deprivation. Their sympathy was translated into tangible compensations. Thanks to the local people, we knew exactly how the seasons were progressing through mainland gardens. We enjoyed the first of the prized Pembrokeshire new potatoes, followed in succession by tomatoes, runner beans, plums and apples, which arrived in parcels slipped to the boatman. The only sad thing as far as we were concerned was that it was a one-way trade. We seemed always to be on the receiving end of other people's generosity, with nothing to give back.

If there were to have been a point of conflict, it should, perhaps, have been with the local fishermen. Logically, we were directly opposed; they wanted access to the best fishing grounds close in to the island, while we wanted the cliffs and their breeding birds to be left undisturbed. In reality, there never was a problem. Only two fishermen worked their boats regularly around Skomer, Jim Aldred and Skip Rudder. Jim was quiet, gentle and extraordinarily hardworking, while Skip was outgoing, full of fun, with a barely concealed wild streak. Although the two men could hardly have been more different, they were united in their love of the sea, and that included the wildlife that surrounded them throughout their working days. They would have hated to cause any disturbance to the cliff-nesting birds, and were happy to bide their time, waiting until the cliffs were empty before fishing the more sensitive areas.

We watched with envy as their boats braved the tide races, hauling in the strings of pots with their yield of crabs.

'We should put out some pots of our own,' Mike insisted. 'An occasional crab would certainly improve our diet.'

So, as soon as we had caught enough mackerel to spare some for bait, we set a few pots in the relatively safe waters off North Haven. It was surprisingly hard work hauling pots, hand over hand, inch by inch, swinging them up into our boat with a great gush of seawater, and all we ever saw for our efforts were conger eels, dog fish, or spindly spider crabs, which went back into the sea unharmed.

We bemoaned our lack of success to Jim and Skip.

'Well, what do you expect?' they said, predictably. 'If you use rubbish for bait, you catch rubbish.'

But, instead of showing professional intolerance of the amateur, they graciously handed over a few precious strips of their own bait: pungent morsels of red gurnard bought from Milford Docks. The transformation in our fortunes was astonishing; we actually began to discover proper, edible crabs in the pots. Gradually, the system mutated so that, instead of giving us the bait, Jim or Skip simply baited our pots along with their own whenever they were passing. I often watched the comings and goings of the fishing boats from the cliff top; it was nice to see a friendly presence, even at a distance. I began to notice that if Jim, thinking himself unobserved, lifted one of our pots and found it empty, he would sometimes take a crab from his own catch and slip it into the pot. If Skip was passing he might call to me on the cliff top. When I scrambled down the slope, he brought the boat in close and threw a couple of crabs ashore. I caught them with a suitably appreciative smile on my face that was supposed to disguise my cowardice as the flailing claws came flying towards me.

One morning, we were in the middle of the island when we were surprised to see Jim trudging towards us carrying a large sack on his back. He had found an octopus in one of his pots, and had been so excited by the discovery that he had put it in a damp sack and brought it up to the house to show us. Disappointed at finding no one home, he had set out across the island to find us, taking the octopus with him. I had never seen one before, and was fascinated as it emerged from the sack, an oddly amorphous thing, whose shape seemed to flow and change, while the mottled brown colours melted across it, growing lighter and darker in chameleon fashion. We watched only for a minute or two before returning the strange creature to the sea.

As we walked together back towards North Haven, I was thinking about the way someone like Jim could retain such an incredible love and fascination for the sea and everything in it. The fact that he worked in that environment, sometimes in awful conditions, had done nothing to make it seem commonplace. His relationship with the sea was very much like ours with the island: however much time he spent there, it would always be fresh and exciting.

We had noticed some exceptionally nice scraps of driftwood washing into North Haven. Mike recognised it as something special even from the cliff top and decided that it was worth taking the dinghy to the far side of the haven to rescue it. Though the planks were small and broken, the wood was mahogany and in much better condition than the battered firewood that usually washed up on our beaches, frayed at the edges into fibrous clumps. We soon discovered that we had found some stray shards from a deck cargo that had been swept overboard from a freighter in a storm. This had sparked a 'Whisky Galore' type frenzy on the mainland, with boat owners and beach combers scouring sea and shore for the valuable timber. Mike was devastated when he realised that fate and the tides had conspired to bring only a few weather-beaten sticks to Skomer. He had a passion for woodwork, but had to make do with waste wood and off cuts. He would never have bought anything like that beautiful West African mahogany.

Skip had been busy chasing the wood, and had managed to collect a nice store of planks. An amnesty was declared, and everyone who had found the wood was told that they could keep it. Mike offered to make a table for Skip; even if he couldn't own such timber, it would be a pleasure to be able to work it. For weeks he devoted all his spare time to it. Without any power tools it was hard, physical work: planing the bruised, dented wood for hours until it ran smooth beneath his fingers, shaping and curving the legs, invisibly joining the heavy planks. When I saw the end result I finally realised why everyone had been so excited by these ragged pieces of scuffed timber. The rich, pinkish-red gloss sank deep into the polished grain giving the patterns an almost three-dimensional quality. It was so magnificent that I was sad to see the table go, though it was almost worth it to see the delight on Skip's face.

The next day Skip came back with a fresh batch of wood: enough for another table for us. Mike began again, laboriously slivering papery coils from the dull wood, while sweat and sawdust trickled over his skin. In the end we had a second, identical, table, although perhaps ours had benefited slightly from the extra practice.

Despite our long periods of isolation there were so many people who shaped our experience of Skomer and made it richer and more rewarding. From our earliest years Chris and Mary Perrins had been a constant presence. In fact, Mike had first met them when he was a teenager on Skokholm. Chris was the Director of the Edward Grey Institute of Field Ornithology in Oxford, and it was mainly his students that came to the island in the summer. He was one of the kindest, most dependable of people, and perhaps the only person I have ever met who seemed to know something about any subject you could mention.

His wife, Mary, was generous, open, endlessly considerate, and one of the few people who truly shared my passion for seals. Over the years we watched their two boys, James and Richard, grow from bright, inquisitive children into unusually pleasant and outgoing teenagers. Preparations for their visits were predictably thoughtful, involving a plentiful supply of cream cakes, fresh fruit from their garden, ice cream for me (buried deep in their luggage among layers of newspaper), a large communal meal to be shared on their first evening, and perhaps a rare book that they had managed to track down for us. The island lit up when they arrived, and we became absorbed into the warm family atmosphere that surrounded them.

Another of the great characters was Dicky Sweet. He came as a voluntary assistant in the aftermath of an appalling road accident that had left him physically and mentally damaged. Still struggling to regain his memory and co-ordination, he returned to Skomer as somewhere he had visited in the past, somewhere that might help to revive his memory. We shared his triumphs and frustrations, applauded his determination never to be beaten by anything, but, most of all, we laughed at his irrepressible sense of humour until the tears streamed down our faces. I shall never forget the lump that came to my throat when he rushed in to show us the first words he had written in the three years since the accident. Skomer was good for Dicky, and he was good for the island.

It seemed that everyone who found their way to Skomer had something special to offer and added to the atmosphere of the island. Among the rigorously hardy outdoor types it was often the slightly more incongruous volunteers that stood out, and perhaps most notable among these were Diana and Gloria. Elegant, refined and wilfully 'un-birdy', they had a no-nonsense practicality which meant that they could turn a hand to anything. Somehow their annual week-long visit always erupted into a seemingly spontaneous, yet carefully orchestrated, party. Their greatest success was organising Christmas, complete with turkey, at the end of summer, in case we missed the real thing.

All things considered, it was incredible how indulgent people were towards us. No one even seemed particularly perturbed by Mike's all-consuming vice, which happened to be wet concrete. He had an insatiable urge to build, and couldn't keep away from the stuff. One of the biggest problems for someone with such ambitions living on an island was transport. It meant that he was forever plotting ways to carry enough materials over from the mainland to fulfil his needs. We grappled with the perils of keeping cement bags dry in the boat and discovered just how full a sand bag could be before it became impossible to lift out of a dinghy with wet, slippery, aching hands.

Mike's most breathtaking feat of excess, however, involved a consignment of concrete blocks. He had one or two major jobs in mind, including rebuilding the boatshed, so he calculated the number of blocks required, and ordered them accordingly. There was an air of happy anticipation as he set off with Terry on the *Arklow* to oversee the delivery of the blocks to Martin's Haven. When he returned early in the evening, the passenger seats had been removed from the deck and the boat was piled high with blocks. Mike finally came ashore, bringing the first dinghy load on to the beach.

'Wow,' I said, as he started passing the blocks. 'You've managed to cram a lot onto the *Arklow*. There can't many left on the mainland.'

'We've hardly started,' he said grimly.

He went on to describe the arrival of an enormous lorry that was barely able to squeeze itself down the narrow track to Martin's Haven. When it reached the beach, the mechanical arm of the lorry lowered one of the stacks of blocks down on to the pebbles. At that point, Mike half expected the lorry to drive away, mission completed. But the arm went back for another stack of blocks, and another, until the entire contents of the lorry had been disgorged at the top of Martin's Haven beach. He never admitted to an error in calculation, but he did claim to have ordered a few spares since it was cheaper to buy in bulk. Whatever the thinking behind it, we had found ourselves with fourteen tons of blocks to be carried down the beach to the dinghy, then ferried out to the *Arklow* and lifted high onto the decks, only to have the process replayed in reverse when the boat reached North Haven.

At such times, it would have been understandable if anyone with a legitimate excuse to be at the farthest corner of the island had taken the opportunity to absent themselves from the dismal proceedings. Strangely, these moments of crisis had exactly the opposite effect. The research students put their essential work on hold and devoted themselves entirely to the problem of the concrete blocks. We couldn't possibly have managed without them. It took a further three days to carry all the blocks across to the island, with the final load of each day coming ashore by torchlight at around eleven o'clock at night.

It was the most terrible, arm-wrenching, knuckle-grazing experience, made worse by the sheer scale of it, the knowledge that each load would be followed relentlessly by another. As the tide sank away, our human chain was drawn out across the beach until we were throwing the blocks from hand to hand, each one jarring against skin and bone. Sometimes, I couldn't understand Mike; it was as though he was constantly seeking out ways to make our life harder. He could never let more than a few months pass without dreaming up some new scheme, each one grander and more daunting than the last.

And then, when it was over, I understood, as I always did in the end. When the last block had come ashore, and we saw the lights of the *Arklow* sliding away over the black, slippery-smooth sea, we were elated. We had achieved, not the impossible, but certainly the highly improbable. It was like climbing a mountain, or any other physical triumph. It wasn't necessarily meant to be enjoyable; the reward came in looking back. After three days, and thousands of blocks, I was delighted that we had done it. And that was why everyone abandoned what they were doing to help. A challenge is compulsive. Who would want to come along when it was over and find themselves on the outside, looking in at what we had achieved? We may not have climbed a mountain, but we had created one, entirely out of concrete blocks.

The trouble with having so many concrete blocks was that they were virtually useless without vast quantities of sand and cement. So we hadn't really reached the summit, just stopped for a rest on the way. But help arrived from an unexpected direction, from the air rather than the sea. We had found ourselves adopted by the RAF station at Brawdy, directly opposite us on the other side of St Brides Bay, about twelve miles away. They had been sending over work parties to spend long weekends helping Mike with another of his great projects, which involved capping the walls of the old farmhouse and buildings, replacing lintels, and generally securing them for the future. At least then they could be preserved as romantic ruins, rather than being allowed to degenerate into heaps of rubble. The real dream, though, was that if they could be frozen in time while their structures were still sound, there was a chance that, eventually, they could be properly restored.

A beneficial side effect of this was that many of the RAF volunteers who came out with the work parties became close friends. When they were off duty, they were ideally placed to catch a lift on a passing helicopter and drop in for coffee. It was during one of these visits that we were chatting to Jim Macartney, a helicopter pilot. Somehow, the conversation had drifted round to the perennial problem of transporting materials to the island. I could almost see the spectacular idea sparking through his mind.

'We spend hours practising with underslung loads,' Jim said. 'It's part of our training. It seems a bit of a waste of time carrying stuff up and down the airfield, when we could be doing something useful like bringing the materials you need out here.'

It was too ridiculously brilliant a solution to have any chance of becoming reality. Life couldn't be that simple.

I should have known better than to doubt Jim. His amiable, soft-spoken manner couldn't disguise the fact that he was one of those people who had a knack of getting things done. It wasn't long before we saw the arrival of the first of many tons of sand and aggregate, packed into old fertilizer sacks which bulged from the underslung net of the helicopter making it look like an enormous, over-stuffed shopping bag. Once the net was deposited on a field in the centre of the island, it meant only a few minutes of furious work to drag the bags clear, ready for the next load.

Nothing can ever be absolutely perfect, though, and even this stunningly efficient procedure had its down side. It meant that the unfortunate aircrew were left with the back-breaking task of loading up the nets on the mainland. We suspected that Jim must have taken an awful lot of flak from his colleagues for coming up with such a bright idea, but he never admitted as much to us.

By the end of the summer, we had a beautiful, block-built shed in North Haven to replace the crumbling, corrugated iron predecessor. Though we referred to it as the boatshed, it was for the engines, flares, life jackets, oars and all the other paraphernalia of boating. I loved the finished building. Outside, it was unprepossessing, being just an oblong structure with windows and a door. The greatest compliment that could have been paid to it would have been to describe it as unobtrusive. Inside, though, it was lovely. Because of the limited space, it was built into the cliff face, so that the fourth wall was made of natural rock. The feeling was of being inside a half-finished sculpture, with smooth, white, artificial walls melting in surreal fashion into the rugged stone.

If so many chance events had not colluded to bring me to Skomer I would probably never have discovered how deeply and intrinsically suited I was to isolation, but it also highlighted a glaring flaw in my personality: I hated boating. Not being in a boat – I loved floating free amid the sound of waves, with the birds and seals so trusting and approachable – but I loathed being dependent on a small boat, with all the practicalities and uncertainties it imposed on us. I came to dread stepping offshore and losing contact with the island: the constant, ill-defined terror that something might prevent me from getting back.

Becoming reliant on that one precarious link was the thing that truly disturbed me as we crossed the threshold from summer into winter, and the fact that Mike so ostentatiously adored everything about boating made me feel more alone with my fears. Over the years we had had so many cross words launching the boat that it was tainted with past history even before we started. The expectation of conflict had become a self-fulfilling prophecy, and we seemed to be left with little choice but to act out our preordained roles. I was glad that the restless weather severely restricted our opportunities for shopping trips, but the time inevitably came when I was forced to brave the sea and everything that entailed.

The moment we reached the boatshed I was fired up and ready to defend myself from unwarranted criticism. The tricky part of the operation began in synthetically polite silence. Lifting one side of the boat trailer each, we swung the boat round the steep curve of the slipway, and then we accelerated on the straight section until we were half running. As we hit the beach I felt the juddering through my bones as the trailer bounced over the pebbles, but it was essential not to lose speed. Then with a startling, bruising jolt the boat slewed sideways and stopped dead. We were jammed hard against a rock: all that precious momentum lost. Mike stomped round to the front of the trailer to see where the wheel was caught, while I nursed my aching hand.

'Oh well, that's it,' he fumed. 'It's stuck solid. We'll never get this moving again.'

Of course, I knew that we would get it moving, we always did, but I also knew that every last step of the way would be a battle with the beach and the rocks.

Despite the relative calm of the sea, there was enough of a surge dragging against the shore to make it impossible for me to hold the boat still. As the waves slid back from the beach the boat was wrenched away from me and then, on the slow, rolling turn of the wave, smashed forward against the rocks.

'Hold it steady,' Mike snapped, as he tried to balance the engine in place at the back of the boat.

'I'm doing my best,' I said, rising to the unreasonable criticism.

The boat made another uncontrolled lurch, grinding against stone with a splintering noise. Mike made some unintelligible exclamation of disgust. It was no good. I couldn't keep the boat off the rocks and stay dry. I took a couple of steps down the shingle slope to get a firm grip closer to the centre of the boat, and I was in control again. On the next wave, a stream of breath-taking cold came flooding down inside my boots. I gasped slightly.

'What on earth did you do that for?' Mike said crossly. 'You'll be soaked all day now.'

'I didn't have much choice. It was either me or the boat. And since I'm obviously the most expendable thing round here . . . '

'All right. We haven't got time for that.'

Hostilities continued until the boat was safely afloat and clear of the rocks, with the outboard motor pushing us gently through the reflections of lichen-bright cliffs.

Mike was in his element, engine humming obediently, boat skimming the water, as he beamed ecstatically round at his little kingdom. He had emerged from under his cloud of ill humour and was doing a very good impression of being an amiable person. I ignored the conciliatory smiles that kept flittering in my direction. I had earned my indignation and had no intention of sacrificing it by indulging in friendly communication. Instead, I stared fiercely down at the water in front of the boat, watching the patterns of colour dissolve away into an endless stream of ripples.

'Do you want to drive?' Mike called temptingly.

I looked up without conveying too much interest and made my way to the back of the boat while maintaining a stance of aloof dignity. The tiller passed from his hand to mine and I perched on the gunwale, gazing into the distance to get a clear view of the way ahead, and to avoid eye contact. The cool breeze trickled over my face, tasting faintly of salt. As we passed Rye Rocks, the basking seals lifted their heads to stare at us. Though I fought against it, a smile twisted the determined set of my lips, and I could no longer pretend to be angry. Mike smiled back at me, looking so genuinely happy that the resentments of boating melted, fleetingly, like the ripples on the water.

There was such a sense of solitude that, at the end of the crossing, it should have been a shock to turn away from the open sea into the calm of Martin's Haven to find someone on the beach waiting for us. Our trips to the mainland were spur of the moment decisions, based on tides and weather, and Martin's Haven is a small, pebbly cove, miles from anywhere, which attracted few visitors in winter. And yet it was not unusual to find Jim Aldred there to meet us, already in place to hold the boat steady as it touched against the shingle.

'What are you doing here?' we asked in amusement, so grateful to see him, as he helped us to unload the gas cylinders.

'Oh, the weather was good this morning, so I had a feeling you might come.'

Of course, he would never mention all the days when he had waited, but no one came.

The October days were bright in the middle, but by mid-afternoon the air had that dull, smoky look of winter, and any illusion of warmth had drained away. I don't know if I was particularly sensitive to the cold, but my horror of an unheated bathroom had never left me since childhood. I couldn't bear climbing out of the warm bath, and sometimes hid under the towel until I had steamed dry, rather than let the air touch my skin. Then central heating had come along and relegated that misery to the past, but the memory of how much I hated it had always stayed strong. Now, here I was, back with the sort of cold, draughty bathroom I thought I had outgrown half a lifetime ago. The laboratory quarters next to the house had a shower, which Mike found very tempting in the winter months when the place was empty. I hated the dark, echoing hollowness of the deserted rooms, and always settled for the slightly greater comfort of our bath.

One evening, Mike disappeared next door for a shower. It was one of those deep black nights, with heavy cloud cover, and a steady breeze blowing: not a gale, but enough to rattle the roof shingles. Once he was gone, I thought that I might as well take the opportunity for a bath. I turned on the taps and watched as the steam wafted thickly into the cold air. Although it left everything running with damp, I hoped that at least it might take some of the chill out of the atmosphere. As I waited for the water to fill the bottom of the bath, I noticed that the seals sounded unusually restless. Their cries echoed from the cliffs and were then carried in on the breeze, so that they seemed to beat against the windows. I turned on the radio and dipped into the shallow water, immersing as much of myself as possible. Gas was too precious to be wasted on heating enough water for a deep bath. I tried to relax, but it was no good. The water was tepid. Once the water temperature outside dropped, the gas heater couldn't cope with the demands of producing a really hot bath.

I gave up any thought of lingering and decided to wash as quickly as I could. Scooping up a handful of water, I poured it down my back to rinse the soap away, shuddering as the rivulets ran like cold fingers over my skin. The noise of splashing water added to the sound of the wind and the seals and the radio, so that I felt slightly smothered, cut off from the outside. I had an uncomfortable feeling that there was something else I should be listening to, something that was trying to force itself through above the other sounds. Then I heard it: definitely not a seal, but a high, wailing human voice. I leapt up, sending a tidal wave of bath water cascading out onto the lino, and switched off the radio. The voice came through loud and clear.

'Help! Help!'

It was Mike.

I grabbed a towel, wrapping it into place as I ran down the hallway. When I stepped outside, the cold slap of night air across my wet skin made me gasp with shock. I proceeded slowly, sliding one foot cautiously in front of the other, feeling for each step in the dark. This gave me an agonizing amount of time to contemplate what I was about to discover. From the desperate sound of Mike's calls I decided it was likely to be something fairly gruesome. The first, rather bizarre, image was of him scalded by the shower, covered in blistered, peeling skin. Then I remembered my tepid bath water and dismissed that idea. There was only one other conclusion: a broken leg. He must have slipped in the shower. If it was only a broken arm, he could have made his own way back home. I groped my way round the corner of the house and, as I left the shelter of its walls, the wind gushed over me, cold as the melt water from a mountain stream. I gasped again, interrupting my mental preparations for calling out the rescue helicopter.

Once I had opened the door of the lab, a faint smudge of light drifting through from the far end of the building allowed me to break into a gentle run.

'Are you all right?' I called.

'No!'

'What's happened?'

I could feel the breath rasping inside my chest.

'The gas cylinder's run out and the shower's gone cold. I'm freezing. Can you change the cylinder for me?'

I was too angry, relieved and cold to think about arguing. I went back outside, feeling my way round to the gas cylinders. The procedure was so routine that I could do it all by touch, but it required two hands to lift the heavy cylinder, and my towel became completely dislodged in the process. It was only then that I wondered why I hadn't told Mike to change his own cylinder.

As I tried to make my way back to the house, I couldn't believe that I had been stupid enough to rush out without a torch. Now that the panic was over, I began to realise how unnerving it was to be marooned in a sea of darkness. Even though my eyes had had time to become accustomed to the dark, I still couldn't distinguish the slightest variation in light and shade. I held my hand in front of my face. Nothing. I blinked my eyes; I couldn't tell if they were open or closed. The dark was spectacular in its completeness. I thought that it must be possible to live an entire lifetime in a world of electricity and street-lights, without ever encountering such intense, impenetrable blackness. I was stranded. There was nothing to be done but shuffle forward, one hand outstretched feeling for obstacles, the other clutching my towel.

I found the cobbled steps leading to the front door quite easily. Their famil-iar, clattery pattern beneath my feet was a comforting reassurance that I had almost made it. I was grasping at the darkness, trying to find the door. It should have been right in front of me. Then the side of my arm hit against the doorframe, and I realised that I was already there, reaching in through the void; in my state of agitation I had raced out leaving the door wide open. Just as I was beginning to feel the relief of being able to step inside, something caused my muscles to lock in terror. I couldn't tell exactly what I had experi-enced, but I knew that someone had moved in the hallway ahead of me. I hadn't seen anything, or heard anything, but the indefinable certainty of another presence was undeniable. My eyes were useless, so I listened hard, but the chaotic thumping of my heart was too distracting.

No matter how much I concentrated, I couldn't find the slightest suggestion that anything was amiss. That only made the situation feel more threatening, since the intruder was obviously hiding deliberately. The urge to be able to stretch out my hand for an electric light switch didn't even occur to me; that was all too far in the past. I didn't know how much longer I could simply stand there shivering, so I tried to convince myself that I had imagined the sensation of movement, even though I knew it wasn't true.

I began to walk into the hallway very cautiously, inch by inch, feeling ahead of me. I was relaxing slightly when my hand touched on something warm and hairy. In that instant, my fingertips deciphered the firmness of bone and the softness of flesh; it was the head of someone crouching low against the wall. A scream cut brutally into the silence, and went on ringing in my ears until eventually I realised that I was the cause of the noise. Above the wail of my own voice I recognised a second sound, the short, staccato rhythm of hooves drumming on floorboards. I knew at once what had happened, and the scream came choking to an abrupt halt.

'Wellington!' There was so much anger and emotion in my voice that the words caught on the inside of my throat. 'Don't you dare come in this house again! Ever!'

But, for once, Wellington seemed to realize the enormity of what she had done. She had slipped past me and out into the night without waiting to be told twice.

When I tried to tell Mike about it later he was blatantly unimpressed, and I could see that the sheer terror of my predicament had failed to register. I suppose you had to be there, standing cold and wet and naked in the dark, to understand. However, I put the incident to good use. On the rare occasions that I recounted the story to amused friends and acquaintances, Mike always squirmed with embarrassment, insisting that he never would have called for help if he had realised I was in the bath. But it seemed a shame to let the minor complication of accuracy spoil such an ideal opportunity to get my own back.

There was a balance in the changing of the seasons: each time one thing was lost, there was something else to take its place. As the birds drifted away, they were replaced almost at once by an influx of seals. The summer weather often ended dramatically with September storms, but the resulting bright, cool air swept aside the persistent heat haze. Even as the evenings started to draw in and the days grew disappointingly short, I was sometimes relieved when the deepening twilight forced Mike to curtail whatever we were working on, and we were allowed to go home for dinner. This equilibrium worked perfectly until late October, and then it fell apart. I hated it when the time came to turn the clocks back. I adapted quite well to the changes of nature, but the abrupt artificiality of losing a whole hour overnight threw everything into confusion. What had been a gradual drift into evening became a black guillotine that sliced off the end of the day. I raged irrationally against the darkness, which always seemed to take me by surprise in coming so soon.

As the years went by, the approach of the end of October played increasingly on my mind. Then, with only a few days to go, I came up with an idea that was so flawless in its simplicity I couldn't believe that it had taken me so long to think of it. I went through it thoroughly in my mind to make sure that there were no obstacles, and when I was convinced that it would work I rushed to tell Mike.

I built up to the subject slowly, so that he would have time to be impressed.

'You know how awful it is every year when the clocks go back, and it starts getting dark in the middle of the afternoon, and the gas lights feel really gloomy?' I asked.

'Yes . . .' Mike said vaguely, as though he might actually have forgotten.

'Well, we don't have to do it any more.'

'What do you mean?'

'We don't do it. We keep our clocks on Summer Time all winter. I mean, there's no reason why we should have to change our clocks just because everyone else does.'

'Don't be ridiculous.'

'What's ridiculous about it?'

'Well, it wouldn't work, for a start.'

'Why wouldn't it work? Give me one good reason why it wouldn't work.'

Of course, he didn't have any reasons, which was probably why he refused to discuss the subject. I was disappointed to see my scheme collapse without a fair trial, but Mike was so uncharacteristically and vehemently opposed to it that I felt compelled to let it drop.

When the day came to change the clocks, I began to realise that there was hope, after all. Mike had forgotten, and I certainly wasn't going to remind him. The critical point came and went, and, while the rest of the country suffered the gloom of GMT, we were still basking in Summer Time. After a couple of days, something (it could only have been the radio) alerted Mike to the fact that we were out of step. He was unexpectedly cross.

'You did that on purpose, didn't you?' he fumed.

I could only grin sheepishly, since a lie would have been completely transparent. He stomped across the room, took the kitchen clock off the wall, and began to alter the time. I watched with growing amazement as the hands moved, not back an hour, but forward.

'There, that's better,' he said, replacing the clock on the wall.

The situation was becoming wonderfully ludicrous, and I knew that I was going to get the blame. I wondered if I dared go along with it, and decided that I did. Mike took off his watch and advanced that, too, by an hour.

'You should do the same,' he said, in case I was harbouring any thoughts of rebellion.

We now had our clocks and watches efficiently synchronised two hours out of line with the rest of country. It didn't matter at all. Mike didn't even seem to find it odd that the evenings had grown lighter rather than darker.

It became a challenge on my part to see how long I could keep him from discovering the truth. It helped enormously that he had no sense of time. He was the sort of person who could 'pop out for five minutes' and return two hours later, convinced that only a few minutes had passed. When he finally realised, three days later, he wasn't quite cross enough not to see the funny side. I never did find out why he was so opposed to the idea in the first place, but I had managed to undermine all his arguments. If he had failed to notice a discrepancy of two hours, the trifling matter of an hour was hardly going to make any difference. So, from then on, we stayed on Summer Time (or Skomer Time, as it became known) and I felt much happier for it.

In the matter of storms, there was a fine line between the exhilarating and the unnerving. There was almost nothing better than a good storm from the right direction, when the sea turned white, and to walk along the cliff top filled me with high-spirited energy. But a shift of even a few degrees in the wind direction could turn a good storm into a threatening one. Just as good storms were invigorating, bad ones were draining; they made me feel anxious and unsettled.

That November, it was a case of a good storm turning into a bad one. It started as a westerly, the best winter wind as far as I was concerned. Soft and mild, the westerlies had all the reach of the open Atlantic to build the sea into deep, powerful waves, but while the storm raged outside, the house was sheltered. Even when the wind gathered so much strength that we could hear it screaming above our heads, the house remained becalmed in a pocket of tranquillity. After three days with the wind touching storm force, the sea had been heaped into mounds like ranks of small hills. The slow determination in these lumbering slopes of water was like a taunting assertion of the power trapped inside them. From the house, we watched them pour in spellbinding succession across the front of North Haven, but the waves couldn't reach right into the bay. Only a little of their strength escaped into the shelter of the haven, where the water undulated with a swell so smooth that it was barely visible until it smashed against the cliffs and dissolved into foam.

On the fourth day, the wind turned to the north, flipping round onto the most exposed face of the house. This combination of weather gave us the worst of all options. The waves were already there, bloated by days of storms, and now the wind was pushing them straight into North Haven. The cliffs that curved around the bay were dwarfed by the impossible size of the waves as they broke against the land, overwhelming everything in a convulsion of spray. Above the wind, I could hear the constant dragging and clattering of sea against shingle: the lingering explosion of surf, and then the rasping intake of breath as the water was sucked back to make way for the next wave.

Late in the evening, the sounds changed. Waves were no longer rolling onto the beach and diffusing their power against the gentle incline. The turbulent incoming tide had met the irresistible stillness of the cliff. Each collision between these two opposing forces resulted in a clash that welled up with the resonance of thunder. Whether it shook the air or the earth I couldn't tell, but I could feel the shock of each blast running through me like a faint buzz of electricity.

Mike couldn't stand any more inactivity.

'I'm going out to look at the boat,' he said.

The boat was tight under the cliff above the landing beach, and tied down with an intricate network of ropes. When Mike returned the news was bad.

'The tide's still coming in, and the waves are breaking over the boat. I think we're going to lose it.'

It is almost impossible to explain how awful those words sounded. The boat was our lifeline, our only physical link with the outside.

'There must be something we can do,' I said.

'I don't think so, but we could go down and have a look.'

Outside, the touch of the wind stinging with sea spray, the smell of damp earth and crushed seaweed, made the whole thing more frighteningly real. I couldn't see anything beyond the narrow stripe of the torch beam as it snagged against the glittering, salty air. Mike stopped and took a rope from the bundle he was carrying. He tied it round his waist and then began to slip another loop round mine. It was only an illusion of safety: perhaps all it meant was that if one of us was lost we would go together.

As we walked down towards the sea, Mike ahead of me disappearing into the dark, the sound of a wave came like the roar of an approaching avalanche, all-consuming, shutting out everything else. Then the noise was everywhere, directionless, unfathomable: water was drumming down on us, hard and cold and startling. As the wave subsided, we glimpsed the boatshed in the torchlight and it was obvious that we were almost too late. Foam was swilling all around, licking at its base. We held back, timing our moment as the dense spume dragged itself back to rejoin the ocean. As we were darting forward into the fleeting lull we heard it coming. There was a great roar of energy coupled with the swoosh of pebbles flowing against each other like liquid. Then came an impact so solid that I felt it shuddering through the ground. I could see the leading edge of the wave coming towards me, sparkling in the torch beam. It reared up above us and on into the darkness.

'Run!' yelled Mike.

He slid the bolt on the boatshed door and we tumbled inside. The crash came immediately, way above our heads, as the wave collided with the cliff face behind the shed. The water was full of pebbles picked up from the beach. It sounded like a lorry load of gravel being tipped from the cliff top down onto the shed roof. The noise went on and on pouring down, as the wave that had broken over us continued to fall back to earth.

We were trapped: it was a long and unnerving hour, watching through the window as the boat was tortured by the waves, before we could risk opening the door. Despite being swamped by the sea, the ropes anchoring the boat had held. Our brave mission to save it had ended in failure but, fortunately, the boat had survived without our help.

Almost as soon as we left the shed, the thick clouds peeled back from the sky to reveal a brilliant disc of moon. The wind was moving the clouds so fast that the change was almost instant. We emerged from our cramped tunnel of torchlight, and found ourselves looking out across the whole of North Haven. Everything was waterlogged; streams of swollen droplets drizzled noisily from the cliff behind us, and a thin film of salt water shimmered beneath our feet as it flowed determinedly back towards the sea.

The moonlight made it look so beautiful. The strangeness of the light gave everything an unfamiliarity that showed the landscape as something new and exciting. The silver-grey sea seemed to be piled high in the bay, higher, I thought, than I had ever seen it before. The stream of white surf that pummelled the cliffs had an intensity that made it appear to glow with a faint luminescence.

As we walked back up the path, I felt elation that was almost a physical lightness. Such solid darkness is oppressive; it crushes you with its weight, making every movement slow and clumsy, magnifying the threat of every sound and sensation. Now, that pressure was lifted away and the island was, once more, glitteringly, spectacularly safe. It was the ever-changing, unpredictable Skomer that I loved so much.

ELEVEN

By the end of winter, it looked as though the island had been stripped bare. The months of wind and rain and salt-spray crushed everything that had thrived through the gentler days of summer. All trace of the previous year was gone, and Skomer was waiting to make a fresh start. This emptiness uncovered the island's deeper layers, highlighting the underlying patterns of its history. I felt acutely aware of the island's past, of the people who had gone before me. It was both a sadness and a comfort to know that in the story of Skomer I would be gone in the blink of an eye.

The past was everywhere. I only had to look towards The Neck to see the ridge of an ancient promontory fort. Every day, when I went to Castle Bay to check the seals, I crossed over it, almost oblivious of its presence. And yet sometimes, when it was at its most imposing, with the low winter sun marking it out in stark contrasts of light and shade, I was struck again by a sense of awe at being surrounded by the fragments of so many different lives stretching back over thousands of years.

One of the things we most enjoyed about Skomer was the people that it attracted. It wasn't just about wildlife. Experts in a variety of fields were drawn to the island, and true enthusiasts invariably inspired us with their excitement, until we began to share some of that passion for the subject. We particularly looked forward to the visits of the archaeologist John Evans and his students from Cardiff University. He always found time to take us round and show us what they were studying. There was nothing to see in the practical sense, since their methods involved only meticulous examination, with no digging or moving of anything, but it was an unforgettable experience to be part of that atmosphere of discovery, listening as the theories were being formulated. It made me realise what an exceptional place Skomer was, almost unique in the completeness of its prehistoric landscape, which remained undisturbed over much of the island.

And when the archaeologists were gone, my perspective on the surroundings that I had thought to be so resolutely familiar would be subtly changed. I saw things that had never been there before. My little island, that seemed fully occupied by two of us, may once have supported as many as two hundred. The lives of these farming communities were laid out in detail beneath my feet, and I had walked over them countless times without noticing. There were some wonderful examples of prehistoric hut circles (probably Iron Age) which were obvious even to me, but, where they had once stood in isolation, I gradually saw unfolding around them the patchwork of enclosures and field systems.

There was hardly any part of the island that didn't show evidence of its former occupation. The roofless farmhouse, with the spikes of its gable ends jabbing into the sky, was simply the most obvious presence, creating an image that dominated the centre of the island, while around it fields dating probably from the eighteenth and nineteenth centuries chequered the land. These 'modern' fields were wide and open; some were still smooth and grassy, only gradually being reclaimed by the swarms of dishevelled vegetation that invaded stealthily from all sides. Their neat, well-built walls had suffered little from the passage of time. Each field had its own name; even the sound of Calves Park or Well Meadow was a hauntingly poetic evocation of the past, while some of the others, like Abyssinia and Banshee Corner, were far more intriguingly exotic.

The new fields overlaid more ancient systems. Walking away from the farmhouse out towards the edge of the island was like stepping back in time. When we reached the remoter areas, we had travelled thousands of years into the past. The remains of smaller prehistoric fields could still be clearly seen; the walls that divided them were more haphazard: ridges of larger stones, with banks of earth at their core. In recent centuries, much of the useful stone had been re-used, and untold generations of rabbits had burrowed into them causing them to crumble, slowly obliterating the painstaking labours of my long-forgotten predecessors.

A wall is such an unremarkable thing, but on the island they felt like some of my strongest links to the past. I was enthralled by the line of stones that stretched across the tip of Skomer Head. To my uneducated eyes this wasn't really a wall at all, but a procession of boulders running side by side. Between each enormous stone there was a gap wide enough to walk through. They served no obvious function, perhaps marking only a ritual boundary, but the line may once have been complete, with the smaller stones between the boulders later being robbed. The sheer size of the remaining chunks of rock left me intrigued to know how and why such efforts had been made to lay them so precisely across the island. But it didn't matter that I might never understand the meaning of the stones; I could feel their power as the setting sun turned them into dark silhouettes against the shining gold of the western sea.

On empty winter days, with the camouflage of vegetation peeled away, these ancient places had a presence that was less apparent in the summer, when the island was overflowing with birds, and there was always too much to be done. The pace of our existence was slower in winter; the peace and bleakness seemed to bring us closer to those past lives. I used to stand inside a ring of stones, and try to imagine how it would be to live within that space. My hands rested on the upright stones that formed the entrance as I wondered who had hauled those heavy objects into place. They had touched these very stones, and now, thousands of years later, I was touching them, reaching through that gap in time. It sent the faint breath of a shiver tingling down between my shoulder blades.

It was much easier to imagine the people who had lived in the old farmhouse. I had even seen photographs of them: ladies, incongruously over-dressed in bustles, standing in the farmyard; demure women in neck-to-ankle dresses sitting side-saddle on horseback; uniformed maids; whiskery men dipping sheep out in the fields. The decaying remnants from that era of farming had been left scattered through the fields, like a child's toys abandoned in the garden at the end of a long summer day. During our earliest explorations of the island we found some of the old horse-drawn implements, including a plough and harrow, a hay rake and mowing machine, discarded in corners of fields, almost obliterated by the thickets of bramble that had grown up to imprison them. One of the first things we did was to cut them free and bring them back to their rightful place at the farm, where they would at least have some protection from further decay.

We could still walk around the fading circle of the horse gin, tracing the path of the animals that would have been harnessed to the wheel that powered the farm machinery in the barn. And from his earliest visits as a teenager, Mike remembered Prince, the last horse on Skomer, left behind to live out its final days on the island when all attempts at farming came to an end soon after the Second World War.

There was something poignant about a gateway, the feeling of following in the footsteps of those who had gone before. Time after time, I paused at a field entrance to touch the wooden gatepost - the textures of the open, crumbling grain and the rough stippling of grey-green lichens - and to feel the connection going back through the years. I knew that I must have shared something with the people who had once lived here, but there was also a sense of guilt that their lives would have been so much harder than ours. They had no outboard motors, VHF radios or tinned food. They worked the land, fighting against its impositions, rather than living with it as we did.

Though the farmhouse would once have been comfortable, even magnificent compared to our simple rooms, and its occupants far more self-sufficient than we were, I wondered whether the farm worker or the maidservant could have understood my love for the island. I was afraid that the daily hardships would have made the luxury of enjoyment impossible. And yet our own lives were much further removed from contemporary reality than they had ever been in the past. Life in an Iron Age hut would not have been very different, whether on Skomer or on the mainland. Even a Victorian would have left few comforts behind, but in the intervening years, while things had changed dramatically on the mainland, life on Skomer remained essentially the same. Without television, electric light, washing machine or telephone, we were set very much apart from the average family on the mainland. And during our tenure of a single decade, the world would go on changing rapidly, leaving us behind.

If I had any lingering doubts, the truth of how far removed we actually were from those simpler times was forcefully emphasised as the winter was drawing to an end. It was dull and cold, with the flat light of early morning just paling the sky, and far too early in the year for us to have any thought of seeing another person. The stillness only added to the drab feeling of the day. Then, out of nowhere, came a rushing noise overhead that made the house tremble. I could only imagine that a freak tornado had crossed our path and was about to suck the roof off.

We pulled the door open to be greeted, not by some force of great destruction, but by a man, in a one-piece orange suit and a yellow helmet, dangling just outside, a few feet above the ground, with a newspaper in one hand and a pint of milk in the other. Our eyes followed the winch cable attached to his back upwards to the helicopter hovering thunderously overhead. A tiny figure at the pilot's window above us grinned and waved. We took the milk and newspaper but the noise precluded any conversation, and the helicopter quickly pulled away with only a brief flurry of concern as the winchman nearly became entangled in our washing line. Then, with a swoop towards the sea in North Haven, the winchman was hauled in, and the helicopter tracked out across the bay, leaving us completely bemused.

'How did they catch us out like that?' I asked. 'It's so peaceful today. We should have heard the helicopter coming for miles.'

Later, the pilot explained that he had deliberately approached the island very high, so that we wouldn't hear, and then descended rapidly over the house. Having the RAF close by meant a great deal to us. It seemed as though one of the entry requirements was an irrepressible sense of humour. I had never come across a more intensely professional and yet good-natured group of people. For them, that incident was simply a practical joke, but to us, fresh milk and a newspaper were almost unknown luxuries at that time of year.

The ravens were among the first birds to return to the island after the winter, and by February they were beginning to settle themselves in. At the far end of The Neck a huge, twiggy nest structure clung to the cliff in a sheltered inlet, where it remained from one year to the next. It appeared that this coarse, but elaborate, example of the intricate art of latticework was undergoing some renovations. This was an indication that the ravens were preparing to lay their eggs, and so we kept a close but discreet eye on them. When we walked out that way, towards the most easterly point of the island, we could see the pair-bond between the birds clearly displayed. They took to the air together, wheeling through the empty blue, exchanging their exuberant 'kronking' calls across the sky.

We made a detailed census of breeding birds; the more we knew of what was happening to the birds, the easier it would be to detect any changes that might be affecting them. The ravens were giving us all the right clues, but there was only one way to be sure that they were actually breeding. We needed to be able to see into the nest to check for eggs. The problem was that the birds had carefully constructed the edifice in such a way as to ensure that this was impossible. We had tried every angle on the cliff top, but the inside of the nest remained hidden. There was, however, a solution, which we had practised to perfection over the years. It involved me lying face down on the ground and then sliding out over the cliff edge until I had a clear view of the nest. This could be achieved only with Mike's assistance.

Since it was a slightly risky operation, the main safety feature was that I should take off my boots so that Mike could get a good grip on my legs. The first time we tried it, I had had an awful feeling that I was going to slide out, leaving him hanging on to my empty boots, so we had introduced this important refinement into the technique. The procedure was that Mike sat with his feet firmly braced against the ground, clinging on to my ankles, while I wriggled out into the void beyond. The outward part of the journey was exhilarating, like flying. Below me, the waves swished cloudy blue against the base of the cliff, where the bubbles of air were being swirled through the water. It was a deliciously giddying sensation. Then, with another push forward, and a craning of the neck, the thrill of seeing the eggs cradled in the soft cup among the knot of twigs. For a few moments, my concentration was all about trying to get the best view, seeing if I could count the eggs, but as soon as those distractions were over, the time always came when I knew had made an awful mistake. The first seconds of trying to get back to a position of safety filled me with panic. My arms flailed helplessly with nothing to grab on to, no way of pushing myself back. There was nothing between me and the distant sea, churning slowly, hypnotically, as if it were trying to suck me down. Then Mike was hauling on my ankles, and I felt myself moving. My hands found some crumbling bits of stone to push against and, suddenly, I was lying on the cliff top, laughing. It was all wonderful again, terror dissolved into euphoria.

That morning, as we watched the birds playing noisily above us, it was obvious that the time had come again to check the nest. Things were clearly well advanced, and the ravens should have begun to lay. The timing was ideal; with both birds away from the nest, we could take a quick look without causing any disturbance. I sat down on the short turf, and began to pull at my left boot. The echo of the sea sounded such a long way down. I felt a sickening reluctance at the thought of finding myself once again suspended in that breathtaking nothingness.

'I don't think it's a good idea to dangle you over the cliff,' Mike said, before I had even got my boot off. 'It's not really safe.'

'No, you're right,' I agreed, surprised at my own sense of relief.

I looked back at that moment with a certain amount of wistful amusement, recognising it as the point where we passed one more of those milestones on the road to growing up.

Once the island began to move out of winter, change came almost daily, and with the return of the puffins, we found ourselves yet again crossing the boundary of the seasons. Within a matter of weeks we would have to begin acclimatizing to the fact that we were no longer alone. We would become soft and pampered, forgetting what it was like to run out of food and to face the storms. Everything would feel safe and easy, because there would always be someone to call on for help. It would be good for us to have company and, almost without exception, we liked the people who came to the island: the students, assistant warden and voluntary helpers. But it was difficult at first to accept that the link between us and the island had been broken, to hear other voices, to see footprints that were not our own, to feel a little more detached from our environment.

There was another change that we had to accommodate that year: Terry had given up boating to return to what I suspected was his true love, farming. The boating arrangements for summer visitors were taken over by the Dale Sailing Company, with Campbell Reynolds at the helm. Campbell was a man with boundless drive and energy, who seemed permanently contented with life. The faint trace of a smile never left his face and the year-round tan was soaked deeply and indelibly into his skin. His quietly lilting voice didn't immediately convey his strength of character. He was the most unflappable man I had ever met, the sort I would like to have around in a crisis.

I had once been out in a boat with Campbell in a storm. As we were coming through Jack Sound, a stretch of sea with a formidable reputation, the waves had tipped the boat so violently that it caused an airlock in a fuel pipe, and one of the engines cut out. I was terrified, but Campbell never lost that half smile. His actions remained calm and unhurried. He didn't even flinch at the prospect of leaving me at the wheel while he went below deck to restart the engine. With only one engine working, the boat pulled itself out of line, and I found it completely unsteerable. Wind and waves and currents were in control; nothing I did with the wheel had the right effect. A couple of times, when we were on a direct collision course with a rock, I called to Campbell for help, screaming into the dark void of the open hatchway, knowing that he wouldn't hear me above the raging noise of the engine. When that failed, I closed my eyes against the impending impact, and opened them again to find that the currents had swept us safely past the obstacle. Campbell didn't emerge until we had crossed the boiling tides of the sound into calmer waters on the other side. He looked around at our new surroundings with a soft smile of satisfaction, obviously never having doubted for a moment that I would get us through.

For us, the boating arrangements were a rare experience of change in our established way of life, but the island went on as ever, unfolding its seasons. Soon the cliffs were thick with birds and, in time, the drab look of winter was washed away by the influx of flowers. Inevitably, even with the new boating regime, there were summer days when the island was isolated by the weather. This was usually as a result of northerly winds, which were bright and cool, sending scatterings of dazzlingly white waves flickering across the gentian-blue water. It was my favourite direction for a summer breeze, clearing the air and pushing the horizon away to infinity. Northerlies sprang up quickly, lifting the surface of the sea into strong, shallow waves, and they were the only winds that could cut off North Haven and Martin's Haven almost instantly.

When we had one of these days of northerly weather, bringing the certainty of no boat from the mainland, the south side of the island remained a refuge of summery calm. The wind skimmed over the cliff tops, cascading down onto the sheltered side and fanning out across the sea in delicately etched patterns, pressing the water smooth rather than churning it into waves. It was one of the rare times when we had a whole summer day in which to lose ourselves completely, and there was a preferred spot for these escapes: Tom's House. This oddly named spit of rock reaching out into the sea was among the island's most striking natural features. The rocky platform was topped with a towering stone arch, and the whole thing was bathed in lichens that turned it as warmly gold as a field of buttercups.

Thin streams of water crossed the path above Tom's House and seeped down to the cliff edge, creating damp, green oases. Following the course of this moisture, sheets of silverweed pressed close against the ground. With sunlight trickling over the frost-pale leaves, like the play of light and shade on water, the plants appeared to flow in rivulets over the short grass.

It was a scramble to get down on to the spit that necessitated edging along a narrow ridge with a steep drop on either side, but it was always worth it. Every single time, the enchantment of the place came back afresh, the delight of finding ourselves truly among the birds. It wasn't a powerfully dramatic encounter, as with the thousands of birds at the Wick, but a quiet and intimate meeting. Stealth and patience brought us close to the things we could usually only glimpse through binoculars. Between the carelessly heaped boulders, razorbill chicks peered out at the daylight. Scaled down ledges, with room for only a few pairs of birds, gave us views of guillemot chicks. The young guillemots and razorbills were almost like replicas of the adults, but impossibly small. They had the same upright, penguin-like shape reproduced in miniature, but their size made them seem unreal, like toys. They also looked softer, slightly unfinished, less robust than the adults. Their colours were more muted and their feathers lacked that deep, protective sheen. The adults were so sleek and polished that the feathers took on the appearance of a smooth, impermeable shell.

Among the golden rocks we were dazzled and sunburnt by the light reflecting all around us from sea and stone. The young birds remained on the island for only a couple of weeks. Soon they would leave, still flightless, still tiny imitations of the adults, to do the rest of their growing up out at sea. It was perhaps just once a year that we would have the chance to catch this fleeting interlude with the chicks.

The cliffs were so captivating, with or without the birds, that it was easy to forget how special the centre of the island was. It had a tranquillity that contrasted with the restlessness of the cliffs, an ever-present sense of the past and, woven through the landscape, its own distinctive mix of birds.

One of the most emotive sounds I have ever heard is the song of the skylark. No bird could sing more clearly of summer. There was always a skylark at the edge of Calves Park, where the track curved round towards the farm, and I had to stop and listen whenever I passed that way. As the bird rose higher and higher into the sky, singing with unrestrained rapture, I could feel it lifting my spirits up with it. Somewhere, half-hidden at the back of my mind, the collective noun I learnt at school, an 'exaltation' of larks, found its meaning. The notes were so sharp and clean that they came trickling back down to the quiet green fields unblemished by the distance they had travelled. The flowing rise and fall of the song had the purity of stream-water undulating over pebbles. It was hard to believe that a small bird soaring so high could sing with such intensity that it sounded close by. I was often confused by this ventriloquism, staring up towards the source of the song until the clarity and emptiness of the sky dazzled me with its sheer blueness, while the speck of a bird remained elusive.

On the brightest days the skylark sang to the sun: the moment a cloud hazed the sky with shadow, the bird fell silent. And so the link is made quite inseparably in my mind between brilliant summer weather and the song of the skylark. Perhaps the real magic of the skylark is that, in remembering it, every day is turned into one of those luminously flawless days that made up all our childhood summers.

Those same large fields in front of the farm were where the lapwings chose to nest: discreetly colourful birds whose deep green feathers were shot through with a rainbow of silky iridescence. Their broad, blunt wings carried them in a bouncing flight pattern, which, at regular intervals, collapsed into a tumbling motion, as though the birds were falling out of the sky. These flights were accompanied by a mewing call, with each short burst of notes rising to a crescendo.

Our regular walks to the farm took us past lapwing nests on either side, but the birds never grew accustomed to our presence. No matter how many times we passed soundlessly by, there was no gradual acceptance that we posed no threat. Every time we used the track the lapwings had to go through the same laborious charade. It involved skimming erratically above the ground with one wing trailing limply, all the time emitting a piteous wailing sound. We were supposed to be distracted away from the nest by the sight of the poor injured bird, and it was a virtuoso performance, which could easily have worked had we not seen it repeated so many times. I only wished that we could have come to some mutual understanding, so that they wouldn't have had to abandon the nest to carry out that touchingly heartfelt display each time our paths crossed.

It was out behind the farm, in the damp areas leading down to North Pond that we most often heard curlews. They were quietly spectacular birds with improbably long, curved beaks, but they were also immaculately camouflaged in broken shades of brown, the colour of fading vegetation. Because the curlews were so carefully lost among the tangled backdrop, we heard them far more than we saw them. Their beautifully evocative calls came flooding in a bubbling cascade through the marshy hollows. Musical, without being melodic, the sound was soft yet ringingly clear, lingering like an echo and then drifting into stillness. It was the sound of evening, of calm at the end of the day, of mellow, muted colours, like the birds themselves.

Another bird of the failing light was the short-eared owl. Although it was a day-flying owl, we saw it most often early the in the morning or late in the afternoon when the sun had lost its strength. There was never any certainty of seeing one of these unpredictable birds; we could only trust in the universal rule that waiting patiently for something was the surest method of keeping it away. But if we loitered, half-hoping to be surprised by an owl, a good place to stand was by the farmyard walls, looking towards the shallow curve of North Valley. The most startling thing about the arrival of the owl was the absolute silence that accompanied it. Before we could look up and catch sight of them, most large birds announced themselves by the sound of their approach: the sharpness of wing feathers slicing through the sky, the wailing of gulls, the raven's grating call, like rock against rock, always came ahead of them. But the owl just materialized, a shadow in the greying air, almost ghost-like in its soundlessness, as though not quite inhabiting our world. The broad wings seemed to offer so little resistance to the air that the bird appeared soft and weightless, an ethereal thing rather than an efficient hunter.

There could be as many as six pairs of short-eared owls nesting on the island, and once the eggs were hatched the birds became much more active. As I watched one, dappled with infinite gradations of brown, gliding in dream-like slow motion above the valley, I knew that it was searching out Skomer voles made careless by the relative safety of the island. The owl was intent on its prey, scanning with keen, yellow eyes, hovering and then plunging. Such consummate stealth would soon bring success. Though I hated to see those plump, furry blobs being snatched away, the rational side of me knew that the food was essential for the white, hissing owl chicks with angry-looking eyes that were waiting among the heather.

The fascination of the contrast between day and night on Skomer was something that could never be dulled by time. The still of dusk as the last calls of the gulls grew fainter and more scattered, gradually gave way to complete quiet. Then, as darkness became deeper and denser, the influx of shearwaters on the blackest of nights held me as spellbound as it always had. The more impenetrable the night, the more overwhelming was the invasion of birds. I would never lose the sense of awe at the sight of so many birds raining out of the sky, covering the ground, filling every inch of space with the sound of their calling and the vibrating hum from thousands of beating wings.

But there was another, more discreet, night-time spectacle that brought a childlike sense of enchantment. I can't exactly explain its appeal except that at first glance it looked so extraordinarily unreal as to be almost magical. This phenomenon lasted for only a few weeks in high summer, so we had to make a special point of not missing it. I had never seen glow-worms before we went to Skomer, and I found the fairy light effect ridiculously beautiful. They shone with a pale, luminous green, making globes of soft light that glinted among the miniature forests of bracken. Each circle of living light was bright enough to conceal the insect hidden behind it, leaving a firmament of disembodied green stars. They shouldn't have existed; they should have vanished the moment I looked too closely, the moment I broke the spell by trying to see behind the illusion. The fact that I could hold them in my hand to study the unexpected brilliance of the light, the way the subtle greenness suffused the skin of my palm, made it only a little easier to believe in them.

Skomer is one of a scattering of islands off the coast of Pembrokeshire. Among the most remote and intriguing of these islands is Grassholm. An uninhabitable place, steeped in legends, its very inaccessibility makes it incredibly alluring. A visit to Grassholm was, by its nature, a rarity. Set amid miles of empty ocean, it was a destination that would have been far beyond the capabilities of our own boat, and so we had to wait patiently to be invited aboard a larger sea-going vessel. The *Dale Princess* made occasional trips, though these were very dependent on good weather and, since the boat was only licensed to carry a small number of passengers so far off shore, places on board were few, but, if there was room, Campbell would take us along as crew.

Grassholm is such a powerful and unique experience that my first encounter with the island stays with me. The eight-mile journey took a couple of hours, thudding over endless waves, but the prospect of that first distant glimpse of the island obliterated any monotony. It is impossible, though, to describe simply seeing Grassholm, because it is a place that touches so vividly on all the senses.

Approaching Skomer by sea would do nothing more than hint at its diversity of landscape and wildlife. Discovering Skomer is a gradual process, a slow unfolding of its layers. Grassholm is dominated by one single and stunning feature, which becomes immediately obvious, even across a mile of ocean - its gannets. I saw it rising from a blank horizon, the only presence in an empty seascape, appearing from a distance as a shapeless mound, the archetypal desert island. It was starkly divided, with one half splashed dazzlingly white where tens of thousands of gannets were crowded onto the gentle seaward slope. A haze of birds shimmered above it, like a swarm of pale bees hovering round a hive. Both the ultramarine sea and the sun-scorched white of the island were made more intense by the contrast they created.

Long before the distant curve of the island had taken on any detail, the air was infused with the faint ammonia smell of seabirds, drifting over the sea towards us. Then the gannets appeared, and I stared up into the transparent blue to watch them. At first they were isolated flares of white, gliding high in the sky, but heading purposefully towards us. Directly overhead, they wheeled round, skimming far above the boat. As they turned, their wings caught the sun with a blinding brightness that flickered into my eyes, already half closed against the brilliance of the sky. Having come out as if to meet us, the gannets escorted us back to the island, flying slowly to keep pace with the boat. And all the time more birds were joining the convoy. As the number of birds accompanying us increased, so too did the strong, sun-warmed smell of the island.

When we scrambled up the rocks onto Grassholm it was like walking through a curtain of noise. We were smothered by the upsurge of sound, which, for a few moments, was disorientating. Many of Skomer's seabirds called with a hard, mechanical rattle, but the gannets magnified this into something otherworldly. The chirring, like the purr of a thousand engines, came washing over us, rising and falling in high-pitched waves.

From the top of the island we could look down across the strange landscape of gannets' nests. There were hundreds of rows of them, each meticulously spaced within beak-reaching distance of the next, so that the slope was smoothly stippled with birds. They spread in a sheet of smothering whiteness that disappeared over the edge of the island and down towards the sea, giving the impression of an infinity of birds. The sun glared back at us from the reflective surfaces of the island, creating an airless heat that was chokingly dense with the smell of seabirds.

To avoid disturbing the gannets while they were incubating, we never went to Grassholm until after the eggs had hatched so that by the time we saw the island there were a large number of chicks at varying stages of development. The smallest chicks, just emerged from the egg, were black-skinned, all sharp angles and unformed wings, with a strangely primitive appearance, like something straddling the boundary between bird and reptile. White down was appearing on the chicks that were a few days old, but the black skin still showed through, like coal dusted with powdery snowflakes. These little, dark creatures looked out of place, small and alien, as they cowered beneath the tide of huge white birds.

Within a few weeks of hatching, the down had thickened, turning the chicks into puffballs of fluff, almost dodo-like with their miniature wings and over-sized beaks. In the heat of the day the island was littered with these young birds as they slept, wings outstretched, heads lolling, often draped half out of the nest, like the toddler that suddenly sprawls headlong into sleep, regardless of its surroundings. Oblivious to the possibility of danger, they flopped lifeless at the feet of their parents, enjoying the only few weeks of blissful irresponsibility in their lives, as the adult birds watched patiently over their tiny territories. By the time they were six weeks old, and swollen by candyfloss down, the chicks appeared larger than the sleek adult birds struggling back to the nest carrying fish for their cuckoo-like offspring. But, already, the black wing feathers were spiking through the clouds of down, hinting at the changes that would lead rapidly to independence. Gossamer wisps from these moulting chicks drifted thickly in the air. It brushed our skin and clung to our hair, reminding me of the late summer explosion of thistles in South Valley.

Close up, the adults had an almost absurd perfection. Their feathers were purest white with stark black markings on the wings. The only colour was on their heads, where a flash of golden ochre faded away towards the neck, like the most expertly applied watercolour washed over crisp, clean paper. Any sense of softness given by this delicate colouring was eclipsed by the piercing intensity of pale blue eyes, highlighted by immaculately penned ink-black lines. Despite the flawlessness of their plumage, on land they couldn't maintain the truly majestic impression that they had commanded when I first saw them sweeping and diving through the air because of their comically short legs ending in enormous, black, webbed feet. These extremities were made all the more ludicrous by a tracery of fine, blue lines outlining their toes.

As my senses grew accustomed to the noise of the densely packed birds and the searing, snow-blinding whiteness, I began to enjoy the chaotic detail of the colony. With the nests so close, it was too tempting for a bird to reach out with its long, pointed beak and delicately pull a particularly appealing strand of something from a neighbouring structure. The result was an ungainly tug of war as the birds battled over a garishly coloured mess of cheap twine.

More serious fights disrupted the intricately ordered pattern of birds. The drift of white broke apart in a flurry of wings as two birds clasped their beaks together, wrestling with determined fury. In such a confined space the fight couldn't remain isolated, and surrounding birds joined in, jabbing their beaks into the fray, until calm eventually returned and the gap healed to its original smoothness.

The intimacy of their living conditions made some form of communication between the birds essential. My favourite of these signals was sky-pointing, an indication to the mate and to the surrounding residents that a bird was about to become airborne. I scanned the colony to find an individual with its neck elongated, head tilted back, beak pointing towards the open sky, as though every muscle was stretched taut with a longing to escape the crowded confusion of the island, reaching up for the freedom of the air above. Then the bird opened up its wings and lifted itself into the sky, gliding effortlessly up from within the close-packed mass of gannets, leaving them unruffled by its departure.

By the end of our visit, the evening sun was beginning to stain the island and its gannets weakly pink. It took away the harshness of the glare, turning it mellow and tranquil. Or perhaps I had just become a little less overwhelmed by the noise and the smell, the astonishing intensity of so many birds. The journey back was no longer shot through with the anticipation of reaching our destination, but gentle in its mix of greys and golds folding over and over in the waves. The real highlight, though, was the rafts of gathering shearwaters, skimming in shadowy streams across the sea.

No trip to Grassholm could be anything less than memorable, but the one that stays in my mind as being different from the others was made not in a large, solid passenger boat, but in a small inflatable dinghy. Tony Bomford was on Skomer making a film about puffins for the Survival television series. He had his own boat for filming and carrying supplies, which seemed to offer an unmissable opportunity for an excursion to Grassholm. The weather was not good when we set out and it quickly began to deteriorate.

With me and Mike, Tony and his assistant Mark crammed into the small inflatable, the journey was extraordinarily uncomfortable. We blundered painfully from one shallow wave to the next as the boat belly flopped across the corrugations. There was enough wind to lift the spray kicked up by the boat and tip it into our faces in a steady, salty gush. The rhythmic battering caused aching in muscles that had never made their presence felt before, and my eyes stung so much from the salt that I could barely see where we were going. The combination was enough to make the journey of a mere hour or two seem interminable.

By the time the rain began to pour down I was almost too wet to notice. It just mingled with the sea spray in a single drenching cascade. But the physical discomforts couldn't quench the excitement of seeing the first gannets. They not only came out to greet us, but were soon diving all around the boat. The gannet's plunge is famous, one of the most thrilling of all encounters with birds. From high in the air those oddly-angled eyes could pick out the shimmering movement of fish below the waves, and they pursued their prey with precision skydiving. The bird swooped down until, at some expertly judged distance from the sea, the wings were folded back, streamlining it into the shape of an arrowhead, and the controlled descent became a high-speed freefall, giving a final rush of momentum as the beak sliced into the water. A small fountain of spray splashed into the air as the surface of the sea shattered, and the bird continued to glide downwards, its outline dissolved into a fluttering trail of white confetti. As they rose again, we saw the occasional metallic-blue iridescence of mackerel in their beaks. I had watched gannets diving countless times before, but nothing could compare to the sensation of being so close to them.

We edged slowly into the lee of the island and cut the engine. The sudden silencing of that persistent drone came as an unexpected relief. Its place was filled by a flood of birdcalls and the soft tapping of rain on water. Only then, in the stillness, did we realise for the first time that the unusual turbulence of the water wasn't caused simply by a combination of exceptionally generous raindrops and the wind-strewn spray from the boat. The sea all around us was bubbling. It was like being afloat in a cauldron of fiercely boiling water. As we stared at the fizzing, splashing sea we realised that we were drifting in a huge shoal of mackerel that was forcing its way up to the surface to feed on an equally impressive swarm of sand eels. The water was alive with the writhing bodies of fish, so close and crowded that I felt I could have dipped my hand in and pulled one out. That was why the birds were plunging so crazily around the boat.

We looked up into the sky to watch as the gannets came skidding through the air towards us. The dark markings of their faces and wings, the outstretched necks and tapered sharpness of their beaks were locked into perfect alignment, as if their whole bodies had fused into a single-minded surge of determination. They pierced the water so close to the boat that the spray from their dives spattered over us. It was breathtaking to be in the middle of a hail of tumbling birds, a once in a lifetime experience, a chance meeting of circumstances that would never come again. For those few minutes we were invisible; the birds were so intent on fishing that we didn't exist. We could watch without being seen. It felt as though we had found the hidden gateway that allowed us to cross the barrier and enter their domain.

The display was electrifying to the point of being unnerving. I had read somewhere that a gannet can strike the water at sixty miles an hour, and with only inches separating us from the birds there was no room for the slightest miscalculation. I fingered the taut skin of the inflatable, reassuring myself that it couldn't be punctured by a bird's beak. If anything should go wrong, the eight miles of sea that separated us from Skomer might as well be a hundred. But this vague sense of vulnerability only heightened the exhilaration, so it was deeply disappointing when the shoal of mackerel melted back into the water and the diving gannets retreated to a more conventional distance.

We could no longer pretend to ourselves that the wind was going to die away, and the waves were already gathering boisterous fringes of foam. The only safe thing was to head straight for home without even visiting the island. As the engine churned back into life, and the tunnel of rain and spray closed in around us, I peered out into the watery greyness through half-closed eyes. Each ridge of sea clanged hard against the bottom of the boat like the mud of a rutted track that had frozen solid. It was going to be a long journey back, but worth every moment to have experienced the briefest and most unforgettable glimpse of Grassholm ever.

As summer progressed, South Valley seemed to detach itself from the rest of the island; it was a secluded pocket of rich growth that drifted away to bask in its own distinct climate. Harsh summer weather could quickly fade the freshness of spring until the island began to look weather-beaten, as though it had forgotten every colour except dusty bracken-green, but South Valley remained a hidden and protected oasis. The crushing, desiccating winds skimmed harmlessly overhead, while the stream running through it provided a flush of moisture, creating a swathe of surprisingly dense, lush vegetation that cut across the parched island. Soft white clouds of hemlock water-dropwort flowers filled the valley like an early morning mist trapped in the hollow. According to Mike, this innocent looking plant was so poisonous that I shouldn't even touch it. This stern warning hit some rebellious streak in me, and, occasionally, when I found myself alone among the froth of plants, I couldn't resist tasting one of the flowers with the tip of my tongue. I lived, of course, but never risked telling the tale.

As the pale shades of spring gave way to the stronger colours of summer, the valley filled with a gushing rill of purple loosestrife that forced its way tall and bright above the jungle of competing growth. At the point where the stepping-stones passed through the stream, water mint crowded round the edge of the path. The mounds of deep green leaves were strewn with puffballs of bluish-lilac flowers. If I accidentally trod on part of the plant, a delicious smell came wafting up, encouraging me to pick a few of the fresh-tasting, spearminty leaves to chew on as I walked. On days of intense sun the atmosphere of South Valley was as motionless and humid as an exotic hothouse. The effect was instantly exhausting, with the air so dense and heavy that it was like walking through something sticky.

Butterflies, drawn irresistibly into this bubble of enhanced summer weather, were scattered thickly among the flowers. Peacocks, small tortoiseshells and red admirals, looked worn out by the demands of their fleeting existence; their wings were faded like a threadbare tapestry. Some even had the v-shaped imprint of a bird's beak branded across their powdery scales, marking an escape that must have been only a wing beat away from death.

Small coppers emerged so frequently through the season that they always looked new and perfect, with a glow of burnished metal that sparked and shone against the dense smudge of green.

As summer drew to a close, the valley filled with thistle down. The sturdy, purple spikes of thistle flowers had been almost unrealistically plump and picturesque, until they finally broke apart into a storm of silky white strands that wandered aimlessly through the air. Each single flower seemed capable of producing an inexhaustible quantity of down, which meandered across the stillness clinging onto anything it touched, frosting it all like a spangling of ice crystals.

The thistle heads unravelled at the merest touch if I ran my fingers over them, and as they dissolved into the air it was like watching another summer slipping away. Summers were such insubstantial things compared to the solid reality of winter. They passed by so quickly, and with the first September gale the island would revert to winter. Few of the research students ever stayed beyond the middle of summer. Their work was mainly with the seabirds and, like their subjects, the students migrated from the island around June or July, which added to the feeling of a season drawing to a close.

Seals were the highlight of late summer days. I could watch them without ever venturing further than the kitchen window, but to see them in a truly spectacular setting meant taking one of my favourite walks to Castle Bay. This was a cove hidden away on the southern side of the Neck and protected by an arc of steep cliffs. There was no easy way in; it could only be reached by using ropes to abseil down from the top of the cliff, but, with a bit of a clamber, it was possible to get unbroken views of the bay. On one side of it, an arm of grass-topped rock reached out into the sea. From there, if I kept low to the ground, I could watch the seals without disturbing them, and this was where Mike eventually built the hide to allow for a more serious study of the seals.

It was a breathlessly still September day, with the sea so pale and translucent that its thin, blue colours mingled with the golden sand of the seabed to create the most alluring shades of watery green. The weather was not ideal for seal watching. Storms pushed them out of the sea to crowd onto the beach for shelter, but when the sun shone and the sea was calm they abandoned the shingle of Castle Bay to wallow in the benign waves. Despite its lack of promise, the day was too beautiful not to lure me out.

I followed the cliffs of South Haven before turning away to walk along the ridge of the promontory fort and through the dwindling remnants of a lesser black-backed gull colony. Even though their numbers were depleted, the gulls were everywhere, diving at my head, ruffling my hair with the swoop of their wings, screeching threats into my ears, making it clear that I was in their territory. The relentlessness of their noise and aggression was distracting, but soon they would be gone for the winter, leaving behind a silence that would seem almost unreal until I had grown used to it again.

As I crossed the top of Castle Bay the needle-fine leaves of thrift made springy cushions beneath my feet, with the memory of dense pink petals now turned to sepia drifts of paper flowers. In sheltered dips of the south-facing slope, random clusters of thrift and sea campion had bloomed again, creating isolated little islands of spring. I edged out onto the spit of rock to get a clear view of the bay. The hollow wailing sounds, drawn out endlessly by the echoes that floated in the stillness, came as a reassuring promise that I would find at least a few seals. The first glimpse of an empty beach was disappointing, but then I saw them, drifting languidly in the turquoise water and scattered over the offshore rocks. Directly below me a young seal was scrabbling at the almost impossible task of dragging itself onto a boulder that jutted through the sleek water in an untidy hummock of matted weed.

It was a rare moment that the seals so obviously appreciated, and I knew I should do the same. Within days, darkly opaque waves were piling up against the shingle, saturating the air with a restless noise. At low tide I might find the beach clustered with almost two hundred seals: plump bodies, grey and round as sea-smoothed stones, arranged within touching distance of each other. The sight of so many animals strewn below me was riveting, but I missed the easy tranquillity that had gone. The waves, edged with a froth of clattering pebbles, permeated the atmosphere with their simmering irritability. Seals pushed closer and closer together by the encroaching sea turned on each other in an endless series of skirmishes. After a few weeks it became hard to remember that the weather had ever allowed us all such peace.

It was strange how quickly the summer was forgotten as it disintegrated into a succession of storms, but at least the bad weather didn't make me feel quite as vulnerable as it had in the early years. My first impression of our house had been of a fragile structure made up of the thinnest slivers of wood. It looked so precariously close to the edge of the cliff that I was sure it would slide into the sea rather than face up to the slightest opposition from the wind. Over time, I had forced myself to trust it a little more, despite the fact that the previous year I had made a discovery that tested my faith in it.

Brinley Hooper, who had been in charge of building the house back in the late fifties, arrived unexpectedly one day on the passenger boat. Even though I had never met him, it was one of those names that had become so familiar over recent years that it sounded like a piece of my own history. I was delighted when he introduced himself at the top of the landing steps, and we walked over to the house together so that he could examine his creation. He stared at it with what I imagined was awed pride. It was only later that I realised he might have been feeling relief to see that it had stood the test of storms so well.

He cheerfully recounted a story that provided an instant solution to a long-running mystery. As the house was nearing completion, the team of builders had returned to the island following a blustery night to find that the structure had moved about three feet off its foundations. Undaunted, they had used tractors to drag the building back into place, and then fixed it down with wire. I had always wondered about the maze of wires criss-crossing the cellar but had never imagined that they played such a vital role in the structural integrity of the house. Had I been told that story on the day I arrived it would have worried me, but now I was prepared to be more forgiving. After all, we had been through hurricane force winds together, and the house had clung on, no matter how bad things got. But perhaps I was allowing myself to slip into a false sense of security.

One of the exceptions to the rule that researchers deserted the island in high summer was Tim Healing. He was carrying out a long-term study of the Skomer vole, and he came for a couple of weeks two or three times a year. This year, he came early in the autumn, when everyone else had gone. He was good company and, since much of his work was carried out at first light, he was more than willing to lend a hand with whatever else was going on around the island.

Almost as soon as Tim arrived the unsettled weather began to deteriorate dramatically. It was an unusual wind, a south-easterly; most of the really bad gales had at least a hint of west in them. This was a spiteful storm that broke through our defences. It sliced its way up through South Haven and then, swelled by the funnelling effects of the cliffs, unleashed its concentrated force against the corner of the house, screeching past with a thin, cold roar that made the windows shudder. Winds usually come in erratic gusts, but this one was unrelentingly continuous, without the slightest modulation of its tone; it had a single-minded determination that was unnerving.

The noise of the wind was so intense that we didn't hear when the roof of the house began to shatter and peel away. We only heard the thump of the front door swinging open and the sound of Tim's voice shouting up the hallway. We ran outside and saw the wooden shingles that tiled the roof splintering and being whipped skyward on the current of wind. There was already a small hole, a little black patch of nothing, for the wind to wheedle its way into. I knew that the larger the tear grew, the easier it would be for the wind to slide beneath it and rip the whole thing apart.

'What are we going to do?' I asked, my throat aching with a sense of impending disaster.

'I'll have to go up there and stop it, before it gets any worse,' Mike said.

'But you can't,' I protested. 'Not in this wind. It's too dangerous.'

I knew he wouldn't listen.

'You two go and get the ladder,' he went on, as though I hadn't spoken. 'I'll find something to patch it with.'

Between us, Tim and I struggled with the ladder. Normally, one of us would have managed it easily, but it wrenched and twisted against our hands in the wind, as though it was trying to escape. By the time we had grappled the ladder into place, Mike returned with some small, square sheets of roofing lead.

Although the wind had seemed as bad as anything I could imagine, incredibly, it was getting worse. As Mike edged his way up to the apex of the roof I could see the wind dragging against him; his hair streamed flat against his head so that he looked like someone swimming under water. I saw him fumbling, trying to hold his position half-lying against the roof as he pulled the hammer and nails out of his pockets. I could see the movement of the hammer hitting against metal, but no noise came back down to us; the wind swept everything away. His grip on the roof was so precarious that I didn't want to watch, but it was irresistibly compulsive. Tim and I were both close in under the house, leaning hard against the ladder to keep it in place, craning our necks outward, trying to see the roof. Tim stepped back to get a better view, but the moment he let go of the ladder, the wind began to tear it out of my hands and I almost lost it. He grabbed it again quickly as it was slithering sideways out of my grip.

Suddenly, there was a heart-stopping development. Mike's coat, despite being heavy and close fitting, whipped inside out over his head. It was grotesquely frightening, and yet comical at the same time. Mike was flailing, blinded and barely able to move his arms. As he struggled to extricate himself, he looked like some strange wounded monster arching and thrashing on the roof, but any residual sense of the ludicrous was crushed by the certainty that he was going to fall. I tried to shout to Tim, ask him what we should do, but, though he was standing next to me, I could barely make myself heard above the noise of the storm.

Fortunately we were spared from attempting any rescue measures as Mike managed to break free and came sliding back down the roof to gutter level.

'I can't hold on up here!' he shouted. 'I need a safety line.'

'How?' I screamed.

'The tractor. Get the tractor, and tie it to that.'

After several repetitions, I understood what we had to do. I drove the tractor round to the front of the house and we fixed a rope to it. A squall of rain came: cold needles, pecking at our skin like biting insects, stinging our eyes, making everything slow and slippery. Somehow, from the shelter of the building, we were able to throw the rope up to Mike, and he tied it round his waist. At least it would keep his coat in place but, other than that, it was useless. I could see it was. It would hold him if he fell towards where Tim and I were standing, but I was sure that the wind would push him the other way, over the apex of the roof.

Despite the difficult conditions, Mike slipped easily into a rhythm of working, seemingly happy with his illusion of safety. I watched his total concentration: everything focused on the noiseless thud of the hammer. The thing I couldn't understand were the spots of red appearing on his forehead, like a scarlet rain blowing into his face and gathering into tiny rivulets that dribbled down towards his eyes. It was only as I stared harder that I began to see the splinters of wood being torn from the frayed edges of the roof shingles and flung up into Mike's face, grazing the skin as they skimmed past. They were moving so quickly that I could barely see them and, despite the blood trickling down his face, Mike didn't seem to be aware of them. He didn't flinch once, or brush at his face with irritation. I couldn't tell if he was too absorbed in what he was doing to notice, or if he didn't dare allow himself to be distracted while his position remained so precarious.

The important thing, though, was that the repair was working; the split in the roof was disappearing under a solid patchwork of lead. I was convinced that it would be strong enough to withstand the storm and I began to let the first sensations of relief infiltrate my anxiety. Mike took the last sheet of lead, preparing to close the hole, and then it would be over. We would be safe again.

As he was trying to position the square of lead, the wind ripped it out of his hands. Despite its weight, it sailed high above the roof and drifted through the air like a scrap of paper. I ran after it, and finally it came to land on a distant grassy bank. I was running with such power; the wind at my back was carrying me along as though I was flying. I would be there in no time. And then the lead took off again, bowling over and over, bouncing across the grass. It was outpacing me, and it was going to escape. I was out of breath, my waterproof clothes were cumbersome and my energy was fading. All I could think was how ridiculous it was that lead should be blowing in the wind, as weightless as a dried-up leaf.

When I caught up with the lead it was scrunched into a ball, like a discarded tissue. It was our last piece, the piece that was going to seal the hole. We had no more. I forced my way back against the tide of the storm, trying to straighten out the lead as I went. When I reached the house, Tim saw the crumpled lead and turned to help me with it. As he let go of the ladder, it immediately began to fall, shoved by the wind. I watched it plunge lethargically towards his head, suspended infinitely in that last fraction of a second before impact, and yet there wasn't time for me to begin to shout a warning before it hit him. I couldn't hear anything, not or own voices, or the pounding of the hammer, but I heard the ladder hit against his skull, clear and hollow and ringing. Tim slumped to the ground, face down, with the ladder on top of him. Time slid to a halt. Even as my hands reached down towards him, there was endless opportunity to watch the mournful raindrops drizzling so slowly over his yellow oilskins, and to think how unbearably sad it was. Surely no one could survive a blow to the head like that.

I tried to lift the ladder off him, but the wind was holding it down. We wrestled: I pulled, the wind pushed, and nothing moved. I could hear Mike's voice: no words, just angry sounds. Tim and I were so close under the house that Mike couldn't see us, and I couldn't see him. I was isolated, the only one left who could help Tim or Mike, and I couldn't manage to do either. As I was about to panic, Tim revived and writhed his way out from under the ladder. I felt weak with relief.

As my initial concern for Tim ebbed away, Mike's voice came back to me. His words were being shredded and snatched away by the wind so that only scattered fragments drifted down to me. The few scraps that I could translate included some very strong language, but I could see that he had every reason to be annoyed. From his perspective it must have appeared that Tim and I had taken the ladder and wandered off, leaving him stranded.

With incredible fortitude Tim continued as though nothing had happened, and we put the ladder back in place. While Mike was nailing down the crumpled piece of lead, I kept glancing sideways at Tim as we held the ladder, trying to take in the miracle of his resurrection and looking for any signs of injury. I decided that, in my alarm, I must have overestimated the enormity of it.

The storm continued to grow, until the south side of the island faded away: the strands of foam vaporizing from the tips of the waves became a white blur of salt that masked the cliffs in a shining fog. By the time the weather calmed Tim's brief visit was over. He headed back to the mainland, and we returned to our state of beloved isolation.

I didn't go to Skomer in search of isolation. Everything had happened so quickly, and there had been so many other things to think about, that I had never considered how much of our time would be spent completely alone. If I had thought about it at all, isolation would have been one of the most outstanding drawbacks of what we were about to do, the price that had to be paid in order to take part in the adventure. It was only later that I realised isolation was, in some senses, the whole point of it. Without that degree of seclusion, we could never have grown so close to the island. We knew every subtle shift in its moods, achieving an intimacy that grew into a feeling of belonging and even possession. The island owned us, and yet also belonged to us. Everything was intensified by that bond; every sunset, every storm, every rainbow, touched some deeper level of emotion because it existed just for us.

For me, there was nothing more inspirational than being part of a rhythm that was untouched by the outside. Anything that broke the pattern, even a fleeting trip to the mainland, was an unwelcome intrusion. I knew it was something that few people would understand, but I had become so captivated by solitude that I had forgotten what it was to need a wider world. Mike adapted so perfectly to isolation because he was a complete enthusiast; he immersed himself in whatever he did to the exclusion of everything else. It was a quality that I both envied and admired, but could never find in myself.

With the wisdom of passing years, I realised that the biggest mistake we made in those first blindingly euphoric days was to believe that we could marry in such haste and set off into the unknown to be thrown so uncompromisingly together. It had all the ingredients for a bitter ending. I had too little idea of what living on island would mean to be able to make a rational decision, although, with hindsight, I don't believe that anyone could predict their reaction to such a way of life until they had experienced it. The fact that it worked for us was no more than an extraordinary piece of good fortune.

I am not sure if it is ever possible to know another person well enough to be confident about being isolated with them for months at a time. It has to be matter of trial and error. By some peculiar chemistry we turned out to be ideally suited to the vagaries of being marooned on a deserted island. I think that one of the main reasons for this was that we were absolute opposites. We had so few similarities that, instead of clashing against each other, our strengths and weaknesses interlocked to make a fairly seamless join. Mike was optimistic, impulsive, impatient, while I tended towards the other end of the spectrum on all those characteristics. I tried to analyse every potential problem before it arose, but Mike could never imagine the possibility that anything might go wrong. He dismissed my convoluted worries with such certainty that they came to seem ridiculous. I calmed him down when his fragile temper snapped; he dragged me out of any impending sulk. Mike was infuriated by any delay or hindrance to his plans, while I was endlessly patient and persuaded him to let things take their natural course. Each of us was the counterweight that balanced the other.

So often, people are intrigued by the mechanics of living in isolation, and if they weren't asking me how I dealt with loneliness, the question was how we managed when we argued, with the obvious implication that two people confined together are bound to spend a lot of time fighting. I didn't really understand it any more than I understood the loneliness question. The fewer intrusions there were from the outside, the less there was to argue about. Life lost most of its irritations; everything became simpler, more light-hearted. We shared a common cause in the island, and, because that mediated every-thing we did, it brought us together. If we did quarrel, there was nothing about being alone that made it intrinsically worse. There were none of the distrac-tions that make it easy to sideline resentments and harbour them indefinitely, so one of us usually said sorry very quickly.

That is not to suggest that we lived in unnatural harmony. The main threat to our good relations was any practical problem that appeared temporarily insurmountable. When things were difficult Mike managed to make it clear that I was the worst possible person to have around at such testing times. It

gave us the components for a really good argument. Whenever we were struggling with the boat trailer stuck fast on the beach I was solely responsible for
our inability to move it. As the trailer ground predictably to a halt I waited
furiously for one of Mike's favourite phrases shouted with condemnatory rage:
'It's no good, *you're* just not strong enough,' or, worse still, 'I wish there were
two of *me*'.

I also found Mike's unflinching single-mindedness, his inability to compro-
mise, extremely frustrating. The summer took up most of our time, seven
days a week, and evenings often consisted of no more than a late meal before
bedtime. It was only the winter that left space for pure recreation. Having
been forced to abandon his first love, sculpture, by the practicalities of moving
to an island, Mike had taken up painting. Sadly, the paint and canvas were
luxuries we could barely afford, but rather than settling on something small
and safe, he always converted his year's supply of canvas into two or three
large pictures. Once the material was stretched over the wooden frames and
primed he was hardly able to wait until it was dry enough to start painting.

Instead of savouring this pastime during his free time, real life was set aside
so he could dash off the picture in couple of days. My pleas went unheard.

'The weather's stunning today, and we'll probably have storms for the next
month. We should do something outside,' I might cajole, watching mesmerized
by the speed at which the brush streaked paint over the canvas.

Mike barely acknowledged me, just pausing to wipe the brush over his
painting smock, adding to the layers of muddled colours absent-mindedly
spattered there as a memento of his past creations. He was utterly absorbed,
lost to reason, painting until the light faded, until he couldn't tell one shade
from another. Then, in the days that followed, with the kind weather having
passed us by, and the storms keeping us trapped inside, he would be distraught
because he had no more canvas. His need to be creating was a craving more
powerful than any physical deprivation, but he was too overwhelmed by the
moment ever to think of rationing. He was always the same, whether it was a
painting to be finished, or a longed-for book that had to be read in a single
sitting. I was only glad that I was in charge of the food, eking out our supplies
to try to ensure that we never actually ran out of anything. I was sure that
Mike's regime would have been one of feast or famine.

During these quieter months, the seal pups were a compelling diversion.
I could never fail to be moved by the arrival of a new pup, slipping into the
world pristine and bewildered. Every one of them had the look of being too

perfect, too vulnerable for such a harsh environment. The main seal beaches were quite close to the house, but there were isolated scraps of boulder beach scattered round the island where pups might be born. These mainly offered inadequate shelter for the pup, and were difficult for us to keep track of because of their inaccessibility.

Though it was not an ideal situation for a seal to give birth, we made a daily check of the Wick. The beach there was a refuge in all but the fiercest storms, but it faced straight into the westerly gales and was cut off from the sea at low tide by the maze of jutting rocks. It was a bleak day, already nearing its end as we made our usual survey of the inlet. The afternoon light was dimming, and the chill was forcing its way in along with the greyness. Finding no pups at the Wick, we cut across towards High Cliff, with the view of South Haven opening out in front of us. The tide was exceptionally low. Around the edges of the bay, the water had seeped and filtered from between the rocks, exposing fringes of naked brown weed glistening in the last of the cold light. It was so extreme that it changed the familiar shape of the bay, and showed us shadows in the water of rocks that were never seen.

As we passed High Cliff, we heard the unmistakable wail of a newborn pup.

'I'm sure there aren't any pups here,' I said

We clambered down the grassy thread of a path to where the unusual tide had uncovered an expanse of boulders tumbling out from the base of the cliff. We began to jump from rock to rock, moving down towards the sea, urged on by the obvious sound of distress. We had almost reached the water's edge when Mike called out,

'Over here!'

The face peering up at me from a deep hole between the rocks was not, as I had expected from the sound of the voice, a white-coated pup, but an animal of a couple of months old. It was as though its terror had sent it back into babyhood, calling with all its might for the mother that had forgotten it.

Perhaps he had stayed too long, basking in the fleeting patches of pale winter sunshine, and then woken to find that the sea had drained away, and been replaced by this unfamiliar landscape of rocks and weed. Somehow he had slipped, tail first, into a deep gully between the rocks and was caught fast in an upright position with his head facing skywards.

Mike reached down into the rocks to grab a handful of blubber on the scruff of the seal's neck and yank it free. The seal, despite the swathes of fat making thick folds around his neck, was remarkably agile. His head moved with the slick cunning of a cobra, so that the jaws were ready to bite Mike's hand, no matter what angle of approach he took. The teeth were intimidating, the jaws as formidable as those of a large dog, and infections from seal bites can cause permanent paralysis of the fingers.

'Give me your jumper,' Mike said. 'If I could get him to bite on it I could grab him with the other hand while he's distracted.'

Mike brought his protected woolly hand provocatively close. The pup snarled and bared his teeth, but wouldn't take the bait.

'This is never going to work,' Mike said. 'We need to get a rope round it, or something.'

Summer evenings linger, but in winter the light falls sharply away. Already, the dull afternoon had the blue-grey feel of twilight. There would be no time to get back to the house, so we searched among the rocks, eventually finding a length of blue rope. Mike began to construct a makeshift noose. The rope was old and weathered, its synthetic strands stiffened by time, and the eroded surfaces snagged against each other. But Mike had a natural ability with knot tying, and the end result looked quite good.

By the time we turned our attention back to the seal, I saw the glint of water encircling its lower body. Mike dropped the loop down over the seal's neck and pulled on the rope. The knot tightened a little, and then the whole thing slipped off, whipping free against the breeze. After a number of failed attempts, the seal was almost submerged in the pool of water that had come seeping rapidly up through the rocks. On an incoming wave the anguished cries were caught and crushed by the cold surge of sea. I could make out the colours of the pup, broken into a shoal of pieces by the rippled water, and I felt sure that the cry was still going on, rising up in a silent stream of bubbles, desperate and hopeless. For the first time, I accepted that we might be going to lose the pup and I felt the faint prickling of tears.

'Your belt!' I said, in a flash of inspiration. 'Try your belt.'

Mike pulled the thick strip of leather from his waist and threaded the free end through the buckle to form a loop. The pup seemed tired, less angry, more resigned to our feeble rescue efforts. In a lull between the waves I felt the breath freeze in my throat as Mike dropped the belt over the seal and the leather began to tighten around it. Mike pulled harder, increasing the pressure slowly, tentatively. The seal was beginning to lift slightly, when the belt snapped free and the animal slumped back between the rocks. He tried twice more, growing ever more cautious as the belt began to pull at the seal's flesh, in case any sudden movement might break that precarious hold. But each time, the seal fell from his grasp.

The waves were coming so frequently over the seal's head that it would soon be beyond our reach. Mike began what was sure to be one of his last attempts. As he felt the seal slipping again, Mike knew that it was too late for caution. Instead of moving tentatively, he snatched hard at the belt and it bit into the flesh, sinking between the folds of blubber. The seal came lurching upward, clear of the hole, and then flopped down onto a smooth, flat rock. Arching its back violently, it propelled itself into the sea where it sank into the smoky greyness, leaving behind only a growing pool of ripples and a sense of calm that felt unnatural after so much drama. I waited for it to reappear, certain that, once it felt the safe embrace of the water, the seal would find the courage to turn and look back. The dully-opaque air had become indistinguishable from the sea, so that the mist-coloured twilight looked infinite. No shiny head appeared in this endless half-light. The pup was gone.

We relied on the tractor more than ever in winter when there was no one else to help us. Without it, life would have slowly ground to a halt. But it wasn't just a necessity, I was truly fond of it, and the fact that it could be temperamental and irritable was no more than a forgivable affliction of old age. One of its most unnerving idiosyncrasies was its habit of rearing up like a startled horse and lifting its front wheels off the ground when we were negotiating the steep track behind the house. And yet, because of our shared history, it was difficult not to find such small tantrums endearing. Having become accustomed to the tractor's foibles on the smooth, open fields in the centre of the island, I had made my first solo run up this perilous piece of track on my twenty-first birthday. It seemed like a particularly good present and had sealed the bond between us.

Despite my affection for the tractor, even I had to accept that our time together might not be indefinite. It was going wrong with increasing regularity and spare parts were becoming almost unobtainable. I think that the tractor had only kept going as long as it had because Mike refused to give in. He was not one to be beaten by any sort of practical problem. In fact, the more he raged and swore and insisted that something was absolutely impossible, the more certain I was that he would find a solution. When the situation with the tractor was desperate he had been forced to mend old parts, or even make new ones, with access to no more than a basic tool kit. We had finally reached the unhappy situation of having a tractor that wouldn't start. That was where our precarious hill came into its own. It meant that we could leave the tractor parked on the slope and roll it down to get it started.

We were in the process of building a rabbit-proof exclosure at the Wick. The island's rabbit population was having a profound effect on the vegetation, and the fenced-off rabbit-free area was an attempt to see what would happen without the impact of the rabbits. We had the fencing wire and posts ready to transport across the island; all we needed was the tractor. Mike trudged up the hill and settled himself in the tractor seat, while I waited by the pile of fence posts preparing to load them. I saw the tractor churning and bumping its way down the muddy slope. Then came that satisfying, clunking roar as the engine began to turn over. I was only half interested, half staring out to sea, when I began to realise that something was wrong. The tractor was running out of space. It was losing speed as the slope grew shallower, and the clunks from the engine were becoming dismally slow and wide apart. Finally, it rolled to a dispirited halt, cold and lifeless.

Mike said something very unpleasant about the tractor, which I thought was unfair, given its age and general good behaviour. He jumped down from the tractor seat.

'Now what?' he demanded, glaring at the poor, inoffensive vehicle.

I knew that he wouldn't welcome an answer, so I continued to stare in silent disbelief. That was the trouble with winter. I loved the challenge of it, but when things went wrong, they really went wrong. There was no prospect of help, since we were unlikely to see anyone for months. If we were going to overcome this, we would have to do it ourselves. The situation appeared to have all the necessary ingredients of a nightmare: a huge machine stranded at the bottom of a slope with nowhere else to go, except over the cliff.

I took solace from the fact that Mike was declaring vociferously that the situation was beyond salvation. He was obviously about to come up with a solution.

'We're going have to winch this thing back up the hill. Do you understand?' he shouted.

It was one of those severely testing occasions where he felt obliged to make it clear that he was cursed with the world's most incompetent assistant. We found ropes, the heavy cliff rescue stakes and a small hand-winch with a ratchet handle. I couldn't see how it was going to work. With the stakes hammered deeply into the ground and the winch connected by an intricate network of ropes, Mike began to click the handle with a slow, regular beat, backwards and forwards, until the rope finally stretched taut and began to pull against the tractor. The thick rubber lugs on the tyres made good hand holds and I tried to force the wheels back up the hill. It took us hours, inch by painful inch. When we started it had seemed hopeless, but eventually we made it.

On the downward descent, the tractor built up speed, the engine began to choke and sputter back to life, coughing a few smudges of dark smoke from the exhaust pipe. The first indication of failure came as the sounds began to die like a fading pulse. It was painful to watch as the slope ran out and the tractor slid to a determined standstill.

Hours later, when we were higher than the coveted position we had allowed to slip through our fingers, where the track was carved into deep gullies by the overflow of water, we had no option but to let the tractor go back down the hill, despite the prospect of failure. My feet slithered as I pushed at the back of the vehicle, and then the huge wheels began to turn. Splashes of mud flicked up into my face. The tractor clattered reluctantly at first over the stones in the deeply rutted track, then, finally, it began to gather speed. The engine choked out a feeble trail of exhaust clouds and, gradually, the staccato splut-tering increased its tempo, harmonizing into a long, rhythmic judder. At the last possible moment the clattering engine broke into a roar of triumph and a fountain of exhaust smoke leapt into the air. The tractor pulled away from me under its own power and I was left standing in its wake. I looked down at my sore, burning hands. The grit from the tyres had been driven into my palms, and was buried so deeply under the skin that it would stay for weeks. But all that really mattered was the fact that we had succeeded.

Winter was the time for beachcombing. The summer was too busy for such idle pastimes and, besides, it was the winter storms that sent the most appeal-ing assortment of oddities tumbling onto our shores. South Haven and its offshoot, Driftwood Bay, were the most suitable sites for treasure hunting. North Haven trapped virtually nothing, and the other bays were too inacces-sible. South Haven was no more than a scramble away, down a steep, slightly crumbling, path. Whenever we went, Wellington and the kids had to come too. They loved racing up and down the windswept track, trying to trip us up on the most precarious sections, and then gambolling like lambs across the rocky shore.

We went down to see what the big tides had brought us. Always, when my feet touched the clattering beach stones at the bottom of the path and the sound echoed back from the great curve of cliff around us, I felt a sense of excitement. We were entering the unknown where anything might be found. This was the point where we touched the outside world: a sweep of ocean that went on, unbroken, all the way to America, carrying the ships that crossed our distant horizons, vague and unreal as shadows. We walked along the strandline while the goats charged on ahead. Thick, leathery ribbons of glossy, brown weed, that had been broken loose by the waves, lay heaped in a ridge along the shore. The sea-smell that came up from the weed still carried childhood memories of the first day of a seaside holiday and the promise that stretched ahead.

The reality of beachcombing was that we rarely found anything of great value; it was all to do with anticipation. My favourite finds came in our early years on the island: two glass fishing floats, one green and one amber. Though purely functional, to me they looked like rare and precious things. When I held them up, with the sunlight streaming through them, they seemed as fragile as soap bubbles, and yet they had obviously seen hard work, before crashing ashore on the rocks, still intact. Perhaps their real beauty lay in the fact that they were the last remnants of a passing era. After those two, we only ever found plastic or aluminium fishing floats. When I saw the glass floats sparkling on the kitchen dresser I was glad to think that I could remember the time just before they disappeared. Another treasured find, for quite different reasons, was a Russian pencil, brand new and unsharpened, inscribed in an indecipherable text. It was a mundane and worthless object but, for me, the fascination was in wondering by what circuitous route it had found its way to Skomer.

We meandered purposefully, kicking occasionally at the weed to discover anything that might lay hidden. Each jab with a foot produced a fresh drift of sea-scent. The tide was low enough for us to make our way across to Drift-wood Bay; Mike leapt easily from rock to weed-slicked rock, while I followed slowly, slithering with ankle-jarring regularity into the gullies between. Drift-wood Bay remained true to its name: for some reason, its sloping shingle gathered plentiful supplies of good, clean wood, while only a minimum of rubbish ever became trapped there. As usual, our return journey was made all the more hazardous by the cumbersome chunks of firewood that we couldn't bring ourselves to leave behind.

As we reached the main beach of South Haven again, I saw a curtain of rain draping down from the clouds and flapping indecisively in the erratic squalls of wind. We ran for the alcove scooped into the cliff at the top of the bay and

Wellington, sensing impending moisture, raced ahead of us. Boojum and Snark came too, for the fun of joining in. The dingy haze whispered faintly against the rocks and smelt of dampness. In the quiet of our retreat, the waves sounded loud against the shore.

The shower passed quickly and, almost at once, the sun shone again. Water dripped down from the cliff above, shimmering across the cave entrance like a beaded curtain, and we walked out through the flickering diamonds into the sunlight. The kids followed, but Wellington, fooled by the drops, stayed trapped inside, bleating furiously at being left alone. Though hardly the most refined of animals, Wellington was as fastidious as a cat when it came to rain. If we were out walking, she would run home bleating with rage as the first splashes hit her.

As soon as we resumed our beachcombing, Mike lunged at something half hidden in the weed.

'This looks interesting!' he exclaimed.

Searching for anything is, by its nature, vaguely competitive, and I went over, slightly enviously, to examine his find. It was a fairly large tin, scuffed and battered from its journey across the rocks.

'It's quite heavy,' Mike said. 'Certainly not empty.'

'What does it say on it,' I asked.

'It's lifeboat stores.' He examined further. 'American.'

We went and sat on a nearby rock to concentrate on the job of prizing the tin apart. After a brief struggle the lid popped off, and, remarkably, there was no water inside. We sorted through the rock-hard biscuits, sickly white chocolate and boiled sweets with ridiculous fascination. It was, to us, like a messenger from another land.

'What are you doing?' I squealed, as Mike unwrapped one of the sweets and began to eat it.

'Just seeing what it tastes like.'

'But you can't,' I protested. 'You don't know where it's been.'

'It's all sealed. Try one.'

He handed me a sweet and, tentatively, I put it in my mouth. It was perfectly ordinary, tasting faintly of orange. We sat side by side on the rock, sucking our sweets and gazing out to sea.

It was one of those moments of true contentment that happen for no particular reason. Dazzling dregs of winter sunlight felt warm against my face. The seals were watching us. Clusters of two or three smoothly rounded heads slid quietly through the water, venturing daringly close, then, with sudden synchronized splashes, they all disappeared at once. Bubbly, filigree fringes of sea were beginning to brush the base of the rock, just below our dangling feet. We didn't want to leave our charmed spot, and sat stubbornly still, as though we could hold back the tide. But, as it always does, the sea eventually won. An oversized surge of foam came flooding in around the rock, and as it receded we jumped clear before the next wave. The sun was slipping down behind the island sending a slab of cold, evening shadow cutting across South Haven, and the sea was rapidly reclaiming its territory. It was time to go home, but tomorrow there would be another tide, and everything that might bring.

If only every day could have been filled with such idyllic interludes, but, unfortunately, the work on the rabbit exclosure took priority. It was a particularly dreary job. Since the fence was to keep rabbits out, the wire had to buried three feet into the ground to prevent them burrowing below it. In reality, we usually hit bedrock long before we had reached anything like that depth. Chipping through the stony soil with a crowbar was dispiritingly slow, and our hands blistered until they bled, but at least something was going our way: as we prepared to load our supplies for another day at the exclosure, the tractor sped down the hill and growled obediently into life. We threw the fence posts, crowbars and sledgehammers into the back, setting off towards the centre of the island and then out behind the farm.

For the last part of the journey, we had to leave the track and drive across rough ground towards the Wick. The storm-flattened bracken lay like a rustling brown blanket over the landscape. The tractor wheels crushed the dry, crackling stems, while the wood and wire bounced noisily in the back. I followed, walking between the lines drawn by the tyres, and, though the tractor was picking its way with tentative caution, I found myself slipping behind. I was in no hurry to reach the Wick and start digging, with the sharp, dry wind rising up over the cliff and spitting dust into my eyes. I stared around taking comfort in the bleakness, the flatness of the sky, the vegetation in its dozens of rusted shades.

We were almost there when the tractor lurched to a halt. Mike swore loudly, disturbing me from my idle enjoyment of the landscape, and I ran over to see what was wrong. By the time I reached the scene, Mike was striding round the tractor peering underneath it from all angles. The frequent muttered curses told me that it was quite bad, but the exact nature of the disaster was difficult to understand. My own amateur assessment of the situation suggested that all four wheels of the tractor were suspended off the ground. But that wasn't possible. I joined Mike, craning my neck at on awkward angle to scrutinize the underside of the tractor, and tried not to make matters worse by asking silly questions. Eventually, I had to speak.

'What's happened?' I asked.

'The tractor's got caught on a rock. Under there, see?'

I didn't see. The rock was still completely camouflaged by the bracken, and the tractor was hovering, as if frozen in the middle of a small, balletic leap.

As the tractor had started to go downhill, the underside had grazed the rock, and then the front wheels had tipped forward down the slope, lifting the back wheels off the ground and leaving the tractor pivoted in mid-air on one jutting point of rock. It looked like an impossible situation to have got into, and even more difficult to get out of. The only thing on our side was that we had inadvertently come well equipped for just such a rescue mission. Mike began throwing spades, wooden posts and a crowbar out of the tractor box and onto the ground.

'Now then,' he said loudly and precisely. 'We're going to build an earth ramp to give the wheels something to grip on.'

The clear, harsh tones warned me that we were entering one of those crises that apparently sent my intelligence levels plummeting.

All the time we were digging the ramps I was listening to the steady purr of the tractor engine, and particularly to the way it hesitated occasionally for a moment too long. I was afraid that at any second it would catch its breath and die. And then we really would be in trouble. It was too old and feeble to start under its own power, and the experience of winching it up the hill was enough to convince me that we would never be able to drag it clear of this spot. We would have to pull it through the rough clutter of rocks and bracken back to the track, and then half way across the island before we could find a slope steep enough to start it again. As we worked, I wondered how long the diesel would last, whether each little cough was the first symptom of the tank running dry.

Finally, we had packed enough earth under the wheels to give them something to cling on to. Mike got into the tractor seat, the engine roared and the wheels began to turn slowly. My sense of triumph faded quickly as I realised that the tractor remained firmly anchored: the movement of the wheels was simply pushing aside the earth that we had piled into place.

'It's still caught on the rock,' Mike called above the engine noise. 'Grab one of those fence posts and try to lever it off.'

I wedged the fence post under the tractor and wrenched with all my might. The tractor wheels continued to turn until they were spinning free above two hollow scoops of earth. Mike eventually accepted the futility of what we were doing and allowed the screech of the engine to slip back to gentle stutter.

'It's no good!' he shouted. 'You're just not strong enough.'

We rebuilt the ramps, packing the earth in as firmly as we could.

'Right,' Mike said. 'This time you can drive. But, remember, if you stall the engine, this tractor will never move again. It'll sit here forever and become a rusting heap.'

With my confidence perceptibly dented, I climbed reluctantly into the driving seat. The engine growled; the tractor moved a couple of inches and then jammed again.

'Come on!' Mike yelled through gritted teeth, as he strained against the fence post.

With the engine noise screeching to a crescendo, I felt certain that I was pushing it too hard. I eased off the accelerator and the tractor dropped back, losing what little ground we had gained. Mike threw the fence post down in anger.

'What on earth did you do that for?' he said.

'I'm sorry,' I wailed. 'I was sure the engine was about to stall.'

'All right. Let's try again,' he said with exaggerated patience. 'I wish there were two of me.'

We tried, and again I lost my nerve, and Mike yelled with justified frustration. We were wearing our ramp away; soon it would need rebuilding.

'Now,' Mike said, 'whatever happens, keep going this time.'

The wheels turned, juddering against the earth, and the sound of the engine rose to a scream that buzzed like a dentist's drill through my head. I looked back to catch a glimpse of Mike. He was in a trance of total concentration, eyes closed, face deep red, beads of sweat stippling his skin. With a howl that released a surge of energy, he poured all his strength into the makeshift wooden lever, and everything lurched forward. The tractor broke free, and I found myself driving cautiously down the slope. I dragged the handbrake on and ran back to Mike. We hugged each other and the anger was already forgotten. We had saved the tractor, our workhorse, and, yes, I have to admit it, our friend.

TWELVE

As we moved into the last days of winter, the ravens returned to their nest sites and called to each other, high above the island, with their deep, rattling voices. It was a wake-up call, a reminder that spring was waiting just out of sight. The time had come again to watch the ravens closely, as they incubated their eggs and fed the nestlings, in the hope that, eventually, we would catch sight of the newly-fledged birds. That was the true moment of success, when the young left the nest and launched themselves into the precarious freedom of the world beyond. Except that year things turned out differently.

It was in early summer that we first encountered The Raven. Despite all he came to mean to us, that was the only name he ever had. Mike found him tumbling helplessly down a steep, grassy bank towards the cliff edge, as a flurry of noisy gulls mobbed him furiously. He had flown too close to the gull colony and been driven away by birds protecting their nests. They had continued to attack him even as he fell, no longer a threat to anything. When Mike slithered down the grass slope after him, the gulls reluctantly left their prey, but remained circling hopefully overhead, mewing gentle threats. He was able to retrieve The Raven as it flailed on the ground, too dazed and battered to fight back.

Mike brought The Raven back to the house, and the wing was so obviously broken that it didn't take more than a cursory examination to tell us that we had just acquired a dilemma. He was one of that year's clutch of young birds, almost full-grown, but with an immature softness about him. His feathers had not yet developed the sleek, metallic-blue gloss that made the adults look invulnerable. Apart from his injured wing, he was too healthy and magnificent a bird to be put down; Mike was determined to save him.

The calm weather was on our side, and so the forlorn raven was bundled into a cardboard box and taken to the mainland to be examined by a vet. When Mike returned, the good news was that there were no other injuries apart from the wing, which had been strapped and would take about six weeks to mend. The sting in the tail was that there was only about a fifty percent chance that he would ever fly again. I never seriously believed in those odds; in my mind they diminished to nothing. I convinced myself that we held the key to his future. If we cared for him well enough, we would eventually be rewarded by the sight of him gliding above the cliffs again.

The immediate difficulty was where he was going to live. Mike, with his usual unstoppable practicality, set about building him a small aviary out of fence posts and chicken wire. Within a few hours the cage, about six feet square, with a wooden shelter to provide protection from the weather, and perches made of driftwood branches, was complete. Peering up from the depths of his cardboard box The Raven looked sullen and aggressive. It was hardly surprising, since his few weeks of life had shown him little reason to trust. He fought fiercely to stay in the box, the only refuge he knew, and when he was transferred to the cage he wedged himself immediately into the dark gap beneath the wooden shelter. All we could see was the occasional glint of beak and eyes looking out at us.

When he had recovered his self-composure enough to be able to venture out into the daylight, The Raven turned all his attention to the band of pink sticking plaster that pinned his two wings together. He obviously resented it as something alien, and therefore unacceptable. His heavy beak proved to be surprisingly dextrous as he used the pointed tip to tease skilfully at the tape. Within half an hour, the binding that the vet had put in place was lying tattered and dirty at the bottom of the cage.

'Now what?' I said. 'The wing will never mend now.'

'It's all right,' Mike replied. 'The vet showed me how to replace the tape.'

He found some thick, green tape and wrapped it round and round the wing tips, binding them firmly together. The disgruntled raven sat on his perch twisting himself into contortions so that he could examine the tape from all angles. When, after a few hours, the tape remained impervious to sustained attack, The Raven had the good grace to give up. He quickly forgot about the tape, and continued to preen the feathers around it as though it had been accepted as part of him.

The following morning, The Raven surprised us. With the palest light of dawn just diluting the darkness, he began to sing. It was one of the most beautiful birdsongs I had ever heard, rippling and melodic. The only sounds I had associated with ravens were the gravelly, reverberating calls that echoed across the sky. I had never realised that these powerful birds also had such gentle songs. It sounded so impossible that I had to get out of bed and go to the window to make sure. There he was on the perch in the middle of his cage, no longer hunched and sulking, but completely absorbed in producing the flowing notes of his song. I went back to bed, comforted by the ridiculous belief that no truly unhappy bird could sing so beautifully.

Every morning after that, he greeted the first light with the same haunting song, and then for the rest of the day he remained silent. As time passed, I found more and more reasons to believe that he was not unhappy. His intelligence, which should have made him particularly resentful of the deprivations of a cage, actually seemed to be an asset. He was alert and bright-eyed, with an insatiable interest in everything. He watched every movement, every coming and going from the house, with absorbed fascination, and was forever busying himself about the cage, as though there were endless things to be done. He had even forgotten to bear any resentment towards us for the cruel way we had shoved him into a box and bound his wings with tape.

The difficult thing was remembering that The Raven was not ours. He had come from the wild and that was where he would always belong. We had him only on the most fleeting of loans. The last thing we wanted was for him to become a tame bird, and so, although it took all our willpower to treat him with such coldness, he was fed, watered and ignored. The greatest excitement of the day was the arrival of his food. His body quivered with ecstatic anticipation, but we couldn't stay to watch him enjoy his meal. We could never allow ourselves to linger too long at his cage or let him associate us with these favourite moments.

The weeks of his recuperation passed quickly, but, as the time for his release approached, I felt my optimism dissolve. The strip of tape around his wings that had once seemed to offer so much hope now looked faintly ludicrous. How could something so simple have worked a miracle? Although the allotted time was over, we hesitated in case a few more days could produce that last bit of magic. And when we could find no more excuses to wait, the wings were carefully cut free. The feathers were slightly ragged at the tips where the tape had gripped them, and, discouragingly, the injured wing drooped lower than the good one. After another day, to let him exercise his wings and recover from the indignity of being handled, we gave him his chance to fly. Somehow, as we took him from the cage, I knew that it was over; my faith in miracles had evaporated. As I had feared, The Raven couldn't manage even a few credible wing beats. He tumbled onto the soft vegetation and scurried into the forest of towering bracken fronds. Mike sprinted up the hill to retrieve him before he was lost beneath the canopy of bracken. A couple more attempts to launch him only confirmed the hopelessness of the situation.

'Don't worry,' Mike said as he put The Raven back in the cage. 'We'll give him a few more days to build up his muscles, and then we'll try again.'

But I already knew. I had seen enough to convince myself that he wouldn't fly again. Some days later we encouraged The Raven to take to the air once more, with the same spectacular lack of success. And suddenly we had taken ownership of him; he was our problem and our responsibility. I had never considered his future, because I had thought only of the time when he would be back among the rocky crags and empty skies. My one hope had been that I might occasionally look up to see him soaring free, and that, perhaps, if he glanced down, some fleeting recognition would pass between us. That would be all that remained of his time in captivity, some faint and clouded memory. Now, with his useless, drooping wing, all prospect of freedom was gone.

The only certainty left was that there was no longer any point in keeping our distance from him. He would have no need of the independence we had been so carefully nurturing in him. Whenever he was fed, or even if we were passing by, we stopped at his cage to talk. We convinced ourselves that he enjoyed the company, and we could find constant fascination in watching such an intelligent bird. Though he now belonged to us, it was too late to give him a name. By that time he was simply and unalterably The Raven; any name that we invented would have been an imposition.

We discovered that he filled his days with his own succession of games. He had a hoard of toys that, with immense skill, he managed to keep hidden. These were mainly smooth, dark, shiny stones that he had unearthed from the floor of his cage. They were buried in pockets beneath the turf, or wedged deeply into crevices between the wood and wire structures. His two favourite trophies were kept in special places, separate from his run of the mill playthings. These treasures consisted of the original fleshy pink sticking plaster that he had torn from his wing, and a rabbit's ear that he had removed from one of his meals. The relish with which he disinterred these objects and examined them, turning them over and over in the tip of his beak with the utmost delicacy, made me think that he was savouring their slightly illicit nature. When he had finished, he would put them away, often retrieving them and moving them several times before he was sure they were really secure. Sometimes, whole days would pass without these horrible things being revived, and I hoped that he had lost interest in them, but always, eventually, they reappeared.

He never seemed to notice his loneliness, but we did. No matter how much of a hurry we were in, it was impossible to pass his cage without at least shouting out, 'Hello!'. One morning, we were rushing across to the landing steps to meet the *Dale Princess*. Mike and I both called 'Hello!' in mid-dash, and The Raven, in a high, croaky voice, said 'Hello' back. We lurched to an abrupt halt and stared at each other. Then we ran to the cage, ducking down to meet The Raven at eye level. 'Hello, hello,' we said encouragingly. The Raven gazed back inscrutably, tilting his head on one side to look at us with polite interest, but he didn't utter a single word.

We were coming close to believing that we had imagined it when, a couple of days later, The Raven spoke again. 'Hello' remained the only word in his vocabulary, but he used it often and with great subtlety of meaning. It served for greetings and partings, the acceptance of food and toys, and as a general social interjection in any conversation. With appalling anthropomorphism, I convinced myself that he knew he was talking to us.

The Raven had one main aim in life, and that was to reach the ends of the string that tied his cage door shut. Two strands of parachute cord dangled down from the knot outside the cage, and The Raven twisted himself into endless contortions trying to reach them. I hoped that it was just an intense curiosity for the unattainable rather than any carefully planned escape attempt. We tried to lure him away with other dangling distractions. Mike tied a strip of canvas, which had been trimmed from the edge of one of his paintings, to the cage roof. It was something to be tugged, twisted and stalked from all angles, and, with the possible exception of the sticking plaster, became his favourite toy. It did nothing, however, to quench his longing for the door strings.

Our time with The Raven would have been remarkably happy but for one inescapable anxiety. We couldn't come to any satisfactory conclusion as to where his future lay. The only thing we were sure of was that he couldn't stay with us. His cage had been an emergency solution for an injured bird. It was never meant to be a permanent home. He needed more than we could give him. We had horrible circular conversations about where he might end up, which left us feeling sad and defeated, as though we had let him down. We thought that perhaps he could go to a zoo, or even, in our more desperate musings, to the Tower of London. But it was all so dismal, and we had no idea if anyone would want an injured bird. I couldn't bear to think of our wild raven, that had fledged from the sea cliffs and now sang to the dawn, in any of those dreary places.

Summer came to an end, the days were shortening, and still no decision had been made. Every evening we stood with him as the light grew dusty and grey, and watched as he ate his rabbit. The weather had defeated the mild sea breezes and a bubble of bitterly cold and dirty-looking air had settled over us. I could feel its thin, brittle touch like a cold compress against my face, sinking right through the skin and making my bones ache. The gloominess of the days, frozen into a high-pressure stillness, became linked in my mind with the dull despair I felt about The Raven's prospects. The only thing that had allowed us to linger so long without being forced into action was the fact that The Raven appeared so completely at ease. His apparent contentment helped to take away the sense of urgency.

It was while we were having another of our discussions on what were likely to be the necessary qualifications for a raven to take up residence at the Tower of London that the solution hit us. It came like a brilliant light, illuminating both our thoughts simultaneously, dazzlingly clear and so perfect that our anxieties dissolved instantly. The Raven didn't have to leave Skomer at all. If our only worry was keeping him confined in a cage, then we would open up the door and set him free. There was nothing on the island that could harm him, no predators for him to fear. We would continue to feed him every day and the cage could be left open for him to use as a shelter whenever he wanted. There was only one problem that we could see: it was too good to be true.

We could hardly wait until the next day to begin the trial. The weather had turned milder, while the air was still and dry; conditions couldn't have been better. We untied the strings, leaving them dangling free, and propped the door wide open. Our vantage point was inside the hallway of the house, crouched behind the front door. The biggest fear was that The Raven would make an escape bid, plunging into the thick vegetation and disappearing forever. We had to make him understand that there was no need for any dramatic break out because he would be able to come and go whenever he wanted. My idea was that he would learn the same sense of freedom as the chickens up at the farm. They were completely free, with the whole island to wander over if they wished, but they never went beyond the farm complex, tucked themselves up in their shed at night, and came running when we went to feed them. I never knew how they learnt the rules of free-range life, but I only hoped that The Raven could do the same. It didn't matter how far he strayed; the important thing was that he remained close enough to accept food from us.

We watched in a state of sickening apprehension, ready to spring at any moment before we lost him. He would be unable to hunt for himself and would almost certainly die on his own. Faced with the reality of actually letting him go, my faith weakened, and I was beginning to feel sure that he wouldn't choose to stay with us. After so long in captivity, all his instincts would be telling him to get as far away as possible. The fragile bond that had grown between us would surely be broken by his craving for the wild.

After an hour or so, the tension had dulled to a cramped, aching boredom. We were stiff with cold and with crouching in our hiding place. The Raven had made not the slightest move to leave the cage, though it was obvious that he knew the door was open. His only interest remained his long-held desire to retrieve the strings. He leant out through the doorway and craned his neck up towards them, while his feet stayed firmly inside. No matter how desperate he was to reach that string, he wouldn't leave the cage. After another hour of watching his odd performance, we were ready to give up.

'I don't think anything's going to happen today,' Mike said stretching wearily. 'We'll close the cage and try again tomorrow.'

I made an attempt to move my heavy, tingling feet. At that moment, The Raven jumped out of the cage and down onto the grass. From our state of listless torpor we were instantly alert and ready for the chase. In another second he had seized the end of the string and leapt back into the cage with the cord still clutched in his beak. That was it; The Raven had won his most hard-fought battle. There was no chance that anything else would tempt him out of the cage, so we wandered over to close the door. 'Hello!' he said as we approached. And the string dropped from his beak, already forgotten. It was the contest that mattered, not the victory.

I was disappointed, because I so wanted to see The Raven free of his cage, and it felt as though our plans had come to nothing. But the more I thought about it, the more positive it seemed. The Raven was obviously happy where he was. It was clear that his days had not been spent plotting his freedom, as I had sometimes feared. The worst outcome would have been to discover that he was desperate to get away. If things could proceed at such a gentle pace, there would be far more chance of moving towards a state of tamed liberation.

The next day it all began again. Everything was as before: the cage door propped open, us hiding in the hallway. Predictably, the only interest The Raven showed in the open door was the greater opportunity it gave him to reach those entrancing strings. But after about an hour, he hopped out onto the grass and looked round. He then set off with a jaunty stride and disappeared from view down by the side of the house. Mike and I went after him as quickly and stealthily as we could. Pressed tight against the house wall, we peered furtively round the corner. The Raven was strutting purposefully away from us. We followed as closely as we dared, stepping slowly and silently over the short winter turf.

Suddenly, The Raven looked back and saw us following him. We froze and he froze, and our eyes held his in an uneasy deadlock. I saw, not our safe, caged bird, but something wilful and unpredictable. This would be the moment when he would panic and try to break free. I was certain that if I moved, even an inch, his trust in us would disintegrate and the scramble for freedom would begin. After a few heart-stopping seconds The Raven turned and strode back towards us. 'Hello!' he called cheerfully, like someone who has had a surprise encounter with an old friend. That one word cut through the tension and, feeling more relaxed, we followed him down onto the tractor track below the house.

These new surroundings obviously delighted him. He began to examine everything with gleeful curiosity, but the carefree behaviour was only a glossy veneer. Just below the surface he was watchful and wary. If we tried to approach him, he immediately tensed and edged away, maintaining the distance between us. I found it odd that he needed to retain a circle of his own inviolable space when, in the cage, he would have come as close as he could to the thin filigree of wire that separated us. It was as though he was remembering a little of what it was to be wild.

Mike and I sat on the cold, dusty path, facing each other, several yards apart. The Raven was calmed by this passivity, and began to tease his way through the precious things scattered round him. When he found something particularly interesting, a sleek pebble, a shiny metal bolt accidentally lost during one of the tractor's frequent repairs, he would bring it to show us. He came swaggering over with immense pride to lay the object in front of one of us and then, after a few seconds, it would be carried over to the other of us and set down for inspection. Finally, he would retrieve it and take it away to keep for himself. There was something slightly unreal about this perky little creature striding between us, something knowing, almost human. He had taken control of the situation and we were meekly following his instructions.

I began to feel elated that the experiment was working so well. As I watched him exploring, I could see no reason why he shouldn't gradually become accustomed to that level of independence, and eventually live happily in his own territory around the house. This blissful ignorance lasted until it was time to return The Raven to his cage. Mike and I both stood up, walking slowly and steadily towards him, with the intention of ushering him towards the cage. He didn't like it. He ducked away from us at every opportunity, scurrying in the wrong direction.

'This is never going to work,' I said. 'We're making him edgy.'

'Well, we've got to get him back somehow,' Mike replied. 'Let's see if he'll follow us.'

We began to walk ahead of The Raven, slinking nonchalantly towards the cage. There were no abrupt movements, nothing to shake his confidence in us, and, unwilling to be left out of the game, The Raven followed. We had found the solution: he did things on his own terms, not ours.

'Come on. Come on,' I coaxed quietly, as I grew increasingly confident of success.

In fact, I had grown so certain of him that I glanced away for a moment, and when I looked back The Raven was no longer with us. He was running, with more speed than I would have imagined possible, towards the edge of the cliff. As I turned to follow him, I realised that it was already too late. There was such determination in his stride. In another few seconds he had reached the cliff edge and launched himself over. I wanted to close my eyes, but it all happened so quickly that I found myself still staring transfixed as he fell. He plunged down towards the rocks, with his wings clasping uselessly at the air. Far below, the waves oozed back and forth, adding to the giddying feeling of sickness that was swilling over me. As he was about to land crumpled at the base of the cliff, I realised that his free fall had slowed into an uncontrolled glide. The Raven came to a halt among the rocks with a fairly restrained crash landing. Immediately, he scurried out of sight into a narrow gully, which at least reassured me that he must be relatively unhurt. Our biggest problem was that he was cut off from us by the tall cliffs on one side and the sea on the other.

'Quick,' Mike shouted. 'Let's get the dinghy.'

We began to run along the narrow cliff path towards the landing beach. My heart was beating so hard that it made a painful throbbing sensation deep in my throat. If there had been time to spare, I would have sat down and cried. The certainty was growing inside me that there was nothing we could do for The Raven. The tide was high and still rising. Soon it would be dark. He could hide from us indefinitely among those rocks, and when the darkness forced us to abandon him, he would surely drown. We reached the slipway and within seconds had dragged the dinghy splashing into the water. As Mike rowed across North Haven the boat rocked in the steady procession of gently arching waves hitting us from the side. All the time I stared ahead for any glimpse of The Raven.

It was not until the dinghy reached the furthest corner of the bay that I caught sight of him. He was at the entrance to a gully, which had been hidden by a rocky promontory. The rock he was standing on was surrounded by water. Behind him, the tumbled boulders disappeared into a shadowy darkness, making a maze of escape tunnels. The Raven was hunched and bedraggled, staring down at his feet and showing no curiosity at our approach, but I knew that he was watching us surreptitiously, ready to dive away as we came too close. Mike slowed the stroke of the oars, dipping them through the water in a series of smooth, quiet sweeps. We were torn between the need for speed and the importance of stealth. We had to get to The Raven quickly, but any rapid movements might drive him away from us.

Mike brought the boat skimming softly to a halt against the rocks, but that was enough to send a hollow echo juddering around us. I grabbed the nearest rock, hugging the boat tight against it to hold it still and prevent any further reverberations. As the water undulated languidly in and out on the lifeless waves, I noticed how brilliantly green the weed-covered rock looked as the sea lapped over it, and how the colour paled and drained to a milky softness as the water was sucked away leaving pockets of air between the filmy layers of weed. I thought how odd it was that my heightened emotions had made even the colours more vivid.

The boat had come to rest next to The Raven. He was within touching distance, but still he refused to look up. I held the boat steady as Mike reached out towards the despondent bird. His hand was tense, the fingers curled, ready to close into a sudden snatch. He was moving with infinite, breath-stopping slowness. The tension was like an elastic band being stretched tighter and tighter, waiting to snap. I knew that the wily raven would be sizing up every-thing, choosing the exact moment to scuttle out of reach. But I was wrong. Before Mike had a chance to grab him, The Raven stepped off the rock and perched himself delicately on Mike's wrist. It was only as Mike was lifting him into the boat that he looked up at us for the first time.

'Hello,' The Raven said, in perfect imitation of an abject apology.

After his scare, I think that The Raven was glad to return to his cage, to live again in a world of clearly defined boundaries. My first feelings were pure delight just to see him there unhurt, but they were soon followed by a desperate sadness. However well things appeared to have turned out, the truth was that we had lost The Raven the day he fell. The fact that he was safely back in his cage couldn't conceal the reality that our hopes of keeping him were over. In constructing our brilliant scheme to set him free, we had considered every possibility, except the most obvious one. A raven, even one with a damaged wing, will always dream of flying. It simply wasn't safe to let him wander so close to the cliff edge. Perhaps he had learned his lesson and frightened himself out of ever jumping over a cliff again, but we would never know. We couldn't take the risk, because the next time he might be killed.

We found The Raven a home on the mainland at a place where injured birds were cared for. It was the right decision, and yet one of the most painful we had ever made. If only he hadn't given the impression of being so happy in his cage it would have been easier to send him away.

Mike made him a small travelling cage, and when the time came for him to leave we retrieved a few of his toys and put them into the new cage. Mike took his favourite strip of bright canvas and tied it inside where he could reach it. I went through these final preparations for his departure in a blur of tears, trying to believe that I was crying only for myself and not for The Raven. He would be all right.

He was extraordinarily quiet and well behaved as he was transferred to the small cage. Perhaps subdued would have been a better word. He was such an intelligent bird that I couldn't help wondering how much he understood of what was happening. We carried him down to the beach and then into our open boat for the journey to the mainland. The day was the most miserable I could imagine, drained of colour, the air saturated with a fine drizzle. As we cut across the fog-coloured waves the pinprick moisture seeped out of the air, trickling down my face and beading on my oilskins. The Raven sat beside me showing little interest.

At Martin's Haven we lifted the cage out onto the damp, glistening pebbles, and a car came edging down the rutted, water-scoured track, ready to take The Raven away. Mike and I found a quiet moment to say goodbye to him before he went. His hunched and dejected posture reminded me very much of the day he had been rescued from the bottom of the cliff. He stared down impassively as we whispered to him through the wire. Then at last he looked up, with pale crescents of misty sky gleaming in his eyes.

'Hello,' he said quietly, for the last time.

The absence of The Raven permeated deeply into our lives. There were all sorts of silly things that I missed: his singing in the morning, the cheerful 'hellos' every time we passed. Outside the house the abandoned cage, stripped even of its toys, stood as permanent reminder of him. The cage, though, was not quite empty. When, occasionally, it was used by a new occupant for a brief period of convalescence, we found some of The Raven's playthings expertly concealed, and, for a second, he was back with us.

I looked for ways to distract myself. It was one of my favourite times of year. The seals were back in full force, crowding onto the beaches, perching precariously on offshore rocks, fighting, playing and producing their pups. It gave the island that feeling of being alive again after the quiet decline of late summer. One of the things I missed, almost as much as The Raven's singing, was the sound of seals gathered on the beach below our window. It had once been part of our winter nights to hear them so close that, in still weather, we could eavesdrop on every pebbly rattle of a seal stirring in its sleep, but since the oil spill, five years before, they had not come back to the haul-out site in North Haven. I never understood how they had been so discouraged from returning. I was certain that there could be no physical trace of the oil remaining, and the animals themselves would be a shifting population, with perhaps hundreds passing through in the course of a season, so it was impossible that they could all be carrying memories of that disaster. But, somehow, they knew that North Haven was no longer an acceptable place.

Only a handful of animals used the beach now. Surprisingly, these consisted mainly of breeding cows and their attendant bulls. There had been no decline in the number of pups born on North Haven beach over the years. It seemed strange that, if the beach was perceived to be in some way tainted, the breeding cows still came. With pups to protect they would have the most reason to stay away. I couldn't rationalise it; I was just so relieved that the breeding animals had not deserted us. Being able to watch the pups daily from my windows was one of the most rewarding experiences of being on Skomer.

My fascination with the seals had grown over the years, and I spent more and more time studying them. Since pups are born during the night, first light is the time for discovering new arrivals. I could never describe myself as a morning person, but some of those cold, early walks were among the happiest of my life. I would find it hard to explain why they were so special, except that there was always a feeling of hope, anticipation and freshness.

It was an unusually dismal November morning, and I set off before the light was fully awake. The air was still heavy with the drab particles of twilight. The full skin-numbing force of the weather didn't hit me until I began to cross the isthmus. It was often like that; since wind from both north and south streamed across that narrow strip of land with equal strength, it usually felt bitterly exposed in winter, whichever direction the weather came from. The search for seal pups began immediately; they could be nestled among rocks below the steep drop to either side of me, and I had to find vantage points that would let me see into the hidden niches among the boulders. If there was a well-concealed pup that had been born during the night I might see other clues, such as the mother just offshore, watching the beach.

That morning there was nothing new, only one pup in North Haven and another in Driftwood Bay, both a few days old. I made a mental note of their condition, but my notebook remained firmly in my pocket, along with my gloved hands. My fingers were too cold and unresponsive to write; I would have to wait until I had generated a bit more warmth from walking. As I left Driftwood Bay behind and cut across towards Matthew's Wick, I could hear the cries of a newborn pup carrying on the wind. The excitement began to ignite inside me, a spark of pleasure that was stronger than all the discomfort of those raw mornings. As soon as I looked down into the inlet of Matthew's Wick I could see the pup, absolutely brand new and still damp. The mother lay sleeping nearby, undisturbed by the constant wailing of the pup.

The sticky fur was clinging to the pup's body. Usually, the white coat gave an illusion of plumpness, but, with the wet fur crushed flat, the shadows of bones beneath the skin were clearly visible. Without their snowdrift fringe of fur, the huge dark eyes that should have been soulful looked only empty. It was a cruel start in life, one that seemed indifferent to comfort and well-being. After being cradled inside its mother for almost a year, the pup had swapped that warmth and darkness for a patch of stones and the harsh, bleak light of a winter morning. It looked too fragile to be lying alone on the sleek, wet pebbles without any shelter from the restless weather. As the cold seeped down round the collar of my coat, I imagined how the thin tendrils of wind must be raking through that damp fur and scraping against the pup's skin.

Eventually, the sleeping mother would wake and feed it. The pup would be so well fed that it would quickly fill out that loose, crumpled skin until it was almost too fat to move. But it would never know what it was to be curled up beside its mother in some warm, dark place. It would never feel the blood-heat of siblings piled around it. The pup was born alone and would stay alone. Soon its mother would have forgotten it. In a couple of weeks, her ties to that one small beach would be broken, and she would be free to wander again, with next year's pup already growing inside her.

I took out my notebook, removed my glove, and began to write. My fingers ached with cold, and their movements were slow and clumsy. In a jagged scrawl I listed the new pup with its mother close by. I would continue to note its progress day by day. Even when the mother was gone, I would still be watching over it, unseen, from the cliff top.

I pulled my glove back on, and headed off towards Amy's Reach. It was not a promising site for seals, but one that had to be checked every morning. The entrance to Amy's Reach was so full of boulders that it was almost inaccessible at low tide. The smooth shingle and relative shelter of Matthew's Wick made it a much more likely choice as a place to give birth. As I expected, the cliffs above Amy's Reach were silent: no newborn baby cries twisting and writhing in the wind. I was surprised, then, to look down and see the unmistakable whiteness of a pup against the dark rocks. It was apparently sleeping, with the mother lying so close that the pup was half hidden, but something was wrong. The pup was too still; I couldn't even see the faint swell of breathing. And the fur was too wet; every crisp claw-mark of its mother's touch remained imprinted on it. The warmth of the body should have dried it just a little.

If I had not seen so many pups over the years, it would have been easy to imagine that it was stillborn, but the mother's behaviour made that impossible. More than once I had seen a cow produce a lifeless pup and then move away without a backward glance. The small white thing was left to be tumbled in the surf and rolled with the torn and broken weed along the strandline: just another scrap of flotsam. In as little as a day, the eyes would be gone, pecked away by the crows to leave blank, staring holes. Then the body would be slit open and the pink, knotted insides dragged out to be feasted on. I knew that a stillborn pup was something to be discarded, not protected, by its mother.

I checked the rest of the bays and inlets round the Neck, finishing at Castle Bay, and then climbed back over the ridge of the promontory fort towards home. At last, I was warm all over, immune to the weather. Even the tips of my fingers felt warm. I was walking easily over the slopes, my legs barely feeling the steepness of the ground. My breathing was steady, not dragging the cold air down into my chest. I loved it in the winter when I walked so much every day that the process became almost painless.

As I crossed the isthmus, fulmars skimmed through the air beside me, just level with the cliff. Though it was only November, they were back already, settling themselves in, preparing for the distant spring. Their calls sounded like streams of jubilant laughter. The effect was so infectiously uplifting that I had to stop and watch them. They soared around me, suspended on motionless, outstretched wings. Fulmars are capable of the most effortless flight I have ever seen, gliding on the air currents with barely more than an occasional flick of their wings to sustain the momentum. Whenever I watched them it made me wish that I could step off the cliff edge and share their freedom of the sky. Occasionally, a bird turned its head to look at me as it whispered past almost at touching distance. They were vaguely gull-like with soft, pink-grey plumage, but any suggestion of elegance was tempered by a thick neck and a clumsy beak, made of mismatched parts, that would have suited a larger bird. As I walked on, the fulmars seemed to follow, scudding at my side, with me and yet absolutely separate.

After breakfast, I went back to Castle Bay with my telescope to watch the seals as they came ashore on the falling tide. I skirted widely round the bay, avoiding the temptation to go close enough to look down. If I were glimpsed on the cliff top, all the seals strewn across the beach would pour in a silvery cascade over the pebbles and plunge into the sea, turning it, momentarily, into a boiling froth. My route took me round to the side of the bay and down over the rocks, where I had to crouch low so that my silhouette wouldn't break the skyline. Mike had made a hide, which was precariously sited on a jagged promontory overlooking the bay. The hide was a wooden box, big enough for me to sit in, with a door on the side that faced away from the seals and a small, hinged flap on the other, that opened up to reveal a viewing slit with a perfect panorama of the bay. The whole structure was held down by a network of heavy ropes firmly anchored to the ground. In fact, there were so many ropes criss-crossing the hide that it looked ridiculous and, the first time I saw it, I laughed at Mike's excessive caution. But, having weathered the shuddering and rattling of the hide through many storms, with the sea thundering below me, I became convinced that there was not a single strand of rope too many.

I unbolted the door, ducked inside and pulled open the wooden flap. I loved that first moment of looking down to see what might be there. Twenty or thirty seals were scattered across the beach: their bodies, in all shades of dappled grey, mimicked the smooth, rounded boulders. At the water's edge, a couple of seals, hard and shiny as polished marble, were newly emerged from the sea. I was looking for yesterday's newborn pup. It should have been somewhere at the top of the beach, safe from all but the highest tides and clear of the lumbering bodies of the adult seals.

When I realised that the pup was gone I felt a mild, protective panic. I searched every corner of the beach with binoculars, and when that failed I began to look for the mother. I found her immediately at the edge of the shingle, lifting the front of her body from the stones and staring intently ahead. The briskness of her movements told me that she was anxious too. She began to make her way up the beach, stopping every few seconds to raise her head and scan the deserted place where her pup had been. Each time she came too close to a seal that had laid claim to one of these ephemeral territories she was met with aggression. Resentful of being woken, they twisted their heads towards the mother in a show of bared teeth and wailing hisses, stretching out flippers tense with aggression and swiping their claws close to her face.

The howls rippled across the beach as the agitation spread, and then, above the discord, I heard the voice of the pup. The mother heard it too. She hesitated, and then continued with such determination that she became impervious to the disapproval unfolding around her. She blundered in a heavy caterpillar-wave, with the wintry light on the sea-bright gloss of her fur making white highlights of every shuddering movement. The tentativeness that made her vulnerable had hardened into an aura of strength.

As the pup emerged from behind a rock, pulling itself forward with its foreflippers and crying in petulant desperation, the mother reached cautiously forward to nuzzle the soft white fur. Reassured that she had found the right pup, she rolled onto her side to let him feed, but lost patience before he had finished. She began to drag herself back towards the sea, with the pup threading in her wake along the path she had cleared through the sleeping seals. As she reached the point where the tips of the waves melted like a watery mirage into the pebbles, she stopped and looked back towards the pup. He had reached the faint, glittering barrier of sea, and could go no further. She turned onto her side, with the white-edged waves lapping her back, creating a pool of calm in front of her. The offer of milk was irresistible and the pup slid forward, breaking through the pale reflections of his mother imprinted on the water.

He swallowed the milk, laced with salt water, until his mother pulled abruptly away. Without her to block the waves, the plumes of white froth began to splash over him. He would have pulled back, but already the sea had taken hold and the stones beneath him were gone. In that moment of fear he had been set free, just as surely as if I had achieved my dream of flight and launched myself from the cliff like a fulmar.

As I watched the pup's uncoordinated body meandering haphazardly, it reminded me of a child making its first tentative attempts to swim without water-wings, paddling wildly, head held carefully out of the water safe from smothering splashes of sea. Even the intense, single-minded perseverance seemed to show the same childlike delight in the achievement. As he approached her, the mother dived deep into the water, and for a second I could see her outline mingling with the fractured patterns of the waves. Then she faded away completely, like the shadow that dissolves as the sun disappears behind a cloud. The pup, glaringly white against the twilight-coloured sea, looked suddenly very small and alone. Unable to follow, his flippers snatched uncertainly at the water. Then his mother broke silently to the surface, reassuring him with her presence, as the rings of rippled water grew around them.

She led the pup back, waiting frequently for him to catch up as he wriggled his tortuous course towards her, and stopped at the water's edge, while the pup, beginning to tire, splashed courageously behind her. As he came within reach of the shore, the smooth curve of a breaking wave arched above his head. I thought it would overwhelm him, but, instead, it scooped him up, holding him beneath the rim of bubbling surf, and swept him onto the beach.

The brief escape into his own element was over, and he was earthbound once more. Like a bird with its wings clipped, he had lost the freedom to soar effortlessly. Soon, he would learn the skills to play carelessly in the water, and then, all too quickly, it would become not a plaything but the source of his survival. His mother would relinquish responsibility for him when he was barely more than two weeks old, and then he would have to find a way of living with the sea, discovering a harmony with it, through the worst of the winter storms that were still to come.

I decided to walk back past Amy's Reach to check on the strange pup I had seen earlier in the day. I found the mother and pup together, seeming hardly to have moved since the morning. The mother was gazing at her pup intently. Though I knew I shouldn't, it was difficult not to interpret the gaze as loving. Most seals would have been content to remain close by in the water, but this animal appeared to be besotted with her pup. The certainty that something was wrong came to me almost like a physical pain.

The pup was still damp, and the fur clung with slimy smoothness to the skeletal structure of its body. The head looked wrong, too: twisted awkwardly. There was no longer any doubt that the pup was dead. It happened. It happened so often that I was almost used to it. But why did it have to happen to an animal with such exceptional maternal feelings rather than one that would have swum away without a backward glance? I began to wander slowly back home, irrationally subdued. After feeling my spirits being set free as I watched the young seal swimming, I had come back to reality, like the pup stranded again on the beach.

Each day I went back and found the mother lying side by side with her still-born pup. In the past, whenever I had touched a dead pup, the absolute stony coldness was somehow shockingly unexpected. But looking down at this pup, I could feel the chill in its body, like the uncompromising cold of winter seas. Its lifelessness radiated from it like an aura, and I could hardly believe that the mother didn't sense it too.

Over at Castle bay, the pup was gaining in confidence. Some pups didn't go near the water until they had reached independence, when discovering the sea had become a matter of life or death, but this pup was ready to swim at every opportunity. It was three days since he had first ventured into the water, and during that time the gawky uncertainty had matured into a streamlined self-confidence. The weather had remained calm throughout the previous days, and the water had settled into a limpid stillness that was quite un-wintry. Cramped in my hide, I peered down at the cluster of seals cast up on the shore, and thought how much their sleeping serenity and flowing shapes, made them look like artfully placed stone sculptures.

The following day the weather broke. As I crossed the isthmus for my early morning check of the seals, salt spray was already spiking the air. This first visit to the beaches, with the prospect of finding new pups, should have been my favourite bit of the day, but as I walked towards Amy's Reach I realised that my enthusiasm had gone. The situation with the stillborn pup and its tenacious mother was becoming more distressing with every day. This would be the fifth day that the mother had spent guarding her lifeless pup and, as far as I could tell, she had not left it alone for a moment.

When I looked down into Amy's Reach I saw that the steep incoming waves were being broken apart by the rocks that blocked the entrance to the inlet. Inside the gully there were no distinct waves, just a dense mass of surf. Through the haze rising up from the water I could see that the two seals were gone from their normal place on the beach. I felt relief, mixed with an odd sadness, to realise that the two had finally been separated. Then I saw them, still together, almost hidden by the thick, creamy foam washing all around them. The pup had been dragged from the beach and become wedged between two large rocks. The desperation of the mother showed in every movement of her body as she sent clouds of water droplets erupting into the air. She was sliding her muzzle beneath the pup's body and trying to lift it free of the rocks. The whole thing had an awful fascination, this grotesquely fierce loyalty towards a pup that had never been able to respond to her. I wanted to stay and watch, to see what the outcome of this struggle would be, but I couldn't. I found it too heartbreaking, and so I walked away.

At Castle Bay I edged my way cautiously down towards the hide with the eddying wind snatching and pushing at me from all directions. It was not until I was settled inside and had a clear view of the beach through the slit in the front that I realised how bad the situation was. Huge waves were driving directly into the horseshoe-shaped bay and rearing up in jagged, effervescent ridges. Where they broke, everything dissolved into a turmoil of white that was almost brushing against the base of the cliff, leaving only the thinnest ribbon of beach glistening in dark contrast. The air was filled with the crashing echo of waves layered one upon another, but I could make out the small, sharp voice of the seal pup. I could see the pale curve of its body pushed right up under the cliff, with no escape. The waves were so vast, consuming and dominating the bay, that the pup was diminished by them, overwhelmed by his surroundings.

Among the thick white curds of foam, the glinting black head of the adult seal was visible. She was in the water close to the pup with her body held sideways to the waves, as if to shield him. Each time one of the tumbling cascades of water vaporized against her, I thought that she would be caught up and smashed into the rocks, but as the confusion of surf ebbed away she was still there, sparkling bright with seawater. One after another the unforgiving slabs of water pounded against her, but she never lost her position. It was as though she was held in place by an anchor somewhere below the waves.

Soft, foamy tongues were beginning to lick against the pup. He cried loudly. Though he had adored the calm seas, he sensed the danger that was now filling the bay. Only the last, gentle reaches of the dying waves were spilling around him, and the froth looked deceptively benign, but I could hear the strength in the rattling drag of the backwash as it pulled away. Then an exceptionally large wave hit the pup, and as the water flooded back towards the sea he was dragged with it. The blunt, white foreflippers were clawing at the gritty shingle beneath the cliff, clinging on to safety, and then the pup lost contact with the shore. Like a leaf caught on a swollen river, he flowed helplessly with the sweep of retreating sea. He was being sucked into the deep, curving belly of the next incoming wave, arched above him ready to break. For a moment the wave hung in an impossible balance. Shades of muted green and grey flowed through the stretched skin of water. It held suspended for an endless fraction of a second, then tipped beyond the point of equilibrium and shattered with an explosion that reverberated through the solid rock of the island. Shards of broken water splintered into the air, as the seething white mound lunged towards the cliff. I glimpsed the pup tangled almost indistinguishably into the surf, appearing, vanishing, wallowing in and out of focus. When the turbulence had calmed enough for me to see clearly, the pup was gone. I stared at the shore until I was dizzied by the endlessly turning patterns of white, but there was no sign of the pup trying to drag himself back onto the pebbles.

I had almost given up hope of seeing the pup alive when something caught my eye further out in the bay. Barely visible amid the streaks of foam it was the pup, his head held defiantly above the water. He was swimming, not back towards the shore, where the waves would crush him against the rocks, but further out to sea. He had made the right choice, but surrounded by so much churning water he looked desperately vulnerable. A few seconds later his mother broke the surface alongside him, and I allowed myself to hope. I didn't know what she could do, but at least her strength and understanding of the sea were with him.

Side by side, they swam towards the mouth of the bay, but remained in the comparative shelter of the enclosed water, riding out the waves like buoys in a harbour. I could see the sleek heads and backs of seals driven from the beach and outlying rocks by the storm. For them it was no more than an irritation, but the pup was risking its life. One in three of the pups born on those beaches wouldn't survive the first three weeks of life, and much of that mortality would be as a result of storms. For all his agility, the pup was not a strong swimmer; he wouldn't be able to hold firm against the waves in the way that an adult could, and soon he would be exhausted.

When the tide had fallen a little, I saw the mother and pup making their way back towards the cliffs, swimming into the area where the sea was completely white with foam. As they approached the shore a breaking wave caught them both; it washed over the mother and she rode above it, but I lost sight of the pup. When I found him again he was being propelled towards the beach on the long, bubbling gush of water that was the remnant of the broken wave. He splashed and scrabbled for a hold on the stones but the sudden out-rush of water pulled him backwards into the path of the next wave, which twisted over, spilling all its weight on top of him. As the pup emerged from beneath the foam, still struggling to gain a hold on the beach, the water sucked him back and I could hardly watch, knowing that he would be smashed and thrown into the waves again. At that moment his mother appeared, slipping effortlessly through the surf and pressing close behind him, preventing the backwash from dragging him away. When the next wave broke, her body sheltered him from some of the impact.

I lost count of the number of waves that poured over them while the pup fought to regain his position on the beach. As each surge fell away he slipped back towards the sea, but his mother stayed close, making sure he didn't lose too much ground. Using her body to protect and guide him, she nudged the pup slowly ashore, until he was able to grasp the stones and drag himself, bedraggled and defeated, to the base of the cliff. He looked like a newborn again, with the camouflage of his fur washed smooth and the frailty of his body showing through. At a few days old he had done well to survive, and it was probably only his mother's tenacity and experience that had carried him through. All I could hope was that the storm would have eased before the next high tide.

It was time for me to go but, with more and more seals hauling themselves out of the water to escape the waves, watching was compulsive. They crammed themselves into every space left bare by the ebbing water. By low tide the beach would be full of seals, their bodies interwoven in a pattern of grey mosaic. When I left the hide I found that my legs were numb with cold and with sitting still for too long. I hadn't noticed the sensation draining away because all the time the pup had been in the sea I had been unaware of every-thing else.

I walked cautiously back up the steep slope, disorientated by the fact that I was unable to feel where I was putting my feet. I thought gloomily that within a few days my toes would be so red and swollen with chilblains that my boots would hardly fit; it was the same every winter. I wanted to go home and warm some life back into my feet before the damage became too bad, but there was one more thing that I had to do. I needed to go back to Amy's Reach to see what had happened to the pup there, though I knew what I would find. The pup would have been washed away, and the mother, with nothing to keep her there, would have deserted the beach.

When I looked over the cliff edge I saw at once that the pup was gone from where it had been wedged between the rocks. I walked further along the cliff to get a better view of the beach and was surprised to find the mother and pup back in their usual place. As always, they were lying side by side. The only difference was that this time the pup was tightly enfolded in its mother's foreflippers. Having watched the drama in Castle Bay, I knew that she must have fought hard to avoid losing her pup to the storm, and she was obviously determined not to let go of it again.

I walked slowly home, but the image of the cold, dead pup clasped against its mother wouldn't leave my mind. I had never seen a seal show that sort of affection, not even for a live pup. Far from accepting that her pup was dead, the longer they were together, the stronger the bond appeared to grow. I was beginning to wonder what it would take to make her relinquish her unhappy obsession.

The following day I could find no trace of mother or pup. It was a relief, but, without knowing what had happened, it felt like an unsatisfactory conclusion. I wondered if the storm had intervened and torn them apart, or if, in the end, she had abandoned her pup willingly to the waves. I wanted to believe that she had somehow come to understand that the pup no longer needed her. I looked across the open water to where the waves had piled together in long, rolling ridges, and I hoped that she was not out there, still searching.

THIRTEEN

December, and although the seal breeding season was definitely sliding into decline, it showed no signs of coming to an end. Pups were still appearing at regular intervals on the beaches around Skomer. The two-month breeding season had been well documented, particularly at colonies further north in Scotland, where most pups were born in October and November, but we had realised that Skomer followed a different pattern. The first pups appeared in September (or occasionally even earlier), and we continued to find newborn animals until the spring. By the time the breeding season dwindled indecisively to an end, perhaps eighty pups would have been born on the island.

Conditions could be so difficult that Skomer had no recent history of being occupied during the winter months and was generally deserted by the end of October. With no evidence to the contrary, the seals had been assumed to fit into the normal two-month breeding pattern. The only oddity was that when people returned at the end of the winter they found newborn pups. These spring pups were recognised as a Pembrokeshire phenomenon, and it was something that I remembered hearing talk of when we first came to Skomer. It was only when we began to stay on the island later into the year that we saw them as marking the end of a continuous winter breeding period. For me, it was one of our more exciting discoveries.

I was becoming so fascinated by studying the seals that it would have been nice if they could have been the only things to occupy my time over the cold, quiet months. Unfortunately, Mike had embarked on an ambitious project to renovate the old 'chalets' at the farm. These offered accommodation for visitors to stay overnight during the summer. They had been converted in the early fifties from the old cow sheds into a row of extremely basic, cell-like rooms, consisting of asbestos partitioning, crumbling concrete floors and iron bedsteads. During the summer, with unstinting help from volunteers, Mike had stripped everything away to leave only the outer stone walls and earth floors. We were now left with the problem of rebuilding them over the winter.

With the days at their shortest and bleakest, the first morning light seeped into the sky as if through a smoky filter as we made our way up to the farmyard to begin work on laying the new floors. We rapidly assumed our customary roles: me mixing the concrete while Mike swiftly and skilfully smoothed it into position. Each time I tried to lift one of the slithering-wet plastic sacks of sand to tip it into the mixer, set unfeasibly high on the back of the tractor, I had to grip so hard to stop it slipping through my hands that it felt as though my fingernails were being wrenched out. I could only keep going by blocking out the enormity of what lay ahead and concentrating my mind and body entirely on lifting just one more bag. As I grew tired, I became careless. Twice I failed to lock the concrete mixer securely back into place, causing it to tip suddenly and unexpectedly, disgorging its contents onto the sheet of plastic that we were using to protect the bowling-green lawn of the farmyard, leaving me on the brink of self-pitying tears.

As the late afternoon light ebbed away and a profound coldness clogged the air, we reached a natural and welcome end: the completion of a whole room. I stopped for a moment of satisfaction, leaning on the doorframe to watch as Mike smoothed the finishing touches into place, slick as icing on a cake. That gave enough time for the chill to come creeping in shuddering waves over skin that was hot and clammy from hard work.

'What are you waiting for?' Mike called crossly, seeing me idling, hands deep in the pockets of my boiler suit. 'There's another floor to be done. We need a fresh mix.'

I was furious, but my protests trickled over Mike's impervious back. It was impossible to do another one in daylight, but he was refusing to give way to mere physical practicalities. We finished the second room by touch alone as the day dwindled to an amorphous shadow, drained of detail. Mike was on his knees in the doorway, working in broad sweeps to iron out the creases in the wet concrete, insisting that the end result would be fine, but all I could see were shades of indeterminate grey turning to black. My hands were too numb to function as I fumbled to clean the tools in icy water.

Before we left the farmyard there was one more important thing to do. I groped round in the dark and managed to retrieve my sandwiches. As we walked home, I struggled to open them with fingers made clumsy by throbbing ache of returning sensation, which was far worse than the anaesthetizing effect of the cold. Mike would never allow anything as frivolous as a lunch break to interrupt the flow of work, so I'd had nothing to eat or drink all day. Weak with hunger, I bit passionately into one of the sandwiches, which consisted of two thick slices of stale bread, crumbly-dry with a sawdust texture, glued together with peanut butter. Disappointingly, it was almost unswallowable. Mike, who had somehow found time to eat his, was eyeing me enviously. Without a word of criticism I passed him one of my sandwiches. It gave me a nice, smug glow of self-sacrifice but, actually, it would have been impossible to eat two of them anyway.

From these unpromising beginnings, this shell of stone and concrete, we moulded Mike's vision of the bright, new rooms that would welcome visitors. They had warm tiled floors and wooden fittings, including simple kitchen units and bunk beds, all hand-made by Mike. We worked throughout the winter, until there was nothing left to remind us of the gloomy cells we had dismantled. The final coat of varnish was brushed onto the gleaming wooden surfaces just in time, and we were ready for the coming spring.

It wasn't only the seasons that shaped the changes on the island. Skomer had so many different layers all interwoven: the transformations from day to night, the visible world above ground and the more secretive one that was hidden beneath our feet. It was sometimes hard to believe that when we walked round the island in late spring there were tens of thousands of birds sitting silently, patiently beneath the earth, with only the occasional wisp of a gurgling sound floating up from a burrow entrance to give them away. The puffin colonies had been buzzing with the activity of rediscovering mates and burrows, and with the delicate rituals of courtship, but this was followed by a quiet time. With one bird deep underground incubating the single egg, and the other out at sea feeding and recuperating from the long, cramped hours spent down inside the burrow, the colonies could be almost empty at the height of the day. Then, towards the end of May, came the turning point. Below ground the eggs began to crack apart, and dark grey, fluffy chicks with glittering black eyes forced their way out of the shells. This alchemy of transformation was, of course, hidden from us, but we still knew exactly when the eggs hatched.

Above ground the signs of the emerging chicks were obvious. As soon as their young had arrived, the puffins could be seen returning to the cliffs with their beaks crammed full of fish. The long, thin sand eels, often a dozen or more, were draped down on either side of the bill like shimmering curtains, and, as the birds moved, sunlight drizzled over the rainbow colours of the fish. This was a definite signal of change since the puffins only carried fish ashore to feed the chicks; their own food would be swallowed as soon as it was caught.

Sadly, the glittering prizes they carried back to the burrows made the puffins vulnerable. Gulls had no scruples about taking fish intended for another bird's young. In fact, some of them learnt to specialise in these easy pickings. It was a problem that had grown worse over the years since I had first started watching puffins. Though the gull colonies were growing, that hardly seemed the reason, since it took only a tiny number of gulls to terrorise a whole puffin colony. It just seemed that more gulls were beginning to discover the advantages of this cruel parasitism.

The gulls positioned themselves at intervals, standing on the slopes behind the puffin colonies, watching intently the comings and goings of the birds below. These prime spaces were eagerly fought for, and I was glad that each marauding bird had to waste a lot of time defending its position rather than attacking puffins. Next to the pristine little puffins, the gulls' assiduously preened feathers looked faintly shabby, and the shine in their yellow eyes was cold. I found myself trying not to hate them.

The puffins' behaviour changed when the gulls were watching over them. They paddled awkwardly from foot to foot and glanced round frequently. In more relaxed times, puffins carrying fish stood for a while outside the burrow displaying their sparkling catch, but that was too dangerous when the gulls were hunting. I watched the puffins grow more and more adept at evasion as the season progressed, while the gulls became increasingly vicious as their attempts at bullying were obstructed. Puffins are not proficient flyers. As they tried to come in to land, the rapid beat of their wings often slowed to a stall at the last moment, and they came thudding heavily to the ground. These crash landings generally brought them to earth a few feet from the burrow, and the remaining distance could be covered at a gentle stroll, but, in order to avoid the gulls, they had to improve their tactics. It was essential that they should reach the burrow, and safety, in the minimum possible time.

The gulls, ever alert, stretching and bobbing their necks to get the best view over the colony, launched themselves the second a puffin carrying fish came in to land. Often, just the sight of a gull bearing down on it was enough to make the puffin drop the fish and hurl itself blindly over the cliff edge. The brightly silvered morsels fell scattered across the ground where the dust immediately quenched their rainbows, making them look dull and dead. The gull snatched the sand eels from the dirt, gulping them down before another bird could make a challenge. As they disappeared into the gull's beak, the slivers of fish appeared to shrivel into something ridiculously small: far too insignificant to be worth fighting for. I could only watch with a sense of helpless rage, knowing that somewhere in one of those burrows a chick was still waiting to be fed.

Some of the puffins learnt to come screeching out of the sky, wings humming with the intensity of their effort, and crash straight into the entrance of the burrow, disappearing into the darkness in one ungainly manoeuvre. The gulls responded to these feats of agility with renewed callousness. They gazed across the bay, singling out the puffin with fish long before it reached land, so that they could be ready to strike as soon as it was close enough. As the puffin felt the security of the burrow closing round it, the gull swooped, grabbing the disappearing tail with its beak and hauling the puffin back to the surface. If the terrified puffin did not immediately discard its catch, the gull shook it until the fish finally fell to the ground and then the puffin was tossed aside.

These pre-emptive strikes gradually moved further out into the bay, giving the puffins less chance of escape. I was sure that I could see the ruthless determination in the eyes of the gulls as they stood on the cliff top tracing the route of the incoming puffin through the sky. Then, when they judged the time to be right, the gulls fired themselves like missiles out into the sky, perhaps travelling half the length of the bay in order to meet their target. The speed of their movement made a sound like the air being sliced open. Sometimes, the puffin was able to swoop away from the gull at the last moment, and the two would skim past each other amid a jarring flurry of wings. Often, the gull outmanoeuvred the puffin, timing the mid-air collision with faultless precision, tilting its body back to strike the puffin with its feet, and sending the fish drifting down in a shower of liquid silver to splash like raindrops on the surface of the sea. If that didn't work, I had even seen gulls catch the leg of a passing puffin in their beaks and spin the helpless bird upside down to ensure that the sand eels were dropped.

These tiny scraps of food spilling down into the water were an irresistible attraction for the scavenging gulls. They came plunging out of the sky to squabble noisily over fish so small that they must have slipped down their throats almost unnoticed. I couldn't understand the efficiency of a strategy that squandered so much time and energy in stealing the occasional beakful of food. To raise a chick that would be strong enough to survive the first winter at sea, the puffins were facing a battle that they struggled to win. I hoped that the added pressure from the gulls would not be enough to tip the balance more heavily against them.

There were a few weeks of the year when everything on the island came together in a brief, transcendent radiance. The spring flowers reached their peak just as the puffins feeding their chicks brought a flurry of drama back to the cliffs after the quiet period of incubation. But even then I could see the thing that would bring an end to this idyllic interlude curled in waiting, ready to pounce. Beneath the juicy-thick stems of bluebells, clenched knots of bracken were forcing their way above ground. They emerged tightly coiled, like the spirals of little green ammonites, primed to unwind and stretch out their fronds. At first they looked innocent, almost beautiful: a delicate filigree of translucent caterpillar-green that made a perfect complement to the milky indigo of the bluebells. But it was an unsustainable harmony. The bracken quickly grew coarse and dark and strong, shading out everything but itself. All spring the island had been a chaos of competing colour, and then there was only green.

My antipathy was, as Mike insisted, misplaced: the bluebells needed the bracken. Though they look strong and luxuriant, bluebells are poor competitors, and in the spring there was a little niche, a window, in which they could thrive. When the bracken closed over them, filtering out the scorching sun, it was also closing the window for other plants that might have displaced them. Bracken has such a complex interplay with some of Skomer's most important species, including shearwaters and Skomer voles, that it cannot be labelled simply good or bad. The vegetation is in a state of change following the era of farming, and time is still unravelling the losses and benefits, but I have gradually learned to see it as part of what makes Skomer unique.

That summer brought a sad parting: we had to say goodbye to our faithful old tractor. Although I had grown extremely fond of it, even I had to accept that it was time for the tractor to go. It had become too difficult to maintain, and in our isolated situation, where we depended on it totally, we needed something more reliable. The biggest problem was how to transport a tractor across the water. I had seen photographs dating from the days when the island was still farmed. One showed a very small tractor on North Haven beach. It had been reduced to manageable pieces on the mainland and carried to the island by boat, where it was reassembled on the beach in time to be driven away before the next incoming tide.

Fortunately, we didn't have to spend too long contemplating the possibility of piecing a three-dimensional tractor jigsaw back together, because the RAF stepped in with an offer of help. The arrival of the new tractor was mixed with sadness. The old tractor felt like part of the island's history, and of ours; I didn't want to see it go. We took it on its last drive up to the flat fields in the centre of the island and waited for the first view of the new tractor sailing through the sky, like a baby suspended from the beak of a stork. The sound came first, and we peered across towards the mainland to glimpse the distant black speck growing in the sky. As the shapes gradually began to crystallize, I was surprised to see how tiny the tractor was as it dangled on its single thread beneath the yellow helicopter.

The aircraft seemed to be moving slowly, gingerly, as it crossed the sounds. We had been warned that if the load began to swing out of control it would endanger the aircraft, and there would be no choice but to let the tractor fall into the waves. At that distance the tractor had the appearance of a shiny new Dinky toy, blue and gleaming, fresh from its box. I was already warming to it in a way that felt disloyal in the presence of our dear departing tractor. Gradually, the tractor came close enough to be placed with the gentlest precision on the track leading up to the farm. Despite my secret hopes for a dignified burial at sea, thanks to the expertise of the RAF, our old tractor swooped safely back to the mainland.

Summer always came to an abrupt end. It wasn't simply the physical end of summer that was carried in on the first big storm, but the end of the season for visitors to the island. This ending was much more precise than the arrival of a storm. It could be dated very reliably from the time of the August bank holiday. August was the busy time for visitors on Skomer, coinciding with one of the quietest periods for wildlife. It was that lull after the birds had left and before the seal pups had begun to arrive, when the bracken, at its most full-blown, monotonous greenness, dominated the landscape. The number of visitors would rise to a crescendo over the bank holiday weekend at the end of the month, but by the following week there would be only a handful, and within a few days the boat would stop running for the winter. It was oddly anticlimactic the way everything came juddering to a halt, but we had grown used to it.

The other influx that occurred at the time of the late summer bank holiday was of scuba divers. Little swarms of inflatable boats came buzzing across from Martin's Haven and clustered round the island. Most of them were attracted to the wreck of a boat called the *Lucy*, lying in deep water off the entrance to North Haven, while a few of the diving craft dispersed to explore the stunning underwater scenery of an area that would eventually be declared one of the first marine nature reserves in Britain.

It was rare to see so much activity, and it felt as if the island was acting as a magnet for every boat in the area. With the hum of outboards and the occasional echo of voices against the cliffs there was a faint sense that Skomer was under siege. I was unsettled by the presence of boats around the island. The birds were sensitive to disturbance, and a single boat in the wrong place could cause enormous disruption. Although it was rare for people to behave really badly, problems sometimes arose through lack of understanding of how fragile the bird colonies could be. My instincts for the island were fiercely protective, so I had to keep reminding myself that there were few birds left to be disturbed. And I knew that within a week we would have returned to a state of almost perfect peace.

Late in the afternoon of the bank holiday we received a radio message from the coastguard. Two divers were missing; the boat waiting to pick them up had failed to find them. A couple of hours had elapsed between the start of the dive and the alarm being raised. The one thing that seemed certain was that they could not still be under water, since they would only have had enough air to stay down for about an hour. We began to search around the island, calling in the help of anyone available, including the voluntary assistants and research students. The boat had been at the entrance to South Haven, off the southern tip of the Neck, when the divers had plunged into the water, and that had been the last anyone had seen of them.

The practice was for divers to stay in pairs to be sure of backup in case of an emergency. Each pair should also have a marker buoy that floats on the surface, attached by a line, so that the waiting boat can keep track of them. The missing pair had done exactly as they should; the only trouble was that the marker buoy had disappeared almost as soon as they entered the water, somehow dragged below the surface.

With so little information about what could have happened to them, all we could do was search the area where they were last seen. The most intricately carved of Skomer's cliffs are on the Neck; it is an area full of inlets and sea caves. We scoured the coastline, gradually moving further and further away from the point where the divers had been lost. It was exhausting climbing up and down the cliffs to explore every hidden place, but we only gave up reluctantly when it became too dark to see. That night I slept badly, with images trapped behind my closed eyelids of being alone amid so much sea, and at first light we began searching again.

We found no trace of them, and I think that was really what we expected. Local theories abounded, but the general consensus was that the divers would have been long gone even before the alarm was raised. They had disappeared on a day of exceptionally high tides, which meant that the currents would have been moving with immense strength and speed. If the divers had surfaced and been caught in one of these tidal streams they could have been carried far away in the first couple of hours before the search began. Everyone agreed that if the bodies were ever found it was more likely to be off the coast of Ireland than anywhere near us.

I believed these grim assurances. The boatmen and fishermen had a knowledge of the sea that was formidably precise. Their lives depended on it. It was in their blood, passed on through the generations, not something that could be learnt in a single lifetime. I remembered poor George Sturley, dragged from the house, still wearing his slippers, to help the coastguard when Mike was lost at sea. He had told them exactly where Mike would be found, and he was right.

So it was over: a sad story with a very unsatisfactory end. Over, but not forgotten. I couldn't get it out of my mind, and I often thought about the two divers and their families. I used to stare out of the side window in the kitchen, where I could get a view to the south, remembering how I had watched the boat that afternoon. It had caught my attention because it had been there for an unusually long time. Most dives last about an hour; this boat had stayed much longer. I hadn't realised then that they were waiting for two passengers who would never return. I felt implicated just by having seen it, almost guilty in an irrational way.

It was fortunate that we had a late return of summer weather. While the energy of storms can wind tensions even tighter, calm, sunny days seem to soak up anxieties like blotting paper. Instead of bringing the usual gales, September turned uncharacteristically soft and mild. It was that point in the year when the weather could collapse completely, becoming cool and stormy, or when the echoes of summer might come whispering back, giving the illusion that winter was still a long way off. I loved a gorgeous September on Skomer because it brought that rare combination of seclusion and fine weather, instead of the usual pairing of storms and solitude. The days didn't have enough warmth to stir up the dull haze of summer, so the air remained sharply clean. All around us the sea glittered pure aquamarine, deep and dark, like the pigment squeezed straight from a tube of watercolour. It met the diluted cerulean blue of the sky in a crisply drawn line. There had been enough rain for the thin-soiled slopes to bloom green again, and patches of heather added a final splurge of colour before everything began to fade into winter.

That September was particularly spectacular because it brought an invasion of butterflies. We were used to seeing large numbers of them on the island, but this was something quite different to the demurely unpretentious gatherings we had grown accustomed to. On hot summer days the sheltered fringes of North Haven were always shimmering with butterflies, mostly graylings and meadow browns. Their muted sepia colours melted unobtrusively into the vegetation. The graylings that scattered themselves across the paths were so self-effacing that their closed wings were carefully tilted sideways to minimise any shadow they might cast, and their marbled patterning was lost against the dust. This camouflage was so effective that they were almost invisible until they took off at our approach, drifting like scraps of confetti on the wind. Then, as summer was ending, there was an influx of brighter and more beautiful butterflies, a blizzard of red admirals and painted ladies stippling the island with crimson and gold.

I saw them first on the ivy that flowed in a thick, glossy drape down the cliff below the house in North Haven. I had been gazing idly down as I walked along the path when the sight brought me to a sudden halt. The ivy, which could normally manage no more than the dullest of off-white flowers, appeared to be smothered in brilliant red and orange blossoms. When I stared more closely I began to see the occasional flutter of movement and realised that the flowers were actually dozens and dozens of butterflies, feeding on the nectar of the late-flowering ivy. The contrasting deep, dark green of the leaves made the butterfly wings glow like fragments of a stained glass window.

These shoals of butterflies had a slightly melancholy beauty. The painted ladies had made their way from warmer climates as far away as North Africa. For as long as the weather continued to masquerade as high summer it suited them perfectly, but as soon as the season showed its true colours, their fragile hold on life could be broken. Those that failed to make the migration back would not survive the winter here.

As the month progressed, the number of seal pups on the beaches gradually increased. Already, the first of the newly moulted pups were finding their independence. Separation from their mothers appeared to be a painless process; the bond was abruptly broken when the mother simply failed to return to feed her pup. Whether the youngster even noticed the change in circumstances I could not tell. By that stage, they were so well fed that they gave the impression of being permanently contented, wriggling to find a comfortable position against the stones, scratching themselves with the claws of their ungainly flippers to send wisps of the moulting white coat meandering into the air, shrugging off the final traces of babyhood. Some might remain in the same spot on the beach for weeks, sleeping or watching as the days slipped lugubriously past, until hunger finally launched them into the world.

The calm weather provided the pups with a brief interlude in which life gave them the illusion of being easy. Looking down from my hide into Castle Bay on a golden autumn day, it was hard to believe what a harsh environment it really was. Just to have survived those first three weeks and passed the threshold into self-sufficiency was an achievement. Despite appearances, the first year would be a difficult one, and many of them would not see the end of another summer. That was why it was such a pleasure to be able to watch them enjoy a fleeting chance of freedom.

At the top of the beach a plump moulter was fast asleep. It had been immobile for so long that the discarded fur had felted together in a white mat around it. The sea was so invitingly sleek that few seals had been enticed by the shelter of the beach, but a group of moulters had gathered round a rock pool taking turns to splash in the shallow water. They had formed a passing alliance for as long as the game lasted, united by a curiosity for their newly discovered surroundings; it was the only time in their mainly solitary lives that they would be able to enjoy a carefree companionship.

Their playfulness was an insatiable urge to explore. Every touch, every taste, every smell was adding to their store of knowledge. The moulter at the top of the beach had woken and was sprawling on its back, neck outstretched, using its mouth to tug at the vegetation that trailed down to the bottom of the cliff. Then it rolled slightly to a new position to savour the sensation as a cascade of water droplets escaping from the island showered down over its face. Below me, a small seal hung lifeless in the water, lapped close against the rocks by the gentle swell of the sea, its head dipped below the waves. I had seen that sort of behaviour often enough to know that the animal was not in trouble. They could drift like that for hours carried by the faint movement of the sea, staring into the greenish half-light as though it held the key to their future.

An adult seal slid out onto the beach with a soft clatter of pebbles. I focused the telescope on her so that I could see every detail of the shiny, dappled fur. As she pulled herself clear of the waves I saw a distinct pink mark on her side. It was the scar of an old, healed wound, and it told me at once that she was an animal I knew well. I loved that moment of rediscovery; it filled me with excitement every single time, as though I had never quite believed that it would happen again. I had studied her, drawn her, detailed her movements for weeks, and then suddenly she was gone. Now I had found her again, the mother of the moulter at the top of the beach, but the ties that bound them had been shaken loose and forgotten. A couple of weeks ago she would have fought passionately to protect him, and now they could lie together on the same beach without any sign of recognition passing between them. That lapse into instant indifference always made me feel irrationally sad.

I was distracted by a small seal that had moved away from the group at the rock pool. It lay on its back among the low tide debris of weed with the slick of shallow water making its fur look almost black. In its mouth it held a stalk of kelp that had broken free, waving it back and forth like a flag on a pole and staring intently at the patterns of the weed fluttering against the blue sky. It was no more than act of idle curiosity, but for a moment that banner shining in the sunlight seemed like a defiant symbol of hope.

If we could find a boat to give us a ride at that time of year, we tried to get out to Grassholm at the end of the season as the last of the young birds were fledging. I will never forget the first time I saw Grassholm without its gannets; it looked almost shocking in its bleakness. The change was obvious as soon as the island came into view: the blaze of white was gone, and so too were the birds that always came gliding slowly, determinedly out to meet us. A cloud of silence hung in the air, the intense loneliness highlighted by the occasional stray cry of a gull. But the most powerful impact of the emptiness came when we reached the island and looked down over the slope where the gannets had been. The whiteness that had been almost too brilliant to look at was replaced by a drab, muddy brown.

Rows of barren nests stretched out across the slope. These were not ephemeral little things to be dismantled by the coming wind and rain of winter. Each one was a substantial mound, accumulated over many years, a minute restructuring of the island's landscape. The remarkable thing was their regularity. The nests were so precisely spaced that the pattern they formed looked artificial, like a man-made structure rather than the random creation of nature. There was also a surprising uniformity in the nests: the ideal design of the flattened hillock, with a faint depression in the middle to cradle the egg, had been reproduced unwaveringly by all the birds. The result was a mesmerizing piece of optical art. Every move of the head created changing patterns of straight lines and diagonals that flowed in perfect alignment down the slope.

It felt strange to be able to walk among the nests, to set foot in that no man's land that had always been protected by an impenetrable thicket of birds. Close-up the nests looked messier than when we stood at the top looking down over the neatly ordered array. Already the rain had washed away the veneer of white, and I saw for the first time how much rubbish had been hoarded by the gannets. The dull khaki-brown landscape that we had seen from above showed itself to be etched with the bright colours of green, blue or orange twine, fragments of fishing net, torn scraps of polythene.

In the silence of an abandoned island there were even a few remaining gannets, young birds ready to fledge. We could see a dozen or so scattered among the thousands of deserted nests. These birds looked distinctly un-gannet-like, despite being almost identical in size and shape to their parents, because their plumage was starling-speckled black. The contrast with the adult birds was so great that I found it hard to see them as the offspring of the huge, white birds that filled the island in summer.

We walked towards the closest bird, moving slowly so as not to cause it too much distress. Its wings flapped, thrashing against the ground, but it did not fly away from us. It couldn't. It was tethered to the nest and, like the other young birds left behind, it was waiting to die. That was why it had been so important for us to be able to make this end of season trip out to the island.

When we were within striking distance, the bird opened its beak and jabbed menacingly to ward us off. The young bird was unexpectedly tall as it stretched its long neck threateningly, but Mike grabbed its beak in a firm hold before it could do any damage. With the bird safely disarmed, I bent down to get a better look. A length of orange string was wrapped round and round the leg and then disappeared into the solid tangle of debris that was the nest. Apart from that, its condition was remarkably good. It must have been well fed before the adult birds had been forced to leave it.

I took over from Mike holding the bird's beak firmly shut while he began to pick at the string with the tip of a knife blade. Strand by strand he teased and cut the string away until leg was free. As I let go of its beak the bird took a few stumbling steps away from us, its foot still clumsy from the numbing restriction of the string. I looked down to where the slash of vivid orange protruded from the bedraggled nest. The twine looked stridently, artificially fresh, not worn or faded, as any natural substance would be. I thought back to the summer, when I had watched two gannets fighting over exactly such a scrap of garishly exotic string, wrenching it from beak to beak in a heartfelt tug of war. How impossible it would be for them to understand that these prized trophies carried back from the sea, and fought over so tenaciously, might eventually kill the chick they had nurtured with such care.

As we moved from one forlorn prisoner to the next, I was dismayed to realise that almost every nest contained some shred of string or plastic, some remnant of discarded rubbish that had probably seemed harmless to whoever had thrown them casually aside, to drift on the waves until they were found by the gannets. And now there they lay, woven innocently into these nests, half hidden and ready to kill. I stared around me. The sea, with its first metallic undertones of hard, wintry blue, went on forever. This little island that we were standing on looked like the only fragment of land in the whole world. It was hard to imagine somewhere more remote, more unspoilt, and yet it was an illusion. Every part of the island had been touched by the indiscriminating nature of pollution.

We walked on across the strange, bleak landscape. The next bird we reached stirred itself into an aggressive flurry of wings at our approach. It presented more of a problem. Instead of the thick twine, a narrow filament of fishing line was biting deeply into the bird's leg, so that the thread had disappeared, buried in the swollen skin. The damage looked more permanent compared to the last bird we had seen; the foot was limp and withered.

I was suddenly overwhelmed by the most profound sense of sadness. To me, Grassholm had always been a perfect place, somewhere that transcended the failings of the world beyond. It was set apart, a bright, white gem shining in an empty ocean. And now I had been shown its ordinariness, the fact that, like everywhere else, it was tarnished by reality. It was something I had hoped never to see.

We finished cutting the birds free, and in a day or two they would be gone. They would take to the sky, their great, speckled wings carrying them into a future that had already been blighted by such an unhappy start in life.

When the boat pulled away from Grassholm, I turned back to watch the small, dark hummock of land slide into the distance. Almost at once my spirits began to lift. As the island dwindled to a speck on the horizon I realised that the memories of what we had just done were fading with it. When I saw Grassholm again it would be summer. The drab, brown, tussocky landscape would be shining white with its tens of thousands of birds, all in their pristine, fresh-painted plumage. And I would see only the pure beauty of such a unique place, just as I always had.

By October we were always alone on Skomer, but that year, for the first time, we had company. George Jones, the assistant warden, had stayed on to help out and Paul Slater, a PhD student, was putting in some late season field-work as part of his study of the rabbit population. Tim Healing had also returned for a couple of weeks to continue his long-term research on the Skomer voles. Their presence would be more welcome than we realised.

I was enjoying being back in the routine of early morning walks to check on the seal pups. As I set off I stopped at the corner of the isthmus. The first strong southerly wind of the autumn had picked up during the night. The air smelt like the rock pools that gather among the weed at low tide, and was studded with specks of salt water. The sound of waves disintegrating against the shore had a fizzing grittiness, smoothed out by the constant muted clamour of the backwash. I stood still, breathing it all in. The unexpected freshness made me realise how long the weather had been calm, and that I actually missed the storms.

I walked towards North Haven, moving cautiously because the stream of air buffeting against my back was forcing me too quickly towards the cliff edge. Somewhere below me there should have been a seal pup; I had been watching it since it was born a few days before. Despite the sudden change in the weather I was not too worried about it. North Haven remained sheltered from the southerly wind. The only sign of the storm on that side was the patterns made by the air as it came eddying over the top of the isthmus, inscribing billowing fan-shapes of scuffed water onto the calm surface. It did not lift the waves, but flattened the sea to an unnatural frosted serenity as it pressed down from above.

The isthmus created the most spectacular anomaly of divided worlds. To my left the water was dark, dense blue and almost motionless, just traced round the edge of the haven with thinnest ribbon of white. To my right the waves stretched the sea into curls of pale-green glass, which turned milky as they tumbled and broke, while the cliffs were obliterated by exploding fountains of foam. The fact that the line separating the two was no more than a narrow strip of land that I could cross in a few steps made the contrasting seas look almost unreal. The storm shook and snatched at me as I followed the cliff line along top of the bay, playing, like someone pretending to push me over the edge and then letting go at the last moment. Soon I found the pup wedged high among the rocks at the top of the shingle, its voice all but washed away on the dregs of the wind. It was safe.

I turned my back on the calm of North Haven, making that brief crossing to the brink of the cliff overlooking the stormy south. The sky was heavy with black clouds, breaking and reforming as they tumbled in the wind. Spikes of sunlight, escaping through the gaps between them, jabbed down into the sea, lighting up the brilliance of the surf. For a second this twisting kaleidoscope of weather held all my attention, but as soon as I glanced down onto the storm-raked curve of sand below me I was gripped by blank terror. There was someone on the beach. My thoughts were racing slightly out of control; my heart was beginning to beat harder. All at once time was very slow and yet much too fast. I tried to assemble some rational ideas. Someone was lying face down close to the water's edge, on a patch of gravelly sand that formed a small smooth space among the boulders. My first impression was that he must have fought his way through the waves, pulling himself to safety on hands and knees, and then collapsed with exhaustion, arms outstretched above his head.

But where was the boat that had brought him? I stared out across South Haven. It was completely wild, the surface streaked by filaments of white dragged from the wave tops. Since there was little chance that a boat could have made it safely into the bay, I began to look for scraps of wreckage, but there was nothing, no clue as to how someone came to be there. These thoughts filtered through my mind in a panicky confusion that lasted no more than a few moments.

I looked back towards the figure on the beach. That second glance told me everything; the shock of it flashed into electrifyingly clear focus. I knew exactly who it was. The moment I took in the details of the wetsuit and the life jacket I recognised it as one of the divers we had been searching for. The impossibility of the situation was spinning in my head, making me feel disorientated. The divers had been lost six weeks before. It was too long ago for this to be happening now. The search had continued for days, until I was sure that, whatever the reason they had failed to return, they had been carried far away from Skomer. One thought drifting to the surface through this maelstrom was that the purple wetsuit and yellow life jacket looked stunningly new and fresh. The radiance of their colours seemed absurd, impossible to reconcile with the cold brutality of death. And yet there was no doubt in my mind. The description fitted too perfectly. This was one of the missing divers.

Once I was certain, it was strange to realise that I felt not fear but relief. There had been no possibility that the divers would be found alive, so surely it was a comfort that they should simply be found. Over the past weeks I had come to realise that there could be few things worse than a loved one vanishing without explanation. Until there were answers, the questions would never end. I was not even sure if it would ever be possible to come to terms with the fact that someone was gone without that final confirmation. However awful, this was for the best.

I turned and began to walk back to the house. No need for panic, no urgency; it was too late for that. But I had not gone far before I began to run. It was almost like a reflex action, beyond my control. By the time I reached the house, my breath was coming in short, hard gasps. I rammed myself against the front door to throw it open, and then heard a series of echoing crashes, which I realised was the sound of my boots thudding against the floorboards in the hall.

'What is it?' Mike called, disturbed by my uncharacteristically clumsy homecoming.

'There's a body,' I said, surprised at the way the words choked breathlessly in my throat. 'A body in South Haven.'

'Come on then,' Mike said calmly. 'We'll go and have a look.'

As we walked across the isthmus I found myself compulsively pouring out every detail I could remember, as if to convince myself that I had not imagined the whole thing. It was already beginning to seem incredible on this beautiful windswept day, on our own peaceful island.

I took Mike back to the exact place on the cliff, and we looked over. It was still there, still startlingly forlorn. We both stared, feeling helpless.

'Don't look,' Mike said, 'or you'll never be able to forget it.'

It was too late for that. I knew that the image of those dazzling colours against the damp, drab stones of the beach would be with me forever. All I could think was how lonely he looked, how very far away from us, as we gazed down, silently appalled at the thought of having to go any closer. And I was so sorry for feeling that way.

'OK then,' Mike said. 'We'd better get back and call the coastguard.'

I guessed that they would use the helicopter to winch him straight off the beach. And then, as far as we were concerned, it would be over.

Back home in the kitchen, Mike radioed St Ann's. They agreed to work out the best course of action and call us back. It was only then that Mike and I turned to the subject that had been troubling us both. This was not the end, but really only half of the story. Two divers had been lost; so what had happened to the other one? They had obviously remained close by all this time, not swept out to Ireland as everyone had predicted. Whatever it was in these changed weather conditions that had brought this body ashore meant that we were also likely to find the second one.

'It would be terrible if we'd got this sorted out and then found another one,' I said.

'Yes,' Mike agreed. 'If they're going to get the helicopter out to us, it would be much better if they could deal with both at once. The trouble is, we can't go out and do anything while we're waiting for this call to come back.'

'I could go,' I said. 'I'll start along the south coast of the Neck.'

'Well, if you're sure you don't mind going on your own . . . '

'No, I don't mind. I'd really prefer to be doing something.'

I checked South Haven first, wondering how the beauty of an hour before could have dissolved into something so desolate. Then I walked along the isthmus and out towards the bays and inlets on the southern edge of the Neck. It was almost the route I would have followed to find the seal pups, but I never would have imagined that it could have felt so bleakly depressing. Each time I reached a suitable point to stop and look over the cliff, I had to spend a few moments gathering my courage, and each time I found nothing I was disappointed. Every small reprieve was only making the situation worse. Unless I found something, the watching and waiting would go on indefinitely.

When I had searched all the obvious places I made my way back towards the house feeling despondent. It was inevitable that the walk down from the Neck would give me a clear view of South Haven beach, but I had made up my mind that I would not look. I should have known that anything so carefully avoided becomes compulsively magnetic. My eyes flickered involuntarily downwards until I saw that the incoming tide had reached the body. Soft foam from the spent waves was billowing round it. I didn't want to watch, but I had to. I needed to work out exactly how far the sea could reach, how much time we had. It would be so awful if we allowed him to be lost to the waves again. I stayed long enough to assure myself that it was only the drawn out wash of the largest waves that had the strength to lift and move him. Each time the body shuddered with the liquid motion of the waves I found myself silently imploring it not to turn over. As long as I couldn't see the face it was so much easier to detach myself from the realities of the person he had once been.

For the second time that day I found myself running in breathless panic across the isthmus.

'How much longer is the helicopter going to be?' I called as I clattered through the kitchen doorway. 'The tide's reached him. We haven't got long.'

'I don't know,' Mike said. 'I still haven't been given a time. I'll call the coast-guard again and tell them things are getting urgent.'

The news from the coastguard was bad; there was no immediate prospect of a helicopter and so, as a temporary solution, the body would have to be moved further up the beach, above the tide. The normal route into South Haven was now cut off by the waves; the only way to reach the body was to use ropes to abseil down the cliff.

'I'll have to go and find help,' Mike said.

It was Paul who drew the short straw, since he happened to be the first person Mike encountered. It was an awful thing to ask of anyone, but Paul could be relied on never to flinch from anything. He was also ideal for the task, being strong, fit and an experienced climber. While the two of them assembled the climbing equipment, I went and found a blanket to wrap the body in. Both Mike and Paul had a look of stoical determination as they disappeared over the edge of the cliff, as though they were trying to harden their minds to what they might find.

They were gone for a long time. While I waited, watching the cliff top, the thoughts I was trying to avoid kept reverberating in my mind. They circled endlessly without ever reaching a conclusion. How could someone disappear, and then reappear six weeks later in almost precisely the same place? At the time, when nothing had been found despite all the searches, the local boatmen had shaken their heads sadly, repeating their wise and comfortable old sayings: 'The sea gives up her dead after ten days.' If the divers were still in the area, submerged somewhere, that was the longest anyone had thought they could remain missing. It unnerved me irrationally to realise that they had stayed so close, that all the times I had looked out of the window at the place where I had seen the boat they had still been there. I had to accept that I would proba-bly never know what had happened.

When Mike and Paul returned, their faces looked sallow and drained; they were visibly shocked. But at least it was over with, and all we could do now was wait for help. We sat in the kitchen transfixed by the faint crackle of the radio. It felt as though everything was suspended, and we couldn't move on until the situation was resolved. We would have no peace of mind until we knew when the helicopter was coming. While we waited, Mike explained what they had found on the beach. I was surprised to discover that there had been enough clues to resolve most of the unanswered questions.

As they came close they saw that the body was tangled in a maze of fine string. The diver had obviously made a desperate, but hopeless, attempt to fight free of this web. All the diving equipment, including the air bottle, had been unbuckled as he tried to extricate himself, but everything had remained firmly attached by the mesh of string. The knife had been taken from its sheath to cut away the tightening knots, but even that had become locked in the endless loops of twine. The life jacket should have been a fail-safe. In an emergency it could be inflated to drag a stricken diver instantly to the surface. This life jacket had been inflated but for some reason had not saved him, possibly because the diver and the string were already inextricably entangled in the weed by that time.

The thing I found most upsetting was that the bottle still had some air in it, but had been discarded in the struggle to break free. Not that it would have made any difference in the end, but it just seemed to crystallize the awful claustrophobic terror of the fight to escape. I had never been a good diver. I was unnerved by the intense physical pressure of the dull, green, twilit water, the constant whispering rush against my ears, and the way my whole body was enveloped in the unnaturalness of breathing. I could understand the fear, almost feel it tightening at the back of my throat.

As we talked, I stared out towards South Haven. The windows had become frosted by the salt spray carried in on the wind. Everything was out of focus, colours shimmering pale. I could see the waves carved thin and translucent by the wind, a smudged, watercolour blur of turquoise and green. At last, a voice from the radio interrupted us. Mike answered at once and the news came through that the helicopter would be with us in a couple of hours.

'But the string?' I asked, when the radio was quiet and we returned to our conversation. 'Where did that come from?'

'Well that's the awful thing. It was the line for the safety buoy. Do you remember back to when we were searching and they told us that the marker buoy had disappeared almost immediately? They obviously became caught in the line and dragged it down with them.'

So, in the end, the thing that was meant to protect them had resulted in the tragedy. The body must have remained tethered to the weed, probably suspended above the sea bed as its natural upward movement was restrained by the string. It was only the storm waves, scooping deep troughs into the water, that had finally reached down far enough to break it free.

Before the two hours had elapsed, the deadline for the helicopter was pushed back a further hour. And so we waited. It was impossible to talk about anything but what had happened on that day back in August. It was compulsive, as though it was vital that we understood it before we could lay it to rest. Although the evidence that Mike had found seemed fairly conclusive, it didn't explain the other diver. How had they both been lost? If one had gone to help the other and then become trapped, they should both have been found still tangled together. The apparent solution to the mystery had only raised a lot more questions.

A call came through from the coastguard. The helicopter had been delayed for another hour. And so it went on; for most of the day the deadline slipped further out of reach until we were told that the helicopter would not be coming. They couldn't risk contaminating the aircraft by carrying a dead body. I suppose that as far as everyone else was concerned, a rescue was about saving someone with a chance of survival; in this situation, we were the only ones who felt an acute sense of urgency. There was still hope, though: the lifeboat would soon be on its way.

I was not surprised when the call came to say that the weather was too rough for the lifeboat to get out. We only had to look down into South Haven to see the impossibility of attempting to do anything from the sea. It meant that the body would have to remain on the beach over night. As the call came to an end, Mike and I glanced across at each other, and we both knew that we couldn't leave him there. Our consciences wouldn't allow us to let someone lie abandoned on the beach like that. It was a ridiculous distinction after six weeks in the sea, but it was something we both felt quite strongly. Besides, there were more practical considerations. The waves had grown dense and powerful; they were pouring onto the beach in long, sweeping convulsions of foam. We couldn't be sure that anywhere in South Haven would remain safe from them.

When Mike radioed the coastguard to say that the body couldn't stay there all night, we were hoping that they would find another way of helping us. Their answer was an unwelcome one. Even over the radio, I could tell by the hesitation in the coastguard's voice that he felt uncomfortable suggesting it.

'Do you think you could find somewhere safe to store the body?'

The image came instantly into my mind of it lying in our spare bedroom. The shock must have flashed across my face, because I saw Mike staring anxiously at me.

'Can you give me a few minutes to work out what we can do?' Mike replied into the microphone.

As he lifted his finger from the transmit button we were cut off again, and we had to make the decision quickly.

'Not in the house,' I said, before I had had time to think clearly.

'No, of course not,' Mike agreed.

We discussed the options. Even getting him up the cliff from South Haven would be difficult. We certainly couldn't transport him as for as the farm; it would have to be somewhere close. The situation felt surreal. I could never have imagined myself sitting in my own kitchen having a serious conversation about where to put a body. Eventually, we decided on the new boatshed; its combination of fresh, white walls and natural stone gave it a nice, almost spiritual, feel.

Mike went and found Paul, George and Tim, to tell them the bad news. It was an awful thing to ask of anyone, but not one of them complained. It was part of the atmosphere on Skomer that no one ever failed to help when things were difficult; I put it down to the island's benign influence. As it would take only four people to do the carrying, Mike banned me from coming down with them and, being a coward, I accepted without much argument. We found ropes and a stretcher, and I watched them go with a guilty sense of relief that I was not with them.

They emerged at last with the stretcher. The solemn procession made its way slowly along the cliff top and down towards North Haven. It was growing dark. The colours of the land were softening into tones of grey, while the sky had the last traces of a dusky pinkness. The whole effect was bitterly sad.

I was resigned to the night ahead, knowing that the body was close by; Mike was definitely more edgy. I was sure that if I had been in such close contact with it I would have found it hard to stay calm. I fell asleep easily; I had always considered it a gift to be able to sleep instantly and anywhere. But after a couple of hours I was jolted awake by a vivid image of the body. I slept again, but the same shocking picture kept waking me with a start. In the end I found myself lying awake and watching the darkness, dreading the first weak signs of dawn. As soon as it was light I would have to get up and go out to the seal beaches. Usually it was a pleasure, each new day bringing a faint excitement. For the first time, I found myself not wanting to go. The strong possibility that I might find another body was beginning to unnerve me. All the positive feelings of the day before had ebbed away during the night.

When I went out into the storm it was as fresh and luminous as the previous morning, but that didn't make me feel any better. I knew at once from the touch of the wind, and the way it was ripping spindrift from the tops of the waves, that we faced another day of waiting. The storm had strengthened during the night. If we had been beyond help the day before, it was certain that no one would be able to reach us now.

I walked to the point where I had looked over into South Haven the previous morning, and stopped. Two more steps forward and I would be able to see the beach. I took a deep breath and forced myself to look down. Of course there was nothing, just the slippery ribbons of brown weed torn out by the waves and discarded in a glistening mound along the tide line. I turned and continued to walk along the top of the bay. Every time a seal broke through between the blue-green curves of water to stare up at me, I felt a momentary electric buzz of panic. Each time I approached a new inlet it was the same: the brief hesitation followed by the determined effort to look down onto the rocks below. It was made so much worse by the fact that the storm was everywhere, grating away all normal sounds, smothering my breath into little choking gasps, imposing its own frenzied sense of restlessness.

Back at home I reported my dismal failure to find the second body, with its unspoken implications of more days of uncertainty stretching ahead of us. Mike confirmed what I already knew: the coastguard had sent a message to say that the lifeboat would not be able to reach us that day. I couldn't understand why it mattered so much, but it did. Mike made things immeasurably worse as he tried to comfort me.

'There's nothing to be afraid of,' he said. 'It's not as though he can get up and start roaming round the island.'

And so the thought, which, until then, had not so much as flickered through my head, was implanted. Somewhere almost beyond the conscious reaches of my mind, this inanimate presence had become mobile.

Later, I went out to the hide above Castle Bay. Instead of being able to concentrate on the seals, I found myself searching obsessively for a figure in a black wet suit, the only description I had for the second diver. Every shadow, every half-seen mirage of a seal beneath the water had to be studied minutely. Suddenly, behind me, the door of the hide began to rattle violently, though it was bolted shut from the inside to keep out the weather. I knew that it was only the wind, but it felt like someone trying to get in. The whole hide was shuddering with the force of it. Then it subsided, and the silence was worse.

I could only see out through a tiny slit in the front, and I was swamped by the absolute certainty that whoever had been shaking door was now coming round to peer in at me. In another second the face would be there, inches away, staring out from inside the hood of a wetsuit. The image was so forceful that I had to cover my eyes. Even when my more rational self had regained control, a faint, claustrophobic panic remained, and I couldn't stay locked inside that wooden box. I packed up my telescope and went home.

This suspension of normality was made worse by the knowledge that, even when it came to an end, everything could start again if we found the second body. We decided on one last determined search of the island as the most useful way to pass the time. Mike retrieved the climbing ropes and went with the others to scour some of the inaccessible caves and ledges. I checked again around the bays on the south side of the island.

Storms brought debris drifting into South Haven, which gathered in sheltered corners of the bay, wallowing in the undulating water. Much of it was weed, scooped up by the waves as they cut deeply into the sea. It coagulated into brown, swampy pools that floated on the surface, and it was through this that the other debris emerged, half hidden. This muddled collection had a certain predictability. There would always be chunks of wood, bleached and abraded by the constant pounding of the waves; knots and skeins of heavy rope; buoys of assorted sizes and colours that had broken free of their tethers. Among all this, was a miscellany of oddments, perhaps discarded from ships half an ocean away. These murky lakes provided infinite scope for fruitless searching.

I settled myself on the cliff top and began to scan with binoculars, inch by inch. The semi-submerged objects, with their ability to metamorphose at each passing palpitation of a wave, were ideal fuel for my skittish imagination. A large, yellow, plastic canister brought horrible echoes of the bright yellow life jacket I had seen the previous day. But the most heart-stopping moment of all was when the flaccid, pink fingers of a rubber glove came groping up through the gloom. In the end, though, despite all our searching and all the concentrated effort of my willpower, the day drew to a close in exactly the same state of uncertainty. We had found nothing and were condemned to go on looking.

The following day was a Saturday. No change, except that the wind was subtly, imperceptibly strengthening, and the swelling waves were growing more powerful with every hour that the storm persisted. The white-streaked sea gave a clear indication that we were facing yet another day without help.

There was no reason why the presence of a dead body should invade every aspect of our existence, but fears do not answer to logic. We found ourselves starting at every unexpected noise, and the nights were even worse. When the blackness closed in around the windows, the outside became a huge, barren place, empty and impenetrable. The thick, clinging darkness and the all-pervasive sound of the wind detached us from any other reality. Every shudder of the house, every flicker of the gaslights, took on an unpleasant significance.

I knew from the look of the weather that there would be no respite for days. I could tell just by standing on the cliff top and feeling its sheer, unflinching force rolling in across all those miles of ocean. But I was wrong. When we listened to the shipping forecast that evening, we realised that the following day was going to bring a brief slackening of the wind; it would no more than an intake of breath before the storm resumed, but it might be enough of a pause to allow a boat to reach us.

The next morning we had the best possible news. Talk of our situation had spread on the mainland and reached Campbell Reynolds: he had decided to come straight out to us. It would take a while, but he would be there. We had an overwhelming feeling of optimism. If we could rely on anyone, it was Campbell.

We went outside. The wind had definitely eased, but the sea had such a weight of movement built into it that the waves were driving in with an unstoppable momentum of their own. There would be no time for them to die back before the storm regained its strength. Any boat would have to come a long way to reach us; they had all gone to sheltered harbours, and most had been taken out of the water for the winter. Campbell would have to make the journey of a dozen or so miles from the sheltered moorings of Dale Roads and out through the violent seas around St Ann's Head. By land it would have been an insignificant distance, but by sea it was quite an undertaking. Even from Skomer we could see the waves, miles away, breaking against the cliffs of St Ann's Head and flaring upward in slow, silent torrents of white. It was not a crossing that I would have wanted to make, but we knew that once Campbell had set his mind on coming it would take a hurricane to stop him.

In the end, it was nothing as dramatic as a hurricane that brought everything to a halt, merely the intricate tangles of bureaucracy. A message came through from the coastguard to say that we did not have permission from the coroner to move the body, and, therefore, it would have to stay where it was. Mike tried desperately to get the decision changed, but there was nothing that could be done. The coroner was on holiday and his deputy could not be contacted on a Sunday. Even if we did finally get permission on Monday, the storm would have picked up again by then and we could be left waiting indefinitely.

I assumed that no one on the mainland understood how it felt to be stranded on an island with a dead body. Without personal experience I could never have imagined the haunting power of something so essentially harmless. It was hard, then, to blame anyone for treating our emergency as a purely practical problem. And in practical terms there could be no sense of urgency. But perhaps I was being too cynical, because someone, somewhere, was on our side. The coastguards took up our case, and eventually secured permission for the body to be moved. By early afternoon we heard that Campbell was on his way.

We watched the boat, far to the south, picking its way towards us, lurching nauseatingly over the waves, and sometimes disappearing in a surge of spray. It looked tiny and vulnerable. We lost sight of it as it entered the bubbling tide race of Little Sound, and, finally, it came gliding smoothly into the relative calm of North Haven. Glistening with salt, it shone bright against the storm-coloured sea. I wasn't sure that I had ever been as glad to see the arrival of any boat in North Haven.

Poor Campbell was furious. Normally so calm and even-tempered, he could not hide his anger. He was horrified to discover what had happened to us over the past few days. If only someone had contacted him, he would have come straight out to the island, whatever of the weather. That was typical of Campbell, but I couldn't help feeling glad that he had not known; the seas that day were about as bad as I would ever want to see a boat the size of the *Dale Princess* take on.

The body had to be ferried from North Haven beach out to the *Dale Princess* in our dinghy. Although, compared to the south side, North Haven gave the illusion of being calm, the water was rocking with a deep swell. It only became obvious how turbulent the sea was when our dinghy started to move cautiously across its surface. With Mike, Paul, George and Tim on board to help with the transfer at Martin's Haven, the *Princess* moved quickly out of the bay, plunging into the rougher seas beyond.

That left just me on the island. Inevitably, the removal of the immediate problem did not dissolve the tension that had built up over the previous days. Feeling acutely alone, I waited, looking down across North Haven from the kitchen window as the grey sky gradually edged closer, shrinking my view out across the sea. Eventually, I saw the boat coming back, labouring hard against the waves. In the shelter of North Haven, the four climbed down into the dinghy, and Mike, seated in the centre, began to row them back towards the shore. With the weather deteriorating and darkness closing in, Campbell was anxious to be on his way. As soon as the passengers had climbed down into the dinghy, the *Dale Princess* began to move quickly back towards the open sea. The storm was definitely picking up again. I saw the squall of wind hit the boat as soon as she was out beyond Rye Rocks. A large sheet of black polythene that had been protecting the deck billowed high into the air and, after a few somersaults, plunged back downwards to sweep thrashing across the surface of the water.

The *Dale Princess* disappeared behind the cliffs as she made her way towards Little Sound. It worried me to think that she faced the difficult journey home with the added handicap of darkness. I would keep the marine VHF radio switched on in the hope of hearing Campbell's final message to the coastguard as he reached the safety of the harbour.

Mike looked downcast when he returned. We were both dismayed to realise that, even now that it was over, we did not feel appreciably better. He described the scene on the mainland: a family rushing their children away from the shingle beach at Martin's Haven as they realised what was being carried ashore on the stretcher. It had been so hopeless and depressing, and he had brought that mood back with him. Then, quite unexpectedly, he started to laugh.

'Did you see what happened as we were rowing back across North Haven?' Mike asked.

'No.'

'Well, I was rowing, sitting facing Paul, with the other two behind me. I glanced up at Paul and saw this look of terror on his face. He was staring at something over my shoulder, and all of a sudden he shouted, "There's a whale! Row faster! Faster!". I was terrified too, by that time, and rowing like crazy. I could tell he was serious, not joking. We were already unnerved by what we'd been doing, and there we were, the four of us crammed into the dinghy, bobbing about on the waves. I glanced back and, although it was getting too dark to see clearly, I could make out something big and black bearing down on us at incredible speed. Paul, kept shouting, "Row! Row faster!", but there was nothing I could do. I was rowing with all my strength and I couldn't make any headway against this thing that was getting closer all the time. It was only when it was almost on top of us that we realised it was just a sheet of black plastic being carried across the water on the wind, but in the half-light it looked so real.'

I was surprised to find that we were both laughing uncontrollably at the image of the dinghy being pursued across the bay by a predatory sea monster. It was exactly what we needed to lift the tension. I knew then that, although we would never forget what had happened, the sadness it had brought would fade.

FOURTEEN

A few days later, George, Paul and Tim left, and we began our winter isolation much later than usual. Over the years, the experience of being so alone had been unexpectedly enriching, giving us a fresh perspective on life. We recognised it as something rare and precious, that few people are given the chance to explore, and we had come almost to crave the loneliness. But that year it felt different; there was a disappointing undertone of emptiness, even a faintly disturbing sense of vulnerability.

In another three weeks Mike would leave to spend a week or more on the mainland for the usual end of year meetings. Several well-meaning messages had reached us insisting that, when the time came, I should not stay alone on the island. I always spent a period on my own in the winter while Mike was away. It was important for me to be able to touch, very briefly, such pure solitude. The experience was unique, a closeness with the island that could never be found in any other way.

I was usually amused by the over-reaction that inevitably greeted any mention of my staying alone on the island, but now I was upset to realise that I was giving serious consideration to the suggestions that I should leave. The problem was not so much what had happened, but what might be yet to come. I still could not walk out to the seal beaches without feeling some uncertain sense of another presence. When I sat in my hide, with the wind twisting and playing against the creaking wooden structure, the atmosphere was faintly menacing. I was isolated from my own senses; my hearing became the drumming of the wind, my vision blinkered to the sliver of bay below me. Every shimmer of movement caught my eye: the graceful pirouetting of weed at the edge of the tide, the effervescent curl of a wave. In the split second before I could unscramble the images, I tensed at each half-seen flicker of light and shade. I told myself over and over again, almost convinced myself, that, whatever I found, I had nothing to fear from it. But I still did not think that I could face the prospect of finding another body when I was alone on the island.

And yet, three weeks is a remarkably long time. Well before Mike was due to go, I knew that I would be able to stay on my own. I loved the island too much to leave and I desperately wanted to continue with the seal research. The weather was calm when we launched the boat. I watched its progress out towards Rye Rocks as it left the water barely disturbed, just fluttering like a sheet of silk. Both sea and sky were the colour of soft rain, but the air was dry. The sound of the outboard motor echoing back from the cliffs was magnified by the tranquillity. It was a winter silence, stripped of the raucous clamour of seabirds. Amid this melancholy calm, the mechanical noise was harshly intrusive. One or two seals followed the boat, heads bobbing up occasionally amid the stream of surf left behind by the propeller. As the boat headed out beyond the rocks strung across the corner of North Haven, and then turned towards the mainland, I could make out Mike's silhouette, arm raised, waving goodbye. Then I lost sight of him behind the cliff.

I began to walk home the long way, climbing up to the top of the track until I had a clear view all the way to Martin's Haven. I decided to wait and watch the boat until it was safely across. First the engine noise disappeared, leaving just the white speck of a boat moving slowly and steadily across the water until it was swallowed by the cliffs of Martin's Haven. It was only then that I felt suddenly and completely alone. It was a detached, slightly hollow, feeling, but I had enough experience of solitude to know that it would pass. I continued to walk sluggishly back to the house, reminding myself that the important thing was to remain calm. Fear would only have the power that I gave it. So long as I never allowed it the chance to take hold, everything would be all right.

And it was all right. Throughout the week the weather was serene and settled, too settled, in fact. I preferred the sea to be ruffled and white enough to ensure that no stray boat would be tempted to make the crossing. Not that it ever happened any more, but in our earliest years the occasional poacher had arrived to bag a pheasant or a rabbit, believing the island to be deserted for the winter. If the weather was rough, as it was most of the time, the possibility of trespassers was one that I didn't have to consider.

It wasn't too difficult being alone, although I scrupulously avoided anything that might unbalance my determined state of calm. In the evening, when I scanned the bookshelves I chose something safe and reassuring to make sure that my imagination would be kept tightly reined in. Even the smallest seeds of panic might take root and grow in the darkness, and in the morning there would nothing to cut them down to size, just me looking out across the solitary days and nights to come. As I sat with the hiss of the gaslights, the gentle crackling of the wood stove, and the howling of seals echoing through the stillness, I didn't want to find myself turning those commonplace sounds into half-heard threats.

It all went well until the day before Mike was due back. A storm began to pick up, and by lunch time I could tell that it was going to be a bad one. At first, the wind came only in erratic little snatches, but each gust had a whine in the tail to show its hidden strength. By the time it was getting dark, the flurries had united and were pummelling steadily against the house. It was a south-easterly, the wind I hated because it caught the side of the building that was lined with large windows. I could hear it crashing through the darkness and rolling over the house like a series of storm waves. At each blast, the house groaned with a sigh of aching timber. When I lit the living room lamp, I could see the huge window warping under the pressure of the wind. The reflected room washed back and forth, stretching and swimming like a mirage in a heat haze. It made me wince to look at it, because I was convinced that the glass was going to break and come splintering over me. Quickly, I drew the thick, lined curtains I had made for the windows, but they couldn't disguise the storm outside. The ideas followed in sequence, like the ripple of falling dominoes: once the glass gave way the wind would come ripping through the rooms, eventually lifting the roof off, and then the house would disintegrate, scattering into the air like shards of balsa wood.

Storms have a profound psychological effect that seems to delve far deeper than the simple fear of the damage they might cause. Storm winds whisper right through your consciousness, stirring up an inescapable, restless anxiety. By late evening my muscles ached from tensing each time the house shifted in the wind. I decided to distract myself by having a bath.

I turned on the taps and, in the unheated bathroom, the steam swirled up in thick, billowing clouds, like summer fog rising off the sea. With a couple of inches of water gurgling round the bottom of the bath, I panicked about wasting too much gas to heat the water and turned the taps off. Reluctantly, I peeled off my layers of clothing and splashed into the dribble of water. It wasn't too bad if I wriggled myself down into the narrow vein of steam, and at least it was quieter in the bathroom; the window faced north and was sheltered from the wind. I tried to concentrate on the radio which was chattering away companionably on the other side of the room, but I found it impossible. Though I had moved away from the direct impact of the storm, I could still hear it roaring all around me, like long, resonating trails of thunder. It sounded submerged and distant, all the more menacing for being slightly concealed.

Although I was barely listening, a quaint, old-fashioned phrase on the radio caught my attention: 'The following programme is not suitable for those of a nervous disposition'. I wondered if that included me, and realised that, under the prevailing circumstances, it probably did. I lifted my head above the parapet and looked across the room towards the radio. Between me and the off button stretched a vast wilderness of cold lino. I slithered back down into the steam. Whatever it is, I told myself confidently, it's not going to be worse than facing the frozen expanse of the bathroom.

When I had been attempting to distract myself by listening to the radio, all I could hear was the storm; now that I was trying to ignore the radio, every single word was wheedling its way into my mind. I found myself intently following the plot of an absurdly gruesome story that would have seemed laughable if I had encountered it at a less vulnerable moment. But it somehow managed to include too many elements that were uncomfortably close to my own fears. Among the more unfortunate details of the plot were an isolated house blacked out by a power cut and held in the grip of a storm, while its occupants were stalked by a long-dead cadaver that had risen from a bath full of water. As I listened to the graphic descriptions of the effects of the water on the bloated and decomposing corpse I knew that I had heard enough. I stood up abruptly and switched the radio off. The silence was immediately filled by the muffled rushing of the storm sounding louder than ever, while the startling flood of air over my wet skin made me shiver.

I dressed quickly, and then made my way tentatively out into the corridor. I could feel the difference as soon as I opened the bathroom door. While I had been shut away on the sheltered side of the house, the weather had deteriorated. A noise, like the drumming of a waterfall, was gushing through the rooms. I was shocked by the intensity of it, by the way it had changed so dramatically in such a short space of time. I went into the kitchen and saw the rain against the window, not individual drops, but an unbroken sheet of water spilling down the glass. The arrival of the rain had given substance to the wind; the saturated air was beating against the house with a new, physical presence. The noise was insistent and unrelenting, confusing my efforts to stay calm. I could no longer interpret the different layers of sound; the flaying of wooden shingles or the cracking of glass would be smothered by the continuous scream of noise. I knew that I had no choice but to check round the whole house.

Though I had no intention of going outside, I took the torch. It would have been too difficult to try to light the gas; in the distant rooms, where the lamps were rarely lit, the gas was slow to travel through the pipes, and I wanted my tour of the house to take as little time as possible. I headed down the short arm of the L-shaped corridor, out to where the rooms were most exposed to the storm. The torchlight made hard-edged, pouncing shadows that leapt out at me from nowhere and then shrank back into corners at my approach. They cowered out of sight behind the furniture and then closed in behind me as I passed. In the studio, where two of the walls were mainly window, the bright beam flared white against the glass, catching the squalls of pale rain that made patterns on the darkness. I looked round quickly, convincing myself that everything was all right, and then moved on to the study.

I could see at once that the force of the wind was driving the water into the room, spitting and gargling around the edges of the window frames. Tiny air bubbles popped and splashed, so that the water boiled up through the fault lines like lava from a miniature volcano. The window sill had flooded and was overflowing in a thin, persistent stream down onto the desk. The puddle was oozing into a stack of documents, which had sucked it up like blotting paper. I tried to shake off some of the water as I spread them out to dry. The paper had curled into ripples, like the corrugated patterns on a sandy beach; ink flowed with the random artistry of wet watercolour. My salvage attempts were only making more of a mess, and with the water still pouring down from the window sill it was hopeless trying to save anything. I would have to find a cloth and sop up the puddles.

As I dabbed at the water I sensed the energy of the storm on the other side of the glass, a few inches from my face; so close that it almost hurt. I was becoming jittery. The noise was so smothering that even if someone had stood behind me and shouted I would not have been able to hear. The darkness surrounding the splash of torchlight was so intense that I could feel its weight pressing down on me. Because I could no longer trust my senses, I had to keep looking round to make sure that nothing was there, but as I turned, each movement of the torch brought spectres of light and shade crowding round me. All the panic that I had kept so tightly contained was about to break free. I was shut off in my own little space of noise and blackness, and it was making me claustrophobic. I wanted to get away from there, away from the worst impact of the storm and back to the gaslight. I spread the papers haphazardly around, hoping they would dry, and dashed out of the study.

As soon as I was back in the hallway I knew that something was wrong. It was too dark. The brightness from the kitchen should have been leaking down the blackened corridor towards me. I hesitated, staring ahead, not wanting to go any further. There was definitely no light, but I would never have deliberately turned it off, leaving the house in darkness. And it is impossible to put a gaslight out accidentally, unthinkingly, like the flick of an electric light switch. So who had turned it off, and who was now waiting for me in the dark?

'Stop it, stop it, stop it!', I shouted silently at myself, snapping the spiral of thought before it had a chance to spin out of control.

There was nothing else to do but go and look. The torch beam went ahead of me into the room. I watched as the shadows darted out of its path, and then I forced myself to follow. I shone the torch up to the gas lamp. It was still in the on position, but there was no hiss of escaping gas. The cylinder must have run out. Usually, the glow from the gas mantle dimmed in warning long before it failed, but I had been gone for so long that the last glimmer of light had shrunk away without me noticing.

I would have to go outside to change the cylinder. That meant braving the screaming wind to carry the heavy, slippery-wet cylinder into place, with no free hand to hold the torch. The dark would be so thick with invisible rain that I would have to feel my way. When I reached the lean-to where the cylinders were connected, on the most exposed side of the house, and slid back the bolt, the wind might wrench the door from my hand, whipping it back and forth until the wood shattered. A fresh surge of wind sent splinters of rain clattering against the window like a handful of gravel, and I knew that I could not go outside. I would go to bed and wait for morning. Everything would look much better in daylight.

Lying in bed, with my knees curled up against my chest and arms folded tight against the cold, I began to feel calmer. The storm seemed more distant now that I was inside the sheltered angle of the L. I had stopped shivering and was drifting comfortably towards sleep when I found myself suddenly and starkly awake. I'd had a horrible thought: if anything happened in the night, I wouldn't be able to put a light on. I remembered the horror films that had haunted my childhood, how it was always darkness and flickering candles that had compounded the terror. Then, I used to lie in bed, with the synthetic flare of streetlights spilling round the curtains, looking at the protrusions on the walls that marked the places where the pipes from the old gaslights had once been, feeling immeasurably grateful for the ever-present safety net of electric light. I comforted myself with the certainty that nothing really bad would have the audacity confront the instant glare of electricity. How appalled that child would have been to see herself now, alone on an island where even the gaslights had faded and died.

Fortunately, the storm was short-lived, and Mike was only a day late returning. Once he was back we realised that we had passed a turning point. For the first time since the morning I had found the body, everything felt normal. While Mike was away our routines had been broken, and we were starting afresh, with the island feeling secure and peaceful again.

Usually, we left Skomer for a period during the winter and spent Christmas with family, but this year we were planning to stay right through. I was particularly looking forward to being able to keep an unbroken record of the seal pups. It would be good to be able to fill in that one last gap in our observations of them. People on the mainland were amused by our tenacity in remaining on the island, though I suspected few could see the appeal of what we were doing. They consulted their extensive knowledge of local history and decided that it was unlikely anyone had spent Christmas on Skomer for many decades, but to me that only made the whole thing special.

We were not the only ones to feel that sense of occasion. We found food parcels left for us on the mainland, full of such old-fashioned things as tinned potatoes and tinned meat pies, and little luxuries, like sugared almonds and sherry. It was very touching. We also began making our own collection of Christmas provisions: a small box of chocolates, nuts, dates. It was the first time such frivolous things had been included among our rigorously practical supplies, and we were so impressed by their rarity that we arranged them on a table, like Christmas decorations, so that we could admire them.

The days were at their shortest, and the weak, diluted daylight had become such a precious commodity that it couldn't be squandered. It meant that if we wanted to walk purely for pleasure we often had to wait until the end of the day, when most of the useful light was gone. We were setting out in a typical late-afternoon twilight when we heard the deep drone of an engine shuddering through the air. The distinctive sound of a helicopter was immediately recognisable, and we hurried up the hill to get a better view. It juddered overhead, slow and low and loud, leading us up towards the centre of the island, where we guessed it was going to land. The helicopter hovered in a barely perceptible crawl just ahead of us, but, though we ran until our legs ached, we seemed to be standing still as it disappeared beyond the ridge of the island. We pushed ourselves even harder as we tried to catch up, and the air felt cold and sharp rasping inside my chest.

As the path levelled out we were able to see as far as the Bread Rock. The winchman was standing on top of the outcrop, waving something in the air. My earthbound legs felt useless as we tried to reach him, and we were too slow. As soon as he was sure we had seen the package, he left it on top of the rock and rose, almost magically, on the fine connecting thread up to meet the helicopter. The aircraft made a few acrobatic twists, swooping low above our heads so that we could make out the crew waving, and then swept rapidly away towards the sea. We watched it go, its lights sparking through the thickening grey of the sky.

With the urgency gone, we walked on slowly, breathlessly, up towards the Bread Rock. We clambered up its rounded slopes and found the long dark package, wrapped in black polythene and yards of sticky tape. I reached out to touch; the prickly feel beneath the plastic was extremely eloquent.

'It's a Christmas tree!' I said.

We were ridiculously excited. Any thought of a walk was forgotten; the tree had to be unveiled at once. Besides, the light had drained away so quickly that it was almost dark, and the prospect of being outdoors was no longer tempting.

We carried the tree into the living room and peeled back the plastic; in one great gulp, that wonderful aromatic scent, with its taste of childhood Christmases, came flooding out. Strewn among the branches were crackers, streamers, balloons and tinsel, along with sprigs of mistletoe and holly. When the tree was lifted clear we found a shoebox, with its lid firmly taped shut.

'What's this?' I asked, picking it up.

It felt very light. Mike took it from me and shook it; no sound emerged.

'I hope it's not fairly lights,' I joked, as Mike began picking at the tape.

The lid came off to reveal two neat rows of coloured lights. We looked at each other and laughed. Charles, the helicopter pilot who had organised this airlift, came in for a lot of teasing over his lack of initiative in sending lights to an island without electricity, but the truth was that we loved them. We set up the tree immediately, and the permanently dim fairy lights took pride of place twined through its branches. They even sparkled faintly in the glow from the gas lamp.

The house had its own distinctive smell, which had become strongly associated with my continuing love of living there. That faintly woody smell greeted me every time I came in from the outside and, strangely, in all those years, it never became so familiar that I forgot to notice it. Sometimes it was mingled with the warmth of baking bread, the mixed-spice smell of narcissi in spring, or wood smoke in the winter. Now, for the first time in the house's history, one more layer had been added: the resinous tang of Christmas.

As Christmas approached, Mike took to shutting himself away in the laboratory next door during the evenings. He had turned it into a woodworking area for the winter, and the floor was covered in soft, pale spirals of wood shavings, which gathered in heaps, like snowdrifts, where he worked. He was always keen for me to admire the progress of any creative venture, and even accepted the occasional word of constructive criticism, but over recent days he had become very secretive, frequently disappearing without explanation. I had my suspicions about what he was doing, and tactfully turned a blind eye to his frequent absences. Over the years he had made me some delightful presents - a tiny writing desk, some intricately carved love spoons - and I was determined not to spoil the surprise.

The pressure had tumbled dramatically during the day, slipping down the barograph in a line of squiggly, blue ink. By nightfall, gusts of wind were slamming into the house with unrestrained fury. All storms are unnerving, but each has its own peculiar way of wheedling under your skin. This wind tormented with its intermittent nature. It settled for periods into a gentle roar that became almost deceptively soothing; then it suddenly reared up, grabbed the house in its teeth and shook it.

I was in the kitchen and Mike had slipped quietly away to his woodwork. There was a jarring noise as a slab of wind hit the house with the force of a solid object. The creaking of wood and a violent crash came almost simultaneously. I felt a rush of cold air sweeping into the room but, as I turned to look, the kitchen door slammed shut with such force that I winced in anticipation of broken glass. I ran out into the hallway to find the carpet flapping like a loose sail, and pictures swinging out into a horizontal position before crashing back against the walls. It was all right. It was only the front door that had blown open. I raced up the corridor and forced the door shut, squeezing out the wind. Calm returned instantly, and in the stillness I realised that I was shaking inside. For a moment I had thought that the house was breaking up. I loved that house, but in the worst of the storms it felt as fragile as a matchstick model.

I went back to the kitchen and tried to concentrate on what I was doing. A few minutes later the door flew open again, reverberating as it bounced against the wall. I made it to the corridor in time to see a picture wrenching itself free and diving onto the floor. Rain jabbed against my face as I reached the doorway. I pushed the door shut, and clicked the latch firmly into place. It felt wrong, because we never locked the door, day or night. There was no need for security and, because it was in the sheltered inner corner of the L-shaped house, the door could withstand almost all winds. I picked up the fallen picture. The glass inside the frame had cracked in a single, neat curve. My nerves were feeling battered, and I thought it might be a good idea to resort to the universal panacea of a bath.

I regretted it almost immediately. The storm had sucked every bit of warmth out of the house, and sharp little draughts were sneaking their way in round the window frames in the bathroom. As I sank down into the shallow pool of bathwater I realised that it was uninvitingly cool. I tried to make the best of it, working the soap into a thick lather, but as I splashed handfuls of water over my back to rinse it, the tepid droplets seemed to crawl over my skin like insects. I shuddered slightly, but I didn't have long to wallow in the discomfort. There was a thumping sound at the front door and Mike's voice, loud and angry, above the storm.

I felt irritated and determined to stay put. That was typical of Mike. He should come in and say what he wanted instead of crashing around making so much noise that I would feel obliged to go running. Then I remembered the front door, the door that was never, ever locked . . . except tonight. I had a hideously vivid image of Mike standing on the doorstep whipped by drenching sheets of rain. He would have no idea why I had locked the door, and would be furious. I leapt out of the bath, barely noticing the torrent of water that accompanied me out onto lino, and hurried down the corridor, stopping only to grab a towel.

When I opened the door, the first thing I noticed was the blood, which was odd given that there was only a faint stream of light trickling down the corridor from the gas lamp in the kitchen. Mike was not angry, as I had imagined, but more distressed. He had been waiting long enough for a small pool of blood to have formed just outside the front door.

'I've cut myself,' he said, rather superfluously, as he barged past me.

I turned and reluctantly followed the trail of glistening red beads up the hallway, feeling slightly sickened by the certainty that so much blood must be a bad sign. He already had water from the cold tap gushing over his hand by the time I reached the kitchen.

'How bad is it?' I asked, squinting through half closed eyes, trying to ascertain the extent of the trauma without exposing myself to the full glare of it. I was pathetically pleased to see that all the fingers were still present.

'I don't know.'

The clear water turned crimson the moment it touched his hand, giving the illusion that pints of blood were gurgling down the plughole. Every time he pulled his hand out of the stream of water blood pooled into the gash, making it impossible to get a clear view of it. I clutched my towel, like a security blanket, to my damp skin.

'I'll go and find some bandages,' I said, glad of the excuse to escape from the scene of the injury.

When the blood flow eased a little, Mike turned off the tap, but even with constant dabbing of cotton wool the wound was barely visible for long enough to get a proper look. Eventually, as I became acclimatized to the quantities of blood, I was able to force myself into enough of a detailed examination to see that it was not too serious. There was a deep, clean slice into the fleshy part of his hand between the thumb and forefinger. It seemed like a bad omen because, as a child, I had always been persuaded that cuts in that unlucky position resulted in lockjaw, and that sort conditioning is hard to shake off. Ideally, it needed a few stitches, but there was no question of calling for help. We knew exactly what we were taking on in accepting that level of isolation, and it would have been unfair to expect other people to come rushing whenever things became slightly difficult. Besides, the storm was probably too bad for rescue to be a viable option.

I tried to apply a bandage. I often browsed through first aid books because I had a persistent fear of finding myself as the only responsible adult in command of a medical emergency, but in real life I had never graduated beyond the occasional sticking plaster. Theory and practice proved hard to reconcile. Mike instructed me patiently as I struggled with coils of tangled bandage. The end result looked quite good, for a few minutes, until the blood came seeping through, making a maroon stain on the clean white cloth.

With the cut safely out of sight, Mike immediately forgot about it. He disappeared back into the storm, leaving me feeling queasy in the wake of so much blood. A few minutes later, he returned looking dejected.

'I'm not really worried about the cut,' he said. 'This is the real disaster.'

He was holding a wooden snail carved in West African mahogany; it was the last small piece of wood from the remnants of the lost deck cargo that Skip had retrieved from the sea and given to us. The snail was beautiful, with the patterns of the wood grain echoing through the sweeping curves of its shell. The only trouble was that the place of one of its delicate antennae was taken by an ugly scar gashed into the wood.

'It was going to be your Christmas present,' Mike said miserably.

'It doesn't matter,' I replied. 'It's still lovely.'

But we both knew that the peculiar, lopsided shape of the head would never work.

Mike put the snail on the table in the living room and sat staring at it despondently all evening. Occasionally, he broke the silence with a few reproachful words.

'It's my own fault. I knew the chisel was getting blunt. I should have stopped and sharpened it, but I thought I'd make a couple more cuts first, and then I slipped . . .'

He broke off, since the conclusion of the sentence was too awful and too obvious. My main concern was for the cut on Mike's hand. No matter how many extra layers of bandage I put on to try to disguise the problem, the blood kept percolating through.

The next day some of Mike's old determination returned. He took the snail away and when I saw it again the head had been remodelled, leaving no suggestion that the poor creature had ever suffered such a horrific accident. The polished wooden shell glowed deep, golden-red, like reflected firelight. I fell immediately in love with the snail, which I named Diggory. To this day, it remains one of my most treasured possessions . . . and Mike still has the scar on his hand.

There was one small anxiety about our lonely Christmas, and that was whether or not we were going to be able to have Christmas dinner. If we failed to get any fresh supplies, our universal emergency stand-by for special occasions, the tin of ham, would prove a sad substitute for a proper dinner. In fact, it would be grim enough to put a damper on the whole day.

It became a tense war of nerves: us against the weather. If we took our chance too early, we would be unable to store fresh food, but if we passed up even a single suitable day, the weather could close in again for weeks, by which time it would all be over. It was an unsettling choice, but, fortunately, we were not forced into making any decisions. There were none of those borderline days when we thought we might just make it. The weather stayed uncompromisingly rough until three days before Christmas, when, almost miraculously, we saw a dawn so calm that the anger had ebbed from the waves.

We waited for the light to brighten a little more and scanned the distance with binoculars to make sure that the half-light was not concealing larger waves further out to sea. It was a lesson we had learnt the hard way. Everything looked fine, but the shipping forecast had been so atrocious that we felt uneasy. We tried calling the coastguard, who assured us that the next storm was still a few hours off. It was all the persuasion we needed to make the crossing.

By that afternoon, we had everything we needed, including the most essential ingredient, the turkey. On the way back to Martin's Haven in the Land Rover I studied every twig and blade of grass, trying to assess how badly the wind had picked up and which direction it was coming from. That same sense of fear overshadowed almost every visit I made to the mainland. My first glimpse of the bay showed tongues of white foam already lurching spasmodically across the water. It was a rough trip back, with waves thudding against the side of the boat and breaking into hard, gravelly spray which the wind caught and flicked into our faces. The sea was building by the moment, and as we tried to land in North Haven the boat was caught by a white-topped wave and driven towards the rocks. I jumped off the bow to prevent a collision, while the wave lumbered cold and heavy around my legs, drizzling into my boots, but I didn't care now that were safely back. A yearling seal, secure in the certainty of its own agility, splashed to the surface next to me, so close that I could hear the hiss of its breath. Its glossy head mingled with the shine of winter-dark sea as it watched us unload our stores. It was enough to make me forget how much I hated boating, and remind me that an easier way of life would be dull compared to this.

We stowed our provisions in the back of the tractor and Mike drove them up, while I walked behind with wet feet sliding inside my boots. Taking the shortcut along the cliff top, I reached the house before him and waited by the side of the track to help unload the tractor. The wind was snatching in fitful gusts past my face. The fact that we had reached home with so little time to spare made me feel all the more elated.

'I don't care,' I shouted into the great emptiness of the sky. 'You can do what you like now.'

The weather took me at my word. The gales picked up again almost immediately, and by Christmas Eve the sea was strewn with dense, white waves. Instead of the usual damp, grey westerlies and south-westerlies, there was a hint of north in the wind. The air was luminously clear, the sea a glass-bright cobalt blue. In the afternoon we walked up to Pigstone Bay, one of the wildest and most exposed places on the western end of the island. The surf had built into a thick foam at the base of the cliff, tumbled into mounds by the waves, like an over-extravagant bubble bath. The low sun was slicing horizontally across the sky, giving everything an unnaturally exaggerated brilliance. Each incoming wave sent clouds of creamy foam streaming up the cliff like an explosion of champagne from a bottle. The white flecks caught the light as they broke free and were carried high on the wind. Then, as they floated back to earth, they became snagged in the vegetation and stroked across our faces and hair, soft and almost warm in the sun. At our feet they gathered in snowdrifts, with the salty sparkle of ice. All around us the artificial blizzard glittered in the shards of wintry light. It was almost impossibly spectacular, like being caught inside the glass bubble of a snowstorm toy.

The whole thing had a feeling of exuberance that made me feel helplessly happy. I couldn't have stopped smiling even if I had wanted to. This was the closest we were ever likely to come to a white Christmas on Skomer; the climate was so mild that, in all of our nine years there, we had never seen snow. It was a perfect moment that evaporated almost instantly. The blaze of winter sunshine, no matter how full of promise, is always brief. Long before the afternoon is over, it loses its strength. The shine went from the waves and the light faded to a cool, smoky red. Suddenly, the wind turned penetratingly cold, and we knew that it was time to go home.

It was too much to expect that Christmas Day could be so flawlessly beautiful. Those days are scattered only sparingly through the winter months. But it was dry, and the grey had a certain brightness to it, which was as much as we wanted. There was no question that I would forget about the seal pups just because it was Christmas morning, but, as a concession to the occasion, we went together to check the seals. There were no new arrivals, but it was still a glorious morning to be out. A small crowd of fulmars had gathered on the crumbling cliffs of the isthmus. They launched themselves into the air and skimmed beside us, like miniature gliders escorting us home. The sound of their euphoric chuckling flowed around us.

Back home, I made breakfast: thick slabs of toasted homemade bread with melting butter and poached eggs. We opened a bottle of champagne provided by one of our benefactors on the mainland, pulled crackers and wore the garish paper hats that unfurled from inside them. Then, while we finished the last of the champagne, we unwrapped our presents, including my immaculate hand-carved snail.

As Christmas had come closer, I began to wonder how it would be possible to set it apart from any other day. After all, it would be just the two of us, alone; nothing would be any different. But, somehow, it turned out to be the most wonderful Christmas. We couldn't have asked for anything more than to be together in the place we loved so much, and I think that we will both remember it as one of the happiest days we have ever spent. It felt like a real Christmas, one that had nothing to do with last-minute panics in crowded shops, or trying to recreate some impossible commercial ideal.

We welcomed the New Year with similarly reclusive pleasure. The mere fact of our solitude gave it an almost mystical quality. At midnight we switched on the marine VHF radio to make contact with the only human voice we had access to. We wished the coastguard on duty a happy New Year, and then listened as the greetings passed between the few ships still at sea. I liked the feeling of being on the periphery of that fragile network of people cast adrift. We went outside to taste the sea air and hear the waves. In the quiet and the darkness, the coming of the New Year felt more profound than it ever could if we had been surrounded by people and noise.

January was cold. Each day the cold consolidated, as though it was sinking deeper and deeper into the land, clinging immovably to the island. First the puddles, and then the ponds, froze. We were not used to such extremes. We lived with storms almost daily, but the temperatures were tamed by the moderating influence of the sea all around us. Intense cold was something that came only fleetingly, and then moved on.

The air was hazy, thin and sharply dry. It did not promise snow, which would have been the one compensation for a breeze so bitterly penetrating that it made my skull and eyes ache. The gaslights raised the temperature in the kitchen slightly, but still I had to warm slivers of butter under the grill before I could spread them. The rest of the house felt inaccessibly hostile; I could hardly bear to face the cutting chill of the other rooms.

When I was walking outside, my steps sliced green trails through the white, crystalline veneer of frost. I became more aware than ever of the extensive network of burrows woven beneath my feet. The frozen ground began to feel so hard and hollow that it had a metallic ring to it. In my imagination I could hear the reverberations running through all those tunnels and chambers carved out underground, created so painstakingly over the centuries. It made me want to stamp my foot with each step, just to hear the strangeness of the sound it made.

On the mainland snow was causing chaos. We listened with fascination, and mild envy, to the radio news reports of atrocious weather, but there was no chance of us seeing so much as a snowflake. The blizzards were on the opposite side of the country to us, in the east of England. But gradually, day by day, they came closer. We followed the progress of the weather as it swept across the country, until, eventually, we could look across the bay and see the distant Preseli Mountains shining with a lustrous, snowy whiteness.

At last! We went to bed that night, almost certain that the snow would have reached us by morning. It was extraordinarily exciting after so many years of waiting, but the reality was far from idyllic. The day began painfully early, while the bedroom was still dark, and the air dense with cold. I was woken by the sound of Mike shuffling about the room, somewhere near the end of the bed. With that first consciousness came the realisation that the cold was breaching a weak point in the bedclothes and slithering in around my shoulders. I snatched the covers tight against my neck.

'I think you'd better get up,' Mike said.

Mike is not a morning person, and was usually happy to wait for me to get up first, so I was immediately disturbed by the sense of urgency.

'What's the matter?' I asked, regretting my fumbled attempt to sit up, which had let more chilled air come rushing in.

'We haven't got any water. The pipe must be frozen somewhere.'

'Can't we leave it till it gets light?'

'No. We'll have to sort it out before it bursts.'

As we stepped outside, the first breath I took was so cold that it slipped down into my lungs with a stabbing pain. I shivered.

'What do we do now?' I asked miserably.

'I'll start by checking the water tank,' Mike said.

He darted up the hill, and I followed carefully, picking my way in his deep, snowy footprints. The torchlight glimmered and sparkled as it brushed across the thick layer of snow.

'This must be the problem,' Mike said, concentrating the puddle of light on a small section of pipe.

For most of its route down to the house the pipe was buried, but one segment showed above ground.

'Right, get me some dry firewood and matches,' Mike said.

'What are you going to do?'

'We're going to have a bonfire.'

'Isn't that a bit drastic?'

'Have you got any better ideas?'

Mike piled the wood over the pipe and lit it. Soon, the weak, liquid flames lapping over the kindling began to take hold, making the wood crackle and spit.

'Now then,' Mike said. 'I want you to go back down the hill and do exactly what I say.'

He spoke slowly and firmly, making it clear that he couldn't quite trust me to follow what he was saying. At the bottom of the hill, half-heard instructions about the sequence of turning taps on and off drifted down to me, and I interpreted them using a certain amount of imagination. I have never understood the intricate rules about taps and airlocks that apply in life's little water pipe emergencies. After running in and out of the house a dozen times, turning taps and trying to listen for further instalments of the instructions, I became convinced that we were trying to thaw the wrong section of pipe. Then, suddenly, I heard the most delightful noise. There was a thumping and gurgling in the pipes, followed by the sound of water gushing into the bath.

By the time we had restored the water, the first faint wash of daylight was seeping into the sky. The smooth sheet of snow gathered up every trace of light, reflecting it back with a weak luminescence that was softly pale, like the surface of the moon. The air was absolutely still, as if it was frozen hard, but from somewhere came a sound like the distant rush of wind.

'What's that noise?' I asked.

Mike gazed up towards the sky.

'Birds,' he replied.

I could make out a faint, sooty shadow blackening the sky as it moved overhead: a dark stream flowing westward.

'You mean those are all birds?' I asked.

'Yes. They must have been forced along ahead of the bad weather as it crossed the country, and now there's nowhere left for them to go.'

'But it looks like thousands of them, and they're all heading straight out to sea. What will happen to them?'

'Let's hope they make it as far as Ireland.'

The day brightened quickly under the clear sky. We layered on as many clothes as we could manage while still remaining mobile, and went out to see the snow. Even with the sun above the horizon, it was startlingly cold. My fingers ached inside my gloves, while my toes stayed disconcertingly numb.

Usually, a brisk walk was enough to bring the feeling back, but not that day. I walked clumsily on strangely absent feet.

The snow was beautiful. I will never know a landscape in the way I had come to know Skomer after nine years, and it was intriguing to see all that familiarity transformed by a glittering quilt of snow. It bulged in thick folds over walls and rocks, smoothing and highlighting, moulding shapes into contrasts of soft curves and hard lines. Some things it emphasised, others it pared away, leaving everything subtly different. The brightness picked out distant features, making the intimate landscape appear expanded and remote. It had a cold untouchability, a forbidding perfection.

On the ground nothing moved. There was not a footprint; not a single rabbit had ventured out of a burrow. The only noise was the high-pitched murmuring from the flocks of birds passing overhead. Then came a loud and almost painfully nostalgic sound, the stridently melancholy wail of geese. Streams of competing notes were all falling over each other. It was wilfully unmelodic, but in that frozen stillness it was stunning. All at once, the birds rose up from their hidden hollow, synchronized into a single pattern of movement. Sharply black and white against the bleached background of a snow-washed landscape, their stark simplicity highlighted the muted scene. We listened to the clamour, like the echo of a memory, as they circled above us and then descended in a slow motion cascade to the shores of North Pond.

As the quiet returned, Mike and I threw our arms round each other. These were not just birds, but almost long-lost friends. For the past three years, a small flock of barnacle geese had arrived on the island in November. They were an oddity, a rarity, having strayed far from their normal wintering grounds. We had expected them to move on almost immediately, but they stayed and became part of the empty landscape. We watched them daily, following their movements and feeding patterns, convinced that a single season would be our only chance of being so close to these ephemeral visitors. So, when they came back in succeeding years, we felt somehow honoured to be chosen by the birds. Then, that snowy winter, they failed to return. We had searched for them almost daily since the end of summer, until, by January, we were certain that we would not see them again. When their haunting, unforgettable cries came cutting through the cold of that spectacular morning, it felt like more than we could have hoped for.

I am ashamed to say that we walked only as far as the farm before accepting defeat. After waiting so many years for the snow to come, I could hardly believe that I would be willing to give in before I had seen the whole of the island, but the cold was more intense than anything I imagined. I could only walk with my head bent, face turned aside, sheltering my skin from the burning cold. At the farm we turned back and saw our two faint sets of footprints drifting endlessly into the distance, the only blemish on the untouched whiteness.

It was a special day that deserved to be marked by some sort of extravagant celebration. At home, I retrieved a carefully hoarded tin of sausages from the store cupboard to cook for breakfast. Under our regime of excessive caution over food supplies, it was an act of pure recklessness. As I cooked, I noticed that Mike was staring thoughtfully out across North Haven. The exceptional weather had given me a false sense of security but, suddenly, I knew what he was going to say, and I also knew that I would not be able to argue against it.

'I think we'd better go across to the mainland,' he said, his eyes fixed on the ice-blue sea that was taut and still, like a frozen lake. 'With the weather like this, we can't risk running out of gas.'

I prodded miserably at a spitting sausage, in a gesture of resentful acquiescence.

After breakfast, Mike set off to walk down to the beach leaving me to bring the tractor. Once I had brushed the snow off the seat, the tractor came instantly to life with a good-natured growl. My hands locked onto the steering wheel, as if soldered in place by the cold. What a waste, I thought crossly, to leave the island on such a magnificent day. But I never wanted to leave, whatever the weather, and some more reasonable part of me knew that Mike was right.

The empty gas cylinders in the back jumped and clattered as I began to ascend the steep hill. Close to the water tank, a band of thick ice had formed across the track. I hesitated for a moment and then ploughed forward, willing the tractor to keep going. The wheels screeched and span, until finally the tractor slid back off the ice. I tried again, twice more, to convince myself that the hill really was too steep and the ice too thick. My first instinct was to switch off the engine and go on foot in search of Mike. My second was not to be so feeble. I edged the wheels up onto the snowy bank at the side of the track, bypassing the slab of ice. The tractor tilted sideways as it moved further onto the slope. As I considered the possibility that it might tip, I realised that I was less afraid of being trapped under a falling tractor than I was of explaining my stupidity to Mike. Then the tractor began to level out, and the wheels were cutting smoothly through the snow back towards the track. The ice was behind me.

I felt quite proud of myself until I reached the beach and realised what a tiny obstacle I had conquered. Water trickling down from the cliff had frozen in a rippling sheet across almost the entire area of the slipway.

'We'll never get the boat across that,' I said, feeling that I had already discovered enough about ice to have the right to be unnerved.

'We'll manage,' Mike said, with the confidence of ignorance.

When we were ready to start wheeling the boat down into the water Mike gave a stern warning.

'If you feel the boat running away from you on the ice, just drop the front of the trailer,' he said, emphatically. 'It'll act like a brake and stop it dead.'

The moment the boat hit the ice we lost it. There was no need for shouted instructions; we both knew immediately that it was out of control, and dropped the trailer. The boat didn't stop. It didn't even slow down. It simply accelerated with shattering speed towards the rocks. I winced, unable to bear the sight of our boat splintering into fragments. Mike acted with more presence of mind. A length of heavy rope snaking out behind the trailer was still within reach. He snatched it, flipping it sideways with such force that the boat pirouetted on the ice, negotiating the right angle bend in the slipway, and came to rest gently on the shingle beach.

The boat was now on the seaward side of the ice. Whatever difficulties that might represent, there seemed no point in abandoning the trip now we had come so far. We dragged the boat across the shingle and set out to sea, with the engine stuttering loudly against the snowy quiet of the cliffs surrounding the bay.

It was almost dusk when we returned, with the opal sea reflecting glimmering images of the cliffs. And still the birds were there, a misty trail and a babble of calls flowing continuously through the sky above us. As we beached the boat I saw that the stubborn barrier of ice still remained. I had stupidly hoped that the problem might somehow have melted away while we were gone. We needed to get the tractor across the ice in order to pull the boat up the beach. Although we could roll the boat and trailer down on our own, it was much too heavy to pull back up. Mike kicked the ice sheet and stamped on it with resounding force. Nothing happened.

'It's not that thick,' he said, confidently. 'It should break up under the weight of the tractor.'

The tractor trundled onto the ice with infinite caution and then slewed violently, skidding sideways down the slope. Its great bulk was unstoppable. In the slow motion panic that comes in moments of disaster, I knew that the tractor would plunge over the edge and down onto the beach below. Instead, it came to an abrupt halt when the carrying box at the back became jammed against the rocks that fringed the slipway. The front wheels were poised on the brink of a sheer drop. For a few seconds we were both shocked into silence, just relieved that the tractor had actually stopped moving. From where I was standing the situation looked insoluble. With the tractor wedged sideways across the slipway, leaving not even a spare inch for manoeuvre, I could see no way out. I was dreading Mike's reaction as he jumped down from the driving seat to inspect the tractor's desperate predicament. When he spoke, he sounded unexpectedly calm.

'If I could manage to free the box and unhitch it from the back, we might have room to move.'

'But whatever we do, we'll never get the tractor back across the ice,' I insisted, 'and the tide's coming in fast, so we can't leave it leave it on the beach.'

We worked for hours until there was nothing but the dazzling glare of tractor lights. Mike hammered and swore and finally freed the tractor box. I clambered through the dark swilling countless buckets of sea water to thaw the ice, but I managed only to blur and soften its shine. The wheels of the liberated tractor span and snarled, making no headway back across the sheet of ice. I dug with my bare hands deep into the fine, sharp gravel at the tideline, grazing the sensitive skin of my fingertips, and threw bucketfuls grit in front of the tractor like an offering of appeasement. Most of it was spat aside disdainfully by the spinning wheels, but eventually, lurching in flashes of crazy movement, dangerously close to the steep drop, the tractor crawled off the ice.

The next day was far less cold, but dense with snow. The frozen stillness had dissolved into more characteristically stormy conditions. When I looked up towards the sky, it was heavy with the immense weight of snow suspended there. Even caught by the strong wind, the flakes drifted with a sense of unhurried calm, an infinite cascade pouring mesmerically down, softly grey. It was only when they touched the smooth layer on the ground that they turned to white.

The crisp, cutting edge had gone from the air, which felt mellow and almost mild. The day before, the frosted turquoise sea had stretched out as far as the distant white strip of mainland. Today we were completely enclosed. The low sky sank down towards us, while the swirling blizzard of snowflakes sealed the tight cocoon. Deep drifts were beginning to build, sculpted by the wind into sleekly elegant shapes. The smooth curves and sharp folds had such perfect definition that they could have been carved from white marble.

The snow was exciting, unknown; its bright, transforming presence was exhilarating. We walked with the downy flakes billowing round us, catching in our hair and beading our skin. When we reached North Pond, we found that it had vanished. The crust of ice had been smothered by snow, so that the pond was lost in the surrounding landscape. We pushed back some of the powdery covering to reveal the swirled, leafy patterns in the opaque, white ice. It looked reassuringly solid, so we stepped out onto it and began to skate, gingerly at first and then with growing confidence. It was like being set free; I could feel myself skidding helplessly away from the constraints of adulthood. Our shouts and laughter drifted only briefly before being caught and held in the clouds of snow. All sounds were deadened as the snow absorbed every trace of an echo.

In such a mood of elation, there seemed no option but to apply ourselves to building a snowman. We worked with an unselfconscious dedication that would have been impossible on the mainland. But there, in our own little world, we barely noticed that we had slipped back into childhood for an hour. When it was finished, plump and already fluffy with the clinging flakes of fresh snow, Mike drew onto it a smile that was curiously full of character. The snowman gazed with the most benign gentleness out across the snow-smoothed island. Reluctantly, we walked away, and when we turned to look back a few moments later it was gone, melted into the overlapping layers of white upon white.

We returned to the house to discover it under siege. Birds were crammed into every space where they could find some scrap of shelter. There were hundreds of them, blackbirds, starlings, thrushes, clustering along the window sills, under the eaves, around the front door. The endless babbling calls were interwoven with the chatter of claws as they scrabbled to find a perch on the wooden surfaces. These were part of the same movement of birds that had been streaming overhead throughout the previous day. They were obviously exhausted and had come to land on the island, which was too thick with snow to offer them adequate food or shelter.

Inside the house we found two birds, battering themselves against the brilliant lure of the window-pane. Their presence was a mystery, until a third bird came scurrying out of the fireplace and we realised that they were coming down the chimney. They threw themselves recklessly from one window to the next before we were able to catch and release them.

Our main problem was how to find food for so many birds. We searched through the fridge and the cupboard, sorting out anything we could spare that might be useful. We sacrificed all our cooking fats, margarine and butter, as well as our store of apples and dried fruit, but it was not enough for the swarm of starving birds, so I cooked huge batches of rice and pasta. As soon as it was cool enough to scatter on the ground, the birds washed over the food in a pool of shuddering wings, bickering noisily as they snatched what they could.

When we went out again and walked towards the isthmus, we noticed the burrows. Almost every burrow had three or four sets of footprints leading into it, spiky little imprints of birds' feet, like lines of hieroglyphics etched into the snow, each one telling a story. Every set of footprints faced the same way, with none of them emerging from underground. There was something about those fragile little marks in the cold that haunted me for months. I imagined the birds deep underground, having abandoned hope of finding food, huddled together for warmth. And there was nothing we could do. Even into the spring and summer I found myself staring at the burrow entrances and wondering how many of those birds ever found their way back out. Were there dozens of forgotten corpses still hidden underground, little desiccated balls of feathers that marked the remains of a life?

We continued past the burrows and down into South Haven. As we approached the water's edge, I could hardly believe what I was seeing. Usually the tide line was marked by a ridge of weed regurgitated by the sea, scattered with scraps of driftwood and rubbish. That day, the dark line was not just weed; woven among the shiny, green-brown fronds were the bedraggled remains of countless small birds. Their feathers had been slicked into clumps by the seawater, and slashes of naked skin showed between the matted strands. When I saw those vulnerable bodies exposed beneath their camouflage of feathers, it seemed impossible that they could have survived the cold even for as long as they had.

These were yesterday's birds: the ones we had seen passing overhead from before the dawn light until long after the day had ended. The dark, shimmering mass had flowed like a single entity, their unity of purpose disguising the fact that each individual bird was on the brink of exhaustion. Somewhere out above the ocean, that determination had deserted them and, unable to go on, they had dropped into the water, where the waves had carried them, slowly retracing their journey, until they washed up on the shore.

From the beach we could see a little way out across the sea into South Haven. The falling snow was twisting in random flurries, like a soft confetti of shredded clouds wallowing in the breeze. As the dense flakes touched the water, they vanished, as if by magic. The muffling blur of snow held back the light, so that the day was almost colourless, and the vignette ahead of me had the look of a grainy, black and white photograph. Part of the graininess came from the flecks of snowflakes, but I couldn't understand why the sea was darkly mottled. Then I realised that the surface of the water was stippled with the bodies of birds. Twisted wings, spiky, dishevelled feathers: a sheet of lifeless birds rocking and shifting with the movement of the waves. So much death all concentrated together.

We climbed back up the steep slope to the top of the isthmus. Even though the day had been relentlessly dull, it was obvious from the growing drabness that the sun had already sunk low in the sky. Then, quite unexpectedly, strands of brilliant light pierced the clouds. Dazzling gold flooded the misty dullness and mingled with the falling snow. I looked down into South Haven at the amazing play of energy, a maelstrom of swirling movement highlighted by this flare of intensely warm light. The winter monochrome had become an aurora of spinning colours.

It was a beautiful moment, one so rare that I would treasure it forever, but most of the pleasure had been taken out of it. The birds clamouring round the house for food, cowering inside the burrows, and eventually washing dead onto the beach in a dull, black tide, had all been a consequence of the weather, one that I could never have imagined. The snow had arrived with such promise, but now we just wanted it to be gone, so that the birds would at least have a chance.

Normality returned swiftly and decisively: mild winds came rushing back, erasing every trace of the snow. The island emerged looking glaringly fresh and green, as though those few days of blanketing monotony had heightened our sensitivity to colour. Our first experience of snow on Skomer had been unforgettably dramatic, but perhaps once was enough.

FIFTEEN

Although we didn't realise it at the time, that snowy winter had brought us to the beginning of what would be our final year on Skomer. We were embarking on our tenth year, and the words that I had used so carelessly during our first week on the island were now echoing back at me across a decade. I had said then that I would like to stay for ten years. I had meant not to set a limit on our tenure but to make it endless, because, at the age of twenty, ten years was literally half a lifetime, and it had sounded then like a way to quantify 'forever'.

But, somehow, those years had passed us by, and I was not a single day closer to wanting to leave. I had only grown more deeply attached to everything that was Skomer, and more hopelessly remote from anything that was outside our limited existence. So, I took comfort from the fact that ten years was an arbitrary number, one that I had snatched from nowhere at a time when I was dazzled by the prospect of embarking on whole new future. I had invented the number and so I could also choose to ignore it.

But that milestone, however intangible, was reminding us that we were reaching the point where it would become difficult to adapt back to mainland life. We had always known that, however much we loved Skomer, one day it would have to come to an end. If we didn't make the move it might soon become impossible. That was the logical side of our discussions; the truth was that I believed I had already passed the point of no turning back. I could no longer even imagine a future without Skomer.

The other problem was that financially we were barely surviving. Even a new pair of wellingtons was a major expenditure that took careful planning. My worn out boots inevitably leaked for the last six months of their life, because I could never justify the luxury of more than one pair a year. For the present that didn't matter, but we were just about beginning to visualise a time when we might be old, penniless and homeless. These vague anxieties were being crystallized into something almost real by the persistent rumours that jobs on some of the best mainland nature reserves would soon be advertised. Such opportunities were rare, and we were being forced to recognise that they represented perhaps our only chance of security.

My escape was to close my mind for as long as I could, and to hope that it would never happen. I am not sure how I would have faced that final spring if

I had known that it was to be our last. Almost since the day I arrived on the island I had felt a sense of blind faith that fate would never part us again. But once the tiniest seeds of doubt are sown they find a fertile place. The feelings of uncertainty were with me, however much I tried to deny them.

As we moved from February into March, we began to watch again for the puffins. It had been a day of flat, dull light, and we were walking back from the farm. The low sun had dropped far enough to escape from beneath the clouds, so that the brightness ricocheted across the water like a skimming stone. The sea was polished steely grey, and every turn of a wavelet glinted like a mirror flash. We were descending the steep slope above the house when Mike stopped abruptly.

'Puffin!' he shouted, pointing with an outstretched hand.

I grabbed my binoculars, and there it was, glistening white against the dark sea.

There was the same surge of elation that we felt every year at discovering that first moment of spring. Then, quite suddenly, I thought how lonely the puffin looked, a single tiny bird dwarfed by the sweep of cliffs. I imagined that I could sense, not its relief at having found its way back across so many miles of sea, but its fear of the land, and I was overwhelmed by a tide of sadness. Perhaps this would be the last time that I would ever watch for the returning puffins. I didn't want to spoil the day by sharing that unhappy thought so, instead, I made a plea silently in my head: 'Please don't let this be the last year; let me see it all again one more time, and then I'll go.' But I knew I didn't mean it. I knew that even in another ten years I would still be asking for just one more year.

I wish that I could look back on that last summer as one of the best, a golden season of endless sunny days like our first, but it turned out to be the worst summer we had known. It wasn't simply a matter of bad weather: some of the things we had feared most during our time on Skomer finally materialised that year. The most immediate and persistent anxiety was Mike's back. It had always been his Achilles heel, the thing that had let him down over the years and caused frequent bouts of pain, but he had refused to give in to it and had never let it stop him doing anything. Then, when we were unloading yet another shipment of concrete blocks, something went more wrong than usual. He must have twisted awkwardly, and, though he kept going at the time, he later admitted that he was seriously concerned about it.

From that point on the pain never went away. It developed, becoming more intrusive and more limiting by the day. There was nothing I could do, and it was awful to watch such misery without being able to help. I also felt guilty, because over the years of lifting, loading and building, I had never suffered any real discomfort. All my aches and pains had been fleeting things. It made me feel that I had not tried hard enough, maybe let Mike take too much of the strain, even though I knew that whenever we had faced a real challenge I always pushed myself to the limit. It was just that Mike always pushed that bit harder.

The pain was so bad that, for the first time, Mike was forced to go to the mainland to see a doctor. He returned with painkillers that didn't work, and a sense of hopeless inevitability that there was nothing more to be done.

Mike had never forgotten that first visit to Skomer with his schoolteacher, and the way it had changed his life so completely. That one glimpse of the island sent his hopes and ambitions soaring in a new direction. Since becoming warden he appreciated even more how much the kindness of that teacher had meant to him, and he nurtured a dream of giving other children the chance of that same experience. Conservation would have a more secure future, if a new generation could understand the need to protect such enchanted places as Skomer. It was, perhaps, one of the most important things we could do. This came together towards the end of our time on the island, when a scheme was established that allowed small groups of schoolchildren to visit at a cost of no more than a nominal boat fare, and I took on the job of guiding these children.

Despite the fact that he could hardly walk, that his back was twisted sideways and one leg dragged slightly, Mike would not be diverted from his main project for that summer. In fact, I have never known Mike to be prevented from doing anything that he has truly set his mind on. He is the most determined, or possibly stubborn, person that I have ever met. That year, he was going to finish building a new set of concrete steps in North Haven, whatever it took. The steps were the point of arrival for all visitors to the island. They ran up to the top of the cliff from the rocks at sea level, where the passenger boat touched against the edge of the island. The old steps were made of wood; a complicated framework that shored up the earth, trapping it in a series of platforms that formed a twisting flight of stairs to the cliff top. The problem was that they required almost daily maintenance during the summer. The dry weather turned the soil to the consistency of sand, and it trickled through every gap in the wooden boards as inevitability as water flowing from a cracked bowl. Added to that, the whole bank was fragile with shearwater burrows; like an ancient piece of timber hollowed out by woodworm holes, it crumbled under the slightest pressure.

Mike was determined to resolve the issue, by replacing the wooden steps with concrete ones. The work had begun the previous year on the lower steps, and he had assured me then that he would only replace the worst sections at the bottom, but now he wanted to do them all, and there was nothing I could do to dissuade him. Perhaps the thought was somewhere in his mind that this might be his last chance, that there might be no more time to realise his vision, but I don't think he would have given way however many years were left.

As always in summer, there was no shortage of help. George, the assistant warden, and the PhD students in their spare time, together with a steady trickle of volunteers, all worked with complete dedication, but Mike would have found it unbearable to direct operations from the sidelines. Despite his physical limitations, he had to be at the heart of the action. The scale of the earthworks, and the sheer quantities of building materials involved, were breathtaking. I had thought that it was a ludicrously impossible enterprise, and yet somehow, day by day, section by section, the steps crept slowly up the side of the cliff. There were so many times when I saw Mike on his knees, because he was unable to stand, digging furiously at the earth with a spade, and I couldn't decide whether he was being incredibly brave or incredibly foolish.

Mike missed his next appointment with the doctor. We woke to the sound of a northerly wind twining itself around the house with a thin, cold whine that sounded like winter, and North Haven was bubbling with short choppy waves. Without even the prospect of pain relief Mike was desolate. As the wind died late in the day I was surprised to see the *Dale Princess* heading for the island; fountains of white spray gushed up on either side of the boat in patterns of rhythmic brilliance as she cut through each successive wave. Campbell had remembered Mike's missed appointment and had contacted the doctor to get a small supply of painkillers.

When Mike finally made his visit to the GP, he came back with the news that he would have to see an orthopaedic surgeon in a few days' time. This felt like progress of sorts, but the mere mention of a surgeon filled me with quiet panic. I was waiting anxiously on the landing steps when Mike returned from this appointment, watching for him to emerge from the wheelhouse, where he would have been chatting with Campbell. He always came out to smile and wave across at me as the boat drew close to land, but that day he did not appear. It was enough to make me fear the worst, without having any idea what the worst might be. When I eventually caught sight of Mike he looked defeated and lifeless. There was not even a flicker of a forced smile. He threw the bow rope across to me, and I pulled steadily against it as the *Dale Princess* slid in sideways to rest against the fenders on the rocks. When the boat was close enough, I caught the side and held it steady as the passengers boarded for their homeward journey. Mike leant across the rails to talk to me.

'What's wrong?' I asked.

'I've got to go straight into hospital. They didn't even want me to come back to the island tonight, but I insisted. I'll have to go in tomorrow, though.'

It was awful. Neither of us had ever left the island overnight in the summer.

As we packed Mike's bag that evening we had none of the right things, but, fortunately, there was a pair of respectable pyjamas tucked away in a drawer for emergencies, which we had jokingly referred to as 'the hospital pyjamas'. I pretended to look on the bright side, in an attempt to push away the crushing atmosphere of gloom.

'At least they're only going to put you in traction,' I said. 'I spent the day worrying that you were going to need some sort of operation. It won't be too bad relaxing in bed for a week.'

They were just words, though, and neither of us really believed them. We actually had no idea what traction entailed, except that it probably bore a striking resemblance to medieval torture, and would feel like being put on the rack.

The main problem was that we both had too much faith in the whole procedure. We were convinced that after a week of immobility, some miracle would have turned the clock back, and everything would be as it was before, when simple things like walking were taken for granted. It had to be that way. Hospital was the last resort. If that didn't put things right, then what would? I am not sure if we ever even considered the possibility of failure.

The first time I went to the hospital, all that faith in the treatment was happily confirmed. The day after Mike left, Campbell sent a note up from the boat telling me to leave the island on the *Dale Princess* that afternoon and he would drive me to the hospital in Haverfordwest. It was three months since I had last left the island. Once the passenger boat re-established our links, Mike made the crossing alone while I remained stubbornly behind, so the mainland spring was something I rarely saw. I was overawed by the luxuriance of it. There was a billowing, overflowing exuberance that took me by surprise. It had been an awful spring, with everything constantly blurred by rain and crushed by wind; in every way the most determined contrast to our first idyllic island summer. On Skomer, the cowed landscape still looked almost as bleak as it had in January. The dried stems of bracken, woven and matted into a crackling shell, shaded the island a drab brown. Even by May, the new spring growth had not received enough encouragement from the sun to force its way up through the dull remnants of winter.

The mainland was vibrant with more shades of green than I could ever begin to find names for. I had forgotten that spring could be like that. In summer leaves are just green, but in spring the newly emerged foliage of each tree has its own radiant colour. It was the colour of freshness; newborn leaves so delicate and translucent that the light filtered through them as though they shone with their own luminescence. Among these swarms of dappled greens were clouds of hawthorn blossom, pure white, like banks of sea fog catching the sun. It was a strange sensation to be so enclosed by the landscape, because on Skomer nothing grew tall and all views were endless. The speckled light, sprinkling and sifting in pale green patterns through the trees, was a perfect distraction from the churning feeling I had inside. I was worried about what I would find when I reached the hospital.

When I finally traced Mike's bed in the large ward, the relief was immediate. The traction bore no relationship to the primitive contraptions I had created in my imagination. His legs were covered in sticking plaster from knee to ankle, and attached to them, dangling over the end of the bed, were things that looked like the weights from old-fashioned kitchen scales. That was all there was to it. Best of all, Mike was smiling. It was a real, happy smile, not a shallow, better-put-on-a-brave-face sort of smile.

'It's working,' he told me at once.

For the first time in what seemed like almost forever, he was out of pain. We talked until I knew I ought to be getting back, and then, as I was leaving, I stopped to ask Mike's advice about things that would be happening on the island the following week.

'Oh, don't worry about that,' he said cheerfully. 'I'll be back before then.'

And he looked so incredibly well that I believed him.

It was dark by the time the boat drew alongside the rocks in North Haven and I jumped ashore. It was a huge relief to feel the island beneath my feet again. I turned to watch the *Princess* go, her lights burning bright holes into the night air. Poor Campbell. That was the first of many times he would have to drop me back on the island late at night after a long day's work. He had wanted me to stay on the mainland with him and his wife, but I needed to be on Skomer, and I think Mike needed to know that I was there, looking after everything in his absence. It must have been hard for Campbell to understand my irrational anxiety at being separated from the island, but, though slightly bemused, he never complained about ferrying me home in the dark.

My optimistic impression of Mike didn't last through subsequent visits. I could hardly admit it, even to myself, but it was slowly becoming clear that things were not as good as I had hoped. I had not realised at first that Mike was taking such high doses of painkilling drugs, but I began to notice that he had often forgotten our last conversation, and sometimes his speech was slurred. I was afraid that the drugs were only masking the underlying problem. We had believed so much in the treatment, convinced ourselves that it was working, and yet I was finding it increasingly difficult to accept that I was looking at someone who was improving.

I said nothing to Mike because I didn't want to dent his trust in his ability to get better, but eventually he confessed to me that the apparent improvement was an illusion. If the weights were removed from his legs, even for a few minutes, the pain was as bad as ever. It was a distressing thing to accept because, even by our most pessimistic reckonings, Mike should have been due to leave hospital in a couple of days. The time was trickling away, and with it went any chance that the treatment might be going to work.

As Mike lay in hospital, summer made little effort to break through, and I faced another day trying to inspire children with an island that had lost its sparkle in a smear of cold drizzle. When I walked on my own I was insulated from the worst of the weather by a full set of waterproofs, but not when I was with the children. They were so badly equipped for the raw elements of Skomer that I felt duty-bound to abandon my own weatherproof clothing. If I was too well protected I might not notice the children becoming cold and wet.

That day, the swimming specks of drizzle thickened rapidly into sheets of rain that flailed in wind. I was preparing to take the children to shelter, but the headmaster insisted that they would rather keep going and make the most of their visit. At a command from him, the children went through the well-rehearsed routine of producing neatly folded waterproof trousers from their rucksacks and slipping them on. That left me as the only one who was embarrassingly under-prepared, with trousers that sopped up the water, so that the wet cloth glued itself uncomfortably to my legs. I couldn't even wear the hood of my jacket since it was too much of a barrier to communication.

Every time we saw the faint images of puffins, blurred and spoilt, like a water colour left out in the rain, the children were endearingly excited. I wished so much that I could show them what Skomer was really like: blue sea with stars of sunlight sparking across it, birds leaving silvery trails as they dived below its glassy surface, flowers cascading like waterfalls over the steep fringes of the island. But it would have been impossible to try to explain. On a day like that, even I could barely believe that it was true.

Although they had been a lovely group of children, I was relieved to deliver them back to the landing steps to catch the boat home. By that stage, my hair was plastered smooth against my head, and my eyes were stinging from the rainwater that had trickled into them. All I could think about was the delight of changing into dry clothes. I waited to help the children onto the boat as it wallowed against the rocks in the faint swell.

'Why don't you come over to the mainland? See Mike?' Campbell called from the wheelhouse.

It was tempting, but totally impractical.

'I can't,' I shouted back.

'Come on, jump on board,' Campbell repeated, every time he caught my eye.

I don't know how he could have been so persuasive. I think it was his calm smile that made everything seem so easy, but, against all my resolve, I jumped down onto the deck as the boat was pulling away. I stared down at my muddy wellingtons and felt immediately uncomfortable about what I had done. I didn't have so much as a coin in my pocket or a comb for my matted hair.

As we pulled out of North Haven the boat swayed and plunged in the deep waves. From the land, the thick mist of rain had dulled everything, camouflaging the contours of the sea. As soon as I felt the boat begin to roll beneath my feet I recognised the smooth swell-waves that come rolling in ahead of a storm. It was a clear signal of bad weather approaching. We had barely left the island, but I knew that I had no chance of persuading the boat to turn back. I rushed into the wheelhouse to join Campbell. A gale warning was crackling out from the ship's radio.

'I'll never get back tonight!' I said, with the panic clearly showing in my voice.

His smile stretched a little wider.

'That's all right,' he replied. 'You can stay with us.'

By the time I reached the hospital the summer evening had sunk into premature twilight. Rain the colour of smoke was oozing miserably down the windows. As I walked down the ward to find Mike, a swoop of wind made the rain rattle against the glass. Mike looked up, amazed to see me when the weather was so obviously spoiling for a storm. And I was amazed to see him because, for the first time, he was not lying flat on his back viewing the world through a mirror. He was no longer in traction, but was curled up on the bed looking small and shrivelled. With the yards of sticking plaster removed from his legs, I could see how the muscles appeared to have wasted, even in that short time. The despair on his face seemed like a reflection of the bleakness outside and I knew that, whatever the reason he had been taken off traction, it was not going to be good news.

In a slurred and halting voice he explained that the traction had made him worse, and that the only option left was an operation to remove the discs. That would mean a long wait in hospital since it would be at least a week even before the necessary x-rays could be done. A week of simply waiting; a week when he could have been on Skomer. In his frustration he had tried to discharge himself from the hospital, only to discover that he could no longer walk. That was the sudden realisation of the seriousness of what was happening. To see him, shrunken and trembling, it was hard to believe the change that had taken place. In a couple of weeks he had gone from being a fit person with a very bad back to someone who looked extremely sick.

As I was leaving the ward I met Charles, one of the RAF helicopter pilots, on his way in to see Mike. As with so many other things, the support from the RAF had proved to be invaluable during Mike's illness. They made sure that he was never without visitors, and, among these, Charles was one of the most frequent and most welcome. He looked at me with slight disbelief and then glanced for a moment towards the pale clatter of rain against the blackened window.

'You won't be going back to Skomer tonight,' he said decisively, and, sadly, I had to agree.

When I went down for breakfast the next morning, I discovered that Campbell had already left for Martin's Haven to check the state of the sea, though I couldn't believe that there would be any chance of making the crossing to Skomer that day. As I sat in the kitchen, eating toast and chatting to Mil,

Campbell's wife, the back door opened and in walked the milkman without even a warning knock. He began a cheerful discussion on the best use for quinces while he checked through the fridge and, deciding that two pints would be plenty for that day, slipped them clinking into place. He then crossed to the sink to collect the empty bottles from the draining board. I sipped my tea, feeling bemused by the intrusion, which seemed so strange compared to life on Skomer, where not even the telephone could interrupt breakfast.

A few minutes later Campbell returned from Martin's Haven, grinning broadly at the awfulness of the weather.

'Well, we won't be able to take you back today,' he said enthusiastically.

I smiled, and hoped that I didn't look too disappointed. The truth was that I was beginning to feel panicky. I should never have abandoned the island like that. Anything could happen, and I wouldn't be there. Campbell poured himself a mug of tea, and I tried to ignore the ringing of the phone, which was an alien and unsettling sound. To my surprise, the call was for me. There was barely time for words such as 'hospital' and 'emergency' to skid through my mind before I discovered that it was Charles on the phone. He said that the rescue helicopter would be on exercise close to Skomer that afternoon; if I wanted to be on the flight, he could pick me up in time for a visit to the hospital and then take me to the airbase. I felt a surge of relief at the thought of going home.

The weather cleared and we drove to the airbase in brilliant sunshine. Despite the strong wind, it was decidedly hot. I had only my heavy clothes and wet weather gear from the day before, which were beginning to feel absurdly inappropriate. Inside, I sat listening to the constantly changing flight plans, and tried to position myself in such a way as to make the wellington boots I was wearing seem as unobtrusive as possible. I was glad when the time came to strap on my life jacket and walk out to the aircraft.

The helicopter rose steeply into the air. At first it was only the popping in my ears that warned of the rapid change of height, but then I realised that we had left the drab airfield buildings far below, and the sea was stretching out endlessly ahead of us. It was so clear that I could immediately pick out the hard outline of Skomer far in the distance. The water was a deep, intense blue, streaked with waves that licked and flared like dazzling white flames across its surface. From so high, the soundless waves appeared to skim the sea, without weight or power. It was hard to believe that those flashes of foam were enough to stop the boat from running.

The slow, hypnotic movement of the sea held me so entranced that only a few seconds seemed to have passed before the island slid into focus beneath us. I pressed close to the window to catch every detail as we sank down towards the mosaic of greens. The aircraft hovered, not even crushing the grass, and I jumped from the open door, ducking my head as I ran clear. The miniature hurricane made a boiling whirlpool of the vegetation around my feet as the thunder of rotor blades heaved the helicopter back into the sky.

And then silence, Skomer's own uniquely noisy silence: the pulse of the sea and the distant, tangled clamour of gulls all calling together. After the excitement of the flight, the sense of being suddenly alone was unexpectedly melancholy. I began to walk towards the house, feeling the strangeness of returning through the fields instead of climbing up from the beach. I had been away long enough to notice the smell again: warm vegetation drying in the sun, salt spray and seabirds. From somewhere high above me, the sharp, bright notes of a skylark came meandering down with the lapping rhythm of waves against the shore. I used a hand to shade my eyes against the painful blueness of the sky and gazed up, higher and higher, to find the bird. It was invisible, but I became so lost in concentrating on the stream of music that, despite everything, I found myself smiling. I walked on over the ridge until the house came into view, and it was only as I stopped and looked down that I realised why this homecoming felt so disappointingly empty. I had lost faith in what was happening, and, though the doubts were almost imperceptible, they were there. A barely audible whisper was telling me that Mike might never be well enough to come back to the island.

As it has a habit of doing in times of crisis, normal life continued, flowing round the edges of the main problem and filling in the gaps. Although a large part of me wanted to give up, I had no choice. The demands of the island continued as though nothing had changed. Among the things that had to be maintained were the visits by the schoolchildren. These had been booked months in advance and I didn't want to let them down. And it probably helped to focus on the positive things that surrounded me. The children were a pleasure to be with: full of questions, and full of the sheer wonder that adults forget. But I was beginning to learn that most children seem to have an innate disinclination for walking. I had to try to keep their attention alive the whole time, pointing out everything from rabbits to oystercatchers, in order to maintain their spirits when there were distances to be covered. I knew that there was no point in trying to interest them in landscapes; it was the detail that fascinated them. They would fail to notice a stunning view, but were enthralled by the stories that I could weave around the shearwater skeletons littering the island, which they inevitably seized upon with gruesome fascination.

The one exception to the no landscapes rule was the bluebells. The sheets of flowers, shimmering like a watery mirage in shades from aquamarine to purple, never failed to grab their attention. I liked to take the children up past the farm and then stop on a ridge where we could look down on the mass of flowers stretching away from us. The effect was of endless blue, because the flowers went on and on, until they appeared to merge with the sea. One day, I brought a cluster of children to this spot and waited. There was a moment of quiet, followed by soft expressions of amazement rippling through the group like the shiver of wind through dry grass. Then I was aware of a small boy at my side, one of the over-boisterous ones that I had already determined to keep a particularly close eye on.

'Oh Miss!' he gasped with unconcealed admiration. 'Did you plant all these?'

There was something in that odd mixture of naivety and enthusiasm that I found very touching, but when I thought about it again later, it made me feel sad that a child should be growing up with no concept of a wild place.

But then again, I was possibly reading too much into it. The concept of an untamed wilderness was something that few children seemed able to master. Despite my efforts, I am sure that some of them left with the idea that they had visited a beautiful park that we had tamed and tidied and stocked with exotic birds. I think perhaps they even preferred to see it that way because it felt so much more secure.

The question I was asked almost more than any other was, 'When are you going to feed the puffins?' Of course, it would have been easier to admit that I would be bringing out the frozen fish as soon as everyone went home, but instead I persisted with the ridiculous story that the puffins caught their own fish out at sea. As we stood at the top of the Wick, with puffins bobbing and strutting around us, bright and polished as clockwork toys, I explained in detail how the birds dived for sand eels, how they could hold the fish in place with their tongues until they had a neat row of them lined up in their beaks. And, even as I was speaking, I could see that I was losing the children's respect. Their faces set into expressions of grim disappointment as I created this elaborate fantasy rather than accepting the inconvenience of letting them wait for feeding time.

I never really understood the working of their young minds, what thoughts or confusions their visit to Skomer would provoke. One afternoon, as we were waiting for the boat to take them back to the mainland, an extremely timid girl came up to me.

'I think you're very brave to stay here at night,' she whispered, blushing at her own boldness in speaking to a stranger.

'There's nothing at all to be frightened of here . . .' I began to explain gently.

'But it's so old!' she interrupted vehemently, with a shudder of obvious disgust.

I didn't dare tell her that, deep down, everywhere was old; she might never have slept soundly again.

I will probably never know whether any of those visits had the same lasting effect that they had on Mike. I do know that at least some of the children remembered long enough to write to me afterwards with their memories of the day. A few even made it back later in the summer, to present me with a drawing of puffins or seals and proudly introduce me to indulgent parents who had been pestered into making the journey. And, occasionally, I couldn't help wondering if, somewhere among those smiling faces, I was looking at a future warden of Skomer.

Mike's condition continued to decline. He reached a low point when the decision was made to transfer him to Cardiff for the operation. He had grown used to having so many visitors in Haverfordwest that he was afraid of being isolated in Cardiff, but I was sure that it was for the best. His sister and her husband were both doctors in the Cardiff hospital, and they would be the most important people to be with him at that time. He was insistent that I should stay on Skomer rather than coming to Cardiff, and I understood that. Whatever else was going on, we felt that the island needed at least one of us to be there.

That evening, after seeing Mike so diminished both physically and mentally, I was completely depressed. He had been in hospital for a month, during which there had been nothing but steady deterioration. There was a huge gaping void in what might be our last summer on Skomer. It was a time when the island changed constantly. Every single hour was precious and they were slipping away. I opened the kitchen window and leaned out. The day was gone, leaving nothing but a smoky blue twilight. I had been too preoccupied to notice how unnaturally still the weather had turned. There was no sound of waves, no stray wisps of wind to blur the perfect mirrored surface of the sea. It stretched out with the muted gloss of polished slate until, somewhere in the half-light, it became sky. The sense of calm overwhelmed me. I was so comforted by the feeling of peace that I invested it with too much meaning. In that absolute quiet I thought I heard some inner voice telling me that everything would be all right.

I should have listened to the more logical part of myself, the part that would deny the existence of any such voices. At the very moment that I was staring out into the stillness, a new disaster was unfolding, ready to break through the equilibrium. The next morning, when I switched on the radio for my regular morning call to the coastguard, I was startled to hear the Skomer call sign being broadcast: they were trying to contact me urgently. I was so concerned about Mike that, at first, the message came as a relief.

'An oil tanker went aground on the Hats and Barrels last night. There's been a spillage, but it's only a light bloom of oil on the water. It's not expected to affect you.'

The coastguard's voice sounded reassuring. The Hats and Barrels was a reef of rocks about fifteen miles to the west of us. At that distance we should have been safe if there was so little oil involved.

Over the next few days I discovered how misplaced that optimism had been. The oil slick went on growing, seeping closer and closer to Skomer. When I first saw the oil it was out towards Grassholm, so far away that it was a barely perceptible shimmer smudged around the distant whiteness of thousands of clustered gannets. In the summer stillness it delicately unfurled, like a sheet of satin, across the water. It was not black and threatening, just a soft, grey sheen, but its innocent appearance didn't make it any less deadly to the island's seabirds. The fact that it had not yet reached us no longer mattered. Grassholm was already surrounded, and there was so much oil in the water that birds travelling out from Skomer to feed would be sure to land in it.

The clean, shiny sea that separated us from the oil could only form a temporary barrier. Inevitably, the oil finally came washing up against Skomer's cliffs. It became caught up in the tide races that swept around the island, coagulating into streams that gushed among the offshore rocks. When I looked down from above, I could see that these iridescent rivers were clotted with thick, black blobs of oil. It was almost unbearable to see this poisonous tide flowing beneath cliffs crammed with birds. For them, nothing had changed. The explosive effervescence of their bubbling growls still echoed against rock and water, flooding the air with sound. They still swished in and out from the cliffs, the sheer determination humming from their wings, their whole existence devoted to the survival of their chicks. For them, nothing would change until they actually touched the oil and it began to penetrate their feathers.

For me, the most painful thing was the feeling of helplessness. All I could do was watch the oil as it washed against the island. In the last spill, when the oil had come on shore, we had been able to attack it physically. A huge amount of the hurt and resentment we had felt at that time had been diverted into the clean-up of the oil. Now I could only count the oiled birds and pick up the corpses that washed onto the beaches.

It was the crystallisation of the fear that had haunted us throughout our years on Skomer. Every summer, when the chicks fledged and the adult birds dispersed out to sea, the sense of loss was mixed with relief that we had escaped for one more season without an oil spill. It was the worst thing that we could imagine: oil at a time of year when the breeding birds were present. Now that it had finally happened, I felt not just rage but a completely irrational guilt. It was as though all the years when we had been trying to protect the birds, and provide a sanctuary for them, counted for nothing. They had come trustingly to what should have been a place of safety, and they had been betrayed.

I couldn't help looking back to the *Christos Bitas* oil spill so many years before, when the seals had been oiled in North Haven. The one thing I remembered about the time of the tanker accident was the exceptionally calm weather. This time had been the same: a stillness so startling that it had made me stop and stare. I knew that the sea could be an unpredictable and terrifying environment, a place where accidents are bound to happen, but both of these small catastrophes came when they should have been least expected. It was as though such easy conditions led to complacency and short cuts. A true accident I think I could have forgiven, but not this.

The scale of what might happen to Skomer's seabird populations was something I found hard to contemplate. What I saw most clearly were the pinpricks of detail: daily incidents that symbolised the vicious, random impact of the oil. One of these came as I was waiting on the cliffs above North Haven for the *Dale Princess*. It was the most peacefully flawless day I could imagine. The water was softly blue, pearl-skinned, like frost. Puffins drifted over it sending slow, smooth ripples fluttering across the surface. Dazzling crystals of sun slid along the crests of wavelets as they rose to meet the shore. All the sounds were warm and summery: the whispered chatter of wave-washed shingle threading through the afternoon lull of birds. Suddenly, materializing as if from nowhere, a heavily oiled puffin came thrashing into the bay. Its body was twisting into wild contortions, as though it was fighting against itself. A small storm of spray clouded the water surrounding it. Startled puffins scattered, running across the sea, with their feet splashing trails of white, their wings dragging hard against the air. Around the apparition, the water was scored by the pale scratch-marks of panicking birds.

After a brief struggle, the puffin was dead, splayed out in jarring stillness. The angular shapes of its dishevelled, oily feathers imprinted a hard-edged silhouette onto fluid undulations of the sea. Soon it was forgotten. The other birds slowly meandered back to fill the empty patch of water around it, and everything was normal again. Except that something had been lost. It was no longer a beautiful afternoon. That tiny, blackened body had cast its shadow over everything.

Early the next morning, I walked across the Neck towards the north coast to make my regular check of the cliff ledges, and the sea below, for oiled birds. It was shortly after sunrise, the grass faintly damp, gulls stirring and wailing lazily, the first scent of warmth in the air. I was trying to close my mind, at least partly, to what I was doing, and feel some of the pleasure of a wonderful morning. It didn't work.

The vibrating calls of seabirds rose up from the edge of the cliff, clattering hard and hollow against the reflective surfaces of rock and water. I leant forward cautiously, out above the opalescent wash of oily waves, trying to see without being seen. On a ledge just below me was a razorbill chick, an engagingly tiny version of its parents. For a moment, I couldn't quite accept that this little thing was covered in oil. Helpless and flightless, it would have waited in that rocky niche to be fed; it could never have come anywhere near the sea or the oil. The contamination could only have come from one of the parent birds. Not even the debilitating effects of oil would have prevented the adult from fighting its way back with food for the chick. Then it would have used its own body to shelter the youngster from danger, and in the process probably killed it.

Irrationally, that oil-smeared chick affected me more than anything I had seen over the past few days. It felt like the most unforgivable desecration of innocence. I turned and rushed from the cliff in such a blur of anger that, inevitably, I fell, thumping onto my knees in the tussocky grass. I knew at once what had happened and looked back to see where my foot had crashed through the top of a shearwater burrow.

'Damn!' I shouted out loud.

I always tried to be so careful about the burrows, and now I was furious with myself. Without bothering to stand up, I wriggled round to the burrow and began sifting through the damage. Almost at once I found the shearwater among the crumbled earth of the broken burrow. I lifted it out, shaking off most of the loose soil.

'I'm sorry.' I said quietly, mainly for my own comfort. 'I hope I haven't hurt you.'

And all the time I was feeling along its legs and wings, reassuring myself that there were no broken bones.

When I was certain that the bird was unhurt, I began scooping out the soft earth, preparing to patch up the burrow and replace the shearwater. Digging with my right hand, I held the bird firmly in my left with its wings closed against its body, feet pressed against the side of my leg, so that it couldn't struggle and hurt itself. As I pushed my fingers through the earth they sank into something warm and sticky. I snatched my hand back and found it smeared in a yellow, viscous slime, spangled with fragments of white shell. It was the shearwater's egg; I had broken it as I fell.

Inside me, something dissolved. I felt a flood of despair choking at the back of my throat, and my eyes were stinging with tears. I picked up a handful of earth and threw it forcefully over the cliff at the dull, oily scum below. It scattered into a fine brown rain and sprinkled down towards the waves. The aggression made me feel better; I threw another handful and another.

'It's your fault,' I screamed at the oil. 'I wouldn't even have been here if it wasn't for you.'

Then I gave in to the tears. But I knew that I was not crying over one shearwater's egg. It was about all the birds dying miserable, pointless deaths, the chicks waiting on ledges or in burrows for adults that would never return with food.

These incidents were small in themselves; the problem was that they were endless. All round the island birds were dying, and, hour by hour, day by day, that number would keep on growing. The oil ebbed and flowed. At times Skomer seemed to be at the centre of a maelstrom of oily tides; at others, the oil retreated, leaving the sea glitteringly blue. These brief periods of remission filled me with unfounded hope, until the turn of the tide brought the oil pouring back. Despite those unrealistic moments of optimism, I knew that the outlook was bleak. The best-informed advice that I could get suggested that oil was trapped and would circulate indefinitely with the tides.

I was desolate, wondering how much longer I could go on watching this slow devastation of the island, when I heard something that I almost dared to believe was good news. The shipping forecast was giving gale warnings for our area. With most of the oil to the north of Skomer, a storm from the south could transform the situation. However promising it sounded, I couldn't risk letting my spirits rise too far. Gales are a rarity in June, and by expecting too much I would be inviting disappointment. If the winds came at all, they would surely blow themselves out in the open seas, and only come limping in to Skomer in depleted little gusts.

The next afternoon I was walking back along Welsh Way, above South Haven. The wind picked up very suddenly. It came in strong, determined bursts that grazed the sleek surface of the sea and whipped tendrils of dust into my eyes. I turned to stare in the direction of the wind. The breaths of air were unnaturally hot against my face. I liked that. It felt wild and unstable, wonderfully threatening. Clouds were already swelling up into the clear sky, billowing in the breeze like black smoke rising from a bonfire. Before I could reach home, the first drops of rain had begun to fall, enormous splashes of water that pitted the earth, spattering it with mud-brown stains.

The intermittent stabs of wind merged into a strong, steady stream, steeped with rain. From the kitchen window I watched as it spilled over the isthmus, rasping patterns of white across the greying sea. Puffins, held aloft on the wind, found new powers of flight. They clustered onto the island, hanging effortlessly in silvered air, cushioned by the wind as they slid to earth. The afternoon dwindled to a colourless twilight, leaving only a faded image of the world outside dribbling down the windowpane.

All night the house shifted restlessly as the storm leant hard into its wooden walls. By morning, the worst of Skomer's troubles were over. The oil had been swept away and dispersed by the churning of the waves. For the next few days, streams of horizontal rain saturated the air, blotting out the view, but as the weather cleared it became apparent that almost every trace of oil was gone. Vanished, too, were the dead and dying birds. The transformation was so dramatic that the aftermath of the storm was like a spectacularly brilliant dawn: truly a new beginning.

The one remaining worry was the birds with stains and smudges of oil, still coming back to the cliffs to feed their young. I had been told to expect the worst, that even the smallest amount of oil on the feathers was so damaging to a bird's insulation that it was unlikely to survive. Every time I made a count of apparently healthy birds with some residue of oil, I felt as though I was recording those already marked out for death. By that reckoning, we were going to lose a lot more birds. Fortunately, that pessimistic prognosis was drawn from experience of winter oil spills, and it became apparent that the return of warm summer weather was likely to give our birds a second reprieve.

I don't believe in miracles, but it felt as though something extraordinary had happened. Just when everything had seemed hopeless, the weather had intervened and spirited the oil away overnight. I couldn't remember a storm like that in June before, although I am sure they must have happened occasionally. The timing was so perfect it was as if help had reached down to us from the sky, and surely Skomer deserved its own small miracle.

SIXTEEN

Throughout the oil spill Mike had remained in hospital. Though confined to bed, he had somehow managed to stay deeply involved, pleading for access to a telephone and raging on Skomer's behalf to anyone who might have some influence. It was one of the few things that could have had enough impact to divert his thoughts from his own situation and to transport him temporarily away from the hospital ward. Though I had needed him desperately on the island, I was glad that he had missed it. He was less stoical than I was when it came to accepting the inevitable, and I think it would have broken his heart to watch helplessly as the birds died.

I was able to make one last visit to him before he was transferred to Cardiff. With the complications of the oil spill and the remaining oiled birds, Mike was more insistent than ever that I should not visit him there. It seemed like the only option, and Mike's sister, Tina, was the most practical and sensible person I knew; I couldn't think of anyone better to be there with him.

As soon as possible after the operation, I crossed to the mainland to call Mike. He was tired and incoherent. We managed a brief conversation before he became too exhausted to hold the phone. The only message that came across clearly was that his resolve had disintegrated. He wanted me to come to the hospital immediately.

On the crossing back to the island I barely noticed the birds skimming in front of the boat, the noise of their wings, the way the sunlight caught in the splashes as they scrabbled across the water. It was normally a sight that filled me with pleasure, despite the fact that I had seen it so many times. That day I was totally preoccupied, wondering what I needed to do before I could leave. By the time the boat reached Skomer, I had decided that I could be ready by the following morning. It would mean relying on a lot of goodwill from the research students who would have to give up their own time to help George, our assistant warden, keep things running smoothly. But I knew I could rely on them: they had never let me down.

I was busy all day. It felt as though there were a thousand things to be thought of and planned for before I felt comfortable about abandoning the island, although it was probably complete arrogance to imagine that I was indispensable. All the time, in the back of my mind, was the sense of one more thing I had to do, something I couldn't put off any longer. I went and found the newspaper that Campbell had given me earlier in the day and began flipping half-heartedly through the pages. Suddenly, I felt a nauseous twist inside my stomach. It was there, hard and real and inescapable. The shadow that had been dulling my happiness ever since the start of the year had finally materialised into something tangible. Having tried to shut it out of my mind for so long, I was now looking at the advertisement for the warden's job on the mainland. I stared blankly at the page, feeling crushed by the realisation that this could be the beginning of the end.

Of course, there was a way out. I simply had to close the paper and convince myself that I hadn't seen it. I could so easily have missed it at such a time of stress and confusion. Mike could never blame me, and by the time he was well enough to take an interest, it would be too late. It was tempting, but I couldn't do it. He would have to make the choice himself, not have the opportunity snatched away from him.

It was about ten o'clock in the evening before I found time to sit down and begin to type out a request for the job application form. It wouldn't take long and then, maybe, I would have something to eat. Every time I had tried to think about food, something new and urgent had sprung into my mind that had to be dealt with immediately before I forgot. I wasn't working efficiently; my mind was leaping off at tangents and taking me with it. Before I had reached the end of the short letter, I was overwhelmed by the urge to switch on the marine VHF radio. Almost at once I heard Skomer's call sign being announced. I called back immediately, but not before I had had time to enumerate the potential catastrophes in my mind. It was a message from my sister-in-law, Anne: she thought I should get to the hospital as soon as possible.

I slipped into a dizzying spiral of panic. I couldn't go now; it was almost dark. But the weather forecast was bad, and by morning the island might be cut off. There were too many conflicting fragments for me to be able to assemble any coherent plan. Trying to concentrate on a logical sequence of ideas was such an effort that my thoughts kept disintegrating, falling apart like a house of cards. I went to find the students. Paul was so decisive that the sense of certainty came as an enormous relief.

'Go now,' he said. 'We'll get the boat ready while you pack a few things.'

The light was no more than a pale luminescence from the distant sea by the time the boat pulled out of North Haven. Ripples made thin, reflective streams across the blackened water. The birds were silent, the air still and cool, with the salty dampness of evening.

My plan had been to spend the night with Campbell and Mil, and then catch the train to Cardiff in the morning. It was only as I approached the house that I began to realise what an awful imposition that would be. It was late, some time close to midnight. They might already be in bed. If I had not seen a light shining from the window, I am not sure that I would have had the courage to disturb them, but the moment the door was opened my apprehension disappeared. It was as though they had been waiting for me to arrive. Without the slightest flurry of awkwardness I found myself settled into an armchair with an enormous glass of wine in my hand. The first mouthful trickled with a burning sensation into my stomach; I remembered that I had forgotten to eat all day. As though she had read my mind, Mil immediately offered to cook me a meal, but I knew that I had already accepted far too much of their kindness and insisted that I had eaten earlier. Soon I was beginning to feel more cheerful than I had for ages. I was touched by the welcome I had received, despite arriving thoughtlessly in the middle of the night. The atmosphere was so comforting that everything began to seem all right. Campbell had been through a similar operation years before, and it gave him the authority to be immensely reassuring.

It was not until the early hours of the morning, lying in bed, that I began to panic. It was that time of night when, under the wrong circumstances, everything can feel bleak and cold and empty. The mellowing effects of wine and company had shrivelled away, and their place was taken by a hollow anxiety. In one of those realisations that comes snapping violently through the barrier of sleep, I was suddenly convinced that something awful had happened, and that I was being protected from the truth until I arrived in Cardiff.

Tina met me at the station, emerging through the blur of people looking cool and elegant in a pink dress and high heels. Instantly, amid these city crowds, my island clothes felt uncomfortably hot and out of place. It made me realise all over again what an outsider I had become.

When I reached the hospital, I could hardly believe how little there was to support my fears. My first impression of Mike was that he was an extremely listless version of himself, not, I realised gratefully, someone who was desperately ill. After an emotional greeting, Mike slipped back into a state of lifeless gloom. Conversation was too taxing, so I tried to distract him by exploring the side ward with its solitary bed.

'What's this?'

I had found his lunch tray. As I lifted the silver-coloured dome covering the plate, the most delicious smell I had ever encountered wafted forcefully into my face. I slammed the dome back down, shutting out the aroma.

'What was it?' I asked, salivating slightly.

'Beef Bourguignon,' he replied with an indifference that bordered on disgust.

'Didn't you want it?'

His only reply was a fleeting glance that seemed to question my sanity. I lifted the lid again. The meal was untouched, right down to the perfect ice-cream-scoop hillock of mashed potato. I still had a food deficit, and the relief of finding Mike reasonably well had startled awake my appetite, which had been lying dormant in recent weeks. My stomach ached with longing for that pool of brown, congealed gravy. I glanced towards the door, wondering how unethical it was for visitors to eat the patients' food. I could probably manage at least a few forkfuls without being seen. My dilemma was solved as a large, cheerful woman, spilling out of the crushed-flat backs of her shoes, came shambling into the room and whipped the tray from in front of me, commenting amiably on Mike's lack of appetite.

Over the next few days, the tension that had been winding up inside me slowly uncoiled. It had been building so gradually that I hadn't noticed how bad it was until I felt it begin to unravel. I realised how wonderful it was to wake up in the morning without immediately thinking about going out to look for oiled birds. But the main reason I was feeling so much better was because Mike's recovery was something close to miraculous. The day after I arrived he was out of bed and sitting in an armchair, and the following day he took a few steps. On the third day, when I saw him shuffling down the corridor to meet me, with that childlike mixture of pride and determination showing in his face, I was so pleased I could have cried.

The only problem was that Mike's recovery began to restore his old, impatient self. As he started to improve, he could no longer bear to think of Skomer without at least one of us there. He knew that he still faced weeks of convalescence, and was becoming almost irrationally anxious for me to go back. Just to placate him, I agreed to leave the following day, even though it was a Monday, when there would be no boat crossing to the island. It was still quite early when the train pulled in to Haverfordwest station. I wandered aimlessly, killing time, and then made my way to the offices of the West Wales Naturalists' Trust, where I was greeted with a buzz of excitement. They were delighted to be the first to tell me the good news: Mike was to be allowed out of hospital the following day. It was unusual for someone to be discharged so quickly after an operation like Mike's, and it was only possible in this case because he would remain under Tina's watchful eye. She had added the sensible proviso that I would have to be there to look after him during the day while she was at work in the hospital. So, Mike's long-awaited freedom depended on me heading straight back to Cardiff.

Since I was already in Pembrokeshire, I decided to stay overnight and then cross to the island to collect a few things for Mike before making my way back. The boat journey was unexpectedly sad. I had been away for only a few days, and yet it felt like forever. The island had changed and moved on without me. It reminded me why I had always refused so stubbornly to leave the island in summer, even for a day. The guillemots and razorbills had gone: the cliffs glared white, marking out the empty ledges. Where a thousand bird calls had been layered, now there was only an echoing stillness. I leant over the rail of the boat and stared at the cliffs sliding past me. Though it was only June, it felt like the end of summer. The vitality of spring was giving way to that sleepy period when only the bracken seemed to flourish. Another season had trickled away, and Mike had missed it all. The cliffs had never looked so deserted, so resonant with silence, because, deep down, I was wondering if I would ever see them crowded with birds again or hear them reverberate with a soaring vibrato of sound. I had never felt that way before, never had to question whether it would all come round again, because I had always been so certain that my future was on Skomer. I shuddered, as if to shake away the thoughts, and went into the wheelhouse to join Campbell.

I was faintly surprised to find the house exactly as I had left it when I fled in such a hurry. It seemed so long ago. In the last few days I had been almost to another world and back. The worst thing was the letter that I had been writing, still unfinished and still scowling at me from the typewriter. Unfortunately, it was not too late to send it. I typed the final sentences and then stuffed it resentfully into my bag, along with the clothes I had packed for Mike.

By the evening I was back in Cardiff, and Mike was already at Tina's house. It was strange to see him in ordinary clothes instead of lying crumpled and half naked under a thin hospital sheet. It was as though I could hardly remember a time when our meetings had not taken place in hospital wards, and even that superficial gloss of normality was enough to make Mike appear almost well again. Over the following days, it was our ability to do simple things together that seemed the most remarkable. Just taking a few cautious steps outside, or walking the length of a supermarket aisle with Mike using the trolley like a Zimmer frame, felt like exotic excursions. Mostly, though, he lay flat on his back on the floor, since it was the only comfortable place to be.

Mike was simply biding his time: his one goal was to get back to Skomer. He had been away so long, and he needed to see the island before the summer was over. In his mind there was only one obstacle in his way, and that was the long zip-mark of stitches running down his back. As far as he was concerned, the day after the stitches were removed he was going home. He was being persuaded that it was too soon to go back, and that he should spend longer on the mainland convalescing, but I supported him completely. I knew that if I had been ill I couldn't possibly start to feel better until I returned to Skomer.

Our main problem was not how we would get back to the island, but how we would get Mike up to the house. Cardiff's smooth pavements were giving him a false sense of mobility, but if we landed by boat in North Haven we had no realistic hope of him being able to climb the cliff path up to the house. It was so frustrating, because all we wanted was for him to be home. Even if he could do nothing except sit at the window to watch the sea and the clouds and the puffins it would be enough, but the cliff remained an insurmountable obstacle.

Once again, it was the RAF that we turned to for help, and they proved to be absolutely dependable. Charles was sure that they would be able to drop us off on Skomer during the course of a routine training flight. Our transfer to the island was arranged for two days after Mike's final visit to the hospital to have his stitches out. In a few more days we would be back on Skomer; it was the most uplifting news I could have hoped for.

On Sunday morning we drove with Tina and the family out to the airbase at RAF Brawdy, and we parted with the most inadequate expressions of gratitude. The truth was that I had no idea how we would have come through such a difficult time without them, but there were no words to say that properly.

When we boarded the helicopter Mike, as the invalid, was strapped securely into a seat at the back, while I was allowed to stand at the front with the pilots. It gave me a wonderful view, out past the curiously old-fashioned looking banks of dials and switches. As soon as the aircraft lifted into the sky, the sea began to unfurl in front of us. It was pale and bright, glinting with sapphires. For a moment I was almost surprised to see it looking so glisteningly perfect, and then I realised that the oil spill was still tarnishing my memories.

The flight was dramatically beautiful as we approached the island. Starlight patterns shimmered below us as the light fractured against the sea, and then, almost at once, the helicopter began to descend with immaculate precision over the isthmus. It hovered inches above the ground so as not to put any weight on the honeycomb of burrows beneath us. I jumped down and Mike followed cautiously behind me. The shuddering roar of the rotor blades allowed only the most perfunctory mimed thank yous, and then the helicopter was gone, dragging its great yellow body back into the sky. We shielded our eyes as all around us the grass seethed and rippled, caught in the centre of a whirlwind, and then the noise quickly receded, its space filled by a cloudburst of gull calls.

We stood still, absorbing the reality that we were finally back on Skomer together. The fact that there had been times when I had begun to believe that it would never happen made it all the more poignant. I took Mike's hand and we walked slowly back to the house.

The next day, Mike insisted on going for a walk. He retrieved the walking stick that had become an indispensable part of him as his mobility declined, and set off doggedly up the steep slope behind the house. I followed, struggling to match his uncomfortably slow pace. As I watched him move ahead of me I could tell that, although he had a lot of recovering to do, he was already walking better than before the operation. At least now he was standing upright. Every hundred yards, or so, I stopped.

'I think that's far enough for the first day. You don't want to overdo it, and don't forget you've got to walk back again.'

But Mike was determined. In the end, we walked a mile or so, as far as the Wick, and settled down among the puffin burrows on the cushions of thrift. Swathes and stripes of whitened rock highlighted the emptiness of the cliff, picking out the places from where hundreds of guillemot and razorbill chicks had already fledged. And yet, even with so many birds gone, the vibrant clamour of seabird sounds still enveloped us. The kittiwakes remained, clinging tenaciously to their haystack nests glued to the cliff face, and the overlapping cadences of their voices chorused around us.

I leant back, resting my weight on my elbows; the fine-leaved thrift felt soft and dry. It was one of those idyllic summer days: deliciously warm without being hot. I closed my eyes and lifted my face up towards the sun to feel the gentle warmth pressing against my skin. An echo of birdcalls swirled up from the cliff. I half opened my eyes to see a sprinkling of kittiwakes spiral like an eddy of snowflakes, starkly white above the deep green of the shaded water. I closed my eyes again, so that the sun-red darkness was filled with nothing but their sound. It was perhaps my favourite of all the seabird calls: the syllables of their own name repeated emphatically over and over, rising and falling, dozens of them dissolving into each other, until the clash of harmonies became almost musical. It was a noise that always evoked the happiness of summer and sea cliffs. Now I heard something deeply melancholy reverberating through those high-pitched wails, something that had never been there before, and I understood why. For the first time in a decade, faint ripples of change had touched our lives, and I was afraid that, like the circles spreading from a pebble dropped in water, they would go on growing. By sending that letter, we had started a process that might eventually take us away from the island.

I stared down at the green slope below me, feeling uncomfortably driven to savour this precious day, because I knew that there might be so few of them left. The rapid whir of a puffin's wings broke free from the medley of sea-cliff noises and the bird came crashing clumsily to the ground in front of me. It righted itself and gazed jerkily around, looking disorientated as if it was surprised at having made contact with the land. As it shook its head, droplets of seawater scattered into the air like beads of pure sunlight. Smooth waterfalls of silvery fish flowed from either side of its beak in iridescent streams. If I had leaned forward I could almost, but not quite, have reached out and touched it. After a few more nervous glances it scurried the last remaining steps to its burrow and ducked out of sight into the underground chamber where the chick would be waiting eagerly for the fish. It was such a commonplace thing, something I saw a hundred times a day, and yet it was so extraordinarily rare and wonderful.

Strangely, I have no recollection of Mike being ill after that day. It was as though coming back to Skomer restored him instantly; he went from being an invalid who could walk only a few cautious steps, to his old, fit self apparently overnight. I know that, in reality, it was not that simple. He faced weeks of physiotherapy exercises, months of residual pain, and years when he couldn't sit in a chair for any length of time, but all I could remember was that once he had achieved that goal of walking to the Wick, there seemed to be nothing that was beyond his capabilities.

The summer was almost gone and it was essential for us to salvage what was left. Daily the number of remaining seabirds diminished. The fringes of North Haven, where rows of puffins had lined the cliff tops, were now almost empty. The only birds that came were those feeding the last of the chicks left inside the burrows. All the bustle and playfulness were gone. The crowds of juvenile birds that hurried with shameless curiosity to inspect each new happening in the puffin colony had given up their vigil and left. Like most of the adult birds, they had dispersed out to sea, the island forgotten for another year. Those few birds that were forced by necessity to come on land were nervous. With the protection of the other birds gone, they stood alone and vulnerable. The incandescent fish in their beaks marked them out as a clear target for any gull.

When night fell I was almost compelled to go out and search for the fledging puffin chicks as they slipped away into the darkness. I had always found it very emotional to watch these fragile birds abandon the relatively safe haven of the island, but now that sense of crossing from the known to the unknown had become confused with my own sadness. The season was so close to an end that each time I stood in the dark, as a silent and unseen witness to these tiny acts of courage, I felt it might be the last time. That was why I had to go out every night until I was sure that the last chick had fledged.

I left the house as soon as it was truly dark, and waited in fear of disappointment. It was a relief when a miniature puffin materialized from the almost invisible entrance to a burrow. With its drab feathers, the bird was barely more than a shadow against the darkness. Its face didn't shine with the brilliant white crescents of the adult's, and its beak was a nondescript wedge of black. It ran in brief, bewildered bursts, clambering between clumps of grass and tangled mats of sea campion. The rough ground was a new and confusing experience; several times the young bird stumbled as it tried to decipher the changing landscape beneath its feet. Then, quite suddenly, it seemed to find its sense of direction, as though it had heard the irresistible call of the sea. The greyish, webbed feet scampered across the turf, growing in strength and confidence with each step. It ran until it had left the cliff top behind, and a void of black sky opened up around it. I could hear the shimmer of its wings beating small and faint against the air as it drifted into the darkness. Then it touched the forgiving surface of the water.

From that moment it was alone. The security of the burrow was left far behind. It would survive only by its own resources; there would be no adult bird to guide or protect it. Perhaps the parents had already abandoned the chick, or perhaps one of them would come at dawn, with its catch of fish, to find the burrow empty.

Somewhere in the black water below me the bird was swimming with a determination it had only just discovered. Ahead of it lay the whole night in which to swim away, because, with the coming of the morning light, the island would be a roost of predators. I imagined it now reaching the entrance to North Haven, crossing the threshold into the open sea, dipping its head beneath the waves, even diving below the surface and feeling the cold water closing over it. Then, as it rose back up to the air, the seawater would disperse into mercury droplets, momentarily silvered by the moonlight as they skimmed over the sleek, new feathers. I waited in the dark until I knew that the fledgling must be gone, and then I turned back towards to the house.

By early August, puffins were such a rarity that I studied every single one that came to land amid the empty burrows in case the chance did not come again. These last remaining birds looked exhausted by the demands of the breeding season. The tips of their anthracite-black wing-feathers were pale, abraded by the months of abuse. Their beaks had lost the pure, translucent colours of newness; time had faded and dulled them, scuffed the shine from those pristine colours. They needed to go back out to sea to renew themselves, to shed the failing feathers and discard the worn out beak-plates. In the spring they would return reborn: so fresh and perfect that they would look almost unreal. But where would I be by then?

Soon the kittiwakes, too, were gone, leaving their ragged nests clutching the rock faces, waiting to be swept away by the first of the late summer storms. The quietness that flooded in to fill the gaps felt like a tangible presence. When I approached the cliffs, the silence struck me more forcibly than the haunting, half-musical cries that I had been hearing all summer.

It was then that the letter came, the next step on the road that was leading us away from the island. I stared at it feeling a sense of both dismay and hopeless resignation. Mike had been invited for a job interview the following month. Skomer could never have been more than an interlude in real life; it was just too good to last forever. I had always known that it must end sometime, and perhaps this was to be it.

With typical resilience, Mike was fit enough to drive our heavy old Land Rover hundreds of miles to attend the interview, and when it was over all we could do was wait; everything that mattered to us was hanging crazily suspended. My heart wanted it to fail; I wanted to believe that I would see another spring on Skomer. My head knew that time was against us. If we stayed much longer on the island it would be impossible for us to absorb the upheaval and start afresh, and, however much we put it off, eventually we would have to learn to face life without Skomer.

Seals were coming back onto the beaches and the first pups were being born. It was as though we were drifting in a sheltered harbour: a gentle interlude before the real harshness of winter set in. The seals brought with them so many memories of past seasons that they represented some sort of stability in that period of uncertainty.

The greatest reward of any early morning walk was to find a newborn seal pup. I approached Castle Bay one morning, listening to the seals rearranging themselves against the pebbles interspersed with the occasional wail of irritation, and feeling slightly disappointed that there was no sound of a pup. Then, as soon as I glimpsed the beach, I felt a heart-fluttering exhilaration as I realised that a new pup had been born during the night. Amid so many seals in various shades of stone colours the starkly white pup was instantly visible, right in the centre of the beach. Almost at once, more by intuition than by logical thought, I knew that the pup was dead. It looked cold; the damp fur sticking to its body was smooth and waxy like a tallow candle. Even its position in the centre of the beach, disturbed by the movements of the other seals, was wrong. It should have been hidden away in some sheltered corner.

I squeezed into my hide, and as soon as the telescope was set up there was no more room for doubt. Despite the pup being so obviously dead, the mother remained fiercely protective. She guarded that section of beach tenaciously, launching herself with a flurry of howls and scrabbling flippers at any seal that came too close. She had given herself a hopeless task since the pup was lying on one of the main routes to and from the beach. The only relief I could see was that the pup would soon be washed away by the incoming tide and the mother would be set free.

I watched the soft tendrils of surf first touch, and then lift, the pup, toying with it before laying it carefully back down. Inevitably, a wave came that was large enough to dislodge the pup and drag it roughly over the shingle, sucking it out into the deeper water. I expected the mother to let it go, vaguely bewildered, but resigned to the loss of her pup. Instead, she followed in a fury of devotion, thrashing clumsily over the beach and sending a hail of water droplets spitting into the air. The moment the sea wrapped around her, the ungainly movements became effortlessly precise as she placed herself between the pup and the incoming waves. The pup's limp body flowed without resistance, undulating to the pattern of the rippling water. Gradually, she was able to nudge the pup back towards the shore. After failing in her attempts to coax it out of the water, she took one of its fore flippers in her mouth and pulled it onto the beach. The only other time I had seen a mother so obviously protecting a stillborn pup had been at Amy's Reach the previous year.

The next day, both seals were gone and, perhaps selfishly, I was relieved. The tide was quite high, and the seals were crowded close together on the remaining strip of beach. It was one of those nearly perfect October days when summer is fleetingly a reality again. The sea was so clear and blue that it had the jewel-like translucence of aquamarine. Seals were lying in the gentle turbulence where the sea met the shore, rocked by the turn of the waves. Others drifted, almost upright, with their heads above the water pointing skyward so that the sun could drench their faces. I was enclosed in their carefree existence where only the moment mattered.

I had been watching for a while when I noticed something brilliantly white on the seabed. It was a liquid image drizzling up to the surface only in fragments. I could see no discernible shape, just colour that drifted fitfully through the waves in broken slivers, but, from the intensity of the whiteness, I was sure that it must be the body of the pup, finally lost or abandoned by its mother. It was a painfully lonely sight.

I returned to my main task of scanning the seals on the beach for any that I might recognise, but I found myself distracted by the dead pup. I kept glancing towards it, and quickly realised that it was not alone. Close by, was the melting, indistinct shape of an adult seal. It was guarding the pup, circling it, darting with sudden determination to warn off any other seal that strayed too close. It was an unusually clear insight into this underwater wilderness, but there it was, unfolding in the bluish light of a glassy sea. I watched until one dissolved image came so close as to touch the other, and I realised that the mother had taken the pup's foreflipper in her mouth and was lifting it towards the surface. The head of the seal broke through, gleaming with seawater. She let go of the pup's flipper and, before it had time to sink, seized it by the scruff of its neck, twisting awkwardly until she had pulled the pup's head clear of the water. Then she released the pup, and it went into free fall, diving in slow motion back towards the seabed. The mother followed, gliding down through the cascading shafts of sunlight that pierced the water and sketched intricate patterns over her body.

A few minutes later it happened again. The sequence was identical in every detail, right down to the last-minute shifting of the grip to the back of the neck, ensuring that the pup's head was lifted clear of the water. Over the following hours it was repeated so many times that I was forced to accept that it was a very deliberate act. I would never have imagined a seal to be capable of such sensitivity of understanding, but, in the end, I could only believe that the mother was aware of her pup's need for air at frequent intervals and was trying to save it from drowning. After so many years, the seals that I knew so well could still find ways to surprise me.

Once the summer was over, letters became a rarity. They gathered in the Post Office for however many weeks it might be before we were able to collect them. Usually, a backlog of mail was pure pleasure, consisting almost entirely of personal letters; we didn't have a lifestyle that involved anything as complicated as bills arriving through the post. Now, however, the prospect of an official-looking letter was filling me with dread.

It was the middle of October when we received confirmation that Mike was to be offered a job on the mainland. My first reaction was a smothering numbness. I thought I had prepared myself, but nothing could really anticipate that agonizing finality. It was over. No more windows of hope; not even the chance of one more spring.

The immediate problems were more practical. We would be leaving at the end of the year, which left us only the stormy winter months to carry everything we owned back to the mainland. I had often said that we would never be able to leave Skomer because we had accumulated so many things it would be impossible to move. It was a joke, of course, with perhaps some element of wishful thinking, but it was not without a grain of truth. The books alone seemed to fill the house. They had trickled across to the island, a few at a time, over a decade. More and more shelves had been built to accommodate them, until they lined the walls like neat rows of memories. But suddenly to see them as a single entity that had to be packed up and shipped back to the mainland was hopelessly daunting. Then there was the beautiful furniture Mike had made, including the table in mahogany three inches thick. And his paintings, not delicate watercolours like mine, but enormous canvases. He never did anything on a small scale.

By normal standards, we still had very little in the way of possessions, but, given that everything had to be carried down a cliff, across a boulder-strewn beach, and then loaded into an open boat, we had an embarrassment of riches. The *Dale Princess* was long gone from Martin's Haven into safer waters for the winter, and, although we were sure that Campbell would have come back to help us, the logistics of trying to handle everything in one large load were too unbearable to contemplate. We decided to tackle the problem in manageable chunks by taking several loads in our own boat.

There seemed no point in leaving it until the last minute, with the days shortening and the weather deteriorating, so we planned to ship off everything that we could live without as soon as possible, and then survive for the last couple of months with only the bare essentials. Then we might at least enjoy our final weeks without the depressing prospect of the move hanging over us.

Packing up the contents of a house is so powerfully nostalgic that there were countless occasions when I wanted to sit down and weep as I delved through the remnants of happier times: times when I could never quite believe that it would all come to an end. Fortunately, the pressure of the task made it impossible to dwell too much or become over-sentimental. A tiny sliver of calm had inserted itself into what should have been one of the most unsettled periods of the year; we had to get everything done quickly, before the weather broke.

Paul, one of the PhD students, came back for a few days to help us, and we crossed with the first boatload in implausibly quiet weather, watched by a gathering of curious seals. On the mainland, we loaded our Land Rover and took everything to Tenby, the home of Richard, onetime Assistant Warden on Skomer. He was expecting us.

'I knew you'd come today,' he called cheerfully as we arrived. 'The weather was too good for you to miss. I'll put the kettle on. I've got a chocolate cake in specially for you.'

I couldn't help thinking that it would be impossible to meet such nice people in the real world.

We made the journeys over several days, packing late into the evening so that we had a load ready for the following morning. It all had to be packed with great care and several layers of waterproofing to secure it for the sea crossing. The heaps of black packages that emerged looked just like those we had brought with us ten years earlier, except that now there were many more of them and they no longer filled me with excitement for what lay ahead. The future was such a blank that I felt as though I was packing my whole existence away, with no idea when or where it would emerge from its wrappings again.

Each morning, the sea was so still that the greens and greys and golds of the lichen-painted cliffs swam in brilliant reflected patterns across the water. Mike carried heavy furniture down the cliff paths like someone who had never known the misery of backache. The boat slid peacefully through places where the waves usually ripped and seethed, and I felt so grateful, because the elements could not have conspired to make things easier for us. We capitalised on this good fortune by ludicrously overloading the boat until there was barely room for us to perch on top of its cargo of boxes and furniture. The mainland cliffs were deserted in winter, but we would have made a bizarre sight had there been anyone to watch as we picked our way across the normally treacherous waters.

We quickly filled Richard's garage and moved on to store the more precious things in the house, turning his rooms into caves of black polythene.

'Are you sure this is all right?' I asked for the third or fourth time. 'We do seem to be invading your space.'

'No, it's fine', Richard insisted. 'So long as you can leave a pathway for me to get to the cooker, and room to sit at the table and eat, I'll be happy.'

I decided that Richard must be the only person in the world who could make a statement like that without the slightest trace of irony.

When everything was transported to Tenby, Paul left for the mainland and we began our last couple of months alone with the island. But there could be no pretence of going back to normal. The house looked drab and bare, bookshelves empty, pictures stripped from walls. There was a definite sense of waiting for the end.

After my morning visits to the seals I was reluctant to go home. Every minute not spent out of doors was time wasted. Soon it would all be gone, and then the only thing that I would truly want would be one more moment standing on those beloved cliffs. I wandered slowly from Castle Bay, held by the magnetic power of the sea, afraid that Skomer was slipping away from me. I stopped and sat down on a slope of lichen-covered rock, pulling my legs up close to my chest to rest my chin on my knees. My hands were at my sides, palms flat down, skin against stone, so that I could feel the physical connection with the island. I looked along the length of the coast across the golden cliffs of Mathew's Wick and Amy's Reach. The day was dull, but not heavily overcast, the weather neither still nor stormy, the sea grey with an undertone of steely blue. The occasional call of a solitary bird cutting through the constant sound of the waves highlighted the winter bleakness. It was a completely nondescript day, and yet completely beautiful. I had never tired of that landscape and I knew that I never would. All I wanted was to spend my life there, absolutely unchanging. I had known from the day we arrived that there would no point in ever trying to find anything better.

I needed to be positive. There must be some good reasons for returning to the mainland. I tried to look back to the time when we were waiting to come to Skomer, when I was afraid just thinking about the things I would be leaving behind. Those doors would open again. The trouble was, I couldn't remember; I could no longer understand how it would feel to care about the superficial things that had no relevance to me any more. I had nothing in common with the twenty-year-old student who had first come here. She was someone I had once known, but had lost touch with a long time ago. Whatever I had left behind then, I had stopped thinking about within the first few weeks of arriving, and now it was all so long-forgotten that I could not imagine ever wanting it again.

One third of my life had been spent on Skomer; it had shaped me, made me into the person I was. I couldn't believe that the mainland had anything to offer me, and I was sure that I had nothing to offer it. I would be an oddity, someone who had not learnt the normal skills of life. All the things I had prided myself on being able to do well would mean nothing on the mainland; all the things I had missed out on would become glaringly obvious. I could drive a tractor but not a car. I could recognise one individual seal on a beach, but I had never even seen a computer. I could lean out over a hundred foot cliff to find a raven's nest, but a crowded street terrified me.

And, although I thrived on solitude, I knew that I would miss the people, too. Despite our isolation, we felt surprisingly integrated into the local community on the mainland; I sensed that people genuinely cared about us, and that we could rely on their support in times of difficulty. I only had to look back to Mike's illness to be sure of that.

Many of those who came to the island as volunteers, students or visitors had become close friends. Perhaps I was being pessimistic, but I could not imagine ever finding so many wonderful people gathered together again. It was something to do with Skomer, a quality that drew in good people and kept them coming back year after year.

When Charles heard about our impending departure, he came up with a plan to give us a glimpse of what lay ahead. We were going to be living in North Wales, a place I knew little about. Charles often went on training exercises in the area to practise flying in the mountains. He suggested that he could pick us up on the way and give us a brief preview of our new surroundings. It was strange, when we waited weeks even to make a trip to the nearest village, to realise that we could travel the length of Wales and back in a matter of hours.

The mountains, when we reached them, were beautiful but overwhelming. Their snow-bright peaks gave them an atmosphere of forbidding remoteness. I thought how much I would enjoy visiting such a spectacular landscape, but how little I was tempted by the prospect of living among such awe-inspiring grandeur.

The training exercise seemed to consist mainly of hovering as close as possible to the towering scree slopes, with the skimming mirage of rotor blades apparently inches from the rock face, and my admiration for the helicopter pilots soared still higher. I felt guilty at being so relieved when we started heading back towards Skomer. As soon as the island came into view I felt a surge of pleasure. I loved it in a way that I knew I could never love anywhere else. It was small, intimate, and it was mine. I could never fall in the same way for a vast, impersonal tract of landscape. I was glad to have had the chance to see where we were going, but it had not made me feel any more resigned to the prospect of moving on.

It was impossible to ignore the fact that Christmas was approaching. Though we were insulated from the excesses of commercialism, we couldn't be totally unaware of what was happening. The problem was that, even if we wanted to celebrate, there was no certainty of making any sort of preparations. After the extraordinary pause in October, when the weather had appeared to suspend all activity, the normal winter regime had resumed. It was not wild, exactly, just interminably restless. There was never a time when we had enough confidence in the weather to make a trip to Haverfordwest. If we were away for more than an hour or two, it would give the sea time to change its mood completely. We might leave it looking merely irritable, and return to find that it wrought itself into a fury of white foam. We were not prepared to waste even one of our last precious days stranded on the mainland; it would have been better to abandon Christmas entirely.

In the end, I had exactly one hour to do my Christmas shopping. We finally made it into Haverfordwest, but the forecast was so bad we couldn't risk staying for long. Mike and I separated in the car park so that we could buy presents for each other.

'Be back here at midday,' Mike said, 'and not a minute later.'

He needn't have been so emphatic; I hated being away from the island, and there was no possibility that I would take any chances with the weather. The pressure of having so little time for such a momentous undertaking meant that the hour slipped by in a few minutes. As the allotted time came to an end, my last hope was the bookshop. There, I found the perfect present almost immediately. It was one of the most beautiful books that I had ever seen. The text was mainly Japanese, but the pictures spoke for themselves. They were stunningly simple photographs - leaves, trees, streams - but unlike anything I had ever seen. It was inspirational. Mike was a brilliant photographer, but I was afraid that he would become disillusioned without Skomer's breathtaking seascapes, or the puffins that crowded round, obligingly posing for pictures. This book was like proof that he would be able to go on taking photographs. I was so delighted with it that I could actually feel my heart beat faster as the thick, glossy pages slipped through my fingers.

Then I saw the price. I suppose I should have known that something as lovely as that book would be horribly, prohibitively expensive. The elation I had been feeling collapsed into the pit of my stomach, and I replaced the book miserably on the shelf. It was time to meet Mike, so I left the shop and hurried down the hill. Immediately, I regretted my decision: that book was a treasure, worth every penny. By the time I reached the car park I felt the loss almost as a physical ache. Despite his stern warnings, there was no sign of Mike. It was all the encouragement I needed; I turned and ran back up the hill.

As I paid for the book, the owner of the shop gave me an approving smile.

'It's worth getting a few of these special books at Christmas,' she said. 'There's always someone who appreciates them.'

She emphasised the word 'special' in a knowing way, as if to imply that it applied as much to the buyer as the book itself. I was glad to have my reckless-ness condoned.

From that time on, I couldn't stop myself looking forward to Christmas. Whenever I could sneak a few private moments, I worked on a Christmas card for Mike. It was a watercolour of a puffin, but in place of the scraps of sea campion or thrift that they sometimes carried in their beaks at nesting time, there was a glossy sprig of holly. I had started to paint it as a joke, but in the end I was delighted to have produced something that seemed to be so much about us and Christmas and Skomer. I was really longing to see Mike's face when he opened the card and the book, and yet even to think of Christmas felt like wishing away our final weeks.

We walked tirelessly during those last days on Skomer. Each contour of the land, every curve of the coastline had to be learned by heart, because, very soon, memories would be the only thing we had left of the island. It was perhaps the last time in our lives that we would be able to explore in that carefree, childlike way, clambering into hidden corners just to see what might be there. The Wick was one of the best of these places, temptingly nerve-racking and full of promise. The run-off of water from the land left the smooth stone slabs glazed with a rippling, oil-slick rainbow of slimy weed, so that they were almost impossible to walk on. We threaded a well-tested route down the incline, following the seams in the rock, until we emerged onto a beach where, by the trick of perspective, the rounded sea-carved pebbles that we saw from above had grown to the size of boulders.

It felt so different to the summer. Gone was the sun-baked air that oozed thickly down our throats. No captive heat, blistering and ricocheting from every surface. It was empty of the thousand bird calls, ringing backwards and forwards among the rocks, and the faint, white drift of down that had been woven indelibly into the atmosphere. Now, listless winter waves tunnelled into the inlet, swelling against the narrowing channel of rock until they fell as foaming breakers on the shore. Cold and stormy sounds echoed around us. The smells, no longer bleached and dried, had turned damp and green.

At the top of the Wick, the crumbling rock had been scooped back to form a shallow cave. Inside, the cave had a musky, toasted smell. A giant log was wedged high above our heads: it had been there for as long as I could remember, thrown by a wave too large for me to contemplate. There were piled planks of sun-dried driftwood, smoothed and rounded by the sea. Hanks of tarry rope were tangled through the debris, some with intricately constructed knots on such an enormous scale that I could never imagine how they had been twisted into shape. The dryness and the trapped scorched scent were a clear indication that the waves had not yet reached into the cave that winter. There was something in the half-forgotten familiarity of it, the warm smell of stone and rope and wood and evaporated sea, that made me think I had stepped into a bubble of last summer, and I could almost hear the birds again. Until that second I could not have described the scent of summer on shingle, but I was suddenly so glad to have rediscovered it. Those were the details that I wanted to find and remember, because I was sure that the more obvious things would always be with me, to be revisited at will.

SEVENTEEN

When Christmas morning came, I realised that it would be impossible to enjoy it. Christmas had been fixed in our minds as the turning point. As soon as it was over we would move into the final stages of packing up and securing everything, to leave the island empty for the rest of the winter. The approach to Christmas had obscured that finality, but once the day arrived I could see beyond it, and I saw clearly for the first time that we really had reached the end.

I was awake early and eventually found myself leaning on the kitchen window sill gazing out across North Haven. It was a dispiritingly gloomy day and yet it was mesmerizing: the fluid, melting patterns of the waves; fleeting, dissolving highlights of foam; seals piercing the rippled skin of water; the loneliness of winter gulls. In the ten years we had been there, that view had never seemed anything less than perfect. Familiarity could never the dull the gloss of something so beautiful. I stared at it a hundred times a day, but every morning it was still the first thing that I wanted to see. I remembered how I had stood in exactly the same spot on the morning after we arrived and had been afraid that such a sense of awe could not survive the test of time. But I had been so wrong. Over the years of standing at that window, watching the sunrise, the puffins returning, the seals swimming with their pups, I had grown to love it more than I ever could when I was a stranger to it all.

I wanted to go out onto the cliffs to look for seals, but I decided to wait for Mike. We would go together, as we had the previous Christmas, probably for the last time. When Mike came into the room, I turned and put on my brightest smile. I didn't want him to see how I was feeling. He smiled back, but I could tell that he was as miserable as I was. And I wondered how I had ever imagined that we could have a happy Christmas.

As we crossed the isthmus I felt the sea breeze against my face, not just the sensation on my skin, but the smell and taste of it. By this point I always felt a faint but growing buzz of exhilaration, no matter how bad the weather. Now, the fact that I had loved these mornings so much became in itself a source of pain. My old sense of well-being had shrivelled into a deep ache that extended from my stomach to the base of my throat.

I glanced down into South Haven. There among the stones was a newly moulted seal pup, dappled silver-grey, perhaps six weeks old. I felt a spark of excitement, bright enough to cut through the gloom. Then, as I looked closer, I saw that something was wrong.

'Can you see that pup?' I asked Mike. 'The top half of its body is green. It looks as though it's covered in paint or something.'

Mike looked down.

'You're right. What on earth has happened to it?'

When we studied it through binoculars we realised that the pup was entwined in a matted web of fine green fishing net.

'We'll go down and see what we can do,' Mike said.

Seconds later we were scrabbling down the steep track towards South Haven.

The seal watched as we approached. We were lucky that it was such a young animal; an adult, no matter how great its distress, would never have waited so patiently for us. As we came close, the pup stretched out its neck, reaching its head as high as it would go, and opened its mouth wide to emit a stuttering hiss from the depths of its throat. It confronted us with such unflinching certainty that I could only believe it had not yet discovered its own vulnerability. Each time we bent closer to try to examine the net a fresh volley of guttural growls poured out as it jabbed its muzzle threateningly towards us.

The only thing we could see clearly was that it was a mess. The net had become entangled in endless loops around the seal as it had fought to free itself. Layer after layer was twisted round its neck and foreflippers, and had pulled so tight that the strands disappeared completely where they bit into folds of skin.

'Well,' Mike said despairingly. 'We're never going to get this lot off without a knife. You'd better go back to the house and get one, while I stay here and keep an eye on him.'

By the time I returned, the seal was looking particularly angry.

'This isn't going to be easy,' Mike said, as he began to remove his coat.

I looked at the large, pointed teeth that were being bared provocatively, and agreed. Young seals in repose are deceptively cute and look about as threatening as a newborn lamb, but this moulter was making it quite clear that it was a wild animal, and one that could defend itself.

Mike flicked his finger across the knife blade, to test its sharpness, and then threw his coat over the seal's head. The two of them wrestled on the ground while Mike tried to single out one of the taut strands of net. Eventually, he managed to slip the knife between the net and the velvety fur, and cut one of the threads. At the same moment, the seal broke free from under the coat and writhed its head round, ready to bite. I screeched a warning and Mike pulled himself clear just in time.

Mike covered the seal's head again and, with most of his weight holding the coat in place, he tackled another of the interlaced strings of net. After one more cut, the seal wrenched itself loose, and Mike darted out of reach as the teeth snapped towards him. Fortunately, the rolls of fat clustered round the seal's neck seriously impaired its agility. An older, slimmer animal would have been able to fight back much more effectively.

We realised that it was going to be a slow process, because Mike was only ever able to cut one or two strands of net before the seal wriggled free. Each time the jaws lurched ferociously into view, my shouted warnings emerged as involuntary squeals of alarm. I was truly scared of what the seal might do if it caught Mike with its teeth, and yet I was on the verge of helpless laughter. The nearer the task came to completion, the harder it grew. The last threads holding the net in place were so deeply buried between the folds of blubber that they were almost impossible to reach. Slowly, one by one, the knife snapped through them; the remains of the net unravelled from around the head and flippers, and the seal was free.

When the net was removed the seal didn't even bother to look up at us. With its newly mobile foreflippers it dragged itself over the rocks and down towards the sea, where it plunged through the curve of a breaking wave and rose again with its soft, pale coat instantly slicked hard and shiny-black. It was wonderful, watching as the seal disappeared among the waves. An hour ago it had almost certainly been facing death, and now it had a chance.

As we walked back up the beach dissecting the daring rescue, we were both laughing, partly from relief that it was over. I was trying to explain how the pair of them rolling on the ground had created a spectacle that managed to be both ludicrous and terrifying. There was also a sense of elation. We both knew that giving the seal a second chance was the most important thing we could have done that day, far better than unwrapping presents. When we reached the top of the cliff, breathless from the climb and from laughing, I realised that my mood was genuine. I wasn't just putting on a radiant exterior so as not to spoil the day. All that dull, cold anxiety had thawed; I was happy and I could tell that Mike felt the same. The seal pup had changed everything, and I knew that we were going to enjoy Christmas.

We had intended to move into our final preparations for leaving as soon as

Christmas Day was over, but we couldn't bear to destroy the atmosphere and so we took Boxing Day as a holiday too. Then everything had to be packed away and closed up. The house would be empty at least until the spring, so it was important to leave everything clean, and sealed against the pervasive atmosphere of the sea. Even a single fingerprint would degenerate into a bloom of mould in the damp, deserted months that were to follow. For days I toured the house with cleaning cloths, effectively obliterating every trace of ourselves. Whoever came next, I wanted them to find it bright and welcoming, just as we had done.

New Year's Day was the date we had settled on for our departure. At least it would give us a chance to see out the old year on Skomer before we set off into a new year and a new beginning. At midnight on New Year's Eve we opened our one bottle of wine and switched on the VHF radio to join in the greetings that were passing between the coastguard and whatever ships were still at sea. Then we went outside to listen. Below us, the liquid flow of shingle was folding against the shore in a soft, hypnotic whisper. Somewhere the breezes were moving past the island, but we were sheltered. The howling of seals, mellowed by distance, was drifting in from beyond the bay. It was a beautiful night. By the time we went to bed, every last thing had been packed so that in the morning we would just have to bundle our bedding into a kitbag and leave.

We were awake long before it was light; perhaps I didn't sleep at all. As I walked through into the kitchen I could feel the misery, solid as a block of ice lodged deep inside my rib cage. I was no longer even thinking of the morning so long ago when I had rushed to this window full of excitement, with the best part of my life about to begin. The sadness now was so heavy that it crushed everything else and concentrated my thoughts into that single moment.

It was still too dark to see outside, but as soon as I opened the window and leant out I knew that we were not going anywhere that day. I could hear the waves tumbling in long, slow, heavy cascades as they hauled a clattering assortment of pebbles up and down the beach. I also knew that Mike would not accept defeat on the basis of such flimsy evidence. A few minutes later he was at my side.

'We can't go,' I said. 'It's much too rough. Listen to the waves.'

He pushed past me and put his head out of the window.

'It's too dark to tell,' he replied. 'We'll have to wait for it to get light.'

The first, almost imperceptible, paling of the darkness showed the surf as a band of silvery luminescence washing up against the cliffs around the edge of the bay. A little more dilution of the blackness picked out foam-streaked waves, rising, twisting, vanishing again, as they pushed rapidly into North Haven.

'It's no good,' I said. 'We're not going to make it today.'

'We'll wait and see what happens when the tide turns. The sea might drop off a bit.'

I knew that he wouldn't give in, but I had already made up my mind that I didn't want to go. Perhaps I was clutching at straws, trying to claw back a few precious hours, one last night, but it was more than that. I didn't want my last memories of the island to degenerate into a bad-tempered battle with the sea. I wanted to leave calmly, with some of the sense of peace that the island had always given me.

By late morning Mike relented. He conceded that there was no chance of the sea subsiding enough to make the crossing possible, and so we abandoned our gloomy vigil at the kitchen window and went outside. After all the rushing to get ready to leave I was overwhelmingly grateful to be allowed this last quiet day. It had felt as though I was being hustled away without time for a proper, dignified goodbye. Being able to go back and visit again the places I thought I had seen for the last time was such a reprieve, as if I had been drowning and then finally gasped fresh air. At that moment, I would have given almost anything for one more glimpse of the island.

When I stared at the familiar landscape around me it was like seeing a map of my own past. There was a sense in which I felt inseparable from the island, as though it was part of me, and I was part of it. Where the rain had made silty hollows in the path, our footprints lay imprinted like the ghostly outlines of our previous walks. For months, ours had been the only feet to follow those paths. It was almost impossible to believe that tomorrow we might not be here, that the footprints would not be renewed, and eventually these ephemeral traces of our presence would be smoothed away by the rain.

On one of the more inaccessible areas of the north coast we clambered down a steep slope towards the sea. At the bottom, suspended above the water, we found a small cave. It was insignificant, just a shallow scoop carved into the rocks, but the most startling thing was that we had not seen it before. It came as reminder that the island could never be completely known by us, and confirmed what I had always believed: no matter how long we had stayed, we could never have outgrown the island because there would always have been something new to discover.

That day was disappointingly short: the featureless, ice-white sky dulled, like charcoal smudged across paper, and we were hurrying to get back before dark. The house had a hollow ring of desertion as our footsteps echoed down the hallway. In the kitchen the gaslight hissed and then purred at the touch of a match as the flame lapped up around the mantle. It was usually such a warm and comforting light, but now it just reflected on the emptiness, highlighting the signs of an abandoned house.

I began shuffling through our food supplies to find something for dinner. Usually, in the middle of winter we tried to make sure that our larder was overflowing, but we had deliberately let our stocks dwindle as we prepared to leave. It had felt like such an awful inevitability that the risk of being stranded had not played its usual part in our planning. Suddenly, I could see the prospect of food running short, and it seemed a ridiculous position to be in after so many years of meticulous caution.

I was still searching disconsolately, and feeling a distinct lack of appetite for everything that was left, when I heard a noise cutting through the soft, insistent boom of the waves. It was faint at first, but swelled rapidly until I was able to recognise the buzz of a helicopter rotor. I opened the window to look out past the impenetrable reflections in the glass and saw at once the cluster of jewel-bright lights suspended in the darkness.

Mike hurried to turn on the VHF radio and a voice came crackling through almost immediately.

'Hello, what are you doing there? I thought you were supposed to be leaving today, but I saw the house lights and came over to have a look.'

It was Cliff, one of the pilots who had given us endless support over the past couple of years. I was so glad to hear his cheerful voice at such a dispiriting time. Mike explained that we were ready to go, but the weather had held us up.

'It's possible I could come over and pick you up tomorrow morning,' Cliff replied. 'I'll see what I can arrange and give you a call later if you keep your radio switched on.'

Then the helicopter lights twisted away and rapidly faded.

We ate our meal and waited by the radio for Cliff to call back. Eventually, the news came through that the airlift was set for the following morning. It imposed a bewildering certainty on us, something I was no longer used to.

But it was good news; though I dreaded leaving, we had had our last peaceful day with the island, and waiting could no longer bring any happiness.

Of course, there was still a chance that something might go wrong. We would have to be abandoned if the helicopter was diverted to an emergency call-out, but I went to bed feeling fairly sure that we would leave in the morning. I lay in the darkness, that pure darkness, uninterrupted by artificial light, that I had come to take for granted. My senses felt detached and disorientated; it was hard to believe that if everything had gone to plan I would no longer be here. Something about the absolute familiarity of my own room, the way I knew these shadow-shapes by heart, struck me with an unexpected force. It made me remember all the times over the years that I had stared at these half-seen outlines and had stubbornly promised myself that, no matter what happened, I would never leave.

As morning approached I heard the sound of the wind gusting against the side of the house. If we had been planning to cross by boat I would already have ruled out the possibility, but I could tell, just by listening, that the wind was not strong enough to stop the helicopter. I left my warm bed reluctantly, shivering in the unheated rooms that I had grown so accustomed to. As soon as I leant out of the kitchen window I saw, even through the darkness, that the day would be clear. There was no rain or fog, which would have been a far greater deterrent to the helicopter than wind.

I took a deep breath to try to calm that dizzying mixture of dread and relief, and prepared myself for the next panic-stricken hours of throwing the final details into place. When the house was ready to be sealed up, I drove the tractor to the farm with one last consignment for the rubbish pit. Everything tidied away; everything clean and sterile and anonymous. The tractor bounced over the steep track behind the house, which had been scored into deep ruts by the winter rains, but I barely noticed the discomfort. All my attention was taken by the reds and golds of dawn as they began to dissolve the bland greyness of the sky. It was spectacular, yet distant and cold, as though I was already losing touch with the island.

In the farmyard, I passed close to the place where Mike had shown me my first Skomer vole. I pulled on the handbrake of the tractor and prepared to jump down. If I had a quick look I would almost certainly find one there. Then, at the last moment, something stopped me. I slipped the tractor back into gear and drove on. The time for reminiscences was gone; it was too late to hold on to the past.

We drove our belongings up to the centre of the island and piled them into a small mound in Calves Park, one of the large fields below the farm. I was surprised at how little we had, impressed almost that we could have lasted so long with so few personal possessions. Then we took the tractor back to North Haven and shut it in the garage. The front door of the house was locked and we walked away.

It was still too early for the helicopter. As I wandered towards the isthmus, I could hear the voice of a newborn seal pup. It was very close. I went to the frail, crumbling edge of the cliff and looked down. There, as though it had been calling me, waiting for me to come, the seal pup was staring straight up into my eyes. As soon as it saw me the pup cried again with a powerfully plead-ing wail.

Usually, the discovery of a pup born in the night was the thing I wished for most when I left the house in the morning. Now it felt like the saddest, most lonely thing I could imagine. Whatever happened to this little, wide-eyed creature, I would not be there to see it. Whether it lived or died, no one would know, no one would care. But, even as we briefly held each other's gaze, I knew that it did not matter whether I was there or not.

'Come on,' Mike said gently. 'We'd better get going.'

I turned away from the pup and began to walk up the hill, slowly, as though I was dragging an enormous weight behind me.

Everywhere I looked, some fragment of the past came reflecting back at me. Each blink of an eye held countless memories that echoed all around uncontrollably. Across the silent slopes of paper-dry bracken, seasons long gone were overlapping one upon another. Bluebells hazed the banks with their muted indigo flowers, while winter storms streaked them with foam. Puffins strummed the air as they skimmed dangerously close to my face. The smell of spring, the heat of summer, the shiver of butterfly wings all filled the air at once. The darkness was effervescent with shearwaters, while the night-time scent of honeysuckle drifted up from the cliffs along with the sound of the waves. The past was filling my head with its pounding resonance, smothering me so that I could not catch my breath. The only way I could control it was to stare down at the ground and think of nothing but placing one foot in front of the other. I watched the crescent of muddy water rise up through the green grass each time the toe of my boot pressed against the ground. I concentrated everything on those mesmerizing patterns of movement and the sheer effort of drawing breath into the constricted tightness of my chest.

When we were about halfway up the hill I paused and made the mistake of glancing back. There it was: the house that I had so resolutely turned away from. Its windows, shuttered against the coming storms, gazed blankly out across the bay, where the sparkle of early morning sun tumbled in the waves like waterfalls of stars. After ten years it was no longer my home. I felt something deep in my chest rise forcibly up to my throat. It was a sob of utter desolation. I was suspended in a fragile balance between composure and helpless self-pity. If I had given in then the tears would have been unstoppable. I took a deep breath, pressed my lips tight shut, and carried on walking. Once more there was nothing but the tread of my feet moving in time to the deep, laboured rhythm of my breathing. And all the time I longed, more than anything else, for the one thing I couldn't do; I knew I could not look back again.

By the time we reached Calves Park there was a sense of unreality. I was insulated by a protective numbness. We chatted about inconsequential things as though it was an ordinary day. This was not how I had expected it to be. All those times over so many years that I had rehearsed this awful moment in my mind, I had imagined leaving by boat. I had felt the unbearable slowness of creeping out across North Haven, watching as, first the house, and then the island, gradually disappeared. This would be quicker and more painless. A boat journey would be saturated with the nostalgia of a whole decade; the helicopter lift would be something quite separate from my familiar experience of the island.

The time was mercifully short before we heard the faint, distant chugging of the rotor blades. We both fell silent and scanned the sky, until Mike picked out the tiny speck of the helicopter, looking much further away than the noise had suggested. We watched it approach, and as it came in to land I shielded my eyes from the whirlwind of downdraught. The noise enclosed us so that all communication was reduced to shouts and signals. I breathed hard to calm myself, and then plunged forward to begin carrying our things to the helicopter. The arrival of outsiders precluded any possibility of a humiliating degeneration into tears. I was glad of that.

When I was strapped into a seat at the back and the helicopter began to rise into the air, it felt as though I was staying still and the island was falling away from me. I watched as it faded, growing ever more remote. The places I had loved were breaking up, forming beautiful shapes and patterns. They were no longer recognisably mine. The helicopter spun round to take us on a final tour of the island. Once, we dipped so low that I could pick out a path with the last of our footprints pressed into the mud. I glanced across at Mike and the look of understanding told me that he was seeing it too.

After a circuit of the island the helicopter soared high into the sky, in preparation for the brief flight across to the mainland. The higher we climbed, the more slowly the waves appeared to be moving, until they took on a dreamlike quality. Then the aircraft veered abruptly as it headed for the mainland and I felt the island slipping from my grasp. The sensation was of being startled awake, and I craned my neck forward, clinging on to the last possible glimpse of Skomer.

In a swirl of noise and confusion the helicopter came to rest in a large, empty field above the cliffs on the mainland. We waved our thanks and goodbyes, watching the helicopter pull away until it left only an awful, wind-grazed silence. I felt so small, dwarfed by the scale of everything: the dark green lushness of the grass, the endlessness of it all. I had a sudden understanding of isolation that I had never recognised within the safe and intimate confines of an island. I stared helplessly towards Mike, and he wrapped his arms around me.

I had finally let go of Skomer, and I knew that I would never see it again, but even in that instant of despair I was shocked to find a tiny glint of light. Until that moment I had thought I was leaving with nothing, but I realised then that I still had the most valuable thing I could take with me: the hope that the island's future was secure. Although the island would change and move on without me, I had faith that it would never be diminished.

Skomer was gone but not lost. Everything the island meant to me, everything it taught me, will be shimmering, always, just below the surface of my thoughts. Sometimes the brightest of these memories will flicker up through the shadows, reminding me that Skomer is part of who I am.

EPILOGUE

We live now in a beautiful place, sometimes romantically described as where the mountains meet the sea. With its dramatic landscape, sheltered wooded valleys and miles of pale-gold beaches, it has everything I could want, everything except a wild sea-cliff. Though I grow to like it more with each passing year, I had to concede long ago that it will never capture my heart. Here I am an observer, detached, looking out through a bubble of glass. It is only when I am on a cliff, with the sea stretching out below, that the real me from the past joins the person I am now and I feel whole again.

My struggle to move on was not helped by the Skomer dreams. They were so real. It was the details that always overcame my doubts and convinced me I was finally back: the fact that I could see and touch the things I thought I had forgotten. If I challenged those dreams and forced myself to wake up, I found myself still in my own bed on the island, reaching down to feel the undeniable sensation of my feet, cold against the familiar floorboards. Of course, I was never really there: I was inadvertently layering dreams within dreams, raising false hopes, so that, when I eventually woke to face yet another day without Skomer, life became a series of disappointments.

I cannot even remember when the dreams stopped, but I think it must have been when the house was demolished. It's hard to believe that a place so full of memories is gone, but perhaps that is why I no longer go back and wander through its rooms. The new house, complete with electricity, would have been one of the more dramatic steps in the slowly evolving changes to life on the island. I always insisted that lack of electricity was not a problem, and in many ways I preferred the simpler way of life it imposed on us. It was that sense of separateness, the way nothing from the past came with us, that helped me to feel so immediately connected to Skomer. If I am honest, though, the lure of a washing machine would probably have proved impossibly tempting.

I am less uncertain about the mobile phone. I would have hated it. Those invisible connections would have left me permanently anchored to the mainland and tarnished the enchantment of isolation. The internet, too, would have held me too firmly in the present, made the outside too immediate, shifted my focus subtly away from the island. Although, on a dark winter evening, as I carefully rationed the last pages of my novel, to be able to wish for a book one moment and hold it my hand the next would have seemed like a mirage made real. It is not that I wanted to live in the past, but Skomer had a timeless quality that set it apart from everything else.

This does not imply that I am troubled by progress. Research now has moved into areas that would have been completely beyond my imagination, and I would have loved to be there, sharing those discoveries. To follow the birds away from the island we had to rely on the chance discoveries of ringed birds, piecing together the fragments with guesswork. Now, in pioneering research supervised by Tim Guilford, shearwaters are fitted with miniature data loggers, and their mysterious journeys can be minutely sketched onto maps. They weave an intricate tracery of lines stretching out from the island in a fine web across the globe. The mist has lifted a little, to show us precisely where they feed and the exact migration routes they follow.

My detailed drawings of seals have been superseded by photographs and satellite tags. Those random sightings I glimpsed, those scattered dots of their lives, will be joined into a complete picture. Archaeologists use lidar images to look deep into the past and see things we could only imagine. Yet none of this can defeat the sense of mystery that still envelops the island like a glittering aura of sea spray. Just as I could never hope to know the island in a single decade, the ongoing discoveries can only reveal the island's complexity.

So many people have contributed to Skomer's fund of knowledge, people like Tim Birkhead, whose guillemot studies began before our time on the island and continue unbroken. The inspiration and driving force behind much of the seabird research has been Chris Perrins. The fact that he has continued to watch over the island, maintaining his personal involvement with projects like the long-term shearwater studies, gives him an almost legendary status in my mind. Whole lifetimes of work and experience have produced something exceptional and invaluable. It is vital that we continue to build on this outstanding resource, and find ways to translate this understanding into better safeguards for the future.

The words of the poem 'No Man is an Island' often turn themselves round in my head, but I always want to alter them to say that no island can ever be 'entire of itself'. 'Our' birds can be threatened by events half a world away, and Skomer can only be secure in the context of protection for the wider environment. If we fail in this, any damage to such a magnificent fragment of our world diminishes us all.

For now, Skomer is thriving. I struggled even to write those words because, in trying to pin down something so ephemeral with such optimism, I fear it may just crumble under the gentle pressure. When we first arrived on the island almost everything had just skimmed its lowest ebb and was on an upward trajectory. It felt as though we were witnessing a peak in numbers, a perfect time to be there. I could never have imagined that we were still at the lowest curve of the trough and most things would go on increasing. Since then, puffins have tripled in number: skittering and skimming around the arriving boat, they probably do more than anything else make the island special in the eyes of visitors. Guillemots have increased sevenfold from a low of about 3,500 birds in the 1970s; those undulating waves of growling calls that echo from the cliffs have swelled to an exuberant roar.

Shearwater numbers have tipped into realms that I would have called fantasy. Our stunning 120,000 pairs of shearwaters have soared to over 300,000. Even allowing for the fact that some of this increase may be attributed to better census techniques, it is a startling change. When I think of the ground and sky so dense with birds, the air clogged with their calls and wingbeats, it is awe-inspiring to imagine so many more birds clustered into that space. The island carries a large proportion of the world's population of Manx shearwaters: an almost unimaginably precious cargo.

Amid this quiet euphoria it is difficult to accept that I have, without even noticing, adapted to the inevitability of decline. I am viewing all this in the context of my own lifetime, and from that perspective I see nothing but success. If I could go back just a generation or two, to the 1930s, I might find as many as 100,000 guillemots – more than four times the number to be seen now. I have heard similar estimates for puffins at the turn of the last century and seen photographs from that era showing the slopes of South Haven thick with birds, where now they only form a thin fringe. I have known about this for almost as long as I have known Skomer, and yet I have always believed that it was something that belonged to the past, not something I could ever hope to see again.

Even this success has to be seen in context. The Atlantic puffin has declined so badly within its European range that it has been declared a vulnerable species. A recent stormy winter killed thousands of seabirds around our coasts, and the increasingly unpredictable climate suggests that these wrecks may become more commonplace. Skomer's insulation from so many underlying threats seems as thin and fragile as a soap bubble.

I feel closest to the island when I am watching seals on Pembrokeshire's beaches. At first I felt like an intruder looking down from the cliff top, but I am ignored or unnoticed by the seals below me. Their sense of vulnerability has dissolved and our worlds have quietly merged. I can see something idyllic in their lives now, replacing the faint undertone of sadness that always seemed to touch them. Pups are no longer left alone on the beaches to cry for hours. They swim in slow spirals, sometimes enfolded in their mothers' flippers, muzzles touching in imitation of a kiss, lost to the dangers around them, and I wonder if it is the lack of fear that allows the mothers to spend so much time with their pups.

On Skomer, I thought that their restless anxiety might stem from the stress of too much competition for the limited space on safe beaches. Pup numbers were increasing, and eventually I was recording numbers more than double those of twenty years previously. I began to fear that Skomer's beaches were at peak capacity, and that overcrowding was causing aggressive behaviour, but I was wrong. Although Pup numbers now are three times those I would have seen, the seals are at ease with each other and barely troubled by people.

I struggled to understand this, but Mike thinks that, with changing attitudes and better protection, it is simply a matter of time: that they are finally forgetting what it is to be persecuted. The past is such a subjective thing. I always saw Skomer as a nature reserve, because that was the status it would have held for almost my entire life. In reality, Skomer was a young reserve, less than twenty years old, and now I have the privilege of looking back down that tunnel of time to see how its position has consolidated.

Then, I was anxious about how Skomer's growing popularity would impact on the wildlife. The wonderfully prescient Aldo Leopold wrote: '. . . all conservation of wildness is self-defeating, for to cherish we must see and fondle, and when enough have seen and fondled, there is no wilderness left to cherish.' And yet, somehow, those who continue to manage Skomer have found a balance between the wellbeing of the island and the people who come to cherish it. The seabirds now seem hardly aware of the visitors who pay their quiet respects. Once-shy razorbills sit patiently as people file past them on the landing steps, while the puffins have taken their renowned boldness to new levels. They give visitors an almost magical insight into somewhere that transcends our ordinary world, and perhaps one close encounter with a puffin will speak more eloquently for conservation than a million words ever could.

Displaying this audacity, a puffin strolled casually across Mike's back as he stretched face-down on the grass above the Wick to take a photograph. Yes, Mike has done the thing I will never find the courage to do: he has gone back.

It was reluctant at first, but he found himself involved in the clean-up following the *Sea Empress* oil spill, and the tide of obligation finally swept him back to Skomer. Once he had broken through that imaginary barrier, the pull became just too strong, and he now visits regularly.

After ten years away, I think Mike was slightly shocked to find the island almost as we left it. He insists that I could go back, that the essence of the place is unchanged, but I know it is not true. My Skomer is gone: it wasn't just a place but also a time, and that is something I could never recapture. Skomer, though, is still there for so many people who have grown to love it. Whether they have discovered it through the pages of a book, or a wildlife programme, by gazing from afar or by visiting the island, it has a way of holding them in its spell. When I fear for its future in an uncertain world, I remind myself that all those quiet voices of support will eventually be heard.

I have written about my Skomer, the Skomer that was: not a straightforward factual account but a personal evocation of an extraordinary place. There are so many good and valid reasons to conserve nature, but perhaps we shouldn't always have to justify ourselves. The truth is that we do feel inexplicable, emotional connections with these wild places, and that is what I wanted to describe. But it is more than that: somewhere like Skomer is uniquely precious in its own right, not simply in terms of what it can give to us.

The Skomer of today is testament to all the people who have demonstrated such unfailing care, to those who have continued to work for the island, to the volunteers and everyone who has contributed to the ongoing research. I left with the slightly optimistic hope that Skomer would somehow hold its course in a sea of change. That vision I took with me now shines more brightly than I would ever have thought possible, and I thank everyone who has been part of that.

Acknowledgements

In trying to distil ten years into a few hundred pages, so much had to be left out, and, with it, the people who made that time special, but I hope that anyone reading this who shared those times with us will accept my thanks for the contribution they made to us and to the island. I wish that there was space to name everyone, but you are all there, between the lines of these pages.

David and Shirley Saunders set the whole thing going through their kindness to Mike in those earliest years. On Skomer, we relied on dedicated voluntary assistant wardens, who often kept coming back year after year. In our later years, assistant wardens, including Richard Gamble, James Perrins and George Jones, provided unfailing support and companionship. Assistance from staff of the Nature Conservancy Council was invaluable, especially Steven Evans, Roger Bray and Ian Tillotson. Most of the PhD students seemed to include assisting the work of the island as an essential part of their studies, and they all meant so much to us. Chris and Mary Perrins, with sons James and Richard, brightened our lives and shared our enthusiasms. All those who came to study the island and were generous enough to share their knowledge made our experience richer, including Professor Denis Bellamy, Tim Healing, Mike Brooke, John Evans and Blaise Bullimore.

I have enormous gratitude for everyone at RAF Brawdy, particularly 22 and 202 squadrons, who took us under their wing, with special thanks to Jim Macartney, Charles Gillow, Cliff Burt, Roger Arrowsmith and that inseparable double act of Pete and Bernie. Campbell Reynolds, together with his wife Mil and family, showed us exceptional and unforgettable kindness. They epitomised the communities surrounding Marloes and Dale who made us feel so immediately welcome. Fishermen Skip Rudder and Jim Aldred were never too busy to help us out. We depended too on the coastguards at Milford Haven, who were a daily presence on the radio and a lifeline through every emergency. Thanks also to Field Studies Council staff from nearby Dale Fort and Orielton, including David Emmerson and Robin Crump.

Heartfelt and enduring thanks to our parents, and to our siblings: Pippa Beech, Anne and Bob Rivett, Mike and Tina Hayward and Jeff and Linda Alexander. I am grateful to Mick Felton of Seren, who showed kindness and understanding to me and my manuscript, making a difficult process easy.

Finally, and most of all, to Mike, that boy who found an island and saw the future: thank you for taking me with you on the adventure.